Eye Movement Desensitization and Reprocessing

EMDR Therapy

Scripted Protocols and Summary Sheets

TREATING ANXIETY, OBSESSIVE-COMPULSIVE, AND MOOD-RELATED CONDITIONS

Marilyn Luber, PhD, is a licensed clinical psychologist and has a general private practice in Center City, Philadelphia, Pennsylvania, working with adolescents, adults, and couples, especially with complex posttraumatic stress disorder (C-PTSD), trauma and related issues, and dissociative disorders. She has worked as a Primary Consultant for the FBI field division in Philadelphia.

In 1992, Dr. Francine Shapiro trained her in Eye Movement Desensitization and Reprocessing (EMDR). She was on the Founding Board of Directors of the EMDR International Association (EMDRIA) and served as the Chairman of the International Committee until June 1999. Also, she was a member of the EMDR Task Force for Dissociative Disorders. She conducts facilitator and consultation trainings and teaches other EMDR-related subjects both nationally and internationally. Since 1997, she has coordinated trainings in EMDR-related fields in the greater Philadelphia area. In 2014, she was a member of the Scientific Committee for the EMDR Europe Edinburgh Conference. Currently, she is a facilitator for the EMDR Global Alliance to support upholding the standard of EMDR Therapy worldwide.

In 1997, Dr. Luber was given a Humanitarian Services Award by the EMDR Humanitarian Association. Later, in 2003, she was presented with the EMDR International Association's award "For Outstanding Contribution and Service to EMDRIA" and in 2005, she was awarded "The Francine Shapiro Award for Outstanding Contribution and Service to EMDR."

In 2001, through EMDR HAP (Humanitarian Assistance Programs), she published, *Handbook for EMDR Clients*, which has been translated into eight languages; the proceeds from sales of the handbook go to EMDR HAP organizations worldwide. She has written the "Around the World" and "In the Spotlight" articles for the EMDRIA Newsletter, four times a year since 1997. In 2009, she edited *Eye Movement Desensitization and Reprocessing (EMDR) Scripted Protocols: Basics and Special Situations* (Springer) and *Eye Movement Desensitization and Reprocessing (EMDR) Scripted Protocols: Special Populations* (Springer). She interviewed Francine Shapiro and co-authored the interview with Dr. Shapiro for the *Journal of EMDR Practice and Research* (Luber & Shapiro, 2009) and later wrote the entry about Dr. Shapiro for E. S. Neukrug's, *The SAGE Encyclopedia of Theory in Counseling and Psychotherapy* (2015). Several years later, in 2012, she edited Springer's first CD-ROM books: *Eye Movement Desensitization and Reprocessing (EMDR) Scripted Protocols With Summary Sheets CD-ROM Version: Basics and Special Situations* and *Eye Movement Desensitization and Reprocessing (EMDR) Scripted Protocols With Summary Sheets CD-ROM Version: Special Populations*. In 2014, she edited, *Implementing EMDR Early Mental Health Interventions for Man-Made and Natural Disasters: Models, Scripted Protocols, and Summary Sheets*. In 2015, three ebooks were published that supplied protocols taken from *Implementing EMDR Early Mental Health Interventions for Man-Made and Natural Disasters: Models, Scripted Protocols, and Summary Sheets*: *EMDR Therapy With First Responders* (ebook only), *EMDR Therapy and Emergency Response* (ebook only), and *EMDR Therapy for Clinician Self-Care* (ebook only). The text, *Eye Movement Desensitization and Reprocessing (EMDR) Therapy Scripted Protocols and Summary Sheets: Treating Trauma- and Stressor-Related Conditions* will be released in 2015. Currently, she is working on *Eye Movement Desensitization and Reprocessing (EMDR) Therapy Scripted Protocols and Summary Sheets: Treating Medical-Related Conditions*.

Eye Movement Desensitization and Reprocessing
EMDR Therapy
Scripted Protocols and Summary Sheets

TREATING ANXIETY, OBSESSIVE-COMPULSIVE, AND MOOD-RELATED CONDITIONS

Edited by

Marilyn Luber, PhD

SPRINGER PUBLISHING COMPANY
NEW YORK

Springer Publishing Company, LLC
11 West 42nd Street
New York, NY 10036
www.springerpub.com

Acquisitions Editor: Sheri W. Sussman
Composition: Newgen KnowledgeWorks

ISBN: 978-0-8261-3167-6
e-book ISBN: 978-0-8261-3168-3
CD-ROM: 978-0-8261-3169-0

15 16 17 18 / 5 4 3 2 1

The author and the publisher of this Work have made every effort to use sources believed to be reliable to provide information that is accurate and compatible with the standards generally accepted at the time of publication. The author and publisher shall not be liable for any special, consequential, or exemplary damages resulting, in whole or in part, from the readers' use of, or reliance on, the information contained in this book. The publisher has no responsibility for the persistence or accuracy of URLs for external or third-party Internet websites referred to in this publication and does not guarantee that any content on such websites is, or will remain, accurate or appropriate.

Library of Congress Cataloging-in-Publication Data
Luber, Marilyn, author, editor.
  Eye movement desensitization and reprocessing (EMDR) therapy scripted protocols and summary sheets. Treating anxiety, obsessive-compulsive, and mood-related conditions / Marilyn Luber.
       p. ; cm.
  Treating anxiety, obsessive-compulsive, and mood-related conditions
  Includes bibliographical references.
  ISBN 978-0-8261-3167-6 — ISBN 978-0-8261-3168-3 (e-book) — ISBN 978-0-8261-3169-0 (CD-ROM)
  I. Title. II. Title: Treating anxiety, obsessive-compulsive, and mood-related conditions.
  [DNLM: 1. Eye Movement Desensitization Reprocessing—methods--Handbooks. 2. Eye Movement Desensitization Reprocessing—methods—Practice Guideline. 3. Anxiety Disorders—therapy—Handbooks. 4. Anxiety Disorders—therapy—Practice Guideline. 5. Interview, Psychological—methods—Handbooks. 6. Interview, Psychological—methods—Practice Guideline. 7. Medical History Taking—methods—Handbooks. 8. Medical History Taking—methods—Practice Guideline. 9. Mood Disorders—therapy—Handbooks. 10. Mood Disorders—therapy—Practice Guideline. WM 34]
  RC489.E98
  616.85'210651—dc23   2015013760.

Special discounts on bulk quantities of our books are available to corporations, professional associations, pharmaceutical companies, health care organizations, and other qualifying groups.

If you are interested in a custom book, including chapters from more than one of our titles, we can provide that service as well.

For details, please contact:
Special Sales Department, Springer Publishing Company, LLC
11 West 42nd Street, 15th Floor, New York, NY 10036-8002
Phone: 877-687-7476 or 212-431-4370; Fax: 212-941-7842
E-mail: sales@springerpub.com

Printed in the United States of America by Bradford & Bigelow.

To Ad de Jongh,
my friend and colleague,
for his insight, guidance, humor, and
for his dedication to EMDR Therapy and the EMDR community

All the evidence that we have indicates that it is reasonable to assume in practically every human being, and certainly in almost every newborn baby, that there is an active will toward health, an impulse toward growth.

—Abraham Maslow, PhD

Contents

PART I
EMDR Therapy and Anxiety Disorders

Specific Phobia

Panic Disorder and Agoraphobia

Use of Specific Procedures in the Treatment of Anxiety Disorders

PART II
EMDR Therapy and Obsessive-Compulsive and Related Disorders

PART III
EMDR Therapy and Mood Disorders

Bipolar Disorder

Major Depression

Postpartum Depression

Contributors

Benedikt L. Amann, MD, PhD, specialized in psychiatry and psychotherapy at the Ludwig-Maximilians University in Munich, Germany. During his training, he initiated scientific projects on bipolar disorder and received grant funding from the Stanley Medical Research Centre. As a research assistant, he spent 1 year each in the Department of Neuropsychiatry and Neurology in London, UK, and in the Bipolar Disorders Unit of Hospital Clinic in Barcelona, Spain. In 2006, he was contracted as the principal investigator for the Ministry of Health in Spain and was named member of the CIBERSAM, the most relevant scientific network to study mental diseases in Spain. Since then, he has been working at the FIDMAG Research Foundation Germanes Hospitalàries, in Barcelona, Spain, with a scientific focus on neuroimaging, clinical studies about mental disorders, and the comorbidity of trauma and severe mental illness. As an EMDR clinician, he founded the Barcelona EMDR Research Group and initiated basic and clinical research on EMDR. He is a member of the Spanish and European EMDR Scientific Committees, author of more than 80 scientific articles in national and international peer-reviewed journals, and lectures regularly at national and international congresses. In 2015, the EMDR Europe Association presented him with the Francine Shapiro Award.

Roser Batalla, PsyD, is a clinical psychologist and EMDR consultant in Barcelona, Spain. She has undergone training in Brainspotting, brief strategic therapy, cognitive behavioral therapy (CBT), EMDR, and neuro-linguistic programming and rhythmic movement therapy and special training for emergencies, catastrophes, and grief work. She works with infants, children, and adults. She is a member of the Barcelona EMDR Research group.

Millia Begum, MD, is a consultant psychiatrist within the National Health Service (NHS) Lanarkshire in the West of Scotland region. She is also an EMDR Europe–approved consultant. She has a keen interest in posttraumatic stress disorder (PTSD) and related conditions. She has worked collaboratively with Therese McGoldrick over the years, publishing research papers and promoting EMDR through joint presentations on various trauma-related topics. She has published with other colleagues in peer-reviewed journals, the most recent being a systematic review of the world literature on Olfactory Reference Syndrome.

Vicky Blanch, PsyD, is licensed in clinical psychology. She is an EMDR facilitator and consultant and she is trained in neuropsychology, hypnosis, brief strategic therapy, and sensorimotor therapy. She has participated in various research projects concerning EMDR and is a member of the Barcelona EMDR Research group.

Karsten Böhm, D Phil, Dipl Psych, is a consultant in EMDR and CBT; EMDR facilitator; and specialist in obsessive-compulsive disorder (OCD), anxiety disorders, and PTSD psychotherapy. He is a member of the German EMDRIA board and also of the German National Guideline Commission on the treatment of OCD. He lectures on psychotherapy for the EMDR Institute Germany, for Institutes for Cognitive Behavior Therapy (in Stuttgart and Basel, Switzerland), for medical councils, and for different congresses (Deutschen Gesellschaft für Psychiatrie und Psychotherapie, Psychosomatik und Nervenheilkunde [DGPPN] Congress Berlin, etc.). He has published a number of articles, chapters, and working materials on the use of EMDR with OCD patients. From 2003 to 2009, he worked as a clinical and ward psychologist at the University Hospital of Freiburg. Currently, he is working as a lead psychologist in Klinik Friedenweiler of Friedenweiler in the Black Forest, Germany.

Keith Brown, BSc(Hons), MB, ChB, MRCGP, FRCPsych, FRCPE, is an honorary professor at Stirling University and a retired consultant psychiatrist. He cofounded and was codirector of the first trauma clinic in Scotland that specialized in the use of EMDR. He has coauthored a number of research papers on EMDR, PTSD, and body dysmorphic disorder. He has served on a number of government advisory bodies related to psychological trauma. He was the chairman of the Scottish Intercollegiate Guideline Network (SIGN), a member of the Scottish Medicines Consortium (SMC), and sat on the advisory board of the British National Formulary (BNF).

Dolors Capellades, PsyD, is licensed in clinical psychology and is an EMDR practitioner. She has undergone training in Brainspotting, brief strategic therapy, CBT, EMDR, and neuro-linguistic programming. For 20 years, she has worked in a private practice focusing on PTSD, attachment disorders, psychosomatic disorders, severe mental disorders, and personality disorders. She is a member of the Barcelona EMDR Research group.

Maria José Carvajal, PsyD, is licensed in clinical psychology and is an EMDR facilitator and consultant. She has undergone training in brief strategic therapy, EMDR, and neuro-linguistic programming. She currently works in the Stress Traumatic Institute in Barcelona, Spain, and is a member of the Barcelona EMDR Research group.

Anna Maria De Divitiis, PsyD, is a clinical psychologist, EMDR facilitator, and approved consultant. She is cofounder of the Italian EMDR Association (Associazione per l'EMDR in Italia) and was on its board of directors for 10 years. She has worked for 26 years as a lead psychologist at Family Planning Centers (NHS) and has conducted Childbirth Preparation Courses with expectant women. She is a trainer of trainers of Childbirth Preparation Course in a number of professional training institutes. She teaches psychotraumatology, attachment theory and psychotherapy, and attention deficit/hyperactivity disorder (ADHD) at the A.T. Beck Institute in Caserta (Cognitive Behavioral Psychotherapy Training Centre). She has taught critical incident stress intervention at the Civil Defense Center in Naples. She has presented several papers and has published articles on EMDR and drug addiction intervention and the prevention of birth trauma and postpartum depression. She has participated in humanitarian projects through the Italian EMDR Association.

Ad de Jongh, PhD, is both a clinical psychologist and a dentist. He is a professor of anxiety and behavior disorders at the Behavioural Science Department of the Academic Centre for Dentistry (ACTA) in Amsterdam, the Netherlands, a collaboration of the University of Amsterdam and Vrije University. He is also an honorary professor at the School of Health Sciences of Salford University in Manchester, UK. He is involved in research investigating the efficacy of evidence-based treatments for the consequences of traumatic events in a variety of target populations, including children, people with intellectual disabilities, and people with complex psychiatric conditions, including psychosis and schizophrenia. He has (co-)authored more than 250 scientific articles and book chapters on anxiety disorders, and their treatment, as well as 5 books, and provides lectures and courses in his field of expertise, both in the Netherlands and abroad. He is an EMDR Europe–accredited trainer. In 2011, he received the outstanding EMDR Research Award from the EMDR International Association.

Franz Ebner, MD, is a specialist in psychiatry and psychotherapy. He is a senior trainer and supervisor in the German EMDR Institute with Arne Hofmann and, since 2000, he has conducted trainings in German-speaking countries, China, and Slovakia. He started as an EMDR facilitator in 1995. From 1998 until 2008, he was the head of one of the first inpatient trauma programs in a psychiatric hospital (Klinik Hohe Mark) in Oberursel, near

Frankfurt, Germany. He has published articles and chapters in two books on EMDR. Currently, he treats trauma patients in the outpatient department for a clinic in Frankfurt and has a private practice.

Isabel Fernández, PsyD, is a clinical psychologist. She is trained in CBT and is a member of the faculty of the Italian School of Cognitive Behavior Therapy. She has worked as a consultant psychologist for the psychiatric ward of Niguarda Hospital in Milan, Italy, conducting clinical research projects. Currently, she is the director of the Psychotraumatology Research Center of Milan and has published various articles and books on trauma and EMDR. She is an EMDR Europe–approved trainer, chairman of the Italian Association of EMDR, and EMDR Europe president. She belongs to the board of directors of the Italian Federation of Scientific Psychological Societies. She has directed and organized emergency psychology interventions in natural and incidental disasters and has worked in cooperation with civil defense and firefighters for debriefing and psychological support concerning the stress of emergency workers. She trains psychology graduates, postgraduates, and clinicians on trauma, EMDR, and crisis interventions.

Francisca García, PsyD, is a clinical psychologist and EMDR trainer. Her specialties are in health, sexology, and sophrology. In 2001, Francisca was a founding member of the Spanish EMDR Association, but her active clinical experience with EMDR dates back to 1998. She is the president of the Spanish EMDR Association and Institute, dedicated to the organization of EMDR trainings and investigation of EMDR. In collaboration with EMDR Italy, she has trained more than 400 Cuban psychologists. She has participated in numerous research projects, and lectures in the fields of education and clinical psychology.

Michael Hase, MD, is a psychiatrist, psychotherapist, EMDR senior trainer, and EMDR consultant. He is head of the Department of Psychosomatic Medicine at the Diana Klinik Bad Bevensen, Germany. From 2007 to 2009, he was head of the Department of Psychosomatic Medicine at the Reha-Centrum Hamburg (former Reha-Zentrum Berliner Tor). From 1986 to 1987, he served as a physician with the Bundeswehr (Federal German Army). He studied neurology and psychiatry until 1992 and worked as a consultant at Lueneburg Psychiatric Hospital until 2007. During that time, he also did research on EMDR in the treatment of addiction. He is a registered specialist in psychotraumatherapy and lecturer at the Training Institute for Psychotherapy in Lueneburg, Germany, and at various institutes in Europe. Since 2011, Dr. Hase has been the president of EMDRIA Deutschland. In 2015, he founded the Lueneburg Center of Stress Medicine. His current research focuses on EMDR for the treatment of depression, National Acupuncture Detoxification Association (NADA) ear acupuncture, and burnout.

Arne Hofmann, MD, is a specialist in psychosomatic and internal medicine. He is a senior trainer and is a trainers' trainer in Europe. He introduced EMDR into the German-speaking countries of Europe after a 1991 residency at the Mental Research Institute in Palo Alto, California, where he learned about EMDR, and went on to head the German EMDR Institute. In 1994, he started the first inpatient trauma program in a psychiatric hospital near Frankfurt, Germany. Later, at the university of Cologne, he assisted in developing aftercare programs subsequent to mass disaster events, such as the 1998 train catastrophe in Eschede, the 2002 school shooting in Erfurt, and the 2004 tsunami in Southeast Asia. He is a founding board member of the German-speaking Society of Traumatic Stress Studies (DeGPT) and EMDR Europe. He also is a member of a German National Guideline Commission on the treatment of PTSD and acute stress disorder. He has published a number of articles, one book on EMDR, and coedited three other books on trauma and EMDR. He has been teaching at the universities of Cologne, Witten-Herdecke, and Peking, and lectures internationally. He received the Ron Martinez Award from the EMDR International Association in 2003 and the first David Servan Schreiber Award of the EMDR Europe Association in 2013.

Ferdinand Horst, MSc, is a licensed clinical psychologist and accredited practitioner in EMDR. He is combining clinical practice, research, and management in the Department of

Psychiatry at St. Elisabeth Hospital, Tilburg, the Netherlands. His specialties are the assessment and treatment of complex (neuro)psychiatric disorders, PTSS, panic disorder, anxiety, and depression.

Maria Lehnung, PhD, is a researcher who works and publishes in the field of brain trauma and developmental issues. She is also a clinical psychologist, working in private practice. She is an EMDR consultant and facilitator. She is involved in recent research on EMDR and depression and has coauthored a number of recent articles and a book on EMDR. She has been teaching at the University of Kiel, Germany.

Peter Liebermann, MD, is a specialist in psychiatry and psychotherapy. He is a senior trainer in Europe. He is a founding board member of the German-speaking Society of Traumatic Stress Studies (DeGPT) and EMDRIA Germany and served as president from 2005 to 2012. Since 2011, he has been the treasurer of EMDR Europe. He also is a member of a German National Guideline Commission on the treatment of PTSD. He has published a number of articles on EMDR and on the aftermath of the Holocaust.

Robin Logie, PhD, is a clinical psychologist in private practice. He is an EMDR Europe consultant and facilitator. He is a member of the board of EMDR Association UK and Ireland and was president of the association for 3 years. Dr. Logie's particular interests include the use of EMDR with OCD, the Flashforward Procedure, and applications of attachment theory. He is extensively involved in EMDR supervision of individuals and groups and contributes to consultants' training in the United Kingdom, as well as running workshops on supervision for EMDR consultants.

Walter Lupo, PsyD, is licensed in clinical psychology and is an EMDR consultant and facilitator. He is one of the founding members of the Clínica Logos in Barcelona and team coordinator of the Psychiatry and Psychology Stress and Functional Medicine Institute Ignacio Umbert, Corachán Clinic, in Barcelona. He is a tutor at the Faculty of Psychology at the Central University, Barcelona. He is a member of the scientific committee of the Spanish EMDR Association, has participated in various EMDR research projects, and is a member of the Barcelona EMDR Research group.

Priscilla Marquis, PhD, is a clinical psychologist and has been practicing EMDR since 1990. She has trained individuals in EMDR around the world in places such as Nicaragua, Bangladesh, and in underserved communities in the United States. She is an EMDRIA-certified consultant. She has published research on the treatment of PTSD with EMDR as part of the Kaiser Permanente Health Maintenance Organization study. She is Obsessive Compulsive Foundation Certified and has been working on OCD and its spectrum disorders since 1996. She has specialized in anxiety disorders since that time. She was the Anxiety Team leader at Kaiser San Francisco from 1997 to 2005. Dr. Marquis currently works as a neuropsychologist and leader of the OCD Spectrum Disorders treatment group at Kaiser San Francisco. She also works in private practice as a consultant and practitioner of EMDR.

Therese McGoldrick, BA, ENBCC650, RMN, is the head of Behavioural Psychotherapy and the Trauma Service with NHS Forth Valley in Central Scotland and an honorary senior research fellow at the University of Stirling. She is an EMDR Europe consultant, an EMDR Institute–approved facilitator, a previous member of the EMDR UK and Ireland Board, and current member of the editorial board of the *EMDR Journal of Practice and Research*. She has a keen interest in research and has coauthored a number of papers published in peer-reviewed journals; in 2003, she received the EMDRIA award for outstanding contribution to research in EMDR. She has presented at national and international conferences on her work and has also been part of humanitarian assistance programs in Bangladesh, Turkey, and Northern Ireland. She sits on the Scottish Trauma Advisory Group (STAG), which advises the Scottish government on trauma-related issues.

Luca Ostacoli, MD, specializes in psychiatry and is an EMDR consultant of the Italian EMDR Association. He is a researcher and teacher at Turin University in clinical psychology and psychotherapy. Since 2001, he has been the head of the University Service of Psychosomatics and Mood Disorders at San Luigi Hospital, Orbassano (Turin). He applies EMDR Therapy in patients who are medically ill and in those suffering from mood, borderline, and psychotic disorders. After the earthquake in Emilia (Italy), he participated in the crisis intervention response, conducting EMDR groups for adults and integrating the group format with individual EMDR, as needed. Furthermore, he has been part of the response team after other acute traumas in the community setting.

Marian Ponte, PsyD, has a degree in psychology from the University in Barcelona, Spain, and has had specialty training in sexuality, at the University of Valencia, Spain. She has worked in the areas of mental health and psychology interventions with immigrants and gives lectures in trauma centers and in universities on sexuality, psychology, trauma, and EMDR, with a focus on physically abused women. She has co-organized EMDR courses in Spain, is a clinical facilitator and supervisor of EMDR, and has participated in various research projects concerning EMDR.

Christine Rost, MD, is a medical doctor with a specialization in gynecology, obstetrics, and psychotherapy. She is an EMDR trainer with the EMDR Institute Germany. Since 1998, she has had a private practice in Frankfurt/Main as a psychotherapist. She specializes in psychotrauma and EMDR.

Maria José Sánchez, PsyD, is licensed in clinical psychology. She is an EMDR facilitator and consultant. She has undergone training in Brainspotting, brief strategic therapy, hypnosis, gestalt therapy, and neuro-linguistic programming. She has participated in various research projects concerning EMDR and is a member of the Barcelona EMDR Research group.

Jesús Sanfiz, PsyD, is a licensed clinical psychologist in Barcelona, Spain, and an EMDR Europe–accredited consultant. His special interests include crisis intervention, the treatment of complex PTSD and PTSD following military trauma, and terrorist attacks. He was involved in humanitarian projects in Africa and Europe. He is cofounder and director of the Stress Traumatic Institute in Barcelona, Spain. He is a member of the Barcelona EMDR Research group.

Antonia Santed, PsyD, is licensed in clinical psychology and is an EMDR facilitator and consultant. She has trained in brief strategic therapy (master level) and has a postgraduate diploma in clinical hypnosis. Currently, she is the director of the Adala Psychological Center and the Barcelona Trauma Institute. Furthermore, she has participated and coordinated various research projects on EMDR.

Christie Sprowls, PsyD, is a psychologist, executive, and personal and work–life balance coach, and has been in independent practice in Austin, Texas, for more than 25 years. Dr. Sprowls is an EMDR trainer affiliated with both the EMDR Institute and the EMDR Humanitarian Assistance Program. She has been presented with two Humanitarian Assistance Awards from the EMDR Institute for her service in disaster sites abroad. Dr. Sprowls travels internationally, speaking, training, and conducting workshops.

Visal Tumani, MD, is a psychiatrist and psychotherapist with a specialty in trauma (DeGPT). She is running and supervising a special outpatient unit at the University Hospital of Ulm for Psychiatry and Psychotherapy for patients with PTSD.

In 2013, Dr. Vincent John Felitti presented Dr. Robert F. Anda and his groundbreaking work on "The Adverse Childhood Experiences Study" (ACE Study) at the EMDR International Association's annual conference in Austin, Texas. The ACE Study is a research study conducted by Kaiser Permanente Health Maintenance Organization and the Centers for Disease Control and Prevention with the purpose of finding out the effects of stressful and traumatic experiences during childhood on adult health (acestudy.org website, 2015). Between 1995 and 1997, more than 17,000 volunteers were recruited into a long-term study to follow up on their health outcomes from a Kaiser HMO. In this cohort, 50% were female, 74.8% were Caucasian, 75.2% had attended college, all had jobs and health care, and the average age was 57 years. What they learned revolutionized our basic understanding of the etiology of mental and physical illness. From the reports of the participants in the survey, they discovered that 63% had at least one childhood trauma, whereas 20% had experienced at least three or more categories of trauma, which were labeled *adverse childhood experiences (ACE)*. ACE included experiences of abuse as in emotional (11%), physical (28%), and sexual (21%); neglect comprising emotional (15%), and physical (10%); growing up in households where a member was mentally ill (19%), in jail or prison (5%); used alcohol and/or drugs (27%), lost a parent due to separation or divorce (23%); or witnessed their mother-treated violently (13%). Felitti and Anda's important discovery was the more categories of trauma experienced in childhood, the greater the likelihood of experiencing high-risk factors in adulthood for alcoholism and alcohol abuse, chronic obstructive pulmonary disease (COPD), depression, fetal death, hallucinations, illicit drug use, ischemic heart disease (IHD), liver disease, risk of intimate partner violence, multiple sexual partners, obesity, poor health-related quality of life, posttraumatic stress disorder (PTSD), sexually transmitted diseases (STDs), smoking, suicide attempts, and/or unintended pregnancies. These are important findings that inform our work as EMDR practitioners.

Felitti and Anda (2009, pp. 77–87), in their chapter "The Relationship of Adverse Childhood Experiences to Adult Medical Disease, Psychiatric Disorders, and Sexual Behavior: Implications for Healthcare," concluded the following concerning adverse childhood experiences:

> The influence of childhood experience, including often-unrecognized traumatic events, is as powerful as Freud and his colleagues originally described it to be. These influences are long lasting, and neuroscientists are now describing the intermediary mechanisms that develop as a result of these stressors. Unfortunately, and in spite of these findings, the biopsychosocial model and the bio-medical model of psychiatry remain at odds rather than taking advantage of the new discoveries to reinforce each other.
>
> Many of our most intractable public health problems are the result of compensatory behaviors like smoking, overeating, and alcohol and drug use which provide immediate partial relief from the emotional problems caused by traumatic childhood experiences. The chronic life stress of these developmental experiences is generally unrecognized and hence unappreciated as a second etiologic mechanism. These experiences are lost in time and concealed by shame, secrecy, and social taboo against the exploration of certain topics of human experience.
>
> The findings of the Adverse Childhood Experiences (ACE) Study provide a credible basis for a new paradigm of medical, public health, and social service practice that would start with

comprehensive biopsychosocial evaluation of all patients at the outset of ongoing medical care.

Dr. Francine Shapiro's Adaptive Information Processing (AIP) model is in keeping with the important findings of Felitti and Anda's ACE Study (Shapiro, 2001, 2002, 2006, 2007). This model is used to guide our clinical practice and show EMDR Therapy's clinical effects. The idea is that the direct reprocessing of the stored memories of the first and other events connected with the problem—as well as any other experiential contributors—has a positive effect on clients' presenting problems. The results of case studies and open trials with various diagnostic categories support this prediction. In fact, many experts have taken the basic Standard EMDR Therapy Protocols reported by Dr. Shapiro in *Eye Movement Desensitization and Reprocessing (EMDR): Basic Principles, Protocols and Procedures* (1995, 2001) and adapted them to meet the particular needs of their clients while maintaining the integrity of EMDR Therapy.

The work on EMDR Therapy and clinical applications, as seen in the chapters in this book, are based on the AIP model. A number of EMDR Therapy clinical applications are mainly case studies or open trials that show promise; however, they are in need of further investigation. The following is a small sample of the types of conditions for which clinicians are using these clinical applications: addictions; anxiety; body dysmorphia; depression; dissociative disorders; excessive grief; family, marital, and sexual dysfunction; intellectual disabilities; pain; phobias; panic; and so on. For more information, visit the EMDR International Association website (www.emdria.org) or the EMDR Institute website (www.emdr.com).

The following are the randomized clinical trials reporting on the effectiveness of EMDR in conditions other than PTSD: adjustment disorder (Cvetek, 2008); bipolar disorder (Novo et al., 2014); fears and phobias (Doering, Ohlmeier, de Jongh, Hofmann, & Bisping, 2013; Muris & Merckelbach, 1997; Muris, Merckelbach, Holdrinet, & Sijsenaar, 1998; Muris, Merckelbach, van Haaften, & Mayer, 1997; Triscari, Faraci, D'Angelo, Urso, & Catalisano, 2011); general symptoms of anxiety and distress (Abbasnejad, Mahani, & Zamyad, 2007; Arabia, Manca, & Solomon, 2011); obsessive-compulsive disorder (Nazari, Momeni, Jariani, & Tarrahi, 2011); and panic disorder (Feske & Goldstein, 1997; Goldstein, de Beurs, Chambless, & Wilson, 2001).

This is the fourth in a series of books dedicated to the better understanding of EMDR Therapy and how the Standard EMDR Therapy principles, protocols, and procedures form the basis for the work that we do as EMDR Therapy clinicians. To understand any subject matter deeply, the rule of thumb is to know the basics so that if a departure from the structure is needed, it is done in an informed manner. The purpose of *Eye Movement Desensitization and Reprocessing (EMDR) Scripted Protocols: Basics and Special Situations* (Luber, 2009a) was to support the structure in Dr. Shapiro's earlier texts (1995, 2001) by showing each step in detail. *Eye Movement Desensitization and Reprocessing (EMDR) Scripted Protocols: Special Populations* (Luber, 2009b) built on that structure and showcased how many experts adapt the EMDR Therapy principles, protocols, and procedures for use with their specific populations, such as children; couples; and patients with dissociative disorders, complex PTSD, addictive behaviors, pain, and specific fears. The next book would have been: *Eye Movement Desensitization and Reprocessing (EMDR) Scripted Protocols and Summary Sheets: Anxiety, Depression, and Medical-Related Issues* to continue to show how expert clinicians are working with EMDR Therapy for anxiety disorders, depression, and medical-related issues. However, in 2011, man-made and natural disasters were coming to the fore and impacting our colleagues experiencing the Tōhoku earthquake and tsunami in Japan; floods in China, the Philippines, Thailand, Pakistan, Cambodia, India, and Brazil; earthquakes in Turkey and New Zealand; droughts and consecutive famines affecting Ethiopia, Kenya, and Somalia; storms in the United States, and so on. In consultation with Springer and EMDR colleagues in the EMDR Humanitarian Assistance Programs worldwide, the decision was made to move up the publication of *Implementing EMDR Early Mental Health Interventions for Man-Made and Natural Disasters*, in book, CD, and e-book formats. It was published in 2014 as an up-to-date collection of the current EMDR Therapy–related responses and protocols for recent trauma events.

In 2012, *Eye Movement Desensitization and Reprocessing (EMDR) Scripted Protocols and Summary Sheets: Anxiety, Depression and Medical-Related Issues* was slated to appear and was originally conceptualized with *Diagnostic and Statistical Manual of Mental Disorder, Fourth Edition* (*DSM-IV-R*; American Psychiatric Association, 1994) in mind; however, by the time publication grew near, *DSM-5* (5th ed.; American Psychiatric Association, 2013) had become the standard. This entailed some reorganization of the structure of the book. However, so much material was involved that it was decided to create three books instead of one. This is the first of a trio of books based on this material: *Eye Movement Desensitization and Reprocessing (EMDR) Therapy Scripted Protocols and Summary Sheets: Treating Anxiety, Obsessive-Compulsive, and Mood-Related Conditions*, with the choice of book, CD, and/or e-book formats. Trauma- and stressor-related issues were separated from this current book and will appear as *Eye Movement Desensitization and Reprocessing (EMDR) Therapy Scripted Protocols and Summary Sheets: Treating Trauma- and Stressor-Related Conditions* (Luber, in press) in late 2015 or early 2016. Medical-related issues, as well, were separated from this current book and will appear as *Eye Movement Desensitization and Reprocessing (EMDR) Therapy Scripted Protocols and Summary Sheets: Treating Medical-Related Issues* (Luber, in press) in 2016.

The following description from *Eye Movement Desensitization and Reprocessing (EMDR) Scripted Protocols: Basics and Special Situations* gives a clear understanding of the evolution and importance of this format:

> *Eye Movement Desensitization and Reprocessing (EMDR) Scripted Protocols: Basics and Special Situations* grew out of a perceived need that trained mental health practitioners could be served by a place to access both traditional and newly developed protocols in a way that adheres to best clinical practices incorporating the Standard EMDR Protocol that includes working on the past, present, and future issues (the 3-Pronged Protocol) related to the problem and the 11-Step Standard Procedure that includes attention to the following steps: image, negative cognition (NC), positive cognition (PC), validity of cognition (VoC), emotion, subjective units of disturbance (SUD), and location of body sensation, desensitization, installation, body scan, and closure. Often, EMDR texts embed the protocols in a great deal of explanatory material that is essential in the process of learning EMDR. However, sometimes, as a result, practitioners move away from the basic importance of maintaining the integrity of the Standard EMDR Protocol and keeping adaptive information processing in mind when conceptualizing the course of treatment for a patient. It is in this way that the efficacy of this powerful methodology is lost.
>
> "Scripting" becomes a way not only to inform and remind the EMDR practitioner of the component parts, sequence, and language used to create an effective outcome, but it also creates a template for practitioners and researchers to use for reliability and/or a common denominator so that the form of working with EMDR is consistent. The concept that has motivated this work was conceived within the context of assisting EMDR clinicians in accessing the scripts of the full protocols in one place and to profit from the creativity of other EMDR clinicians who have kept the spirit of EMDR but have also taken into consideration the needs of the population with whom they work or the situations that they encounter. *Reading a script is by no means a substitute for adequate training, competence, clinical acumen, and integrity; if you are not a trained EMDR therapist and/or you are not knowledgeable in the field for which you wish to use the script, these scripts are not for you.*
>
> As EMDR is a fairly complicated process, and indeed, has intimidated some from integrating it into their daily approach to therapy, this book provides step-by-step scripts that will enable beginning practitioners to enhance their expertise more quickly. It will also appeal to seasoned EMDR clinicians, trainers and consultants because it brings together the many facets of the eight phases of EMDR and how clinicians are using this framework to work with a variety of therapeutic difficulties and modalities, while maintaining the integrity of the AIP model. Although there are a large number of resources, procedures and protocols in this book, they do not constitute the universe of protocols that are potentially useful and worthy of further study and use.
>
> These scripted protocols are intended for clinicians who have read Shapiro's text (2001) and received EMDR training from an EMDR-accredited trainer. An EMDR trainer is a licensed mental health practitioner who has been approved by the association active in the clinician's country of practice. (Luber, 2009a, p. xxi)

In 2012, the CD-ROM versions of the original 2009 books were published in a different format (Luber, 2012a, 2012b). Included in the CD-ROM were just the protocols and summary sheets (the notes were not included, but are available in the 2009 texts in book form). As explained in the preface of *Eye Movement Desensitization and Reprocessing (EMDR) Scripted Protocols With Summary Sheets (CD ROM Version): Basics and Special Situations* (Luber, 2012a):

> The idea for *Eye Movement Desensitization and Reprocessing (EMDR) Scripted Protocols: Summary Sheets for Basics and Special Situations* grew out of the day-to-day work with the protocols that allowed for a deeper understanding of case conceptualization from an EMDR perspective. While using the scripted protocols and acquiring a greater familiarity with the use of the content, the idea of placing the information in a summarized format grew. This book of scripted protocols and summary sheets was undertaken so that clinicians could easily use the material in *Eye Movement Desensitization and Reprocessing (EMDR) Scripted Protocols: Basics and Special Situations*. While working on the summary sheets, the interest in brevity collided with the thought that clinicians could also use these summary sheets to remind themselves of the steps in the process clarified in the scripted protocols. The original goal to be a summary of the necessary data gathered from the protocol was transformed into this new creation of data summary and memory tickler for the protocol itself! Alas, the summary sheets have become a bit longer than originally anticipated. Nonetheless, they are shorter—for the most part—than the protocols themselves and do summarize the data in an easily readable format…
>
> The format for this book is also innovative. The scripts and summary sheets are available in an expandable, downloadable format for easy digital access. Because EMDR is a fairly complicated process, and often intimidating, these scripted protocols with their accompanying summary sheets can be helpful in a number of ways. To begin with, by facilitating the gathering of important data from the protocol about the client, the scripted protocol and/or summary sheet then can be inserted into the client's chart as documentation. The summary sheet can assist the clinician in formulating a concise and clear treatment plan with clients and can be used to support quick retrieval of the essential issues and experiences during the course of treatment. Practitioners can enhance their expertise more quickly by having a place that instructs and reminds them of the essential parts of EMDR practice. By having these fill-in PDF forms, clinicians can easily tailor the scripted protocols and summary sheets to the needs of their clients, their consultees/supervisees and themselves by editing and saving the protocol scripts and summary sheets. The script and summary sheet forms are available as a digital download or on a CD-ROM, and will work with any computer or device that supports a PDF format.
>
> Consultants/Supervisors will find these scripted protocols and summary sheets useful while working with consultees/supervisees in their consultation/supervision groups. These works bring together many ways of handling current, important issues in psychotherapy and EMDR treatment. They also include a helpful way to organize the data collected that is key to case consultation and the incorporation of EMDR into newly-trained practitioners' practices. (Luber, 2012a, p. iv)

This text is divided into three parts with 10 chapters that cover working with *anxiety disorders*, including specific phobia, panic disorder, and the use of a specific procedure in the treatment of anxiety disorder; *obsessive-compulsive and related disorders*, including obsessive-compulsive disorder, body dysmorphic disorder, olfactory reference syndrome, and hoarding behaviors; and *mood disorders*, including bipolar disorder, major depression, and postpartum depression. To address the specific needs of their populations, authors were asked to include the types of questions relevant for history taking, helpful resources and explanations needed in the preparation phase, particular negative and positive cognitions that were frequent in the assessment phase and for cognitive interweaves, other concerns during phases 4 (desensitization) through 8 (reevaluation), a section on case conceptualization and treatment planning, and any pertinent research on their work.

In Part I, "EMDR Therapy and Anxiety Disorders," the first chapter for "Specific Phobia" is by Ad de Jongh, on "EMDR Therapy for Specific Fears and Phobias: The Phobia Protocol." This is an updated version that originally appeared in *Eye Movement Desensitization and Reprocessing (EMDR) Scripted Protocols: Special Populations* (de Jongh, 2009) and includes an important addition on the "Flashforward Procedure." Under "Panic Disorder and Agoraphobia," Ferdinand Horst and Ad de Jongh's chapter, "EMDR Therapy Protocol for Panic Disorders With or Without Agoraphobia," points to the connection of panic attacks with the patient's perception of it as a life-threatening experience as the inspiration to work within the EMDR Therapy framework. In the section on "Use of Specialized

Procedures in the Treatment of Anxiety Disorders," Robin Logie and Ad de Jongh's chapter, "The Flashforward Procedure," introduces us to a very helpful way of addressing worst-case scenarios that have been resistant to resolution. This new procedure is included in a number of chapters in this book, because of its helpfulness in reframing and reprocessing difficult situations.

Part II, "EMDR Therapy and Obsessive-Compulsive and Related Disorders," used to be included in Anxiety Disorders in *DSM-IV* (American Psychiatric Association, 1994) and now has its own section in *DSM-5* (American Psychiatric Association, 2013). Karsten Böhm—who is on the German National Guideline Commission for the treatment of OCD—introduces us to the use of EMDR Therapy and OCD in his chapter, "Obsessive-Compulsive Disorder and EMDR Therapy." Therese McGoldrick has been an early proponent of the use of EMDR Therapy with body dysmorphic disorder. With her colleagues Millia Begum and Keith Brown, she introduces us to a "Body Dysmorphic Disorder and Olfactory Reference Syndrome EMDR Therapy Protocol." Priscilla Marquis and Christie Sprowls bring their wealth of knowledge of EMDR and the treatment of OCD spectrum disorders to their chapter, "EMDR Therapy and Hoarding: The Hoarding Protocol."

In Part III, "EMDR Therapy and Mood Disorders," the first section on "bipolar disorder contains the chapter "The EMDR Therapy Protocol for Bipolar Disorder." It is by the Barcelona EMDR Research Group under the tutelage of Benedikt L. Amann, and including Roser Batalla, Vicky Blanch, Dolors Capellades, Maria José Carvajal, Isabel Fernández, Francisca García, Walter Lupo, Marian Ponte, Maria José Sánchez, Jesús Sanfiz, Antonia Santed, and Marilyn Luber. It is based on the results of a controlled, randomized, single-blind pilot study with 20 bipolar I and II patients with subsyndromal symptoms, and a history of various traumatic events (Novo et al., 2014). The section "Major Depression" includes the chapter "DeprEnd©—EMDR Therapy Protocol for the Treatment for Depressive Disorders," by Arne Hofmann, Michael Hase, Peter Liebermann, Luca Ostacoli, Maria Lehnung, Franz Ebner, Christine Rost, Marilyn Luber, and Visal Tumani. DeprEnd© is the result of a European network of depression researchers who created the EDEN Study—a multicenter randomized study in Germany, Italy, Spain, and Turkey—and offers an elegant and helpful way to address major depression. The last two chapters, in the section "Postpartum Depression," by Anna Maria de Divitiis and Marilyn Luber, include "EMDR Therapy Protocol for the Prevention of Birth Trauma and Postpartum Depression for the Pregnant Woman," and "EMDR Therapy Group Protocol for the Prevention of Birth Trauma and Postpartum Depression for Pregnant Women." These chapters are helpful in primary prevention in an individual or group setting *to reduce or avoid* exposure to risk factors and to *enhance* clients' defenses to prevent or minimize the effects of exposure to risk factors by encouraging their optimal participation in the process of childbirth and strengthening their resilience to reduce the negative effects of stressors experienced during childbirth.

Appendix A includes the scripts for the 3-Pronged Protocol that include past memories, present triggers, and future templates. This section helps clinicians remember the important component parts of the Standard EMDR Therapy Protocol to ensure fidelity to the model. Furthermore, it allows practitioners to copy the protocols and put them in clients' charts. Appendix B includes an updated version of this author's "EMDR Summary Sheet" (Luber, 2009a) and the EMDR Therapy Session Form to assist in easy retrieval of important client information and the most important components of EMDR Therapy sessions. A summary sheet that serves as a checklist showing the important steps needed in these protocols accompanies each of these chapters, with a CD-version format also available to provide mobile access.

Eye Movement Desensitization and Reprocessing (EMDR) Therapy Scripted Protocols and Summary Sheets: Treating Anxiety, Obsessive-Compulsive, and Mood-Related Conditions, in the manner of its predecessors, offers EMDR Therapy practitioners and researchers a window into the treatment rooms of experts in the fields of anxiety, obsessive-compulsive, and spectrum disorders, and mood-related conditions. It is designed to apply what we are learning through research and to support the increasing knowledge and capabilities of clinicians in the method of EMDR Therapy.

References

Abbasnejad, M., Mahani, K. N., & Zamyad, A. (2007). Efficacy of "eye movement desensitization and reprocessing" in reducing anxiety and unpleasant feelings due to earthquake experience. *Psychological Research, 9*, 104–117.

ACE Study website. (2015). www.acestudy.org

American Psychiatric Association. (1994). *Diagnostic and statistical manual of mental disorders* (4th ed., text rev.). Washington, DC: Author.

American Psychiatric Association. (2013). *Diagnostic and statistical manual of mental disorders* (5th ed.). Arlington, VA: American Psychiatric Publishing.

Arabia, E., Manca, M. L., & Solomon, R. M. (2011). EMDR for survivors of life-threatening cardiac events: Results of a pilot study. *Journal of EMDR Practice and Research, 5*, 2–13.

Cvetek, R. (2008, March). EMDR treatment of distressful experiences that fail to meet the criteria for PTSD. *Journal of EMDR Practice and Research, 2*(1), 2–14.

de Jongh, A. (2009). EMDR and specific fears: The phobia protocol single traumatic event. In M. Luber (Ed.), *Eye movement desensitization and reprocessing (EMDR) scripted protocols: Special populations* (pp. 575–610). New York, NY: Springer.

Doering, S., Ohlmeier, M.-C., de Jongh, A., Hofmann, A., & Bisping, V. (2013). Efficacy of a trauma-focused treatment approach for dental phobia: A randomized clinical trial. *European Journal of Oral Sciences, 121*, 584–593.

EMDR Institute website, www.emdr.com

Felitti, V. J., & Anda, R. F. (2009). The relationship of adverse childhood experiences to adult medical disease, psychiatric disorders, and sexual behavior: Implications for healthcare. In R. Lanius, E. Vermetten, & C. Pain (Eds.), *The hidden epidemic: The impact of early life trauma on health and disease.* Cambridge, UK: Cambridge University Press.

Feske, U., & Goldstein, A. (1997). Eye movement desensitization and reprocessing treatment for panic disorder: A controlled outcome and partial dismantling study. *Journal of Consulting and Clinical Psychology, 36*, 1026–1035.

Goldstein, A. J., de Beurs, E., Chambless, D. L., & Wilson, K. A. (2001). EMDR for panic disorder with agoraphobia: Comparison with waiting list and credible attention-placebo control condition. *Journal of Consulting and Clinical Psychology, 68*, 947–956.

Luber, M. (Ed.). (2009a). *Eye movement desensitization and reprocessing (EMDR) scripted protocols: Basics and special situations.* New York, NY: Springer.

Luber, M. (Ed.). (2009b). *Eye movement desensitization and reprocessing (EMDR) scripted protocols: Special populations.* New York, NY: Springer.

Luber, M. (Ed.). (2012a). *Eye movement desensitization and reprocessing (EMDR) scripted protocols with summary sheets (CD ROM Version): Basics and special situations.* New York, NY: Springer.

Luber, M. (Ed.). (2012b). *Eye movement desensitization and reprocessing (EMDR) scripted protocols with summary sheets (CD ROM Version): Special populations.* New York, NY: Springer.

Luber, M. (Ed.). (2014). *Implementing EMDR early mental health interventions for man-made and natural disasters: Models, scripted protocols and summary sheets.* New York, NY: Springer.

Muris, P., & Merckelbach, H. (1997). Treating spider phobics with eye-movement desensitization and reprocessing: A controlled study. *Behavioural and Cognitive Psychotherapy, 25*, 39–50.

Muris, P., Merckelbach, H., Holdrinet, I., & Sijsenaar, M. (1998). Treating phobic children: Effects of EMDR versus exposure. *Journal of Consulting and Clinical Psychology, 66*, 193–198.

Muris, P., Merckelbach, H., van Haaften, H., & Mayer, B. (1997). Eye movement desensitization and reprocessing versus exposure in vivo. *British Journal of Psychiatry, 171*, 82–86.

Nazari, H., Momeni, N., Jariani, M., & Tarrahi, M. J. (2011). Comparison of eye movement desensitization and reprocessing with citalopram in treatment of obsessive-compulsive disorder. *International Journal of Psychiatry in Clinical Practice, 15*, 270–274.

Novo, P., Landin-Romero, R., Radua, J., Vicens, V., Fernandez, I., Garcia, F.,...Amann, B. L. (2014). Eye movement desensitization and reprocessing therapy in subsyndromal bipolar patients with a history of traumatic events: A randomized, controlled pilot-study. *Psychiatry Research, 219*(1), 122–128.

Shapiro, F. (1995). *Eye movement desensitization and reprocessing: Basic principles, protocols and procedures.* New York, NY: Guilford Press.

Shapiro, F. (2001). *Eye movement desensitization and reprocessing: Basic principles, protocols and procedures* (2nd ed.). New York, NY: Guilford Press.

Shapiro, F. (2002). *EMDR as an integrative psychotherapy approach: Experts of diverse orientations explore the paradigm prism.* Washington, DC: American Psychological Association Press.

Shapiro, F. (2006). *EMDR: New notes on adaptive information processing with case formulation principles, forms, scripts and worksheets.* Watsonville, CA: EMDR Institute.

Shapiro, F. (2007). *EMDR: Part 1 training manual.* Watsonville, CA: EMDR Institute.

Triscari, M. T., Faraci, P., D'Angelo, V., Urso, V., & Catalisano, D. (2011). Two treatments for fear of flying compared: Cognitive behavioral therapy combined with systematic desensitization or eye movement desensitization and reprocessing (EMDR). *Aviation Psychology and Applied Human Factor, 1*, 9–14.

Acknowledgments

The idea for—what has become—these new texts began in 2010 after editing two books on EMDR Scripted Protocols. I was thinking about all of the clinical creativity of my colleagues and how important it is to support their work. Ad de Jongh and I were sitting together at an EMDR Europe conference and talking about how to include some of the fascinating research that colleagues have been doing in Europe, especially in the Netherlands. We decided that addressing trauma-, anxiety-, depression-, and medical-related issues would be most illuminating and helpful to our EMDR community. I began developing this project and, in due course, signed a contract with Springer Publishing in November 2010.

On March 11, 2011, the world stepped in by way of the Tōhoku earthquake and tsunami in Japan, and our EMDR community mobilized to help our Japanese colleagues. I pulled together the Recent Event protocols we had worked on in *Eye Movement Desensitization and Reprocessing (EMDR) Scripted Protocols: Basics and Special Situations* to send to the members of EMDR Japan. An international group of concerned EMDR practitioners rallied to support them through webinars, including Ignacio Jarero to teach his team's EMDR-Integrative Group Treatment Protocol (EMDR-IGTP); Elan Shapiro, to teach his and Brurit Laub's Recent-Traumatic Episode Protocol (R-TEP); and Carol Martin, who facilitated donations through EMDR HAP's website. As a result of this process and other catastrophes, I thought that it would be helpful to have a place where all of the updated EMDR work on recent traumatic response would be available, and proposed this to my editor, Sheri Sussman. Ever resourceful, pragmatic, and cognizant of the importance of helping our colleagues respond to recent events, she was enthusiastic and convinced Springer management to switch the deadlines so that *Implementing EMDR Early Mental Health Interventions for Man-Made and Natural Disasters: Models, Scripted Protocols, and Summary Sheets* preempted the earlier contracted book.

By the time that *Implementing EMDR Early Mental Health Interventions for Man-Made and Natural Disasters: Models, Scripted Protocols, and Summary Sheets* was delivered in 2013 and published in 2014, the *DSM-IV* (American Psychiatric Association [APA], 1994) had transitioned to the *DSM-5* (APA, 2013), so I had to reorganize the current project. Sheri and I also decided to separate this book into three volumes: Treating Anxiety, Obsessive-Compulsive, and Mood-Related Conditions; Treating Trauma and Stressor-Related Conditions; and Treating Medical-Related Issues. I want to acknowledge the help of Ad de Jongh and Arne Hofmann in this process. These supportive and knowledgeable friends and colleagues assisted me in setting up a new structure for the project and suggested some of the content.

I want to recognize the joint efforts of the 31 authors of these 10 chapters from seven countries (Germany, Italy, The Netherlands, Spain, Turkey, United Kingdom, and United States) to complete *Eye Movement Desensitization and Reprocessing (EMDR) Therapy Scripted Protocols: Treating Anxiety, Obsessive-Compulsive, and Mood-Related Conditions*. I owe a great debt to each one of them for the time and energy that they devoted to this project. However, in many cases, our efforts went beyond that. The joy of interaction with my intelligent and creative colleagues is the essence of this effort and is one of the reasons that I continue to edit and work on these chapters. Experiencing their perspectives widened my own as I learned how they cope with the dilemmas of working with their particular population. I hope this text will inspire the clinicians who read it and help them to think about their clinical challenges within the context and structure of EMDR Therapy.

I would like to thank Springer Publishing for the faith that they have demonstrated by publishing this body of work. I would like to acknowledge Sheri W. Sussman—always—for her support, dedication to these projects, and always finding a way to help me as I work within my own time limitations dealing with my practice, my life, and the inevitable book deadlines. She never fails to meet my requests with thoughtfulness and a smile—even in some of the more challenging circumstances. Thank you, Sheri, this book would have been impossible without you.

My consultation groups have always been a point of inspiration and feedback for some of the questions I have had with concept and content. I would like to acknowledge Bernie Epstein, Jane Hart, Kelly Jude, Dave Kannerstein, Diane Koury Alessi, Stephanie Lunt, Kathy Miller, Marie Manzo, Bobby Posmontier, and Sarah Trotta for their feedback on my updated summary sheets, and for sharing their wisdom as clinicians in the consultation groups.

I would like to thank and acknowledge the Western Massachusetts EMDR Regional Group for choosing me as their keynote speaker in May 2014. Their invitation was for me to speak about these four books (now six) on scripted protocols. I had not had the occasion to step back and review this body of work in which I had been engaged for nearly a decade, and they gave me a reason to do so. As I did, I looked at the basic statistics for the 6 books and found that there are approximately 135 authors, 126 chapters (including some updates of the same chapter), from 14 countries on 6 continents (although this may shift a bit before everything is submitted)! Thanks to Jim Helling, my keynote was titled, "EMDR Protocols and EMDR Practice: A Clinician's Journey Toward Mastery." It was a challenge to prepare an overview of this amount of work; however, I focused on recent trauma, the importance of self-care for practitioners, and an overview of the books themselves. I came up with eight important take-home messages about the process of my work that I shared with my Western Massachusetts audience:

- *Know the basics*: EMDR Therapy is a psychotherapy approach and how you conceptualize your client's issue is critical. Know the AIP, the EMDR 3-Pronged Protocol, the EMDR 11-step procedure, and the eight EMDR Therapy phases.
- *Pay attention*: Make sure you are paying attention to all aspects of your clients' presentation, such as their body language, facial expressions, tone of voice, how they interact with you, and how you feel in their presence.
- *Keep your eye on the ball*: Know the client's goals, create the treatment plan together, and reevaluate at intervals.
- *Keep it simple*: The Standard EMDR Therapy Protocol is robust. Use it as your standard as well as the eight phases. Use other EMDR Therapy protocols when the Standard EMDR Protocol is not the best option, as in special situations and/or special populations, while keeping the Standard EMDR Therapy Protocol always in mind.
- *Consult to grow*: Work within your area of expertise, talk to your colleagues, check the *Journal of EMDR Practice and Research* and the Francine Shapiro Library to see what others are doing, get supervision to learn about a new area of expertise, and consult when you are triggered and it persists.
- *Remember where you come from*: You bring your unique self to the art and science of your therapeutic work, so learn EMDR Therapy and the basics. Always remember yourself and your own unique style. EMDR Therapy becomes yours when you integrate your style with the basic tenets of EMDR Therapy.
- *Take care of yourself*: Take a personal, professional, and spiritual life review at intervals. Notice what you do to take care of yourself and notice if you are not taking care of yourself so that you can ask for help. Keep a list of symptoms of vicarious trauma/burnout and check to see if you are showing signs or symptoms. Have a buddy and check in with each other at intervals.
- *Connect with the EMDR community*: EMDR Therapy is prevalent worldwide. Connect with your EMDR Association and your EMDR Therapy community group locally. Volunteer for Trauma Recovery: EMDR HAP and create a Trauma Recovery Network (TRN) in your region. WE NEED YOU!

I would like to add two more take-home messages in keeping with the importance of adding research into our clinical work:

- *Use assessment measures*: Utilize assessment measures to follow your clients' progress and outcome.
- *Contribute to research*: Individually or in conjunction with a larger group, set up your study. Reach out to the EMDR Research Foundation for help with your project.

Throughout the process of writing these books, there have been a group of friends and colleagues who have been a consistent source of encouragement and inspiration. Thank you Elaine Alvarez, Michael Broder, Catherine Fine, Robbie Dunton, Irene Geissl, Richard Goldberg, Arlene Goldman, Barbara Grinnell, Barbara Hensley, Donald Nathanson, Mark Nickerson, Zona Scheiner, Howard Wainer, Stuart Wolfe, and Bennet Wolper.

I would like to recognize Barbara J. Hensley for her enormous contribution of the Francine Shapiro Library (FSL). The FSL has been a constant resource for me especially while writing these books from the moment it was online.

As always, I would like to thank Francine Shapiro. Her gift of EMDR Therapy to the world and to me has been incomparable.

I would like to remember my "Aunt" Sis Eisman and "Uncle" Henry Rosenfeld, both of whom passed away early in 2015. They would have loved to see this new book come to fruition.

I would like to acknowledge and thank the people who are involved in my daily life, helping me in so many invaluable ways that allow me both to have a "day" job and to indulge my interest in writing. They are Harry Cook, Rose Turner, and Dennis Wright. My overwhelming thanks to Lew Rossi, who has kept my computers working, even in the shadow of disasters and major catastrophes. I want to acknowledge my miniature schnauzer dog, Emmy Luber, who has been part of my writing from the beginning and always reminds me to take a break and connect with her. Thank you to Shirley Luber, my mother, who has been the primary audience for all I have written from kindergarten to my dissertation and into the present.

I would also like to acknowledge Bob Raymar, who has recently come back into my life after 45 years and changed it in so many ways. Thank you, Bob, for your caring and assistance: listening to my very long keynote, being infinitely patient, always finding time to comment on what I have written, lending me your insightful and discerning perspective and for showing me that the essence of someone can last over time.

I would like to recognize my friend and colleague, Ad de Jongh, by dedicating this book to him. I have known Ad from the early days of EMDR Therapy and he has been an extraordinary resource in the EMDR Therapy community. He has worked to uphold the standard of EMDR Therapy in the Netherlands and taught his colleagues and his students the importance of working within the scientific model by developing the Dutch EMDR Association (one of the largest), hosting continuing education, teaching university students, promoting EMDR Therapy, and helping put together the publication, "EMDR Nieuwsbrief." He is responsible through his own work and his students for a great deal of research on a wide range of topics, especially with anxiety disorders, and with challenging populations, such as patients presenting with psychosis, intellectual disabilities, and so on. He has presented nationally and internationally and won many awards for his work. Most recently (2014), he was awarded the EMDR Research Award from EMDRIA. For me personally, he has been a friend, collaborator, and someone to whom I can turn to discuss ideas and get valuable feedback. Thank you, Ad, for all that you have done for the EMDR community and for me.

I

There are three chapters in Part I: EMDR Therapy and Anxiety Disorders; these chapters are Specific Phobia, Panic Disorder, and Use of Specific Procedures in the Treatment of Anxiety Disorders. Thus, this part is not to be considered a complete representation of anxiety disorders.

Alan Goldstein was one of the first psychologists to see the possibilities of Eye Movement Desensitization and Reprocessing (EMDR) Therapy for the treatment of anxiety disorders. He presented a paper titled *The Role of Eye Movement Desensitization and Reprocessing in the Treatment of Panic and Agoraphobia* at the Fourth World Congress on Behaviour Therapy in Queensland, Australia, in July 1992. Not long after this, Sanderson and Carpenter (1992) wrote the first article on phobias in the *Journal of Behavior Therapy and Experimental Psychiatry*, Kleinknecht (1993) reported on the rapid treatment of blood and injection phobias with EMDR, and Bauman and Melnyk (1994) published their study on eye movements and tapping in the treatment of test anxiety in the same journal. Goldstein and Feske (1994) published a series of case studies on EMDR and panic disorder in the *Journal of Anxiety Disorders*.

Specific Phobia

By 1993, Ad de Jongh and Erik ten Broeke began publishing their findings on specific phobias. Their coauthors included colleagues, namely de Roos, Renssen, van der Meer, Serra, Holmshaw, Doering, and van den Oord. Their first work appeared in the Dutch journal *Tijdschrift voor Directieve Therapy and Hypnose* and since then they have published the following:

- *Three books* (de Jongh & ten Broeke, 2003/2013; de Jongh & ten Broeke, 2011; ten Broeke, de Jongh, & Oppenheim, 2008/2012) and 17 book chapters
- *Thirteen articles in Dutch vetted journals* (de Jongh & ten Broeke, 1993, 1994, 1996, 1998, 2001a, 2001b, 2001c, 2002a, 2002b, 2007; ten Broeke & de Jongh, 1993, 1995, 1997)
- *Eight articles on EMDR and phobias in international journals* (de Jongh & ten Broeke, 1998, 2007, 2009b; de Jongh, ten Broeke, & Meijer, 2010; de Jongh, ten Broeke, & Renssen, 1999, 2001; de Jongh, ten Broeke, & van der Meer, 1995; de Jongh, van den Oord, & ten Broeke, 2002)
- *Two articles in the EMDRIA Newsletter* (de Jongh & ten Broeke, 2000a, 2000b)

In 2009, Ad de Jongh and Erik ten Broeke wrote, "EMDR and the Anxiety Disorders: Exploring the Current Status" for the *Journal of EMDR Practice and Research*'s Special Section on the 20th Anniversary of EMDR. Their article was based on *Diagnostic and Statistical Manual of Mental Disorders–Fourth Edition*'s (*DSM-4*) criteria so their review of obsessive-compulsive disorder (OCD)—with the advent of *DSM-5*—would now be part of another category of disorders. They hypothesized that EMDR Therapy would be an excellent treatment for many of the anxiety disorders because these conditions often start as a result of adverse life events (for panic disorder and agoraphobia, see Kleiner & Marshall, 1987; for social phobia criteria, see American Psychiatric Association, 2000; for specific phobias, see de Jong, Fransen, Oosterink-Wubbe, & Aartman, 2006; Oosterink, de Jongh, & Aartman, 2009; for generalized anxiety disorder (GAD), see Roemer, Molina, Litz, & Borkovec, 1997), and/or these patients suffer from posttraumatic stress disorder (PTSD)-type symptoms (for panic attacks, see McNally & Lukach, 1992; for specific phobias, see de Jongh et al., 2006).

Although in vivo exposure has proven to be the treatment of choice for many specific phobias (Wolitzky-Taylor, Horowitz, Powers, & Telch, 2008), there is increasing support to show that EMDR is effective for fears and specific phobias in controlled case reports (e.g., de Jongh, 2012; de Jongh et al., 2002; Lohr, Tolin, & Kleinknecht, 1996) and case-controlled studies (de Jongh, Holmshaw, Carswell, & van Wijk, 2010); uncontrolled case reports as well are describing positive results (e.g., de Roos & de Jongh, 2008; de Jongh & ten Broeke, 1994, 1998; Kleinknecht, 1993; Marquis, 1991).

Despite the promise that EMDR Therapy holds for the treatment of a specific phobia, there are only three randomized controlled outcome studies concerning the treatment of spider phobia by the same group: Muris and Merckelbach (1997); Muris, Merckelback, Holdrinet, and Sijsenaar (1998); and Muris, Merckelbach, van Haaften, and Mayer (1997). The early studies reported that EMDR Therapy showed some significant changes in the Subjective Units of Disturbance (SUD) scale; however, in vivo exposure showed superior results in participants' approach behaviors and reducing avoidance behaviors. These studies did *not* follow the Standard EMDR Protocol in the following ways: lack of the future template; not preparing patients for the confrontation with anxiety-eliciting stimuli or situations, for example, not teaching self-regulatory skills; limited treatment spent on processing; and inadequate number of sessions. Therefore, these studies and their results are *not* accurate representations of EMDR Therapy.

Ad de Jongh's "EMDR Therapy for Specific Fears and Phobias: The Phobia Protocol" is an updated version of a chapter that appeared in *Eye Movement Desensitization and Reprocessing (EMDR) Scripted Protocols: Special Populations* (Luber, 2009). De Jongh is thorough in his presentation of how to work with this population with a protocol that has been used in clinical practice and research projects (e.g., de Jongh et al., 2002; Doering, Ohlmeier, de Jongh, Hofmann, & Bisping, 2013). During Phase 1, he reviews the criteria for Specific Phobia, elicits what triggers the fear and helps identify the expected consequences, assesses the validity of the catastrophe, provides practical information about the fear or phobia, determines attainable treatment goal/goals, and identifies the touchstone event, the ancillary event/events, the most frightening events, and the most recent events related to the specific fear. In Phase 2, he explains EMDR Therapy and teaches distraction techniques for anxiety management between sessions. Phases 3 to 6 follow the Standard EMDR Protocol. He introduces the "Flashforward Procedure" (see Chapter 3) and addresses future concerns intensively through the installation of the future template, a video check, and in vivo confrontations. Closure is important and homework is in support of maintaining changes in between sessions. Reevaluation is a time to check the homework and the progress the client is making in between sessions.

Panic Disorder and Agoraphobia

EMDR Therapy could be very helpful in treating panic disorder and agoraphobia. In the sparse research available, researchers found that most clients benefited from EMDR Therapy by showing a decrease in panic attacks, severity of anticipatory anxiety, and general signs of distress (de Jongh & ten Broeke, 1996; Fernandez & Faretta, 2007; Feske & Goldstein, 1997; Goldstein, de Beurs, Chambless, & Wilson, 2001; Goldstein & Feske, 1994). Although further research by Feske and Goldstein (1997) with a randomized controlled study where EMDR was compared with a protocol without eye movements and a wait-list condition looked promising at first, the effects did not hold up after a 3-month follow-up. In 2001, Goldstein et al. investigated the efficacy of EMDR compared to association and relaxation therapy (ART): although EMDR Therapy was significantly better versus the wait-list group on the severity of panic and agoraphobic criteria, there was no difference on cognitive assessment and number of panic attacks.

Shapiro (1999) argued that more preparation is needed to get a positive outcome; this contention is supported by Fernandez and Faretta's work (2007) with a woman with panic disorder where they increased the preparation phase to six sessions, resulting in remission of her symptoms and maintenance of her changes on a 1-year follow-up. In 2009, Leeds gave a critique of the difficulties with past research in order to come up with alternatives: his two models of treatment for panic disorder and panic disorder with agoraphobia. He asks for a treatment plan that addresses this population's difficulty dealing with deep feelings, which includes "concrete anxiety management skills, resource development and installation for self-soothing and affect tolerance and then initially targets their panic attacks," although these hypotheses must be investigated. According to Leeds, patients need a sense of mastery and confidence in the EMDR Therapy process, including a good enough sense of trust in the therapeutic relationship by reprocessing memories of the first, worst, and most recent panic attacks, before addressing "the core painful affects" that support the structure of the panic attacks and agoraphobia. An abbreviated version of this model can be found in his 2012 *Journal of EMDR Practice and Research* article "EMDR Treatment of Panic Disorder and Agoraphobia: Two Model Treatment Plans." The question is whether this is true. A recent study on PTSD in patients with psychosis or schizophrenia showed that EMDR Therapy can be applied safely and effectively without any form of preparation prior to memory processing (even without the Safe Place exercise) and even with a vulnerable group like those with as severe a psychiatric condition as psychosis (van den Berg et al., in press). The same holds true for panic disorder with agoraphobia. Results of a randomized controlled trial comparing EMDR Therapy with cognitive behavioral therapy (CBT; introceptive exposure) for patients suffering with this condition showed that EMDR Therapy is efficacious even if the patients are treated without much preparation (van der Horst et al., in preparation). However, there are two studies and it is best to err on the side of caution if the client needs more preparation.

Ferdinand Horst and Ad de Jongh address the subject of EMDR and panic disorder in their chapter "EMDR Protocol for Panic Disorders With or Without Agoraphobia." They point out the importance of determining the first and/or worst panic attack memory, the most recent memory, and other panic attack memories as appropriate targets for EMDR, as well as additional stressful life events that do not meet the criteria for PTSD but could be important for the development of panic disorder. In particular situations where processing has occurred and the client is still avoiding the situations where it would be difficult to escape (agoraphobic memories), they suggest the Flashforward Procedure.

Use of Specific Procedures in the Treatment of Anxiety Disorders

This last chapter in this section is "The Flashforward Procedure" by Logie and de Jongh (2014), which showcases the use of a specific procedure for the treatment of anxiety disorders. The Flashforward Procedure is considered the operationalization of anticipatory fear, which has its focus on the future and is considered to be the second prong of the 3-Pronged Protocol. Because many conditions specifically pertain to fear of future catastrophic events as being an important part of the condition, the Flashforward Procedure could be helpful in addressing specific phobias, OCD, body dysmorphic disorder, hypochondriasis, psychosis and schizophrenia, PTSD, and anorexia nervosa.

The term "flashforwards" was first used by Holmes, Crane, Fennell, and Williams (2007) to explain the cognitive processes underlying suicidal thinking to improve treatment for patients who have suicidal imagery of a future suicide attempt. They posited that the current images appear like flashforwards to suicide, echoing flashbacks in PTSD by also possessing sensory qualities, feeling real and compelling, and being rich in detail. They suggested targeting several imagery features, such as changing the flashforward outcome to an alternative to suicide, reducing imagery reality and preoccupation, reducing comfort, or "imagery rescripting."

As Engelhard, van den Hout, Janssen, and van der Beek (2010) reported in their article, "Eye movements reduce vividness and emotionality of 'flashforwards,'" their goal was "to examine whether eye movements, indeed, reduce vividness and emotionality of visual images about feared future events compared to a no dual-task (exposure only) condition, in a non-clinical sample under controlled conditions." They postulated that eye movements, in keeping with the working memory account (Andrade, Kavanagh, & Baddeley, 1997; Gunter & Bodner, 2008; van den Hout et al., 2001), would affect not only the vividness of past images but future-oriented ones as well; their findings upheld their hypothesis. In 2011, Engelhard et al. studied whether eye movement also affects recurrent, intrusive visual images about potential future catastrophes (flashforwards) in a sample of female undergraduates who reported such intrusions. The results were positive for less vividness of the intrusive images after recall with eye movement in comparison to just recall, with a comparable trend for emotionality.

De Jongh and ten Broeke (2009b) wrote that 20 years after EMDR's introduction, there was little data to support the efficacy of EMDR Therapy for anxiety disorders other than PTSD. At that time, randomized outcome research was available only for panic disorder with agoraphobia and spider phobia. The outcome of this research reported that EMDR Therapy was less effective than exposure-based interventions (evidence-based interventions) but more effective than no-treatment control conditions or nonspecific interventions. De Jongh and ten Broeke concluded that even these results were flawed, as the studies used incomplete protocols or limited courses of treatment, so that the true success of EMDR Therapy with anxiety disorders remained a question.

In 2011, Triscari, Faraci, D'Angelo, Urso, and Catalisano improved their research and had two treatment conditions (CBT with systematic desensitization or EMDR Therapy) for patients with aerophobia. Patients were randomly assigned to these two experimental groups in a before- and after-treatment research design. The effectiveness of each group was evaluated comparing the pre- and post- levels of flying within subjects; comparison of the posttreatment scores between groups was done as well. Results showed the efficacy of each model with significant improvement in both conditions. In the best test of what EMDR Therapy could mean in treating specific phobias until now, Doering, Ohlmeier, de Jongh, Hofman, and Bisping (2013) compared 31 dental phobic patients randomly assigned to two conditions (EMDR or wait-list control). Results showed significant reduction in dental anxiety and avoidance behavior as well as symptoms of PTSD; at a 1-year follow-up, 83% of the patients were in regular dental treatment. Their findings suggested that processing memories of past adverse dental experiences can be helpful for patients with dental phobia.

De Jongh and ten Broeke (2009b) quoted from de Jongh, ten Broeke, and Renssen (1999):

> The empirical support for EMDR with specific phobias is still meager; therefore, one should remain cautious. However, given that there is insufficient research to validate any method for complex or trauma related phobias, that EMDR is a time-limited procedure, and that it can be used in cases for which an exposure in vivo approach is difficult to administer, the application of EMDR with specific phobias merits further clinical and research attention (pp. 69–70)....Now, 10 years later, not much seems to have changed, and it has become even clearer that these conclusions pertain not only to specific phobia but also to the full spectrum of anxiety disorders, except PTSD. (p. 139)

Currently, 6 years later, there is not much change in the state of research with anxiety disorders from de Jongh and ten Broeke's 2009 report. EMDR Therapy remains at the crossroads of acceptance; without gold-standard research on anxiety disorders, the future in this area will be severely limited.

To support the use of these protocols, summary sheets accompany each of these chapters to create a reminder of the salient points in the chapter and to provide a place to enter data for patients.

References

American Psychiatric Association. (2000). *Diagnostic and statistical manual of mental disorders* (4th ed., text revision). Washington, DC: Author.

Andrade, J., Kavanagh, D., & Baddeley, A. (1997, May). Eye-movements and visual imagery: A working memory approach to the treatment of post-traumatic stress disorder. *British Journal of Clinical Psychology, 36*(2), 209–223. doi:10.1111/j.2044-8260.1997.tb01408.x

Bauman, W., & Melnyk, W. (1994, March). A controlled comparison of eye movements and finger tapping in the treatment of test anxiety. *Journal of Behavior Therapy and Experimental Psychiatry, 25*(1), 29–33. doi:10.1016/0005-7916(94)90060-4

de Jongh, A. (2012). Treatment of a woman with emetophobia: A trauma focused approach. *Mental Illness, 4*(1) 10–14.

de Jongh, A., Fransen, J., Oosterink-Wubbe, F., & Aartman, I. H. A. (2006). Psychological trauma exposure and trauma symptoms among individuals with high and low levels of dental anxiety. *European Journal of Oral Sciences, 114,* 286–292.

de Jongh, A., Holmshaw, M., Carswell, W., & van Wijk, A. (2010). Usefulness of a trauma-focused treatment approach for travel phobia. *Clinical Psychology Psychotherapy.* doi:10.1002/cpp.680

de Jongh, A., & ten Broeke, E. (1993). Een nieuwe behandelingsmethode voor angst entrauma's: Eye Movement Desensitization and Reprocessing. *Tijdschrift voor Directieve Therapie en Hypnose, 13,* 161–170.

de Jongh, A., & ten Broeke, E. (1994, June). Opmerkelijke veranderingen na één zitting met eye movement desensitization and reprocessing: Een geval van angst voor misselijkheid en braken—[Noteworthy changes after one session with eye movement desensitization and reprocessing: A case of fear of nausea and vomiting]. *Tijdschrift voor Directieve Therapie en Hypnose, 14*(2), 90–102.

de Jongh, A., & ten Broeke, E. (1996, April). Eye movement desensitization and reprocessing (EMDR): Een procedure voor de behandeling van aan trauma gerelateerde angst [Eye movement desensitization and reprocessing (EMDR): A procedure for the treatment of trauma-related anxiety]. *Tijdschrift voor Psychotherapie, 22*(2), 53–64. doi:10.1007/BF03079287

de Jongh, A., & ten Broeke, E. (1998). Treatment of choking phobia by targeting traumatic memories with EMDR: A case study. *Clinical Psychology and Psychotherapy, 5,* 264–269.

de Jongh, A., & ten Broeke, E. (2000a). Why and how to use "in vivo exposure" in EMDR. *EMDRIA Newsletter, 5*(3), 18.

de Jongh, A., & ten Broeke, E. (2000b). The use of "exposure" in EMDR. *EMDRIA Newsletter, 5*(4), 4–8.

de Jongh, A., & ten Broeke, E. (2001a). Eye Movement Desensitization and Reprocessing (EMDR): Effectieve behandeling van psychisch trauma. *Fysioscooop, 27*(4), 27–30.

de Jongh, A., & ten Broeke, E. (2001b). EMDR bij de behandeling van PTSS na verkrachting. *Directieve Therapie, 21,* 229–245.

de Jongh, A., & ten Broeke, E. (2001c). Eye Movement Desensitization and Reprocessing (EMDR): Kortdurende behandeling van psychotrauma. *GGzet Wetenschappelijk, 5*(3), 15–21.

de Jongh, A., & ten Broeke, E. (2002a). Verwerking van schokkende gebeurtenissen met Eye Movement Desensitization and Reprocessing (EMDR). *Psychopraxis, 4*(1), 21–27.

de Jongh, A., & ten Broeke, E. (2002b). Eye Movement Desensitization and Reprocessing (EMDR): Geprotocolleerde behandelmethode voor traumatische belevingen. *Tijdschrift van de Kinder en Jeugdpsychotherapie, 29*(3), 46–60.

de Jongh, A., & ten Broeke, E. (2003). *Handboek EMDR: Een geprotocolleerde behandelmethode voor de gevolgen van psychotrauma.* Lisse, The Netherlands: Swets & Zeitlinger.

de Jongh, A., & ten Broeke, E. (2007). Treatment of specific phobias with EMDR: Conceptualization and strategies for the selection of appropriate memories. *Journal of EMDR Practice and Research, 1*(1), 46–57.

de Jongh, A., & ten Broeke, E. (2009a). Linksom met EMDR [Left with EMDR]. In E. ten Broeke, de Jongh, A., & H.-J. Oppenheim (Eds.), *Praktijkboek EMDR: Casusconceptualisatie en specifieke patiëntengroepen* (pp. 53–69). Amsterdam, The Netherlands: Pearson.

de Jongh, A., & ten Broeke, E. (2009b). EMDR and the anxiety disorders: Exploring the current status. *Journal of EMDR Practice and Research, 3*(3), 133–140. doi:10.1891/1933-3196.3.3.133

de Jongh, A., & ten Broeke, E. (2011, November). *Vraagbaak EMDR: Oplossingen en tips voor EMDR-behandelingen [Toolbox EMDR: Tips and advice for difficult EMDR treatments]*. Amsterdam, The Netherlands: Pearson.

de Jongh, A., & ten Broeke, E. (2013). *Handboek EMDR: Een geprotocolleerde behandelmethode voor de gevolgen van psychotrauma* (6th ed.). Amsterdam, The Netherlands: Pearson Assessment and Information B.V. [ISBN 978 90 265 2243 7].

de Jongh, A., ten Broeke, E., & Meijer, S. (2010). Two method approach: A case conceptualization model in the context of EMDR. *Journal of EMDR Practice and Research, 4,* 12–21.

de Jongh, A., ten Broeke, E., & Renssen, M. R. (1999). Treatment of specific phobias with eye movement desensitization and reprocessing (EMDR): Protocol, empirical status, and conceptual issues. *Journal of Anxiety Disorders, 13,* 69–85.

de Jongh, A., ten Broeke, E., & Renssen, M. R. (2001). Treatment of specific phobias with Eye Movement Desensitization and Reprocessing (EMDR): Protocol, empirical status, and conceptual issues. *Zhurnal practikuyuscego psihologa [Journal of the Practicing Psychologist], 7,* 182–200.

de Jongh, A., ten Broeke, E., & van der Meer, K. (1995). Eine neue entwicklung in der behandlung von angst und traumata: Eye movement desensitization and reprocessing (EMDR) [A new development in the treatment of anxiety and trauma: Eye movement desensitization and reprocessing (EMDR)]. *Zeitschrift für Klinische Psychologie, Psychopathologie und Psychotherapie, 43*(3), 226–233.

de Jongh, A., van den Oord, H., & ten Broeke, E. (2002, December). Efficacy of eye movement desensitization and reprocessing in the treatment of specific phobias: Four single-case studies on dental phobia. *Journal of Clinical Psychology, 58*(12), 1489–1503.

de Roos, C., & de Jongh, A. (2008). EMDR treatment of children and adolescents with a choking phobia. *Journal of EMDR Practice and Research, 2*(3), 201–211. doi:10.1891/1933-3196.2.3.201

Doering, S., Ohlmeier, M.-C., de Jongh, A., Hofmann, A., & Bisping, V. (2013). Efficacy of a trauma-focused treatment approach for dental phobia: A randomized clinical trial. *European Journal of Oral Sciences, 121,* 584–593.

Engelhard, I. M., van den Hout, M. A., Dek, E. C. P., Giele, C. L., van der Wielen, J. W., Reijnen, M. J., & van Roij, B. (2011, May). Reducing vividness and emotional intensity of recurrent "flashforwards" by taxing working memory: An analogue study. *Journal of Anxiety Disorders, 25*(4), 599–603. doi:10.1016/j.janxdis.2011.01.009

Engelhard, I. M., van den Hout, M. A., Janssen, W. C., & van der Beek, J. (2010, May). Eye movements reduce vividness and emotionality of "flashforwards." *Behaviour Research and Therapy, 48*(5), 442–447. doi:10.1016/j.brat.2010.01.003

Fernandez, I., & Faretta, E. (2007, February). Eye movement desensitization and reprocessing in the treatment of panic disorder with agoraphobia. *Clinical Case Studies, 6*(1), 44–63. doi:10.1177/1534650105277220

Feske, U., & Goldstein, A. (1997). Eye movement desensitization and reprocessing treatment for panic disorder: A controlled outcome and partial dismantling study. *Journal of Consulting and Clinical Psychology, 36,* 1026–1035.

Gauvreau, P., & Bouchard, S. P. (2008). Preliminary evidence for the efficacy of EMDR in treating generalized anxiety disorder. *Journal of EMDR Practice and Research, 2,* 26–40.

Goldstein, A., & Feske, U. (1994, October–December). Eye movement desensitization and reprocessing for panic disorder: A case series. *Journal of Anxiety Disorders, 8*(4), 351–362. doi:10.1016/0887-6185(94)00023-9

Goldstein, A. J., de Beurs, E., Chambless, D. L., & Wilson, K. A. (2001, June). Treating panic disorders with EMDR. *Clinician's Research Digest, 19*(6), 3.

Gunter, R. W., & Bodner, G. E. (2008, August). How eye movements affect unpleasant memories: Support for a working-memory account. *Behaviour Research and Therapy, 46*(8), 913–931. doi:10.1016/j.brat.2008.04.006

Holmes, E. A., Crane, C., Fennell, M. J. V., & Williams, J. M. G. (2007). Imagery about suicide in depression—Flash-forwards? *Journal of Behavior Therapy and Experimental Psychiatry, 38*(4): 423–434. [PMC free article] [PubMed]

Kleiner, L., & Marshall, W. L. (1987). The role of interpersonal problems in the development of agoraphobia with panic attacks. *Journal of Anxiety Disorders, 1,* 313–323.

Kleinknecht, R. A. (1993). Rapid treatment of blood and injection phobias with eye movement desensitization. *Journal of Behavior Therapy and Experimental Psychiatry, 24,* 211–217.

Leeds, A. (2009). *A guide to the standard EMDR protocols for clinicians, supervisors, and consultants.* New York, NY: Springer.

Leeds, A. (2012). EMDR treatment of panic disorder and agoraphobia: Two model treatment plans. *Journal of EMDR Practice and Research, 6*(3), 110–119. doi:10.1891/1933-3196.6.3.110

Logie, R. D. J., & de Jongh, A. (2014). The "flashforward procedure": Confronting the catastrophe. *Journal of EMDR Practice and Research, 8*(1), 25–32. doi:10.1891/1933-3196.8.1.25

Lohr, J. M., Tolin, D. F., & Kleinknecht, R. A. (1996). An intensive design investigation of eye movement desensitization and reprocessing of claustrophobia. *Journal of Anxiety Disorders, 10,* 73–88.

Luber, M. (scripted by). (2009). Current anxiety and behavior protocol. In M. Luber (Ed.), *Eye movement desensitization and reprocessing (EMDR) scripted protocols: Basics and special situations*. New York, NY: Springer.

Marquis, J. N. (1991). A report on seventy-eight cases treated by eye movement desensitization. *Journal of Behavior Therapy and Experimental Psychiatry, 22*, 187–192.

McNally, R. J., & Lukach, B. M. (1992). Are panic attacks traumatic stressors? *American Journal of Psychiatry, 149*, 824–826.

Muris, P., & Merckelbach, H. (1997). Treating spider phobics with eye-movement desensitization and reprocessing: A controlled study. *Behavioural and Cognitive Psychotherapy, 25*, 39–50.

Muris, P., Merckelbach, H., Holdrinet, I., & Sijsenaar, M. (1998). Treating phobic children: Effects of EMDR versus exposure. *Journal of Consulting and Clinical Psychology, 66*, 193–198.

Muris, P., Merckelbach, H., van Haaften, H., & Mayer, B. (1997). Eye movement desensitization and reprocessing versus exposure in vivo. *British Journal of Psychiatry, 171*, 82–86.

Oosterink, F. M. D., de Jongh, A., & Aartman, I. H. A. (2009). Negative events and their potential risk of precipitating pathological forms of dental anxiety. *Journal of Anxiety Disorders, 23*, 451–457.

Roemer, L., Molina, S., Litz, B. T., & Borkovec, T. D. (1997). Preliminary investigation of the role of previous exposure to potentially traumatizing events in generalized anxiety disorder. *Depression and Anxiety, 4*, 134–138.

Sanderson, A., & Carpenter, R. (1992). Eye movement desensitization versus image confrontation: A single session crossover study of 58 phobic subjects. *Journal of Behavior Therapy and Experimental Psychiatry, 23*, 269–275.

Shapiro, F. (1999). Eye movement desensitization and reprocessing (EMDR): Clinical and research implications of an integrated psychotherapy treatment. *Journal of Anxiety Disorders, 13*, 35–67.

ten Broeke, E., & de Jongh, A. (1993). Eye movement desensitization and reprocessing (EMDR): Praktische toepassing en theoretische overwegingen. *Gedragstherapie, 26*, 233–254.

ten Broeke, E., & de Jongh, A. (1995). Eye movement desensitization and reprocessing (EMDR): 'Gewoon' imaginaire exposure? *De Psycholoog, 30*, 459–464.

ten Broeke, A., & de Jongh, A. (1997). EMDR bij de behandeling van type II psychotrauma: een casus. *Tijdschrift voor Psychiatrie, 39*, 249–255.

ten Broeke, E., de Jongh, A., & Oppenheim, H. (2008; 3ᵉ herziene druk 2012). *Praktijkboek EMDR: Casusconceptualisatie en specifieke patiëntengroepen*. Amsterdam, The Netherlands: Pearson Assessment and Information B.V. [ISBN 978 90 265 2255 0]

Triscari, M. T., Faraci, P., D'Angelo, V., Urso, V., & Catalisano, D. (2011). Two treatments for fear of flying compared: Cognitive behavioral therapy combined with systematic desensitization or eye movement desensitization and reprocessing (EMDR). *Aviation Psychology and Applied Human Factor, 1*, 9–14.

van den Berg, D. P. G., de Bont, P. A. J. M., van der Vleugel, B. M., de Roos, C., de Jongh, A., van Minnen, A., & van der Gaag, M. (In press). Prolonged exposure versus eye movement desensitization and reprocessing versus waiting list for posttraumatic stress disorder in patients with a psychotic disorder: A randomized clinical trial. *JAMA Psychiatry, 72*(3), 259–267.

van den Hout, M., Muris, P., Salemink, E., & Kindt, M. (2001). Autobiographical memories become less vivid and emotional after eye movements. *British Journal of Clinical Psychology, 40*(2), 121–130.

van der Horst, F. H. C., den Oudsten, B. L., Lobbestael, J., de Jongh, A., & de Vries, J. (In preparation). *Cognitive behavioral therapy vs eye movement desensitization and reprocessing for treating panic disorder: A randomized clinical trial.*

Wolitzky-Taylor, K. B., Horowitz, J. D., Powers, M. B., & Telch, M. J. (2008). Psychological approaches in the treatment of specific phobias: A meta-analysis. *Clinical Psychology Review, 28*(6), 1021–1037.

EMDR Therapy for Specific Fears and Phobias: The Phobia Protocol

Ad de Jongh

Introduction

When a person starts to demonstrate an excessive and unreasonable fear of certain objects or situations that in reality are not dangerous, it is likely that the person fulfils the criteria for specific phobia as stated in the *Diagnostic and Statistical Manual of Mental Disorders*, 5th edition (*DSM-5*; American Psychiatric Association, 2013). The main features of a specific phobia are that the fear is elicited by a specific and limited set of stimuli (e.g., snakes, dogs, injections, etc.); that confrontation with these stimuli results in intense fear and avoidance behavior; and that the fear is "out of proportion" to the actual threat or danger the situation poses, after taking into account all the factors of the environment and situation. Symptoms must also now have been present for at least 6 months for a diagnosis to be made of specific phobia. The *DSM-5* distinguishes the following five main categories or subtypes of specific phobia:

- Animal type (phobias of spiders, insects, dogs, cats, rodents, snakes, birds, fish, etc.)
- Natural environment type (phobias of heights, water, storms, etc.)
- Situational type (phobias of enclosed spaces, driving, flying, elevators, bridges, etc.)
- Blood, injury, injection type (phobias of getting an injection, seeing blood, watching surgery, etc.)
- Other types (choking, vomiting, contracting an illness, etc.)

Research

Evidence suggests that with respect to the onset of phobias, particularly highly disruptive emotional reactions (i.e., helplessness) during an encounter with a threatening situation have the greatest potential risk of precipitating specific phobia (Oosterink, de Jongh, & Aartman, 2009). Regarding its symptomatology, some types of specific phobias (e.g., those involving fear of choking, road traffic accidents, and dental treatment) display remarkable commonalities with posttraumatic stress disorder (PTSD), including the reoccurrence of fearful memories of past distressing events, which are triggered by the phobic situation or object, but may also occur spontaneously (de Jongh, Fransen, Oosterink-Wubbe, & Aartman, 2006).

Although in vivo exposure has proven to be the treatment of choice for a variety of specific phobias (Wolitzky-Taylor, Horowitz, Powers, & Telch, 2008), results from uncontrolled (e.g., de Jongh & ten Broeke, 1994; de Jongh & ten Broeke, 1998; de Roos & de Jongh, 2008; Kleinknecht, 1993; Marquis, 1991) and controlled case reports (e.g., de Jongh, 2012;

de Jongh, van den Oord, & ten Broeke, 2002; Lohr, Tolin, & Kleinknecht, 1996), as well as case control studies (de Jongh, Holmshaw, Carswell, & van Wijk, 2011) show that eye movement desensitization and reprocessing (EMDR) can also be effective in clients suffering from fears and phobias. Significant improvements can be obtained within a limited number of sessions (see de Jongh, ten Broeke, & Renssen, 1999 for a review).

EMDR Therapy may be particularly useful for phobic conditions with high levels of anxiety, with a traumatic origin or with a clear beginning, and for which it is understandable that resolving the memories of the conditioning events would positively influence its severity (see de Jongh et al., 2002).

The aim of this chapter is to illustrate how EMDR Therapy can be applied in the treatment of specific fears and phobic conditions. The script has frequently been used in both clinical practice and research projects (e.g., de Jongh et al., 2002; Doering, Ohlmeier, de Jongh, Hofmann, & Bisping, 2013). For example, a series of single-case experiments to evaluate the effectiveness of EMDR for dental phobia showed that in two to three sessions of EMDR treatment, three of the four clients demonstrated a substantial decline in self-reported and observer-rated anxiety, reduced credibility of dysfunctional beliefs concerning dental treatment, and significant behavior changes (de Jongh et al., 2002). These gains were maintained at 6 weeks follow-up. In all four cases, clients actually underwent the dental treatment they feared, most within 3 weeks following EMDR Therapy treatment.

Similar results were found in a case control study investigating the comparative effects of EMDR Therapy and trauma-focused cognitive behavioral therapy (TF-CBT), among a sample of 184 people suffering from travel fear and travel phobia (de Jongh et al., 2011). TF-CBT consisted of imaginal exposure as well as elements of cognitive restructuring, relaxation, and anxiety management. In vivo exposure, during treatment sessions, was discouraged for safety and insurance reasons, but patients were expected to confront difficult situations without the therapist (e.g., returning to the scene of the accident, self-exposure to cars, or other anxiety-provoking cues). Patients were considered to have completed treatment when it was agreed that patients' improvements had plateaued or they were unlikely to make significant further progress in treatment. The mean treatment course was 7.3 sessions. No differences were found between both treatments. Both treatment procedures were capable of producing equally large, clinically significant decreases on measures indexing symptoms of trauma, anxiety, and depression, as well as therapist ratings of treatment outcome.

The efficacy of EMDR Therapy was also tested in a randomized clinical trial among 30 dental clients who met the *DSM-IV-TR* criteria of dental phobia, and who had been avoiding the dentist for more than 4 years, on average (Doering et al., 2013). The participants were randomly assigned to either EMDR or a wait-list control condition. Clients in the EMDR Therapy condition showed significant reductions of dental anxiety and avoidance behavior as well as in symptoms of PTSD. These effects were still significant at 12 months follow-up. After 1 year, 83% of the clients were in regular dental treatment.

The Diagnostic Process

Treatment of a fear or a phobic condition cannot be started if the therapist is unaware of the factors that cause and maintain the anxiety response. Therefore, one of the first tasks of the therapist is to collect the necessary information. This is usually done by means of a standardized clinical interview, such as the Anxiety Disorder Interview Scale (ADIS-R), which is primarily aimed at the diagnosis of anxiety disorders (DiNardo et al., 1985). This clinical interview has two important aims:

- To gain insight into the interplay of factors on several possible problem areas, including the possibility of *secondary gain issues*; that is, the extent to which the client derives positive consequences by avoiding anxiety-provoking situations, such as losing a job or receiving extra attention and consideration from others.
- To establish the relative importance of the interrelated problems that many of these clients have and how they are related to the diagnosis-specific phobia. For example, it

may be that a client's claustrophobia is not very specific and occurs in a variety of situations; in this instance, it may be wiser to consider (or to rule out) the possibility of the diagnosis panic disorder, as this condition generally requires more elaborate treatment.

To further enhance the reliability of the diagnostic process, it is often desirable to use valid and standardized diagnostic measures. These can be of help in getting a clear picture of the severity of the anxiety, in detecting other possible problem areas, and in making it possible to evaluate the course of treatment. Many examples of useful self-report questionnaires for fears and specific phobias can be found in Antony, Orsillo, and Roemer's practice book (2001).

Another factor of significance is the motivation of the client. For example, it is important to find out why the client seeks treatment at this particular time. Different issues that affect motivation are as follows:

- *Self versus forced referral.* There may be a marked difference in effectiveness of the treatment depending on whether the client requested referral himself or was forced into it (e.g., "My wife said she would leave me if I did not get my teeth fixed").
- *Past experience with therapy.* Also, clients' experiences of therapy in the past may determine their attitudes toward treatment. If, for whatever reason, it did not work in the past, it is useful to find out why and to attempt to discriminate between genuinely fearful reluctance and lack of effort.
- *Comorbid psychiatric issues.* The therapist should remain aware that comorbid psychiatric illness, such as severe depression, might be a contributing factor toward a lack of motivation.
- *Low self-esteem.* If the phobic client suffers from feelings of low self-esteem, which, in the opinion of the therapist, contribute to a large extent to the client's avoidance behavior, the self-esteem issue may be resolved first and becomes a primary target of processing.

The Phobia Protocol Single Traumatic Event Script Notes

Phase 1: History Taking

During Phase 1, history taking, it is important to elicit certain types of information.

Determine to What Extent the Client Fulfills the DSM-5 Criteria of Specific Phobia

Identify the type and severity of the fear and to what extent the client fulfills all *DSM-5* criteria for specific phobia.

Identify the Stimulus Situation (Conditioned Stimulus, CS)

An important goal of the assessment is to gather information about the current circumstances under which the symptoms manifest, about periods and situations in which the problems worsen or diminish, and about external and concrete (discriminative) anxiety-provoking cues or CS. The therapist should also be aware of other types of anxiety-producing stimuli, including critical internal cues, for example, particular body sensations (e.g., palpitations), images, and negative self-statements (e.g., "I can't cope").

Identify the Expected Consequence or Catastrophe (Unconditioned Stimulus, UCS)

To understand the dynamic of the client's fears or phobia, it is necessary to determine not only the aspects of the phobic object or situation that evoke a fear response (the CS), but also what exactly the client expects to happen when confronted with the CS and then the UCS (for a more elaborate description, see de Jongh & ten Broeke, 2007). For example, a dog phobic may believe that if he gets too close to a dog (CS), it will attack him (UCS), whereas an injection phobic may believe that if she has blood drawn (CS), she will faint or that the needle will break off in her arm (UCS).

The most commonly used method to elicit this type of information is to ask the client a series of open-ended questions that can be framed in the context of hypothetical situations (e.g., "What is the worst thing that might happen, if you were to drive a car?") or actual episodes of anxiety (e.g., "During your recent appointment with the dentist, what did you think might happen?"). If the client remains unspecific about the catastrophe (e.g., "then something bad will happen"), it is useful to respond with more specific questions (e.g., "What exactly will happen?" or "What bad things do you mean?") until more specific information is disclosed ("I will faint," "I will die," "I will suffocate," etc.).

Please note that the UCS, being the mental representation of the catastrophe the client fears, should refer to an event that automatically evokes a negative emotional response. It is not always immediately clear where this information might have come from; that is, when and how the client ever learned that her catastrophe (e.g., fainting, pain, etc.) might happen. The therapist should be aware of the following possible events that may have laid the groundwork for the client's fear or phobia:

1. A distressing event the client once *experienced herself*. For example, she might have fainted in relation to an injection (traumatic experience) at an early age.
2. A horrific event the client once *witnessed* (vicarious learning). For example, witnessing mother's extremely fearful reaction to a needle.
3. An unpleasant or shocking event the client *read or heard about* that happened to someone or from learning otherwise that injections or anesthetic fluid can be dangerous (negative information).

Assess Validity of Catastrophe

The severity of a client's fear or phobia is reflected in the strength of the relationship between the stimulus and the patient's perceived probability that the expected negative consequence would actually occur. This relationship can simply be indexed using a validity of catastrophe rating (in this case, the validity of catastrophe that expresses the strength of the relationship between the CS and UCS in a percentage between 0% and 100%, using an IF-THEN formula. For example, IF (…"I get an injection," CS), THEN (…"I will faint"). Such a rating could be obtained before and after each EMDR session. The general aim of the EMDR treatment of the phobic condition would then be to continue treatment until the client indicates a validity of catastrophe rating as low as possible.

Provide Information About the Fear or Phobia if Necessary

If adequate information about the dangerousness of the object, the animal, or the situation is lacking—and the client has irrational and faulty beliefs about it—it is of paramount importance that the practitioner provide appropriate and disconfirming information to the contrary. However, some clients need to be guided past the initial awkwardness or need for such education. For example, if the client's lack of knowledge of the phobic objects (e.g., about airplanes and their safety) is likely to play a part, it may be wise to spend some time on this aspect first, and suitable reading material should be provided where appropriate.

Determine an Appropriate and Feasible Treatment Goal

There are a wide variety of treatment goals, from simple goals to more global or complex goals. An example of a limited goal for a needle-phobic individual might be pricking a finger, while a more global goal might be undergoing injections or blood draws, while remaining confident and relaxed. Generally speaking, treatment is aimed at reducing anxiety and avoidance behavior to an acceptable level and at learning how to cope. Goals can be formulated concerning both what the therapist would like the client to achieve during a single therapy session and what exactly the client should manage to do in natural situations when confronted with the phobic object. Clearly, the treatment aim is set in consultation with the client and will depend both on the client's level of commitment and the therapist's clinical judgment about what seems realistic or ecologically feasible. However, sometimes clients formulate a treatment goal that is not within their reach, unnecessarily difficult, or simply dangerous, such as a person with a dog phobia who set himself the target of acquiring the ability to spontaneously pet all sorts of dogs. A more appropriate aim of treatment, however, could be the ability to walk outside without having to change direction because of the appearance of a dog. The therapist should be clear about the objectives for each session but also be prepared to adapt to unexpected happenings.

Identify the Conditioning Experience

In general, with regard to the procedure, the memories of the meaningful and disturbing past events (i.e., the first, possible earlier ancillary experiences and other relevant events that had a worsening effect on client's symptoms) are used as a focus for a series of subsequent EMDR Therapy (basic protocol) procedures that are applied separately, each involving a distinct target memory.

   The first target that has to be identified is the origin; that is, the memory of the event that has caused (or in the patient's perception clearly worsened) the fear (e.g., being bitten by a dog in case of a dog phobia, or having undergone a horrific medical or dental treatment that led to a medical phobia).

Check for Possible Earlier (Ancillary) Experience

Check whether this is indeed the first event. If not, identify the incident when the fear was felt for the first time.

Identify Other Relevant Experiences

The assessment should focus not only on the experiences pertinent to the development of the phobia per se, but also on *all* other, subsequent meaningful events that contributed to the fear. The therapist needs to check for related memories of events that could be considered as "collateral damage"; for example, being ridiculed by peers when the patient reacted with extreme fear when confronted with a small dog. These kinds of experiences are likely to have had an effect on an individual's self-image and self-worth in general and therefore may also have to be addressed.

Phase 2: Preparation

The reprocessing work should not start until rapport and trust have been established and the client has been introduced to EMDR Therapy; that is, what EMDR Therapy is and what the client can expect to happen. A basic example (Shapiro, 2001) of what therapists can say is given in the script that follows. Clearly, the explanation could be changed, based on the current state of knowledge on trauma and trauma resolution, as well as certain personality characteristics, such as age and sophistication of the client.

   Another well-established guideline, when using EMDR, is the preparation of the client for EMDR Therapy. To this end, it is important to make sure that the client is not afraid of her own fear reactions, since many phobias entail a fear of fear. If the client has never been able to deal with fear adequately, these things have to be worked out before targeting any traumatic memory. One helpful way to deal with it is to apply self-control procedures before a confrontational method such as EMDR Therapy is used. In particular, training a client in the use of distraction may be a way of challenging the client's faulty beliefs (for example, the perception that she can exert no control over her anxiety). Later in therapy, distraction can be used as an immediate anxiety-management strategy. Examples of distraction techniques include mental exercises such as counting backward from 1000 in 7s, remembering a favorite walk in detail, and so on. In the case of a child, distraction can be applied, for instance, by thinking of animals beginning with each letter of the alphabet in turn. One of the benefits of using distraction is that once the client feels confident with its use, these skills are helpful to direct his attention away from thoughts concerned with possible catastrophic happenings or with evaluating his own performance.

It is essential to explain how important it is to prepare oneself for possible discomfort and any between-session disturbance and to practice with what has been learned. This makes it more likely that the client will become proficient and confident in the utilization of such techniques.

There are indications that blood or injury phobics display an atypical symptom pattern in which an initial increase in heart rate and blood pressure is followed by a sudden drop and sometimes fainting. In such cases, it may be important to teach clients the Applied Tension Technique, as this procedure takes into account the diphasic response pattern that is considered to be characteristic of this type of phobia (Öst & Sterner, 1987). This tension technique teaches clients to tighten their muscles, which seems to counteract the drop in blood pressure. This tension–relaxation cycle should be repeated several times within each practice session. If the therapist has access to equipment for measuring blood pressure, it may be instructive to demonstrate the effect of the tension technique to the client. The client should be requested to start practicing the tension technique prior to the actual beginning of the EMDR treatment. Practicing should be done several times throughout the day. If the client has a medical condition that could be affected by the procedure, such as hypertension, she should consult a physician prior to practicing this technique. It is important to note that when the client has headaches during the practices, the strength of the tension should be decreased.

Phase 3: Assessment

Target Selection

Select a target image (stationary picture) of the memory. (See Phase 1: History Taking: Determine an Appropriate and Feasible Treatment Goal for the series of targets that have to be processed.)

Obtaining Negative Cognition (NC) and Positive Cognition (PC)

The selection of cognitions within the EMDR Therapy treatment is an idiosyncratic process and will greatly depend on the client and the specific characteristics of the target event. For example, the clinician should be sure that cognitions meet the following criteria:

- Appropriate for the issue
- Formulated in the here and now
- Connected to the target image
- Convey the present state about the current belief in relation to the past event, such as "I am out of control," not a statement of what was experienced in the past such as "I was out of control"
- Describe the actual experience in terms of a belief statement (e.g., NC: "I am prey") and not the emotional state (e.g., NC: "I am desperate")
- Are found in the control domain (e.g., "I am helpless," "I am powerless," "I am not in control"); in the majority of the cases, it is the NC of the memory of the conditioning experience

Therapists will discover in their work with clients suffering from phobic conditions that certain categories of cognitions pertain to specific types of fears, for example:

ANIMAL TYPE PHOBIAS

I am powerless	I am in control
I am weak	I am strong
I am prey/in danger (e.g., dogs and insects)	I am safe
I am a coward	I am okay

SITUATIONAL TYPE AND NATURAL ENVIRONMENT TYPE PHOBIAS

I am a coward	I am okay
I am powerless	I am in control

BLOOD-INJURY-INJECTION TYPE PHOBIAS

I am a number, a piece of meat	I am okay
I am powerless	I am in control

The main criteria of the PC selection are the following:

- Level of meaning parallels (in the same cognitive domain) the NC
- Empowerment of the individual (e.g., "I can handle it")
- Ecologically valid or feasible (e.g., PC: *not* "I have control over the spider")

In case it appears necessary to address other relevant memories (see Phase 1: History Taking: Determine an Appropriate and Feasible Treatment Goal), the therapist should take into account that the NC and PC of these targets may have different cognitive domains (e.g., within the self-worth domain rather than within the control domain).

Phase 4: Desensitization

Apply the Standard EMDR Protocol for All Targets

The Standard EMDR Protocol is used to process all targets. There is, however, one difference. To adequately tap into the memory network, it is most useful to have a somewhat different strategy for going back to target than is recommended for using the Standard EMDR procedure. More specifically, after having gone back to target, the client is asked to focus on *the most salient detail* of the target; that is, the aspect that (still) provokes the most disturbance. Therefore, the client may need time to connect emotionally with the disturbing material, but as soon as the client has decided what aspect is now perceived as most disturbing, bilateral stimulation (BLS)[1] is introduced. Such a strategy of using a clear focus on the aspects of the target image by which the affect is triggered has proven to be an excellent way to facilitate a connecting of the nodes in the fear network that still have to be processed, often effectively activating a new flow of associations.

The work in Phase 4 follows the Standard EMDR Protocol. This procedure is to be repeated until the subjective units of disturbance (SUDs) = 0. Then the PC is installed. Each traumatic event associated with the problem that is not reprocessed during the normal course of the first target must be processed using the Standard EMDR Protocol until the SUDs reach an ecological 1 or 0 and the PC is installed.

---

[1] Although this term is often used in relation to EMDR, support for bilaterality as a necessary condition for effectiveness in EMDR Therapy has a weak empirical base. It might be more appropriate to use the term "working memory taxation" in this respect (see de Jongh, Ernst, Marques, & Hornsveld, 2013).

Phase 5: Installation

The work in Phase 5 follows the Standard EMDR Protocol.

Phase 6: Body Scan

The work in Phase 6 follows the Standard EMDR Protocol.

Check the Other Targets

See Phase 1: History Taking: Determine an Appropriate and Feasible Treatment Goal and decide whether it is still necessary to reprocess these experiences (SUDs when bringing up the memory > 0). If the SUD is > 0, continue with other memories that may still contribute to or "fuel" the client's current phobic symptoms.

Check Whether the Client Has (Still) Any Disaster Image About the Future (Flashforward)

After all old memories—that currently "fuel" the fear—have been resolved, check whether the patient has an explicit disaster imagined about the future (called a *flashforward*). What does the patient think will happen to her, in the worst case or "doom scenario," if what is feared cannot be avoided? If the client has a flashforward with a SUD > 0, continue with the Flashforward Procedure (Logie & de Jongh, 2014).

Check for Future Concerns

INSTALLING A FUTURE TEMPLATE

If all targets (Phase 1: History Taking: Determine an Appropriate and Feasible Treatment Goal), including the flashforward, have been successfully processed, as well as current triggers, clients may still have to anticipate future situations in which the former stimuli are present (e.g., a dental treatment situation) and in which they need to interact with these stimuli. To check whether clients are fully capable of that, and to prepare for a future confrontation with the (former) anxiety-provoking object or situation, they are asked to mentally progress in time to identify a specific mental image of a typical future situation by which the fear prior to this session certainly would have been triggered. This may be a situation that clients usually avoid because of fear or a situation that they, until now, were not able to enter or to undergo without fear.

For the future template, it is useful to have clients select a picture of a situation in which they behave and feel in the way they really want it to happen. The goal of this procedure is merely to check that there are no future relapse triggers anymore and to prepare the client for future confrontations with the situation, thereby further increasing the feelings of self-confidence. From a practical point of view, clients are requested to hold in mind their picture and to visualize this scene as well as possible, while keeping in mind a standard PC (e.g., "I can cope," or "I can handle it"). Next, the BLS is introduced. This is continued as long as clients report a strengthening of validity (until validity of cognition or VoC = 7). Thus, when this form of installation procedure has succeeded, clients fully believe that they are able to deal with their mental representation of the experience.

The therapist continues with this procedure (instruction and VoC rating), until the future template is sufficiently installed (VoC = 7).

If there is a block, meaning that even after 10 or more installations, the VoC is still below 7, there probably are more targets (probably a flashforward target) that have to be identified and addressed. The therapist should use the Standard EMDR Protocol to address these targets before proceeding with the template (see Worksheets in Appendix A). Also evaluate whether clients need any new information, resources, or skills to be able to comfortably visualize the future coping scene. Introduce this needed information or skill.

Video Check

After the incorporation of a positive template for future action, the clinician asks the client to close his eyes, and to run a mental video. That is, the client imagines himself in the future and mentally runs a videotape of the time between the present session and a next possible (but successful) confrontation with the anxiety-provoking stimulus or situation (e.g., an upcoming dental treatment: waking, going to the dentist, taking a seat in the waiting room, etc.). The client is asked to identify any disturbing aspect in the mental video and is instructed that as soon as any disturbance arises during the running of the videotape, he should stop, open his eyes, and inform the therapist.

Next, these disturbing aspects are targeted with BLS, where appropriate. This is done by holding in mind the same PC as was used in the previous step ("I can handle it"), while a long set is administered.

The mental videotape is repeated until it can be viewed entirely without distress.

To provide the clinician with an indication regarding clients' self-efficacy, have them rate their response on a VoC scale from 1 to 7. This procedural step may give the clinician feedback on the extent to which the goals have been met.

If the client is able to play the movie from start to finish with a sense of confidence and satisfaction, the client is asked to play the movie once more from the beginning to the end, while BLS is introduced and the PC "I can handle it" is installed. In a sense, this movie is installed as a future template.

In Vivo Confrontations

PREPARE THE CLIENT FOR IN VIVO CONFRONTATIONS

It is likely that, through the application of the previous steps of the EMDR procedure, the meaning or severity of the initial event has been effectively reappraised. Yet, it could be that clients are not completely convinced of their ability to cope with a future encounter with the phobic stimulus. Sometimes, clients have avoided certain activities for so long that they no longer know how to behave and how to feel secure in their formerly phobic situation. If this is the case, it is important that the therapist identify and counter existing irrational beliefs that contribute to a sense of threat and anxiety, for instance, by the use of in vivo exposure assignments or behavioral experiments.

If clients are actually confronted with the stimuli that normally would evoke a fear response and clients gain an experience that the catastrophe they fear does not occur, this would help to demonstrate that their fears may be unfounded.

A behavioral experiment is an excellent opportunity to test if the treatment effects are generalized to all associated triggers or aspects of the situation. To this end, real-life exposure to the anxiety-provoking stimulus after successful reprocessing of the traumatic memories may further strengthen the believability of the PC, as the NC (and other still existing assumptions and beliefs) is contradicted by the consequences of acting in new ways.

As with any of the other steps in the phobia protocol, the in vivo exposure part should be a joint venture of client and therapist. Unforced willingness must be ensured. Some gentle persuasion is certainly permissible, but it must be clear to the client that nothing will happen against her will during the confrontation with the phobic stimuli or situation. Also, unexpected introduction of new fearful material is counterproductive, as this can both damage confidence and lead to a revision of estimates of the likelihood of threat and increased caution.

IN VIVO EXPOSURE

In vivo exposure is applied to reduce avoidance and promote the opportunity to evoke mastery through observing that no real danger exists. All varying stimulus elements within a situation should be explored. Therefore, the eliciting situation should hold the client's attention. For instance, a person fearful of high places could be encouraged to be on the roof of an apartment building that is not too distressful while paying attention to what is happening on the street or to certain objects such as trees, cars, and people.

It is essential that the therapist help the client pay attention to features of the phobic object or situation that are positive or interesting while being exposed to them.

It is important to anticipate various possibilities regarding elements that can be manipulated to ameliorate or to intensify the impact. It is this author's experience that it is helpful to make variations with regard to the stimulus dimensions such as action, distance, and time. That is, in a real-life confrontation, for example with an animal, the animal can be induced to be more or less lively, close or more distant, to be positioned with its head to the client or not, and during a long or a more limited period of time. If necessary the therapist can demonstrate to the client how the therapist would handle the feared object (e.g., by petting a dog).

The therapist should make sure that confrontations are repeated so that the reduction in distress is fully consolidated before moving on. Thus, the overall aim is to foster confidence in a general ability to cope despite variations in circumstances.

The therapist should act in such a confident and relaxed manner that the client feels prepared for any eventuality. Check the results by assessing the validity of the catastrophe.

Phase 7: Closure

At the end of every session, consolidate the changes and improvement that has occurred by asking the client what has been learned during the session.

Planning Self-Managed Homework Assignments

After the therapy has been concluded, the therapist makes it clear that it is important to keep practicing during daily life in order to ensure that the changes are maintained.

Clients should be told to stop any current avoidance behavior as much as possible, and to consider each confrontation with the feared stimulus as an opportunity to put the newly acquired skills into practice. By using self-managed assignments, clients should be encouraged to incorporate as many critical situations in real life as possible. This allows clients to gain self-confidence through overcoming their fears on their own, learning of new and more independent and appropriate ways of coping, and perceiving further progress. Thus, dependence on the therapist should certainly be avoided. Clients are expected to confront situations regularly and alone on the basis of agreed homework tasks. These may include taking a holiday flight, visiting a dentist for a check-up, opening a window of the house on summer days when wasps are flying, using elevators, meeting people with dogs, climbing towers in cases of height phobia, or swallowing solid food in cases of choking phobia.

With regard to blood phobia, the procedure is different in that clients are instructed to practice the Applied Tension Technique (see Preparation Phase) in real-life situations, while exposing themselves to their anxiety-provoking stimulus as much as possible, such as watching violent films with bloodshed, paying visits to a blood bank, and talking about blood-related topics.

Phase 8: Reevaluation

The length of the interval between sessions will depend on several factors, including the nature of the problem, the frequency with which significant eliciting situations are encountered, and the availability of the therapist and the client. It is sometimes inevitable that clients experience a relapse. In many cases, this is due to the fact that clients now expose themselves to situations that they avoided for a long period of time. Also, a spontaneous return of fear should be expected to occur during the interval between sessions. This may lead to increased arousal, which in turn could render clients disappointed about the improvements that they expected, thus interpreting this as a signal that their problems will only worsen. It is therefore important to label their behavior in a positive sense and to redefine the relapse as a challenge to put into practice what is learned.

After application of the phobia protocol, there may still be a need for additional targeting and other strategies to ensure that the treatment goals are met. An evaluation of what still remains to be done should be made at the beginning of the next session. Clients are asked about their current symptoms and about their progress in terms of success in carrying out homework tasks. It is advisable to always evaluate in terms of clients' SUDs level on the already processed material.

If the disturbance level has increased, these reverberations should be targeted or otherwise addressed. An extra test should be carried out by checking that the patient does not have any flashforward that is emotionally charged and thus has to be processed.

Further, the therapist should assess the necessity of teaching clients additional self-control and other relevant exercises that could further enhance their ability (e.g., the Applied Tension Technique) to confront the former anxiety-provoking situation in real life. Repeated rehearsal and reinforcement for success must be emphasized. To encourage hope and foster engagement in treatment, it is crucial that therapy sessions and homework assignments furnish experiences of success that clients can attribute to themselves. In this respect, these successes provide clients with direct experiential evidence that anxiety can, through their own effort, be controlled. Clinically, it is often observed that once clients manage to realize even a small achievement, the vicious circle of dependency, low self-esteem, avoidance, and further anxiety is broken. Therefore, it is important to work toward attainable and personally gratifying goals.

The Phobia Protocol Single Traumatic Event Script

Phase 1: History Taking

Determine the Type of Fear and Its Severity

Say, *"What is the fear or concern that has brought you in today?"*

_____

_____

Say, *"Does this fear or concern seem excessive or unreasonable to you?"*

_____

_____

If so, say, *"Tell me about it."*

_____

_____

_____

_____

Identify the Stimulus Situation (CS)

An important goal of the assessment is to gather information about the current circumstances under which the symptoms manifest, about periods and situations in which the problems worsen or diminish, and about external and concrete (discriminative) anxiety-provoking cues or CS. The therapist should also be aware of other types of anxiety-producing stimuli, including critical internal cues, for example, particular body sensations (e.g., palpitations), images, and self-statements (e.g., "I can't cope").

Say, *"Describe the object or situation that you are afraid of."*

_____

_____

_____

_____

Or say, *"What exactly do you need to see, hear, or feel in order to get an immediate fear response?"*

_____

_____

_____

_____

Say, *"What exactly about* _____ (state the object or situation) *triggers your fear most?"*

_____

_____

_____

_____

Say, *"Which incident caused your fear of* _____ (state the object or situation)*?"*

_____

_____

_____

_____

Identify the Expected Consequence or Catastrophe (UCS)

To understand the dynamic of the clients' fears or phobia, it is necessary to determine not only the aspects of the phobic object or situation that evoke a fear response (the CS) but also what exactly clients expect to happen when confronted with the CS and then the UCS.

Say, *"What are you afraid of that could happen when you are exposed to* _____ (state the object or situation: CS)*?"*

_____

_____

_____

_____

Say, *"Which incident caused your fear of* _____ (state the catastrophe the client expects to happen)*?"*

_____

_____

_____

_____

Assess Validity of Catastrophe

Say, *"Is it true you are saying that IF you would be exposed to* _____ *(state the phobic object or situation) THEN you would* _____ *(state the catastrophe the client fears will happen)?"*

_____

_____

Say, *"On a scale from 0% to 100% where 0% means it is completely false and 100% means it is completely true, how true does this feel that this will happen?"*

0%   10%   20%   30%   40%   50%   60%   70%   80%   90%   100%

(completely false)   (completely true)

Provide Information About the Fear or Phobia if Necessary

If adequate information about the dangerousness of the object, the animal, or the situation is lacking—and clients have irrational and faulty beliefs about it—it is of paramount importance that the practitioner provide appropriate and disconfirming information to the contrary. However, some clients need to be guided past the initial awkwardness or need for such education.

Say, *"What do you know about the relative dangerousness of* _____ *(therapist fills in the information specific to the phobic stimulus with which he or she is dealing)? Since there are other people that are not that fearful as you of* _____ *(state the phobic object or situation), wouldn't it be wise to spend some time investigating whether it is really as dangerous as you think it is? Just to be sure that you don't overestimate the probability of the danger or that something bad will happen to you. I mean, even if it appears to be more dangerous to be exposed to* _____ *(state the phobic object or situation) than you think it is now, it is important to find out, don't you think? Thus, let's look for the information we need. Where shall we start?"*

_____

_____

_____

_____

Determine an Appropriate and Feasible Treatment Goal

Say, *"Based on all that we have been talking about, let's discuss our goal(s) for treatment. What is the goal and how will you know when you have reached your goal?"*

_____

_____

_____

_____

Identify the Conditioning Experience

The first target that has to be identified is the origin; that is, the memory of the event that has caused the fear (e.g., being bitten by a dog in case of a dog phobia, or having undergone a horrific medical or dental treatment that led to a medical phobia).

Say, *"What we have to figure out now is what memories are crucial to understand your fear. I assume that you were not born with this fear. So your fear started due to a certain event or series of events. Through these experiences you have learned to fear _____ (state what learned to fear, for example, 'a dog'). These experiences are, as memories, still active. One could say that every time you are exposed to a difficult situation such as _____ (state client's difficult situation, or, for example, 'a walk in a park,' or 'being exposed to a dog'), memories of a former 'damaging' event, such as _____ (state client's former damaging event, for example, being bitten by a dog), are—consciously or unconsciously— triggered and reactivated. With EMDR, I will help you to resolve these memories, so that they lose their emotional charge. Once these memories become neutral, they will no longer stand in the way of your entering certain situations that might be related to your fear of _____ (state the client's fear) and thereby increase your confidence in doing so. To find the right memories, I'll ask you to search in your mind through time, like a time machine, to determine which event on your timeline has started, or has aggravated, your fear."*

Say, *"To begin with, which incident caused you to be afraid of _____ (state the stimulus or CS)?"* Or, in other words, *"When did this fear begin?"*

_____

_____

_____

_____

Or say, *"When did you notice this fear for the first time?"*

_____

_____

_____

_____

Or say, *"What incident causes you to be afraid of _____ (state the feared consequence or UCS)?"*

_____

_____

_____

_____

Check for Possible Earlier (Ancillary) Experience

Check whether this is indeed the first event. If not, identify the incident when the fear was felt for the first time.

Say, *"Is this indeed the first incident related to this fear? I mean, are you absolutely sure you did not have this fear or phobia prior to this incident?"*

_____

_____

_____

_____

Identify Other Relevant Experiences

Say, *"What other past experiences might be important in relation to the acquisition or worsening of your fear or phobia?"* For example, *"After what event/s did the fear get worse?"* or *"Which other experiences gave rise to how fearful you are now?"*

_____

_____

_____

_____

Phase 2: Preparation

Explanation of EMDR Therapy

Say, *"When a trauma occurs, it seems to get locked in the nervous system with the original picture, sounds, thoughts, and feelings. The eye movements we use in EMDR seem to unlock the nervous system and allow the brain to process the experience. That may be what is happening in REM or dream sleep—the eye movements may help to process the unconscious material. It is important to note that it is your own brain that will be doing the healing and that you are the one in control."*

Teach distraction techniques for immediate anxiety management between sessions such as the following:

Say, *"Please describe out loud, the content of the room, with as much detail as you can."*

_____

_____

_____

_____

Distraction techniques also include mental exercises such as counting backward from 1,000 in 7s, remembering a favorite walk in detail, and so on. For example, say the following:

Say, *"Please count backward from 1,000 by 7s."*

_____

_____

_____

_____

Or say, *"In detail, tell me about a favorite walk that you took."*

_____

_____

_____

_____

In the case of a child, distraction can be applied, for instance, by thinking of animals beginning with each letter of the alphabet in turn.

Say, *"Think of an animal that begins with the letter A."*

_____

_____

_____

_____

Say, *"Great, now let's continue finding the names of animals using the rest of the alphabet. What would the name of an animal be for the letter B?"*

_____

_____

_____

_____

Continue education about the process.

Say, *"These exercises that we have been practicing may help you distract yourself when you are dealing with anxiety-provoking situations. It is really important for you to prepare yourself for possible discomfort, between sessions, by practicing these exercises. The more you practice, the better you will get at them."*

Teach the Applied Tension Technique for blood or injury phobics who often have an initial increase in heart rate and blood pressure that is followed by a sudden drop or fainting.

For clients with blood or injury phobias:

Say, *"Please make yourself comfortable. Now, tense all of your muscles in your body, including those in your arms, torso, legs, and face. Please increase this tension. Now hold this tension (for about 15 seconds) until there is a warm feeling in your head. Okay? If so, release the tension and let your body return to its normal state (for about 30 seconds)."*

_____

_____

_____

_____

This tension–relaxation cycle should be repeated five times within each practice session.

Say, *"You can start practicing the tension technique this week, as we will begin our EMDR treatment next time. Practicing means doing the technique several times throughout the day. If you have hypertension, it is wise for you to check with your physician before practicing this technique. If you experience any headaches during the practices, decrease the strength of the tension."*

Phase 3: Assessment

Target Selection

Select a target image (stationary picture) of the memory. (See Phase 1: History Taking: Determine an Appropriate and Feasible Treatment Goal for the series of targets that have to be processed.)

Say, *"What picture represents the most disturbing part of this incident now?"*

_____

_____

_____

_____

Obtaining the NC and PC

The following are examples of the types of NCs and PCs seen with specific phobia clients:

ANIMAL TYPE PHOBIAS

I am powerless	I am in control
I am weak	I am strong
I am prey/in danger (e.g., dogs and insects)	I am safe
I am a coward	I am okay

SITUATIONAL TYPE AND NATURAL ENVIRONMENT TYPE PHOBIAS

I am a coward	I am okay
I am powerless	I am in control

BLOOD–INJURY–INJECTION TYPE PHOBIAS

I am a number, a piece of meat	I am okay
I am powerless	I am in control

NEGATIVE COGNITION

Say, *"What words best go with the picture that express your negative belief about yourself now?"*

_____

_____

POSITIVE COGNITION

Say, *"When you bring up the picture of the incident, what would you like to believe about yourself now?"*

_____

_____

VALIDITY OF COGNITION

Say, *"When you bring up the picture of the incident, how true do those words _____ (repeat the positive cognition) feel to you now on a scale of 1 to 7, where 1 feels completely false and 7 feels completely true?"*

    1   2   3   4   5   6   7

(completely false)   (completely true)

Identify Emotion, SUD Level, and Location of the Feeling

EMOTIONS

Say, *"When you bring up the picture* (or incident) *and those words _____ (state the negative cognition), what emotion do you feel now?"*

_____

_____

SUBJECTIVE UNITS OF DISTURBANCE

Say, *"On a scale of 0 to 10, where 0 is no disturbance or neutral and 10 is the highest disturbance you can imagine, how disturbing does it feel now?"*

    0   1   2   3   4   5   6   7   8   9   10

(no disturbance)   (highest disturbance)

LOCATION OF BODY SENSATION

Say, *"Where do you feel it* (the disturbance) *in your body?"*

_____

_____

Phase 4: Desensitization

Apply the Standard EMDR Protocol for All Targets

Say, *"I would like to ask you to be a spectator who is observing the things that are happening to you from the moment you start following my hand. Those things can be thoughts, feelings, images, emotions, physical reactions, or maybe other things. These can relate to the event itself, but also to other things that seem to have no relationship to the event itself. Just notice what comes up, without trying to influence it, and without asking yourself whether it's going well or not. It's important that you don't try to keep the image that we will start with in mind all the time. The image is just the starting point of anything that can and may come up. Every once in a while, we will go back to this image to check how disturbing it still is to look at. Keep in mind that it is impossible to do anything wrong, as long as you just follow what's there and what comes up. If you want to stop, just raise your hand."*

Then say, *"Bring up the picture and the words* _____ (repeat the NC) *and notice where you feel it in your body. Now follow* _____ (state BLS)."*

_____

_____

This procedure is to be repeated until the SUDs = 0. Then the PC is installed. Each traumatic event associated with the problem, that is not reprocessed during the normal course of the first target, must be processed using the above protocol until the SUDs reach an ecological 1 or 0 and the PC is installed.

Note: This protocol uses a different strategy to go back to target than in the Standard EMDR procedure.

Say, *"When you go back to the original incident, on a scale of 0 to 10, where 0 is no disturbance or neutral and 10 is the highest disturbance you can imagine, how disturbing does it feel now?"*

0	1	2	3	4	5	6	7	8	9	10

(no disturbance)   (highest disturbance)

If the SUD is 1 or higher, options are as follows:

Say, *"Look at the incident as it is now stored in your head. What aspect of it is most disturbing?"*

_____

_____

Or say, *"What is there in the picture that is causing the* _____ (state the SUD level)*? What do you see?"*

_____

_____

Then say, *"Concentrate on that aspect. Okay, have you got it? Go with that."*

_____

_____

Do sets of eye movements or other BLS until SUD = 0.

Phase 5: Installation

Install the PC

Say, *"As you think of the incident, how do the words feel from 1 being completely false to 7 being completely true?"*

1   2   3   4   5   6   7

(completely false)   (completely true)

Say, *"Think of the event and hold it together with the words* _____ (repeat the PC). *Go with that."*

_____

_____

Continue this procedure until the VoC is 7.

Phase 6: Body Scan

Say, *"Close your eyes and keep in mind the experience that you will have in the future. Then bring your attention to the different parts of your body, starting with your head and working downward. Any place you find any tension, tightness, or unusual sensation, tell me."*

_____

_____

If any sensation is reported, the therapist introduces BLS. If it is a positive or comfortable sensation, BLS is used to strengthen the positive feelings. If a sensation of discomfort is reported, this is reprocessed until the discomfort subsides. Finally, the VoC has to be checked.

Say, *"As you think of the incident, how do the words feel from 1 being completely false to 7 being completely true?"*

1   2   3   4   5   6   7

(completely false)   (completely true)

Check All Other Targets

See Phase 1: History Taking: Determine an Appropriate and Feasible Treatment Goal and decide whether it is still necessary to reprocess these experiences (SUD when bringing up the memory > 0).

Say, *"Okay, let's check the next target that is in your list* _____
(state the next target). *On a scale of 0 to 10, where 0 is no disturbance or neutral and 10 is the highest disturbance you can imagine, how disturbing does it feel now?"*

0	1	2	3	4	5	6	7	8	9	10

(no disturbance)   (highest disturbance)

If the SUD is > 0, continue the procedure and start at Phase 8: Reevaluation.

Check for any "Flashforward" Still Fueling Client's Anticipatory Anxiety

THE FLASHFORWARD PROCEDURE

The Flashforward Procedure addresses clients' irrational fears and anticipatory anxiety responses, which might persist after the core memories of past events have been fully processed. What does the patient think will happen to her, in the worst case or "doom scenario," if what is feared cannot be avoided?

Say, *"We have now dealt with all the events from your past that seem to have been feeding into your current problems and these are no longer distressing you. But, it could be that you are still left with some fear and dread of what might happen in the future, which has been left behind, even after all the past events have been dealt with. If so, we are going to focus on the future, and what it is that you are dreading, using the same procedure as we used for the past events."*

Determine the Flashforward

Step 1: Identify the Catastrophic Event

Say, *"We need to figure out what kind of image is in your head that makes you scared about a future confrontation with what you fear. What is the worst thing you could imagine happening? Basically, we should look for your ultimate doom scenario."*

_____

_____

If necessary, the therapist asks additional questions, for example:

Say, *"What do you imagine might go wrong if you* _____
(state the concern, such as 'come across a dog,' 'have a dental treatment,' 'climb a tower,' etc.)?"

Say, *"If you had a terrible nightmare about* _____ (state the concern, such as 'driving your car to work on a busy road'), *what would the most disturbing picture look like?"*

_____

_____

continued

Step 2: Follow the Event to Its Ultimate Conclusion

Say, *"Why would this be so terrible for you?"*

_____

_____

Say, *"What would be the worst thing about that?"*

_____

_____

Repeat as necessary until the client cannot identify anything worse.

Step 3: Make a Detailed Picture of Flashforward

Image

The therapist might then ask the client to make a still picture of this scene. Ask that the picture be as detailed as possible.

Say, *"Exactly what would _____ (the flashforward identified above) look like?"*

_____

_____

Or say, *"What can you see in that?"*

_____

_____

If clients still have more than one picture, they are asked to contrast these images, for example, by saying the following:

Say, *"If you were forced to choose, what would be most disturbing for you now: the picture of _____ (state the first example of what is disturbing, for example, your dying), or the picture that _____ (state the other disturbing problem, such as the situation of being unable to care for your family)?"*

_____

_____

Negative Cognition

Say, *"What words go best with that picture _____ (state the flashforward) that express your negative belief about yourself now?"* or *"When you think of _____ (state the flashforward), what negative thought do you have about yourself now?"*

Note: The therapist can suggest, "I am powerless."

_____

_____

continued

Positive Cognition

> Say, *"When you bring up the* _____ *(state the flashforward), what would you like to believe about yourself now?"*

> Or suggest, *"I am in control/ I can deal with it/ I can handle it."*

_____

_____

Validity of Cognition

> Say, *"When you bring up the* _____ *(state the flashforward), how true do those words* _____ *(repeat the positive cognition) feel to you now on a scale of 1 to 7, where 1 feels completely false and 7 feels completely true?"*

> 1   2   3   4   5   6   7

> (completely false)   (completely true)

Emotions

> Say, *"When you bring up* _____ *(state the flashforward) and those words* _____ *(state the negative cognition), what emotion do you feel now?"*

_____

_____

Subjective Units of Disturbance

> Say, *"On a scale of 0 to 10, where 0 is no disturbance or neutral and 10 is the highest disturbance you can imagine, how disturbing does it feel now?"*

> 0   1   2   3   4   5   6   7   8   9   10

> (no disturbance)   (highest disturbance)

Location of Body Sensation

> Say, *"Where do you feel it* (the disturbance*) in your body?"*

_____

_____

Continue Phases 4 to 5 according to the Standard EMDR Protocol. For Phase 6, do the body scan and add the video check:

> Say, *"This time, I'd like you to imagine yourself stepping into the scene of a future confrontation with the object or a situation for which the future template was meant* (e.g., making a trip on an airplane, meeting an unknown person, a dog, a dentist*). Close your eyes and play a movie of this happening, from the beginning until the end. Imagine yourself coping with any challenges that come your way. Notice what you are seeing, thinking, feeling, and experiencing in your body. While playing this movie, let me know if you hit any blocks. If you do, just open your eyes and let me know.*

continued

> *If you don't hit any blocks, let me know when you have viewed the whole movie."*

_____

_____

If clients encounter a block and open their eyes, this is a sign for the therapist to instruct clients to say the following:

> Say, *"Say to yourself 'I can handle it' and follow my fingers"* (or other form of BLS).

If clients are able to play the movie from start to finish with a sense of confidence and satisfaction, clients are asked to play the movie once more from the beginning to the end, while eye movements are introduced and the PC "I can handle it" is installed. In a sense, this movie is installed as a future template.

> Say, *"Okay, play the movie one more time from beginning to end and say to yourself, 'I can handle it.' Go with that."*

Do this until the movie can be played without any blocks or significant disturbances.

Continue Phases 7–8 according to the Standard EMDR Protocol.

Check for Future Concerns

INSTALLATION OF THE FUTURE TEMPLATE

If all targets (Phase 1: History Taking: Determine an Appropriate and Feasible Treatment Goal), including the flashforward, have been successfully processed, as well as current triggers, clients may still have to anticipate future situations in which the former phobic stimuli are present (e.g., a dental treatment situation) and in which they need to interact with these stimuli. To prepare for that, clients are asked to mentally progress in time to identify a specific mental image of a typical future situation by which the fear, prior to this session, certainly would have been triggered. This may be a situation that clients usually avoid because of fear or a situation that they, until now, were not able to enter or to undergo without fear.

> Say, *"Okay, we have reprocessed all of the targets that we needed to that were on your list. Now let's anticipate what will happen when you are faced with _____ (state the anxiety-provoking object or situation). Think of a time in the future and identify a mental image or photo of a typical situation that would have triggered your fear prior to our work together. What would that be?"*

_____

_____

> Say, *"I would like you to imagine yourself coping effectively with _____ (state the fear trigger) in the future. Please focus on the image, say to yourself, 'I can handle it,' notice the sensations associated with this future scene, and follow my fingers (or any other BLS)."*

_____

_____

Say, "*To what extent do you believe you are able to actually handle this situation* (VoC) *on a scale of 1 to 7, where 1 feels completely false and 7 feels completely true?*"

1   2   3   4   5   6   7

(completely false)   (completely true)

The therapist continues with this procedure (instruction and VoC rating) until the future template is sufficiently installed (VoC = 7).

If there is a block, meaning that even after 10 or more installations the VoC is still below 7, there are more targets that have to be identified and addressed. The therapist should use the Standard EMDR Protocol to address these targets, before proceeding with the template (see Worksheets in the Appendix). Also, evaluate whether clients need any new information, resources, or skills to be able to comfortably visualize the future coping scene. Introduce this needed information or skill.

Say, "*What would you need to feel confident in handling the situation?*"

_____

_____

Or say, "*What is missing from your handling of this situation?*"

_____

_____

Video Check

After the incorporation of a positive template for future action, the clinician asks clients to close their eyes, and to run a mental video.

Say, "*This time, I'd like you to imagine yourself stepping into the future. Close your eyes and play a movie from the beginning until the end. Imagine yourself coping with any challenges that come your way. Notice what you are seeing, thinking, feeling, and experiencing in your body. While playing this movie, let me know if you hit any blocks. If you do, just open your eyes and let me know. If you don't hit any blocks, let me know when you have viewed the whole movie.*"

_____

_____

If clients encounter a block and open their eyes, this is a sign for the therapist to instruct clients as follows:

Say, "*Say to yourself 'I can handle it' and follow my fingers* (or other form of BLS)."

The mental videotape is repeated until it can be viewed entirely without distress.

Say, "*Please repeat the video until it can be viewed entirely without distress.*"

To provide the clinician with an indication regarding clients' self-efficacy, have them rate their response on a VoC scale from 1 to 7. This procedural step may give the clinician feedback on the extent to which the goals have been met.

Say, *"As you think of the incident, how do the words feel from 1 being completely false to 7 being completely true?"*

1   2   3   4   5   6   7

(completely false)   (completely true)

If clients are able to play the movie from start to finish with a sense of confidence and satisfaction, clients are asked to play the movie once more from the beginning to the end, while BLS is introduced, and the PC "I can handle it" is installed. In a sense, this movie is installed as a future template.

Say, *"Okay, play the movie one more time from beginning to end and say to yourself 'I can handle it.' Go with that."*

_____

_____

In Vivo Confrontations

PREPARE THE CLIENT FOR IN VIVO CONFRONTATIONS

If clients are actually confronted with the stimuli that normally would evoke a fear response and clients gain an experience that the catastrophe they fear does not occur, this would help to demonstrate that their fears may be unfounded. A behavioral experiment is an excellent opportunity to test if the treatment effects are generalized to all associated triggers or aspects of the situation.

Say, *"Many clients appear to avoid certain activities for so long that they no longer know how to behave and how to feel secure in this situation. To be able to help further alleviate your fears and concerns, it is important that you learn to counter the negative belief that contributes to this sense of threat and anxiety. Therefore, you need to actually test the catastrophic expectations you have that fuel your anxiety in real life. I would like to ask you to gradually confront the objects or situations that normally would provoke a fear response. It may seem odd, but if you have a positive experience and it appears that the catastrophe you fear does not occur, it helps you to further demonstrate—or to convince yourself—that your fear is unfounded."*

Say, *"I want you to understand that nothing will happen against your will during the confrontation with the things that normally would evoke fear. The essence of this confrontation is that it is safe."*

IN VIVO EXPOSURE

This is done to reduce avoidance and evoke mastery while observing that no real danger exists. It is essential that the therapist help clients pay attention to features of the phobic object or situation that are positive or interesting while being exposed to it.

Say, *"Please describe the most notable features of the situation. Are you noticing any interesting elements about _____ (state the phobic object or situation)?"*

_____

_____

It is our experience that it is helpful to make variations with regard to the stimulus dimensions such as action, distance, and time.

Say, *"Isn't it interesting to notice that now that you are confronted with this _____ (state the object or situation) _____* (state the catastrophe the client normally would have feared to happen) *does not occur?"*

_____

_____

Say, *"Do you notice that your anxiety is not as physically harmful as you might have expected?"*

_____

_____

Say, *"These emotional reactions will subside and fade over time. Therefore, it is important that you continue exposing yourself to the feared stimuli as long as you feel that you have achieved a certain degree of self-mastery. Please note that you are gradually learning to feel that you are capable of handling a certain level of anticipatory anxiety with confidence."*

The therapist should make sure that confrontations are repeated so that the reduction in distress is fully consolidated before moving on.

Check the results by assessing the validity of the catastrophe.

Say, *"If you would encounter _____ (state the phobic object or situation) again, on a scale from 0% to 100% where 0% means it is completely false and 100% means it is completely true, how true does this feel that this will happen?"*

| 0% | 10% | 20% | 30% | 40% | 50% | 60% | 70% | 80% | 90% | 100% |

(completely false)   (completely true)

Phase 7: Closure

At the end of every session, consolidate the changes and improvement that has occurred.

Say, *"What is the most positive thing you have learned about yourself in the last hour with regard to _____ (state the incident or theme)?"*

_____

_____

If the cognitions are not already on the identity level, say the following:

Say, *"What does this say about yourself as a person?"*

Say, *"Go with that."*

_____

_____

Install with eye movements until there are no further positive changes.

Next, check the results by assessing the validity of the catastrophe.

Say, *"If you would be exposed to _____ (state the phobic object or situation), on a scale from 0% to 100% where 0% means it is completely false and 100% means it is completely true that this will happen, how true does this feel?"*

0%   10%   20%   30%   40%   50%   60%   70%   80%   90%   100%

(completely false)   (completely true)

Next, an explanation is provided about the coming three days concerning agreements, diary, and contact information.

> Say, *"Things may come up, or, they may not. If they do, great, write it down and it can be a target for next time. If you get any new memories, dreams, or situations that disturb you, just take a good snapshot. It isn't necessary to give a lot of detail. Just put down enough to remind you so we can target it next time. The same thing goes for any positive dreams or situations. If negative feelings do come up, try not to make them significant. Remember, it's still just the old stuff. Just write it down for next time."*

Planning Self-Managed Homework Assignments

After the therapy has been concluded, the therapist makes it clear that it is important to keep practicing during daily life in order to ensure that the changes are maintained.

> Say, *"It is very important to keep practicing with exposing yourself to difficult situations during your daily life in order to maintain the changes that you have experienced."*

> *Each time that you have a chance to see* _____ (state the feared stimulus), *it is an opportunity for you to practice these new skills that you now know how to do. So, the more that you encounter* _____ (state the feared stimulus), *the better you can get at* _____ (state the goal). *Your brain learns to do new behaviors by practicing."*

By using self-managed assignments, the client should be encouraged to incorporate as many critical situations in real life as possible. This allows clients to gain self-confidence through overcoming their fears on their own, to learn new and more independent and appropriate ways of coping, and to perceive further progress.

> Say, *"Please make sure to put yourself in as many critical situations in real life as possible. The more that you do this, the more you will gain in self-confidence as you overcome your fears and learn more independent and appropriate ways of coping and see your own progress."*

> Say, *"Make sure to write down your responses when you are practicing your new skills. Sometimes, even with the skills, you might find that you re-experience your fear. I want to tell you that this can happen sometimes, and it is not unusual. What you can do at that time is to note what has led up to the feeling, what is going on around you, and what you did to help yourself handle the situation. Jot down some notes about what happened as soon as you can so that you won't forget what happened and then bring them to the next session so that we can figure it out."*

For clients with blood phobia, say the following:

> Say, *"Please practice the Applied Tension Technique in real-life situations as much as possible, while exposing yourself to* _____ (state anxiety-provoking stimulus). *That may, for example, be talking about blood-related topics with friends, watching a medical documentary, a violent film with bloodshed, or paying a visit to a blood bank."*

Phase 8: Reevaluation

Evaluate whatever is left to be done.

Say, *"What have you been noticing since our last session?"*

_____

_____

Say, *"What are the current symptoms (if any) you have been noticing?"*

_____

_____

Say, *"What kind of progress have you noticed, especially in terms of the homework?"*

_____

_____

Say, *"As you think back on the target that we were working on last time, on a scale of 0 to 10, where 0 is no disturbance or neutral and 10 is the highest disturbance you can imagine, how disturbing does it feel now?"*

0   1   2   3   4   5   6   7   8   9   10

(no disturbance)   (highest disturbance)

If the disturbance level has increased, these reverberations should be targeted or otherwise addressed.

If the client has relapsed, say the following:

Say, *"As we spoke about before, it is not unusual to experience a relapse, as you expose yourself to situations that elicit your response. This is because you have exposed yourself to situations that you have been avoiding for a long period of time. You might have even noticed a return of some fear and become disappointed because you had expected improvements and now feel that your problems have only worsened. However, I see it really as a challenge that will allow you to put into practice what you have learned. What are your thoughts about what I am saying?"*

_____

_____

The therapist should assess the necessity of teaching the client additional self-control techniques or other relevant exercises that could further enhance the client's ability to confront the former anxiety-provoking situation in real life.

Say, *"So what other resources do you think might be helpful in assisting you to deal with this situation?"*

_____

_____

Repeated rehearsal and reinforcement for success has to be emphasized.

Say, *"As we have discussed before, the more you practice putting yourself in these situations that have provoked your fear over a long time, and use all that we have worked on, the more you will be able to overcome your problem."*

To encourage hope and foster engagement in treatment, it is crucial that therapy sessions and homework assignments furnish experiences of success that clients can attribute to themselves.

Say, *"I can see that through all of the work you did between sessions that you are really working hard _____ (reinforce what the client has done that has been successful)."*

_____

_____

Summary

This chapter illustrates how EMDR Therapy can be applied in the treatment of fears and specific phobias. These conditions are highly prevalent in the general population, and are characterized by an unreasonable and severe fear related to exposure to specific objects or situations, which tend to result in active avoidance of direct contact with these stimuli.

Clients with specific phobias display commonalities with PTSD in that they often experience vivid and disturbing memories of earlier events associated with the beginning of their fears. Activation of these mental representations plays an important role not only in the symptomatology of fears and phobias, but also in the process contributing to the maintenance and aggravation of clients' symptoms. EMDR Therapy has been shown to be capable of resolving such memories, alleviating clients' fears, and successfully reducing clients' avoidance tendencies (de Jongh et al., 1999, 2011; Doering et al., 2013).

Like most other anxiety disorders, for specific phobia there are treatment approaches that have been found to be effective, particularly those with a cognitive behavioral signature. Although there always should be good reasons to deviate from such evidence-based treatment standards, EMDR has proven to fulfill a pivotal role in resolving memories of past events that started the fear or phobia, or those that still contribute to the severity of the client's fear response (de Jongh, Ernst, Marques, & Hornsveld, 2013), particularly when these are likely to be activated when the clients are confronted with their phobic stimuli. Contrariwise, in many instances EMDR Therapy could profit from elements of CBT that add significant practical value and elevate the effectiveness of its use. That is the reason that in the present phobia protocol, EMDR is used for the processing of memories, while cognitive behavioral procedures (e.g., applied tension and in vivo exposure)—that are meant to teach clients to confront their feared stimuli until they feel they have achieved a degree of self-mastery that is needed to feel comfortable with handling these situations—are included as well.

References

American Psychiatric Association. (2013). *Diagnostic and statistical manual of mental disorders* (5th ed.). Arlington, VA: American Psychiatric Publishing.

Antony, M. M., Orsillo, S. M., & Roemer, L. (2001). *Practitioner's guide to empirically-based measures of anxiety*. New York, NY: Kluwer Academic/Plenum.

de Jongh, A. (2012). Treatment of a woman with emetophobia: A trauma focused approach. *Mental Illness, 4*, e3. doi:10.4081/mi.2012.e3

de Jongh, A., Ernst, R., Marques, L., & Hornsveld, H. (2013). The impact of eye movements and tones on disturbing memories of patients with PTSD and other mental disorders. *Journal of Behavior Therapy and Experimental Psychiatry, 44*, 447–483.

de Jongh, A., Fransen, J., Oosterink-Wubbe, F., & Aartman, I. H. A. (2006). Psychological trauma exposure and trauma symptoms among individuals with high and low levels of dental anxiety. *European Journal of Oral Sciences, 114*, 286–292.

de Jongh, A., Holmshaw, M., Carswell, W., & van Wijk, A. (2011). Usefulness of a trauma-focused treatment approach for travel phobia. *Clinical Psychology and Psychotherapy, 18*, 124–137. doi:10.1002/cpp.680

de Jongh, A., & ten Broeke, E. (1994). Opmerkelijke veranderingen na één zitting met eye movement desensitization en reprocessing: Een geval van angst voor misselijkheid en braken—[Noteworthy changes after one session with eye movement desensitization and reprocessing: A case of fear of nausea and vomiting]. *Tijdschrift voor Directieve Therapie en Hypnose, 14*(2), 90–102.

de Jongh, A., & ten Broeke, E. (1998). Treatment of choking phobia by targeting traumatic memories with EMDR: A case study. *Clinical Psychology and Psychotherapy, 5*, 264–269.

de Jongh, A., & ten Broeke, E. (2007). Treatment of specific phobias with EMDR: Conceptualization and strategies for the selection of appropriate memories. *Journal of EMDR Practice and Research, 1*(1), 46–56.

de Jongh, A., ten Broeke, E., & Renssen, M. (1999). Treatment of specific phobias with eye movement desensitization and reprocessing (EMDR): Protocol, empirical status, and conceptual issues. *Journal of Anxiety Disorders, 13*(1–2), 69–85.

de Jongh, A., van den Oord, H., & ten Broeke, E. (2002). Efficacy of eye movement desensitization and reprocessing in the treatment of specific phobias: Four single-case studies on dental phobia. *Journal of Clinical Psychology, 58*(12), 1489–1503.

de Roos, C. J. A. M., & de Jongh, A. (2008). EMDR treatment of children and adolescents with a choking phobia. *Journal of EMDR Practice and Research, 2*(3), 201–211.

DiNardo, P. A., Barlow, D. H., Cerny, J. A., Vermilyea, B. B., Vermilyea, J. A., Himadi, W. G., & Waddell, M. T. (1985). *Anxiety Disorders Interview Schedule-Revised (ADIS-R)*. Albany, NY: Center for Stress and Anxiety Disorders.

Doering, S., Ohlmeier, M.-C., de Jongh, A., Hofmann, A., & Bisping, V. (2013). Efficacy of a trauma-focused treatment approach for dental phobia: A randomized clinical trial. *European Journal of Oral Sciences, 121*, 584–593.

Kleinknecht, R. (1993). Rapid treatment of blood and injection phobias with eye movement desensitization. *Journal of Behavior Therapy and Experimental Psychiatry, 24*(3), 211–217.

Logie, R., & de Jongh, A. (2016). Flashforward. In M. Luber (Ed.), *Eye movement desensitization and reprocessing (EMDR) scripted protocols and summary sheets: Treating trauma, anxiety and mood-related conditions*. New York, NY: Springer.

Lohr, J. M., Tolin, D. F., & Kleinknecht, R. A. (1996). An intensive design investigation of eye movement desensitization and reprocessing of claustrophobia. *Journal of Anxiety Disorders, 10*, 73–88.

Marquis, J. N. (1991). A report on seventy-eight cases treated by eye movement desensitization. *Journal of Behavior Therapy and Experimental Psychiatry, 22*, 187–192.

Oosterink, F. M. D., de Jongh, A., & Aartman, I. H. A. (2009). Negative events and their potential risk of precipitating pathological forms of dental anxiety. *Journal of Anxiety Disorders, 23*, 451–457.

Öst, L.-G., & Sterner, U. (1987). Applied tension: A specific behavioral method for treatment of blood phobia. *Behaviour Research and Therapy, 25*, 25–29.

Shapiro, F. (2001). *Eye movement desensitization and reprocessing: Basic principles, protocols and procedures*. New York, NY: Guilford Press.

Wolitzky-Taylor, K. B., Horowitz, J. D., Powers, M. B., & Telch, M. J (2008). Psychological approaches in the treatment of specific phobias: A meta-analysis. *Clinical Psychology Review, 28*(6), 1021–1037.

Ad de Jongh
SUMMARY SHEET BY MARILYN LUBER

Name: _____ Diagnosis: _____

Medications: _____

Test Results: _____

☑ Check when task is completed, response has changed, or to indicate symptoms.

Note: This material is meant as a checklist for your response. Please keep in mind that it is only a reminder of different tasks that may or may not apply to your incident.

Purpose: To illustrate how EMDR Therapy can be applied in the treatment of specific fears and phobic conditions.

Phase 1: History Taking

Diagnostic Interview (e.g., Anxiety Disorder Interview Scale)

MOTIVATION ASSESSMENT

_____ Self-Referral   _____ Forced Referral

Failed Past Therapy: ☐ Yes   ☐ No

If yes, what happened? _____

_____

Comorbid Psychiatric Issues: ☐ Yes   ☐ No

(Other comorbid issues may contribute to lack of motivation) _____

_____

Low Self-Esteem: ☐ Yes   ☐ No

Low self-esteem can contribute to client's avoidance behavior and may also have to be resolved, and to become a target of processing accordingly.

DETERMINE THE TYPE OF FEAR AND THE SEVERITY

Fear: _____

_____

Fear Excessive/Unreasonable: □ Yes   □ No

Explain: _____

_____

IDENTIFY THE STIMULUS SITUATION (CONDITIONED STIMULUS, CS)

"Describe the object/situation that you are afraid of" _____

_____

"What do you need to see, hear, or feel in order to get an immediate fear response?" _____

_____

"What about _____ (the object/situation) *triggers your fear the most?"*

_____

"Which incident caused your fear?" _____

_____

IDENTIFY THE EXPECTED CONSEQUENCE/CATASTROPHE (UNCONDITIONED STIMULUS, UCS)

Expected consequence: _____

_____

Incident that caused your fear: _____

_____

ASSESS VALIDITY OF CATASTROPHE

"Is it true that you are saying that IF you would be exposed to _____ (state the phobic object or situation) *THEN you would* _____ (state the catastrophe the client fears would happen)?"*

(0–100%) = _____

PROVIDE INFORMATION ABOUT THE FEAR OR PHOBIA IF NECESSARY

"What do you know about the relative dangerousness of _____ (fill in the information specific to the phobic stimulus with which the client is dealing)? *Since there are also people on this planet that are not that fearful as you of* _____ (state the phobic object or situation), *wouldn't it be wise to spend some more time in investigating whether it is really that*

dangerous as you think it is? Just to be sure that you don't overestimate the probability of the danger or that something bad will happen to you. I mean: even if it appears to be even more dangerous to be exposed to _____ (state the phobic object or situation) than you think it is now, it is important to find out, don't you think? Thus, let's look for the information we need."

"Where shall we start?"

_____

_____

DETERMINE AN APPROPRIATE AND FEASIBLE TREATMENT GOAL

Treatment goal: _____

"How will you know when you reach your goal?" _____

_____

IDENTIFY THE CONDITIONING EXPERIENCE

"Incident causing fear/incident when you noticed this fear for the first time":

_____

CHECK FOR POSSIBLE EARLIER ANCILLARY EXPERIENCE

"Are you sure you did not have this fear/phobia prior to this incident?" _____

_____

IDENTIFY OTHER RELEVANT EXPERIENCES

Other relevant experiences. *"After what event/s did the fear get worse?"/"Which other experiences led to how fearful you are now?"*

_____

_____

Phase 2: Preparation

Rapport and trust established in therapeutic relationship:	☐ Yes	☐ No
Explanation of EMDR as in the Standard EMDR Protocol	☐ Yes	☐ No

Teach Distraction Techniques

Describe content of room in detail:	☐ Yes	☐ No
Count backward from 1000 by 7s:	☐ Yes	☐ No
Describe favorite walk in detail:	☐ Yes	☐ No

For Children:

Animal names (A–Z)	☐ Yes	☐ No

For Blood/Injury Phobic Patients:

> Applied Tension Technique: □ Yes   □ No

> *"Please make it comfortable for yourself. Now, tense all of your muscles in your body, including those in your arms,…torso,…legs,…and face … Please increase this tension…Now, hold this tension* (for about 15 seconds), *until there is a warm feeling in your head. Okay? If so, release the tension and let your body return to its normal state* (for about 30 seconds)."

This tension–relaxation cycle should be repeated five times within each practice session.

> *"You can start practicing the tension technique this week, as we will begin our EMDR treatment next time. Practicing means doing the technique five times throughout the day, practicing five tension-relaxation cycles per time. If you have hypertension, it would be wise for you to check with your physician before practicing this technique. If you experience any headaches during the practices, decrease the strength of the tension."*

> Client can handle own fear reactions: □ Yes   □ No

Phase 3: Assessment

Target/Memory/Image: _____

NC: _____

PC: _____

VoC: _____ /7

Emotions:_____

SUD: _____ /10

Sensation: _____

Phase 4: Desensitization

Apply the Standard EMDR Protocol for All Targets

Note: This protocol uses a different strategy to go back to target.

> SUD: _____ /10; if the SUD is 1 or higher:

Options: *"Look at the incident as it is now stored in your head."*

> *"What aspect of it is most disturbing?"*

> *"What is there in the picture that is causing the SUD = _____ /10?"*

> *"What do you see?"*

> *"Concentrate on that aspect. OK, have you got it? Go with that."*

Do BLS until SUD = 0.

Phase 5: Installation

Install the PC.

Original PC:

Use original PC: _____

New PC:

Use new PC (if new one is better): _____

VoC: _____ /7

Incident + PC + BLS

Phase 6: Body Scan

Unresolved tension/tightness/unusual sensation: _____

_____

Unresolved tension/tightness/unusual sensation + BLS

Strengthen positive sensation using BLS.

If there is more discomfort, reprocess until discomfort subsides + BLS. Then repeat body scan.

VoC: _____ /7

Check the other targets to see if it is still necessary to reprocess these experiences.

Other Targets	Age	SUD	SUD Post
1. _____	_____	___ /10	_____ /10
2. _____	_____	___ /10	_____ /10
3. _____	_____	___ /10	_____ /10
4. _____	_____	___ /10	_____ /10
5. _____	_____	___ /10	_____ /10

Check for any Flashforward Still Fuelling Client's Anticipatory Anxiety

Check whether there is still anticipatory anxiety regarding the phobic object or situation. If so, ask the client to bring up a fantasy (image) of the most catastrophic outcome of a future confrontation with the phobic object or situation that would explain why the client is so anxious or terrified (see Expected Consequence/Catastrophe that was identified earlier).

Step 1: Identify the Catastrophic Event

"We need to figure out what kind of image is in your head that makes you still scared about a future confrontation with what you fear. What is the worst thing you could imagine happening? Basically we should look for your ultimate doom scenario."

_____

_____

Step 2: Follow the Event to Its Ultimate Conclusion

"Worst thing about it?"

continued

Step 3: Make a Detailed Picture of Flashforward

Use this as a target for processing with the Standard EMDR Protocol (SUD = 0; VoC = 7).

Target/Memory/Image: _____

NC: _____

PC: _____

VoC: _____ /7

Emotions: _____

SUD: _____ /10

Sensation: _____

Video Check

"This time, I'd like you to imagine yourself stepping into the future. Close your eyes, and play a movie from the beginning until the end. Imagine yourself coping with any challenges that come your way. Notice what you are seeing, thinking, feeling, and experiencing in your body. While playing this movie, let me know if you hit any blocks. If you do, just open your eyes and let me know. If you don't hit any blocks, let me know when you have viewed the whole movie."

If blocks, say, "I can handle it," and BLS. Repeat until whole movie can be viewed entirely without distress.

VoC: _____ /7

If client can play movie from beginning to end with confidence and satisfaction, play the movie one more time from beginning to end + BLS: ☐ Yes   ☐ No

Check for Future Concerns

INSTALLATION OF THE FUTURE TEMPLATE

Image of situation triggering your fear prior to our work together: _____

_____

Image of coping effectively with/or in the fear trigger in the future: _____

_____

PC: ("I can handle it") _____

Sensations: _____

+ BLS

VoC (able to handle the situation): _____ /7
Install until VoC = 7

Blocks/anxieties/fears in future scene: _____

1. _____

2. _____

3. _____

Do BLS. If they do not resolve, ask for other qualities needed to handle the situation.

Other new information, resources, or skills to comfortably visualize coping in the future:

1. _____
2. _____
3. _____

If blocks are not resolved, identify unprocessed material and process with Standard EMDR Protocol:

1. _____
2. _____
3. _____

Target/Memory/Image:_____

_____

NC: _____

PC: _____

VoC: _____ /7

Emotions: _____

SUD: _____ /10

Sensation: _____

Video Check

"This time, I'd like you to imagine yourself stepping into the future. Close your eyes, and play a movie from the beginning until the end. Imagine yourself coping with any challenges that come your way. Notice what you are seeing, thinking, feeling, and experiencing in your body. While playing this movie, let me know if you hit any blocks. If you do, just open your eyes and let me know. If you don't hit any blocks, let me know when you have viewed the whole movie."

If blocks, say "I can handle it," and BLS. Repeat until whole movie can be viewed entirely without distress.

VoC: _____ /7

If client can play movie from beginning to end with confidence and satisfaction, play the movie one more time from beginning to end + BLS: ☐ Yes ☐ No

In Vivo Confrontations

PREPARE THE CLIENT

"Many clients appear to avoid certain activities for so long that they no longer know how to behave and how to feel secure in this situation. To be able to help you further alleviate your fears and concerns, it is important that you learn to counter the negative belief that contributes to this sense of threat and anxiety. Therefore, you need to actually test the catastrophic expectations that you have that fuel your anxiety in real life. I would like to ask you to gradually confront the objects or situations that normally would provoke a fear response. It may seem odd, but if you have a positive experience, and it appears that the catastrophe you fear does not occur, it helps you to further

demonstrate—or to convince yourself—that your fear is unfounded. I want you to understand that nothing will happen against your will during the confrontation with the things that normally would evoke fear. The essence of this confrontation is that it is safe."

Client agrees to in vivo exposure: □ Yes   □ No

IN VIVO EXPOSURE

This is done to reduce avoidance and evoke mastery while observing that no real danger exists. Pay attention to features of the phobic object or situation that are positive or interesting while being exposed to it:

Description of most notable features of the situation: _____

_____

Thoughts during in vivo exposure: _____

_____

Thoughts someone who is not afraid would think in the situation: _____

_____

It is helpful to make variations with regard to the stimulus dimensions "action," "distance," and "time."

"Isn't it interesting to notice that now that you are confronted with this _____ (state the object or situation) _____ (state the catastrophe the client normally would have feared to happen) does not occur?"

□ Yes   □ No

"Do you notice that your anxiety is not as physically harmful as you might have expected?"

□ Yes   □ No

Importance of practice.

Check with VoC (0–100%): _____

Phase 7: Closure

Most positive thing learned: _____

_____

PC: _____

+ BLS

Check with VoC (0–100%): _____

Normal closure: □ Yes   □ No

Planning Self-Managed Homework Assignments

Have clients expose themselves to difficult situations in daily life to maintain the changes.

"It is very important to keep practicing with exposing yourself to difficult situations during your daily life in order to maintain the changes that you have experienced. Each time you have a chance to see _____ (state the feared stimulus), it is an opportunity for you to practice these new skills that you

now know how to do. So, the more that you encounter _____ (state the feared stimulus), the better you can get at _____ (state the goal). Your brain learns best to do new behaviors by practicing."

"Please make sure to put yourself in as many critical situations in real life as possible. The more that you do this, the more you will gain in self-confidence as you overcome your fears and learn more independent and appropriate ways of coping and see your own progress."

For clients with blood phobia, say the following:

"Please practice the 'applied tension technique' in real-life situations as much as possible, while exposing yourself to _____ (state anxiety-provoking stimulus). That may, for example, be talking about blood-related topics with friends, watching a medical documentary, a violent film with bloodshed, or paying a visit to a blood bank."

"Make sure to write down your responses when you are practicing your new skills. Sometimes, even with the skills, you might find that you reexperience your fear. I want to tell you that this can happen sometimes, and it is not unusual. What you can do at that time is to note what has led up to the feeling, what is going on around you, and what you did to help yourself handle the situation. Jot down some notes about what happened as soon as you can so that you won't forget what happened and then bring them to the next session so that we can figure it out."

Phase 8: Reevaluation

Noticed since last session: _____

_____

Current symptoms: _____

New material: _____

_____

SUD: _____ /10

If disturbance level increased, target it.

If relapse:

"As we spoke about before, it is not unusual to experience a relapse as you expose yourself to situations that elicit your response. This is because you have exposed yourself to situations that you have been avoiding for a long period of time. You might have even noticed a return of some fear and become disappointed because you had expected improvements and now feel that your problems have only worsened. However, I see it really as a challenge that will allow you to put into practice what you have learned."

"What are your thoughts about what I am saying?" _____

_____

New resources needed: □ Yes   □ No

_____

_____

Give praise for accomplishments: □ Yes   □ No

EMDR Therapy Protocol for Panic Disorders With or Without Agoraphobia

Ferdinand Horst and Ad de Jongh

Introduction

Panic disorder, as stated in the *Diagnostic and Statistical Manual of Mental Disorders*, fifth edition (*DSM-5*; American Psychiatric Association, 2013) is characterized by recurrent and unexpected panic attacks and by hyperarousal symptoms like palpitations, pounding heart, chest pain, sweating, trembling, or shaking. These symptoms can be experienced as catastrophic ("I am dying") and mostly have a strong impact on daily life. When panic disorder is accompanied by severe avoidance of places or situations from which escape might be difficult or embarrassing, it is specified as "panic disorder with agoraphobia" (American Psychiatric Association, 2013).

EMDR Therapy and Panic Disorder With or Without Agoraphobia

Despite the well-examined effectiveness of Eye Movement Desensitization and Reprocessing (EMDR) Therapy in the treatment of posttraumatic stress disorder (PTSD), the applicability of EMDR Therapy for other anxiety disorders, like panic disorders with or without agoraphobia (PDA or Pathological Demand Avoidance), has hardly been examined (de Jongh & ten Broeke, 2009).

From a theoretical perspective, there are several reasons why EMDR Therapy could be useful in the treatment of panic disorder:

1. The occurrence of panic attacks is likely to be totally unexpected; therefore, they are often experienced as distressing, causing a subjective response of fear or helplessness. Accordingly, panic attacks can be viewed as life-threatening experiences (McNally & Lukach, 1992; van Hagenaars, van Minnen, & Hoogduin, 2009).
2. Panic memories in panic disorder resemble traumatic memories in PTSD in the sense that the person painfully reexperiences the traumatic incident in the form of recurrent and distressing recollections of the event, including intrusive images and flashbacks (van Hagenaars et al., 2009).
3. Besides the panic attack itself being a threatening experience, there are indications that PDA often develops after other stressful life events (Faravelli & Pallanti, 1989; Horesh, Amir, Kedem, Goldberger, & Kotler, 1997).

The same research group (Feske & Goldstein, 1997; Goldstein, de Beurs, Chambless, & Wilson, 2000; Goldstein & Feske, 1994) conducted almost all of the studies concerning the use of EMDR Therapy in the treatment of PDA. They found a decrease in panic complaints and anticipatory anxiety in most clients treated with EMDR (Goldstein & Feske, 1994). These studies are limited by the extent to which the EMDR procedure was applied, because in the description of the procedure some essential parts of the current EMDR protocol were lacking (de Jongh & ten Broeke, 2009).

The purpose of this chapter is to illustrate how EMDR Therapy can be applied in the treatment of panic disorder with or without agoraphobia. In this chapter, the EMDR protocol for panic disorders with or without agoraphobia is scripted; it is based on the Dutch translation (ten Broeke & de Jongh, 2009) of the EMDR protocol of Shapiro (2001).

DSM-5 Criteria for Panic Disorder With and Without Agoraphobia

Before identifying suitable targets for EMDR Therapy in the treatment of panic disorder with or without agoraphobia, it is important to determine whether or not the client has panic attacks and meets all *DSM-5* (American Psychiatric Association, 2013) criteria of a panic disorder with or without agoraphobia.

Panic attacks are recurrent and unexpected and include a surge that may range from intense discomfort to extreme fear cresting within minutes. They are accompanied by at least four or more of the following physiological symptoms: paresthesias (tingling sensations or numbness); sensations of heat or chills; experiences of dizziness, lightheadedness, unsteadiness or weakness; queasiness or abdominal upset; chest pain or distress; feeling of choking; unable to catch breath or feeling smothered; trembling or quaking; perspiring; and fast or irregular heartbeat. There are also intense cognitive distortions such as feelings of unreality (derealization) or being disconnected from oneself (depersonalization); fear of going crazy or losing control; and/or fear of dying.

In order to meet the criteria, a person must be either continuously worrying about having another panic attack or their consequences (such as losing control, having a nervous breakdown, etc.) or significantly changing behavior to avoid having another panic attack over the period of 1 month after the attack. If the symptoms can be ascribed to the physiological effects of a substance (such as a medication or drug abuse) or another medical condition (such as cardiac disorders or hyperthyroidism) or another mental disorder (such as social anxiety disorder or specific phobia), panic disorder is not diagnosed.

In contrast to *DSM-IV-TR* (American Psychiatric Association, 2000), where panic disorder is diagnosed with or without agoraphobia, the *DSM-5* considers agoraphobia as an independent disorder. Therefore, agoraphobia is diagnosed irrespective of the presence of panic disorder. This diagnosis includes a separate *DSM-5* code for agoraphobia. In case both disorders are present, both should be assigned. Agoraphobia is characterized by fear about situations related to being in enclosed or open spaces, being in line or in a crowd, being outside of the home alone or using public transport. These situations are difficult because in the event of panic symptomatology, the fear is that escape might be difficult and help might not be available is predominant leading to the avoidance of these situations or the need for the presence of another person. The fear or anxiety that is felt is out of proportion to the actual situation itself; this includes when another medical condition is occurring as well. This type of fear, anxiety, or avoidance lasts 6 months or more, impairs functioning in social, occupational or other areas of functioning and is not explained by other mental disorders.

Measurement

Standardized Clinical Interview

To determine whether a client suffers from panic disorder with or without agoraphobia, and its severity, a standardized clinical interview, such as the Structured Clinical Interview for *DSM-IV* Axis I disorders (SCID-I; First, Spitzer, Gibbon, & Williams, 2002), should be administered. The answers to the questions reveal whether the client suffers from panic disorder and/or other anxiety disorders, like PTSD, depression, specific phobia, or generalized anxiety disorder that are more prominent and possibly require other treatment. (At the time the present chapter was written, an updated version for *DSM-5* was not yet available).

Mobility Inventory

When a client is diagnosed with panic disorder with agoraphobia, the Mobility Inventory (Chambless, Caputo, Jasin, Gracely, & Williams, 1985) can be administered to determine the severity of the disorder. This inventory is a self-report questionnaire to measure the degree of agoraphobic avoidance across 27 situations. These situations are subdivided according to whether the client is encountering them with a trusted companion or alone.

Agoraphobic Cognitions Questionnaire

To identify the intensity of a client's catastrophic cognitions when feeling anxious or tense, the Agoraphobic Cognitions Questionnaire (Chambless, Caputo, Bright, & Gallagher, 1985) can be used. This questionnaire has 14 catastrophic cognitions, divided into two subscales, which include anxiety about physical consequences and anxiety for social consequences.

Panic Disorder With or Without Agoraphobia Protocol Script Notes

Identifying Useful EMDR Therapy Targets

When identifying useful targets for EMDR Therapy in the treatment of panic disorder with or without agoraphobia, any experience in the client's panic history that "fuels" the current pathology can be used; these experience include memories of event(s) after which the complaints—panic, anticipatory fear responses, and avoidance tendencies—originated and/or worsened, and are experienced as still emotionally disturbing today (for a proper case conceptualization, see de Jongh, ten Broeke, & Meijer, 2010). Examples are panic attack memories, traumatic memories, and/or agoraphobic situations.

Panic Attack Memories

As mentioned earlier, panic attacks are likely to occur totally unexpectedly, and clients experience them as life threatening, causing a subjective response of fear or helplessness. Therefore, based on Shapiro's Adaptive Information Processing (AIP) model that negative thoughts, feelings, and behaviors are the result of unprocessed memories, it is a logical step to determine the first and/or worst panic attack memory, most recent memory, and eventually other panic attack memories as suitable targets for EMDR Therapy. When reprocessing of the panic attack memories is completed, it can be expected that these memories will no longer fuel the panic disorder symptoms and that such symptoms will alleviate or dissolve.

Traumatic Memories

Besides the panic attack itself being a threatening experience, there are indications that panic disorder with or without agoraphobia often develops after other stressful life events (e.g., the loss of a loved one, a serious accident, or a divorce). These life events as such, most of the time, do not meet (full) PTSD criteria, but could be considered precursors for the start and development of the panic disorder. Based upon the assumptions underlying the AIP model, it could be hypothesized that panic disorder symptoms will reduce or dissolve following the processing of the underlying traumatic memories/life events.

Agoraphobia Memories

Clients with panic disorder often develop agoraphobia. Since the agoraphobia develops after the start of the first and/or worst panic attack, it can be expected that, in the most ideal situation, the severity of the symptoms characterizing the agoraphobia (e.g., avoidance of a certain situation) will be reduced when the panic attack memories are completely processed. But, when the anticipatory anxiety for clients' typical agoraphobic situations does not dissolve, it is important to determine the presence of other (disturbing) memories of past events that possibly keep the agoraphobic fears vivid.

In certain cases, clients who have been treated with EMDR Therapy and who no longer experience panic attacks still avoid situations where there would be difficulty in escaping if the need arose. It seems that they have avoided certain activities for such a long period of time that—even without panic attacks—they do not know how to behave and feel secure in situations that would precipitate their agoraphobic symptoms. The most logical step is to apply EMDR Therapy to client's most feared catastrophic future event (the client's so-called flashforward; see Chapter 2).

If the client's flashforward has been fully processed and the Validity of Cognition (VoC) of the flashforward in combination with the Positive Cognition (PC; "I can handle it") has reached 7, it should be evaluated whether or not the potentially agoraphobic situations are no longer avoided, as would be expected. If not, the client should be supported and assisted to encounter the agoraphobic situations in order to convince herself that the fear is unfounded. In these instances, in vivo exposure might still be needed to (gradually) confront the client with the situation so that she can experience the nonoccurrence of the catastrophe she fears.

Panic Disorder With or Without Agoraphobia Protocol Script

Currently, no official guideline is available for the treatment of panic disorder with or without agoraphobia using EMDR Therapy. In the present protocol, the authors used the theoretical perspective discussed earlier to give direction to identifying suitable targets in the treatment of panic disorder. This scripted EMDR Therapy protocol for panic disorder with or without agoraphobia is largely based on Ad de Jongh's chapter "EMDR and Specific Fears: The Phobia Protocol Single Traumatic Event" in *Eye Movement Desensitization and Reprocessing (EMDR) Scripted Protocols: Special Populations* (Luber, 2009), *Eye Movement Desensitization and Reprocessing (EMDR) Scripted Protocols with Summary Sheets: Special Populations* (Luber, 2012), and the "Two Methods Model for Establishing Case Conceptualizations for EMDR" (de Jongh et al., 2010).

Phase 1: Client History

Determine to what extent the client fulfills the *DSM-5* criteria of a panic disorder with or without agoraphobia (American Psychiatric Association, 2013).

Identify the Targets

FIRST PANIC ATTACK/STIMULUS SITUATION

Identify the first panic attack or stimulus situation.

Say, *"Please describe your first panic attack that you remember."*

_____

_____

_____

Check whether this is indeed the first panic attack.

> Say, *"Is this indeed your first panic attack? I mean, are you absolutely sure you don't remember having had a panic attack prior to this incident?"*

_____

_____

WORST PANIC ATTACK/MOST REPRESENTATIVE EXPERIENCE

Identify the worst panic attack or most representative experience.

> Say, *"Please describe the worst panic attack you remember."*

_____

_____

_____

MOST RECENT PANIC ATTACK

Identify the most recent panic attack.

> Say, *"Please describe the most recent panic attack."*

_____

_____

_____

IDENTIFY OTHER EXPERIENCES RELEVANT TO THE ONSET OF THE PANIC DISORDER

Identify other experiences relevant to the onset of the panic disorder.

> Say, *"What other past experiences might be important in relation to the onset of the panic disorder you have? Please describe."*

_____

_____

_____

> Or say, *"If the panic attacks started with a traumatic event, which one was that?"*

_____

_____

_____

> Or say, *"Do the panic attacks remind you of another specific event?"*

_____

_____

_____

Or say, *"Do you remember having been exposed to any traumatic (other) event prior to the start of your first panic attack?"*

_____

_____

_____

Introduce the Timeline

Introduce the timeline for the client's panic and trauma experiences.

Say, *"Let's draw a timeline of your panic history and traumatic experiences until now. The horizontal line represents the time, and the vertical line the severity of the symptoms."*

Help the client draw the timeline on a piece of paper.

Expected Consequence/Catastrophe

Identify the expected consequence or catastrophe (e.g., physical consequences, like "I must have a brain tumor" and/or social consequences, like "I am going crazy").

Say, *"What are you afraid could happen when you get a panic attack?"*

_____

_____

_____

If the client meets the criteria of agoraphobia, say the following:

Say, *"What are you afraid could happen when you are confronted with or exposed to _____ (state the agoraphobic situation)?"*

_____

_____

_____

Assess the Validity of Catastrophe

State the reality of the fear of exposure and assess the percentage of fear that a client feels if exposed to the agoraphobic situation using the VoC score.

Say, *"Is it true you are saying that IF you would be exposed to _____ (state the agoraphobic situation) THEN you would _____ (state the catastrophe the client fears would happen)?"*

_____

_____

_____

Say, *"On a scale from 0% to 100%, where 0% means it is completely false and 100% means it is completely true, how true does this feel?"*

0%   10%   20%   30%   40%   50%   60%   70%   80%   90%   100%

(completely false)   (completely true)

Treatment Goal

Determine an appropriate and feasible treatment goal(s).

> Say, *"Based on all that we have been talking about, let's discuss our goal(s) for treatment. What is/are the goal/s and how will you know when you have reached your goal(s)?"*

_____

_____

_____

_____

_____

Addictive Medications

Assess for any addictive medications.

> Say, *"Are you using benzodiazepines?"*

_____

_____

If yes, and client is using benzodiazepines, say the following:

> Say, *"Would you be willing to stop or to reduce your benzodiazepine consumption before starting EMDR Therapy?"*

_____

_____

_____

Phase 2: Preparation Phase

Explanation of EMDR Therapy

Explain EMDR Therapy to the client.

> Say, *"When a negative and distressing event, like a panic attack, occurs, it seems to get locked in the nervous system with the original picture, sounds, thoughts, and feelings. The eye movements we use in EMDR seem to unlock the nervous system and allow the brain to process the experience. Those eye movements may help to process the unconscious material. It is important to remember that it is your own brain that will be doing the healing and that you are the one in control."* (Shapiro, 2001)

Teach Working Memory Taxation Techniques

Teach working memory-taxing methods for immediate anxiety management between sessions, such as the following:

> Say, *"Please describe out loud the content of the room with as much detail as you can."*

_____

_____

The types of exercises that tax clients' working memory include mental exercises such as counting backward from 1,000 by 7s, remembering a favorite walk in detail, and so on. For example, try the following:

Say, *"Please count backward from 1,000 by 7s."*

_____

_____

Or say, *"In detail, tell me about a favorite walk that you took."*

_____

_____

In the case of a child, distraction can be applied, for instance, by thinking of animals beginning with each letter of the alphabet in turn.

Say, *"Think of an animal that begins with the letter A."*

_____

_____

Say, *"Great, now let's continue finding the names of animals using the rest of the alphabet. What would the name of an animal be for the letter B?"*

_____

_____

Continue finding the names of the animals with the rest of the alphabet.

Say, *"These exercises that we have been practicing may help you when you are dealing with anxiety-eliciting situations. It is really important for you to prepare yourself for possible discomfort between sessions by practicing these exercises. The more you practice, the better you will get at them."*

Phase 3: Assessment Phase

Past Memories. Target Selection

Select a target image (stationary picture) of the memory. (See Phase 1: Client History for the series of targets that have to be processed. It is recommended to start with the first and/or worst panic attack.)

Say, *"You've just told me how this event is present in your mind. Now I'm asking you, <u>at this moment</u>, if you look at it <u>right here and right now</u>, what is the most disturbing picture of this memory? Look at it, as if it's a film, and stop it, right at that second, so it becomes a picture. We are looking mostly for a picture with you in it. It's not about what you found most disturbing <u>at that time</u>, but what is <u>now, at this moment</u>, the most disturbing picture to look at, including pictures that show what could have happened."*

_____

_____

If it helps, you can also ask these questions:

Say, *"So you're looking at yourself from a distance?"*

_____

_____

Say, *"What does this picture look like?"*

_____

_____

Negative Cognition

Obtain the NC and PC.

Say, *"What words go best with the picture that express your negative belief about yourself now?"*

Note: The NC, most likely and most preferably, is "I am powerless." Suggest this NC if the patient does not come up with this by himself.

_____

_____

Positive Cognition

Say, *"When you bring up the picture of the incident, what would you like to believe about yourself now?"*

Note: The PC, most likely and most preferably, is "I can handle this." Suggest this PC if the patient does not come up with this by herself.

_____

_____

Validity of Cognition

Say, *"When you bring up the picture of the incident, how true do those words _____ (repeat the PC) feel to you now on a scale of 1 to 7, where 1 feels completely false and 7 feels completely true?"*

1   2   3   4   5   6   7

(completely false)   (completely true)

Identify emotion, SUD level, and location of the feeling.

Emotions

Say, *"When you bring up the picture* (or incident) *and those words _____* (state the NC), *what emotion do you feel now?"*

_____

_____

Subjective Units of Disturbance

Say, *"On a scale of 0 to 10, where 0 is no disturbance or neutral and 10 is the highest disturbance you can imagine, how disturbing does the picture* (or incident) *feel now?"*

0	1	2	3	4	5	6	7	8	9	10

(no disturbance)   (highest disturbance)

Location of Body Sensation

Say, *"Where do you feel it* (the disturbance) *in your body?"*

_____

_____

Phase 4: Desensitization Phase

Hold your hand in front of the patient's eyes.

Say, *"Look at my fingers* (or fingertips).*"*

Say, *"I want to ask you to be a spectator who is observing the things that are happening to you from the moment you start following my hand. Those things can be thoughts, feelings, images, emotions, physical reactions, or maybe other things. These can relate to the event itself, but also to other things that seem to have no relationship to the event itself. Just notice what comes up, without trying to influence it, and without asking yourself whether it's going well or not. It's important that you don't try to hold onto the image that we will start with or keep it in mind all the time. The image is just the starting point of anything that can and may come up. Every once in a while we will go back to this image to check how disturbing it still is to look at. Keep in mind that is impossible to do anything wrong, as long as you just follow what's there and what comes up."*

_____

Then say, *"Bring up the picture and the words _____ (repeat the NC) and notice where you feel it in your body. Now follow my fingers with your eyes (or other BLS)."*

_____

This protocol uses a different strategy to go back to the target than in the Standard EMDR procedure, in that the authors would like to identify explicitly what type of aspects are still causing the existing disturbance.

Say, *"Please go back to the picture that we started with as it is now stored in your head. How disturbing is it now to look at the picture, on a scale from 0 to 10, where 0 is not disturbing at all, and 10 is as disturbing as it can get?"*

0	1	2	3	4	5	6	7	8	9	10

(no disturbance)   (highest disturbance)

If the SUD is 1 or higher, options are as follows:

Say, *"What aspect of the picture is causing that disturbance/tension* (you may name the number, e.g., *'What is there in the picture that is causing the 4?')."*

_____

_____

Or say, *"What is there in the picture that is causing the* _____ (state the SUD level)? *What do you see?"*

_____

_____

Then say, *"Concentrate on that aspect. OK, have you got it? Go with that."*

Repeat the "Back to target" procedure until SUD = 0.

If SUD = 0, say the following:

Say, *"Are you absolutely sure that there isn't a little bit of disturbance or tension somewhere? If so, try to let it affect you."*

_____

_____

If necessary, continue the desensitization until the original picture feels completely neutral. Then continue with installation.

Phase 5: Installation Phase

Install the PC

Say, *"How does* _____ (repeat the PC) *sound?"*

_____

_____

Say, *"Do the words* _____ (repeat the PC) *still fit, or is there another positive statement that feels better?"*

_____

_____

If the client accepts the original PC, the clinician should ask for a VoC rating to see if it has improved:

Say, *"As you think of the incident, how do the words* (the PC) *feel from 1 being completely false to 7 being completely true?"*

    1   2   3   4   5   6   7

(completely false)   (completely true)

Say, *"Think of the event and hold it together with the words* _____ (repeat the PC). *Go with that."*

_____

_____

Continue this procedure until the VoC = 7.

Check the Response and the Symptoms Regarding the Previous Processing

If, after the previous steps, the client still suffers from symptoms such as panic attacks or agoraphobic fears that persist after all memories of all past events that could be identified as contributing to the current symptoms have been fully processed, the Flashforward Procedure (Logie & de Jongh, 2014; see Chapter 3 in this volume) should be applied. This procedure addresses clients' irrational fears and anticipatory anxiety responses/triggers and is focused on the mental representation that represents the worst possible outcome of a confrontation with the object or situation that provokes the fear.

Check the Other Targets

See Phase 1: Client History and decide whether it is still necessary to reprocess these experiences (i.e., SUD when bringing up the memory > 0).

Say, *"OK, let's check the next target that is in your list* _____ *(state the next target). On a scale of 0 to 10, where 0 is no disturbance or neutral and 10 is the highest disturbance you can imagine, how disturbing does it feel now?"*

0   1   2   3   4   5   6   7   8   9   10

(no disturbance)   (highest disturbance)

Phase 6: Body Scan

Say, *"Close your eyes and keep in mind the experience* (e.g., a panic attack) *that you will have in the future. Then bring your attention to the different parts of your body, starting with your head and working downward. Any place you find any tension, tightness, or unusual sensation, tell me."*

_____

_____

If any sensation is reported, introduce eye movements.

If it is a positive or comfortable sensation, a new set of eye movements is introduced to reinforce the positive sensation.

If a sensation of discomfort is reported, this is reprocessed until the discomfort subsides. Finally, the VoC has to be checked.

Say, *"As you think of the incident, how do the words feel, from 1 being completely false to 7 being completely true?"*

1   2   3   4   5   6   7

(completely false)   (completely true)

Present Triggers. Flashforward

After all old memories that currently "fuel" the fear have been resolved, check whether the patient has an explicit disaster image about the future. What does the patient think will happen to him, in the worst case, if what is feared cannot be avoided?

> Say: *"What we have to figure out now is what you fear will happen* (will go wrong) *when you are confronted with* _____ (object or situation that is avoided). *So basically, what catastrophe do you expect to happen, that prevents you from doing what you want or need to do? What is that 'doom scenario' or 'worst nightmare' that's in your head?"*

_____

_____

Let the client create a still image of this disaster scenario and process this mental representation with the Standard EMDR Protocol (SUD = 0, VoC = 7). Here the NC is the standard: "I am powerless" (in relation to the disaster image), and the PC is the standard, "I can deal with it" (the image).

Future Template

For installing the future template, instruct the patient by asking her to imagine a future situation that—until now—has been avoided (or experienced with a lot of anxiety) and/or has been anticipated with extreme anxiety because of the fear of getting a panic attack. In this situation, the preferred behavior is expressed. When doing so, check for catastrophic aspects in the picture. If so, ask the patient to make a picture in her mind without these "disasters."

Install the Future Template

> Say, *"OK, we have reprocessed all of the targets that we needed to do that were on your list. Now, let's anticipate what will happen when you are faced with* _____ (state the (agoraphobic) fear). *What picture do you have in mind?"*

_____

_____

_____

_____

> Say, *"I would like you to imagine yourself coping effectively with* _____ (state the fear trigger) *in the future. Bring up this picture and say to yourself: 'I can handle it', and feel the sensations. OK, have you got it? Follow my fingers* (or any other forms of BLS)."

_____

_____

> Say, *"Bring up the picture again. On a scale from 1 to 7, where 1 feels completely false and 7 feels completely true, to what extent do you think you can manage to really do it?"*

1   2   3   4   5   6   7

(completely false)   (completely true)

Install with sets of eye movements until a maximum level of VoC has been achieved.

If there is a block, meaning that even after 10 or more installations, the VoC is still below 7, there are more targets that have to be identified and addressed. The therapist should use the Standard EMDR Protocol to address these targets before proceeding with the template (see Worksheets in Appendix A). Also, evaluate whether the client needs any new information, resources, or skills to be able to comfortably visualize the future coping scene. Introduce this needed information or skill.

Say, *"What would you need to feel confident in handling the situation?"*

_____

_____

Or say, *"What is missing from your handling of this situation?"*

_____

_____

Use BLS. If blocks are not resolved, identify unprocessed material and process with the Standard EMDR Protocol.

Video Check (Future Template as Movie)

Say, *"This time, I'd like you to imagine yourself stepping into the scene of a future confrontation with* (the object or the situation for which the future template was meant; e.g., a confrontation with a dog). *Close your eyes and play a movie of this happening, from the beginning until the end. Imagine yourself coping with any challenges that come your way. Notice what you are seeing, thinking, feeling, and experiencing in your body. While playing this movie, let me know if you hit any blocks. If you do, just open your eyes and let me know. If you don't hit any blocks, let me know when you have viewed the whole movie."*

_____

_____

If the client encounters a block and opens her eyes, this is a sign for the therapist to instruct the client as follows:

Say, *"Say to yourself 'I can handle it' and follow my fingers* (introduce a set of eye movements)."

To provide the clinician with an indication regarding the client's self-efficacy, ask her to rate her response on a VoC scale from 1 to 7. This procedural step may give the clinician feedback on the extent to which the goals have been met.

Say, *"As you think of the incident, how do the words* (restate the PC) *feel from 1 being completely false to 7 being completely true?"*

1   2   3   4   5   6   7
(completely false)   (completely true)

If the client is able to play the movie from start to finish with a sense of confidence and satisfaction, then the client is asked to play the movie once more from the beginning to the end, BLS is introduced, and the PC "I can handle it" is installed. In a sense, this movie is installed as a future template.

Say, *"OK, play the movie one more time from beginning to end and say to your-self, 'I can handle it.' Go with that."*

_____

_____

In Vivo Confrontations

Prepare the client for in vivo confrontations.

Say, *"Many clients with a panic disorder with agoraphobia appear to avoid cer-tain activities for so long that they no longer know how to behave and how to feel secure in this situation. To be able to help further alleviate your fears and concerns, it is important that you learn to counter the negative belief that contributes to this sense of threat and anxiety. Therefore, you need to actually test the catastrophic expectations you have that fuel your anxiety in real life. I would like to ask you to gradually confront the* (agoraphobic) *situations that normally would provoke a fear response. It may seem odd, but if you have a positive experience and it appears that the catastrophe you fear does not occur, it helps you to further demonstrate—or to convince yourself—that your fear is unfounded."*

Say, *"I want you to understand that nothing will happen against your will dur-ing the confrontation with the things that normally would evoke fear. The essence of this confrontation is that it is safe. Do you understand? Do you have any questions?"*

_____

_____

In Vivo Exposure

In vivo exposure is done to reduce avoidance and evoke mastery while observing that no real danger exists. It is essential that the therapist help the client pay attention to features of the (agoraphobic) situation that are positive or interesting while being exposed to it.

Say, *"Please describe the most notable features of the situation. Are you noticing any interesting elements about* _____ (state the situation)*?"*

_____

_____

To identify negative thought content, say the following:

Say, *"What are you thinking as you pay attention to* _____ (state the situation)*?"*

_____

_____

To cognitively reconstruct the situation, say the following:

Say, *"How would someone who is not afraid of* _____ (state the situa-tion) *view or evaluate this situation?"*

If needed, give advice to help the client cope with both the situation and his own mental and body sensations.

Note: It is helpful to make variations with regard to the stimulus dimensions such as action, distance, and time.

Say, *"Isn't it interesting to notice that now that you are confronted with this _____ (state the situation) _____ (state the catastrophe the client normally would have feared to happen) does not occur?"*

_____

_____

Say, *"Do you notice that your anxiety is not as physically harmful as you might have expected?"*

_____

_____

Say, *"These emotional reactions will subside and fade over time. Therefore, it is important that you continue exposing yourself to the feared stimuli as long as you feel that you have achieved a certain degree of self-mastery. Please note that you are gradually learning to feel that you are capable of handling a certain level of anticipatory anxiety with confidence."*

_____

_____

The therapist should make sure that confrontations are repeated so that the reduction in distress is fully consolidated before moving on. Check results by assessing the validity of catastrophe.

Say, *"If you would encounter _____ (state the situation) again, on a scale from 0% to 100%, where 0% means it is completely false and 100% means it is completely true, how true does this feel that the situation is still catastrophic?"*

0%   10%   20%   30%   40%   50%   60%   70%   80%   90%   100%

(completely false)   (completely true)

Phase 7: Positive Closure

At the end of every session, consolidate the changes and improvements that have occurred.

Say, *"What is the most positive thing you have learned about yourself in the last hour with regard to _____ (state the incident or theme)?"*

_____

_____

If the cognitions are not already on the identity level, say the following:

Say, *"What does this say about yourself as a person?"*

Say, *"Go with that."*

_____

_____

Install with BLS until there are no further PCs.

Next, check the results by assessing the VoC.

> Say, *"If you would be exposed to* _____ (state the situation), *on a scale from 0% to 100% where 0% means it is completely false and 100% means it is completely true, how true does this* (the PC) *feel?"*

> 0%   10%   20%   30%   40%   50%   60%   70%   80%   90%   100%

> (completely false)   (completely true)

Explain the expectations for the time in between sessions, which may include any contracts, diary keeping, and contact information.

> Say, *"Things may come up or they may not. If they do, great. Write it down and it can be a target for next time. If you get any new memories, dreams, or situations that disturb you, just take a good snapshot. It isn't necessary to give a lot of detail. Just put down enough to remind you so we can target it next time. The same thing goes for any positive dreams or situations. If negative feelings do come up, try not to make them significant. Remember, it's still just the old stuff. Just write it down for next time."*

Planning Self-Managed Homework Assignments

After the therapy has been concluded, the therapist makes it clear that it is important to keep practicing during daily life to ensure that the changes are maintained.

> Say, *"It is very important to keep practicing with exposing yourself to difficult situations during your daily life in order to maintain the changes that you have experienced."*

> *"Each time that you have a chance to see* _____ (state the feared stimulus), *it is an opportunity for you to practice these new skills that you now know how to do. So, the more that you encounter* _____ (state the feared stimulus), *the better you can get at* _____ (state the goal). *Your brain learns to do new behaviors by practicing."*

Phase 8: Reevaluation

> Say, *"Make sure to write down your responses when you are practicing your new skills. Sometimes, even with the skills, you might find that you reexperience your fear* (e.g., a panic attack). *I want to tell you that this can happen sometimes, and it is not unusual. What you can do at that time is to note what has led up to the feeling, what is going on around you, and what you did to help yourself handle the situation. Jot down some notes about what happened as soon as you can so that you won't forget what happened and then bring them to the next session so that we can figure it out."*

Evaluate whatever has not been completed.

> Say, *"As you think back on the target that we were working on last time, on a scale of 0 to 10, where 0 is no disturbance or neutral and 10 is the highest disturbance you can imagine, how disturbing does it feel now?"*

> 0   1   2   3   4   5   6   7   8   9   10

> (no disturbance)   (highest disturbance)

If the disturbance level has increased, these disturbances must be targeted or otherwise addressed.

The therapist should assess the necessity of teaching the client additional self-control and perhaps relaxation techniques or other relevant exercises that could further enhance his ability to confront the former anxiety-provoking situation in real life.

> Say, *"So, what other resources do you think might be helpful in assisting you to deal with this situation?"*

_____

_____

Repeated rehearsal and reinforcement for success should be emphasized. To encourage hope and foster engagement in treatment, it is crucial that therapy sessions and home-work assignments furnish experiences of success that clients can attribute to themselves.

> Say, *"I can see that through all of the work you did between sessions that you are really working hard* (reinforce what the client has done that has been successful)*."*

_____

_____

Summary

The purpose of this chapter is to illustrate how EMDR Therapy can be applied in the treatment of panic disorder with or without agoraphobia. There are indications that this condition often develops after other stressful life events (Faravelli & Pallanti, 1989; Horesh et al., 1997). Literature argues that panic attacks themselves are often experienced as distressing, causing a subjective response of fear or helplessness, which therefore can be viewed as life-threatening experiences (McNally & Lukach, 1992; van Hagenaars et al., 2009). Furthermore, panic memories accompany reexperiences of the traumatic incident and therefore resemble traumatic memories as in PTSD (van Hagenaars et al., 2009). Effectiveness of EMDR Therapy in the treatment of PTSD is well examined. However, research on the effectiveness of EMDR Therapy for other anxiety disorders is scarce. Thus, currently no official guideline is available for the treatment of panic disorder with or without agoraphobia.

Therefore, this chapter showed how EMDR Therapy can be applied in the treatment of panic disorder with or without agoraphobia. In this chapter, the EMDR Therapy scripted protocol for panic disorders with or without agoraphobia is based on the Dutch translation (ten Broeke & de Jongh, 2009) of the EMDR Therapy protocol of Shapiro (2001).

References

Chambless, D. L., Caputo, G. C., Jasin, S. E., Gracely, E. J., & Williams, C. (1985). The Mobility Inventory for Agoraphobia. *Behaviour Research and Therapy, 23*, 35–44.

de Jongh, A., & ten Broeke, E. (2009). EMDR and the anxiety disorders: Exploring the current status. *Journal of EMDR Practice and Research, 3*, 133–140.

de Jongh, A., ten Broeke, E., & Meijer, S. (2010). Two method approach: A case conceptualization model in the context of EMDR. *Journal of EMDR Practice and Research, 4*, 12–21.

American Psychiatric Association. (2013). *Diagnostic and statistical manual of mental disorders* (5th ed.). Arlington, VA: Author.

American Psychiatric Association. (2000). *Diagnostic and statistical manual of mental disorders* (4th ed., text revision). Washington, DC.

Faravelli, C., & Pallanti, S. (1989). Recent life events and panic disorder. *American Journal of Psychiatry, 146,* 622–626.

Feske, U., & Goldstein, A. J. (1997). Eye movement desensitization and reprocessing treatment for panic disorder: A controlled outcome and partial dismantling study. *Journal of Consulting and Clinical Psychology, 65,* 1026–1035.

First, M. B., Spitzer, R. L., Gibbon, M., & Williams, J. B. W. (2002). *Structured clinical interview for DSM-IV-TR axis I disorders, research version, client edition. (SCID-I/P).* New York, NY: Biometrics Research, New York State Psychiatric Institute.

Goldstein, A. J., de Beurs, B. E. Chambless, D. L., & Wilson, K. A. (2000). EMDR for panic disorder with agoraphobia: Comparison with waiting list and credible attention-placebo control conditions. *Journal of Consulting and Clinical Psychology, 68,* 947–956.

Goldstein, A. J., & Feske, U. (1994). Eye movement desensitization and reprocessing for panic disorder: A case series. *Journal of Anxiety Disorders, 8*(4), 351–362.

Horesh, N., Amir, M., Kedem, P., Goldberger, Y., & Kotler, M. (1997). Life events in childhood, adolescence and adulthood and the relationship to panic disorder. *Acta Psychiatrica Scandinavica, 96,* 373–378.

Logie, R., & de Jongh, A. (2014). The "Flashforward procedure": Confronting the catastrophe. *Journal of EMDR Practice and Research, 8*(1), 25–32.

Luber, M. (Ed.). (2009). *Eye movement desensitization and reprocessing (EMDR) scripted protocols: Special populations.* New York, NY: Springer.

Luber, M. (Ed.). (2012). *Eye movement desensitization and reprocessing (EMDR) scripted protocols with summary sheets: Special populations.* New York, NY: Springer.

McNally, R. J., & Lukach, B. M. (1992). Are panic attacks traumatic stressors? *American Journal of Psychiatry, 149,* 824–826.

Shapiro, F. (2001). *Eye movement desensitization and reprocessing: Basic principles, protocols, and procedures.* New York, NY: Guilford Press.

ten Broeke, E., & de Jongh, A. (2009). *Praktijkboek EMDR: casusconceptualisatie en specifieke patiëntejagroepen.* Amsterdam, The Netherlands: Pearson.

van Hagenaars, M. A., van Minnen, A., & Hoogduin, K. A. (2009). Reliving and disorganization in posttraumatic stress disorder and panic disorder memories. *The Journal of Nervous Mental Disease, 197,* 627–630.

SUMMARY SHEET:
EMDR Therapy Protocol for Panic Disorders
With or Without Agoraphobia

Ferdinand Horst and Ad de Jongh
SUMMARY SHEET BY MARILYN LUBER

Name: _____ Diagnosis: _____

☑ Check when task is completed, response has changed, or to indicate symptoms or diagnosis.

Note: This material is meant as a checklist for your response. Please keep in mind that it is only a reminder of different tasks that may or may not apply to your client.

Introduction

EMDR Therapy and Panic Disorder With or Without Agoraphobia

Why eye movement desensitization and reprocessing (EMDR) could be useful in the treatment of panic disorders:

1. Can be viewed as life-threatening experience
2. Resemble traumatic memories in posttraumatic stress disorder (PTSD) including recurrent and distressing recollections of the event, intrusive images, and flashbacks
3. Develops after stressful life event

DSM-5 Criteria for Panic Disorder With or Without Agoraphobia

Panic Attacks

Panic attacks are recurrent and unexpected and include a surge that may range from intense discomfort to extreme fear cresting within minutes. They are accompanied by at least four or more of the following physiological symptoms:

- paresthesias (tingling sensations or numbness);
- sensations of heat or chills;
- experiences of dizziness, lightheaded, unsteadiness, or weakness;
- queasiness or abdominal upset;
- chest pain or distress; feeling of choking;
- unable to catch breath or feeling smothered; trembling, or quaking;
- perspiring;

- fast or irregular heartbeat;
- intense cognitive distortions such as feelings of unreality (derealization) or being disconnected from oneself (depersonalization);
- fear of going crazy or losing control;
- and/or fear of dying.

In order to meet the criteria, a person must be either continuously worrying about having another panic attack or their consequences (such as losing control, having a nervous breakdown, etc.) or significantly changing behavior to avoid having another panic attack over the period of 1 month after the attack. If the symptoms can be ascribed to the physiological effects of a substance (such as a medication or drug abuse) or another medical condition (such as cardiac disorders or hyperthyroidism) or another mental disorder (such as social anxiety disorder or specific phobia), panic disorder is not diagnosed.

Agoraphobia

Agoraphobia is characterized by fear about situations related to being in enclosed or open spaces, being in line or in a crowd, being outside of the home alone or using public transport. These situations are difficult because in the event of panic symptomatology, the fear is that escape might be difficult and help might not be available is predominant leading to the avoidance of these situations or the need for the presence of another person. The fear or anxiety that is felt is out of proportion to the actual situation itself, this includes when another medical condition is occurring as well. This type of fear, anxiety, or avoidance lasts 6 months or more, impairs functioning in social, occupational, or other areas of functioning and is not explained by other mental disorders.

Measurement

- ☐ Standardized Clinical Interview
- ☐ Mobility Inventory
- ☐ Agoraphobic Cognitions Questionnaire

Panic Disorder With or Without Agoraphobia Protocol Script Notes

Identifying Useful EMDR Therapy Targets: Any Experience That "Fuels" the Current Pathology

Panic-Attack Memories (Unexpected, Experiences as Life Threatening, Subjective Response of Fear or Helplessness)

Target: First, worst, and most recent panic attack memory

Traumatic Memories

- ☐ Process underlying traumatic memories/life events.
- ☐ Flashforward: If still not sufficient because client is avoiding activities even without panic attacks and does not know how to feel secure, check the most feared catastrophic future event/flashforward.
- ☐ Check to see if client can deal with agoraphobic situations.
- ☐ If not, use in vivo exposure.

Agoraphobic Memories

Usually decrease after panic attack memories have been completely processed.

Panic Disorder With or Without Agoraphobia Protocol Script

Phase 1: Client History

Diagnosis: _____

_____

Identify the Targets

FIRST PANIC ATTACK/STIMULUS SITUATION

Target/Memory/Image: _____

_____

WORST PANIC ATTACK/MOST REPRESENTATIVE EXPERIENCE

Target/Memory/Image: _____

_____

MOST RECENT PANIC ATTACK

Target/Memory/Image: _____

_____

IDENTIFY OTHER EXPERIENCES RELEVANT TO THE ONSET OF THE PANIC DISORDER

Relevant past experiences related to the onset of the panic disorder _____

_____

_____

Panic attack started with traumatic event _____

_____

_____

Panic attacks remind client of another specific event _____

_____

_____

Exposed to any traumatic event prior to the start of the first panic attack _____

_____

_____

Introduce the Timeline

"Let's draw a timeline of your panic history and traumatic experiences until now. The horizontal line represents the time, and the vertical line the severity of the symptoms."

Expected Consequence/Catastrophe

Identify the expected consequence/catastrophe if you get a panic attack: _____

_____

_____

Identify the expected consequence/catastrophe if confronted with or exposed to the agoraphobic situation:

_____

_____

Assess the VoC

"Is it true you are saying that IF you would be exposed to _____ (state the agoraphobic situation) THEN you would _____ (state the catastrophe the client fears would happen)? _____"

"How true does it feel (0–100%)?"

Treatment Goal

Goal(s): _____

_____

_____

How you know when goal is reached: _____

_____

_____

Addictive Medications

Benzodiazepines	☐ Yes	☐ No
Stop benzodiazepines before EMDR	☐ Yes	☐ No

Phase 2: Preparation

Explanation of EMDR Therapy

"When a negative and distressing event, like a panic attack, occurs, it seems to get locked in the nervous system with the original picture, sounds, thoughts, and feelings. The eye movements we use in EMDR seem to unlock the nervous system and allow the brain to process the experience. These eye movements may help to process the unconscious material. It is important to remember that it is your own brain that will be doing the healing and that you are the one in control."

Teach Working Memory Taxation Techniques for Anxiety Management

☐ Orientation—(describe room in detail)
☐ Counting—(count backward from 1,000 by 7s)
☐ Details of walk
☐ Name animals (A to Z)

Phase 3: Assessment

Past Memories

Target Selection

"You've just told me how this event is present in your mind. Now I'm asking you, _at this moment_, if you look at it _right here and right now_, what is the most disturbing picture of this memory?

Look at it, as if it's a film, and stop it, right at that second, so it becomes a picture. We are looking mostly for a picture with you in it. It's not about what you found most disturbing <u>at that time</u>, but what is <u>now, at this moment</u>, the most disturbing picture to look at, including pictures that show what could have happened."

Note: NC usually "I am powerless"; PC usually "I can handle this."

FIRST PANIC ATTACK/STIMULUS SITUATION

Target/Memory/Image: _____

_____

NC: _____

PC: _____

VoC: _____ /7

Emotions: _____

SUD: _____ /10

Sensation: _____

WORST PANIC ATTACK/MOST REPRESENTATIVE EXPERIENCE

Target/Memory/Image: _____

_____

NC: _____

PC: _____

VoC: _____ /7

Emotions: _____

SUD: _____ /10

Sensation: _____

MOST RECENT PANIC ATTACK

Target/Memory/Image: _____

_____

NC: _____

PC: _____

VoC: _____ /7

Emotions: _____

SUD: _____ /10

Sensation: _____

IDENTIFY OTHER EXPERIENCES RELEVANT TO THE ONSET OF THE PANIC DISORDER

Target/Memory/Image: _____

_____

NC: _____

PC: _____

VoC: _____ /7

Emotions: _____

SUD: _____ /10

Sensation: _____

Phase 4: Desensitization

"Look at my fingers/fingertips. I want to ask you to be a spectator who is observing the things that are happening to you from the moment you start following my hand. Those things can be thoughts, feelings, images, emotions, physical reactions, or maybe other things. These can relate to the event itself, but also to other things that seem to have no relationship to the event itself. Just notice what comes up, without trying to influence it, and without asking yourself whether it's going well or not. It's important that you don't try to hold onto the image that we will start with or keep it in mind all the time. The image is just the starting point of anything that can and may come up. Every once in a while we will go back to this image to check how disturbing it still is to look at. Keep in mind that is impossible to do anything wrong, as long as you just follow what's there and what comes up. Bring up the picture and the words _____ (repeat the NC) and notice where you feel it in your body. Now follow my fingers with your eyes (or other BLS).*"*

Dutch strategy for going back to target:

> *"Please go back to the picture that we started with as it is now stored in your head. How disturbing is it now to look at the picture, on a scale from 0 to 10, where 0 is not disturbing at all, and 10 is as disturbing as it can get?"*

SUD: _____ /10
Introduce according to EMDR Standard Protocol.
If SUD = 1 or more, continue processing.
If SUD continues to be 0 after 2 sets of BLS, go to the installation phase.

Phase 5: Installation

PC: ☐ Completed

New PC (if new one is better): _____

VoC: _____ /7

Incident + PC + BLS

Check the other targets to see if it is still necessary to reprocess these experiences.

Other Targets	Age	SUD	SUD Post
1. _____	_____	__ /10	____ /10
2. _____	_____	__ /10	____ /10
3. _____	_____	__ /10	____ /10
4. _____	_____	__ /10	____ /10
5. _____	_____	__ /10	____ /10

Check the Response and the Symptoms Regarding the Previous Processing

If symptoms persist after processing these identified targets, use the Flashforward Procedure that addresses clients' irrational fears and anticipatory anxiety responses/triggers and is focused on the mental representation that represents the worst possible outcome of a confrontation with the object or situation that provokes the fear. See below.

Check the Other Targets

> "OK, let's check the next target that is in your list _____ (state the next target). On a scale of 0 to 10, where 0 is no disturbance or neutral and 10 is the highest disturbance you can imagine, how disturbing does it feel now?" _____ /10

Phase 6: Body Scan

> "Close your eyes and keep in mind the experience (e.g., a panic attack) that you will have in the future. Then bring your attention to the different parts of your body, starting with your head and working downward. Any place you find any tension, tightness, or unusual sensation, tell me."

If positive, add BLS.
If negative/discomfort, reprocess until discomfort subsides.

Check VoC: _____ /10

Present Triggers

Flashforward

"What we have to figure out now is what you fear will happen (will go wrong) when you are confronted with _____ (object or situation that is avoided). So basically, what catastrophe do you expect to happen that prevents you from doing what you want or need to do? What is that 'doom scenario' or 'worst nightmare' that's in your head?"

Use this as a target for processing with the Standard EMDR Protocol (SUD = 0; VoC = 7).

Target/Memory/Image: _____

_____

NC: I am powerless (in relation to the disaster image)

PC: I can handle it (the image)

VoC: _____/7

Emotions: _____

SUD: _____ /10

Sensation: _____

Future Template

Installation of the Future Template (Image)

Image of coping effectively with/or in the fear trigger in the future: _____

_____

PC: (I can handle it) _____

Sensations: _____

+ BLS

VoC (able to handle the situation): _____ /7

Install until VoC = 7.

If VoC continues to be > 7, there are more targets to be identified and addressed using the Standard EMDR Protocol.

Blocks/Anxieties/Fears in future scene: _____

1. _____

2. _____

3. _____

Do BLS. If they do not resolve, ask for other qualities needed to handle the situation or what is missing.

1. _____

2. _____

3. _____

Use BLS. If blocks are not resolved, identify unprocessed material and process with Standard EMDR Protocol.

1. _____

2. _____

3. _____

Target/Memory/Image: _____

_____

NC: _____

PC: _____

VoC: _____/7

Emotions: _____

SUD: _____ /10

Sensation: _____

Video Check (Future Template as Movie)

> Say, *"This time, I'd like you to imagine yourself stepping into the future. Close your eyes and play a movie from the beginning until the end. Imagine yourself coping with any challenges that come your way. Notice what you are seeing, thinking, feeling, and experiencing in your body. While playing this movie, let me know if you hit any blocks. If you do, just open your eyes and let me know. If you don't hit any blocks, let me know when you have viewed the whole movie."*

If block(s), say, "I can handle it," and BLS. Repeat until client can go through the whole movie entirely without distress.

VoC: _____ /7

If client can play movie from beginning to end with confidence and satisfaction, play the movie one more time from beginning to end + BLS: ☐ Yes   ☐ No

In Vivo Confrontations

"Many clients with a panic disorder with agoraphobia appear to avoid certain activities for so long that they no longer know how to behave and how to feel secure in this situation.

To be able to help further alleviate your fears and concerns, it is important that you learn to counter the negative belief that contributes to this sense of threat and anxiety. Therefore, you need to actually test the catastrophic expectations you have that fuel your anxiety in real life. I would like to ask you to gradually confront the (agoraphobic) situations that normally would provoke a fear response. It may seem odd, but if you have a positive experience and it appears that the catastrophe you fear does not occur, it helps you to further demonstrate—or to convince yourself—that your fear is unfounded."

"I want you to understand that nothing will happen against your will during the confrontation with the things that normally would evoke fear. The essence of this confrontation is that it is safe. Do you understand? Do you have any questions?"

Client agrees to in vivo exposure: ☐ Yes   ☐ No

In Vivo Exposure

This is done to reduce avoidance and evoke mastery while observing that no real danger exists.

Pay attention to features of the phobic object or situation that are positive or interesting while being exposed to it:

Description of most notable features of the situation: _____

_____

Negative-thoughts thinking during in vivo exposure: _____

_____

Thoughts someone who is not afraid would think in the situation: _____

_____

It is helpful to make variations with regard to the stimulus dimensions "action," "distance," and "time."

"Isn't it interesting to notice that now that you are confronted with this _____ (state the object or situation) _____ (state the catastrophe the client normally would have feared to happen) does not occur?
                                                                          ☐ Yes   ☐ No

"Do you notice that your anxiety is not as physically harmful as you might have expected?"
                                                                          ☐ Yes   ☐ No

Importance of practice: *"These emotional reactions will subside and fade over time. Therefore, it is important that you continue exposing yourself to the feared stimuli as long as you feel that you have achieved a certain degree of self-mastery. Please note that you are gradually learning to feel that you are capable of handling a certain level of anticipatory anxiety with confidence."*

Check with VoC (0–100%): _____

Phase 7: Positive Closure

Most positive thing learned: _____

_____

PC/What does this say about yourself as a person (identity domain)? _____

_____

+ BLS

Check with VoC (0–100%): _____

Explain expectations between sessions:

> *"Things may come up or they may not. If they do, great. Write it down and it can be a target for next time. If you get any new memories, dreams, or situations that disturb you, just take a good snapshot. It isn't necessary to give a lot of detail. Just put down enough to remind you so we can target it next time. The same thing goes for any positive dreams or situations. If negative feelings do come up, try not to make them significant. Remember, it's still just the old stuff. Just write it down for next time."*

Planning Self-Managed Homework Assignments

> *"It is very important to keep practicing with exposing yourself to difficult situations during your daily life in order to maintain the changes that you have experienced."*

> *"Each time that you have a chance to see* _____ *(state the feared stimulus), it is an opportunity for you to practice these new skills that you now know how to do. So, the more you encounter* _____ *(state the feared stimulus), the better you can get at* _____ *(state the goal). Your brain learns to do new behaviors by practicing.*

Phase 8: Reevaluation

"Make sure to write down your responses when you are practicing your new skills. Sometimes, even with the skills, you might find that you reexperience your fear (e.g., a panic attack). I want to tell you that this can happen sometimes, and it is not unusual. What you can do at that time is to note what has led up to the feeling, what is going on around you, and what you did to help yourself handle the situation. Jot down some notes about what happened as soon as you can so that you won't forget what happened and then bring them to the next session so that we can figure it out."

SUDs of Incident: _____ /10

New material: _____

_____

If disturbance level increased, target it.

New resources needed: ☐ Yes   ☐ No

_____

_____

Emphasize the need for rehearsal and reinforcement   ☐ Yes   ☐ No

Give praise for accomplishments   ☐ Yes   ☐ No

Reprocessed necessary targets   ☐ Completed

Reference

American Psychiatric Association. (2000). *Diagnostic and statistical manual of mental disorders* (4th ed., text revision). Washington, DC.

The Flashforward Procedure

Robin Logie and Ad de Jongh

Introduction

The standard Three-Pronged Protocol for Eye Movement Desensitization and Reprocessing (EMDR) Therapy guides the overall treatment of the client (Shapiro, 2001). It consists of a "three-pronged" (past, present, and future) approach in which initially past events, then present issues, and finally anticipated future situations are targeted in therapy. The generic divisions of the targets are defined as follows:

- *Past:* The past experiences that have set the groundwork for the pathology are fully processed.
- *Present:* Some triggers can still remain active, even though the original traumas have apparently been processed. These triggers may be fed by some residual information from earlier events that have not been completely processed, or may be due to second-order conditioning.
- *Future*: In the third prong of EMDR Therapy, called the "Future Template," treatment helps the client to visualize successfully managing an anticipated future event.

The Flashforward Procedure

The Flashforward Procedure has appeared to be an effective application of EMDR Therapy to deal with the second prong ("present") of the three-pronged approach. It is a procedure to address clients' irrational fears and anticipatory anxiety responses that persist after the core memories of past events have been fully processed. Even though the client's focus is on the future, the fears are experienced in the present, triggered by negative, irrational thoughts with a catastrophic content. To this end, these are considered to be current fears, suitable for processing in the second prong.

It has been shown that employing eye movements, and related working memory tasks, typically results in an amelioration of the emotionality and vividness of memories, not only for resolving unprocessed memories underlying posttraumatic stress disorder (PTSD), but also for those memories playing a crucial role in the development and maintenance of other mental conditions (de Jongh, Ernst, Marques, & Hornsveld, 2013). It is also important to note that EMDR Therapy has not only been found to be efficacious in the processing of mental representations of distressing events that happened in the *past*, but also of potential mental representations in the *future*. Two subsequent analogue studies have shown that mental representations about potential future catastrophes can be processed in the same way as past events (Engelhard et al., 2011; Engelhard, van Uijen, &

van den Hout, 2010). This has opened new opportunities for the treatment of a wide range of mental conditions in which mental imagery regarding the future plays a pivotal role (see later). Further details regarding the theoretical and research background of the Flashforward Procedure are described in a paper by these authors (Logie & de Jongh, 2014).

Uses for the Flashforward Procedure

In most cases, the Flashforward Procedure should only be employed once all past traumatic events, relating to the current symptoms in question, have been fully resolved utilizing the Standard EMDR Protocol in the usual way. When it appears that the client still experiences anticipatory fear of confrontations with certain objects or situations, this should alert the therapist, first, to the possibility of unexplored past traumatic events that remain to be processed. Once all memories of relevant past events have been fully resolved, or it is not possible to identify any past events that appear to be at the root of or meaningfully relevant to the current symptoms, it would then be appropriate to use the Flashforward Procedure.

There are other times when the use of the Flashforward Procedure could be indicated:

1. *Disruptive feared event*: Use of the Flashforward Procedure might be indicated when a future feared event is so disruptive to normal life that the client is either not sufficiently motivated to consider past events or is incapable of doing so.
2. *Client skepticism*: EMDR Therapy aimed at targeting clients' expected doom scenario or *flashforward* might be indicated if it is necessary to convince skeptical clients of the benefits of EMDR Therapy by first demonstrating it with some current issue with which they are preoccupied, and they are initially unwilling to accept that looking at past events may be the key to unlocking their problems.
3. *Unable to identify past trauma*: It may not be possible, with certain clients, to identify any past trauma or negative experience that appears to be at the root of their current symptoms.
4. *Flashforward as only EMDR Therapy target*: In some cases (e.g., simple conditioned fears) targeting solely the irrational fear(s) and/or anticipatory anxiety response(s) by using the Flashforward Procedure is sufficiently potent to effectively alleviate the client's symptoms.

Psychological Conditions Appropriate for Use of the Flashforward Procedure

Besides the aforementioned experimental studies, to date there are no clinical data from well-controlled studies about the effectiveness of focusing on individuals' flashforwards. Yet, the fear of future catastrophe is a key component in several psychological conditions. The following list gives the major examples, though it is certainly not exhaustive:

- *Obsessive-compulsive disorder (OCD)*: This disorder relates to preoccupation with, and avoidance of, future events that the client deems to be catastrophic (e.g., being contaminated, house in flames). In one of their case studies, Böhm and Voderholzer (2010) describe using EMDR to target and successfully process a future scenario in which a female client with OCD believed that she will be punished in hell.
- *Specific phobias*: The fear of future events is also clearly a major component in specific phobias (de Jongh, 2009; de Jongh & ten Broeke, 2007, 2009; de Jongh, ten Broeke, & Renssen, 1999; de Jongh, van den Oord, & ten Broeke, 2002). The use of EMDR Therapy in the treatment of phobias is supported by controlled research (e.g., Doering, Ohlmeier, de Jongh, Hofmann, & Bisping, 2013; Triscari, Faraci, D'Angelo, Urso, & Catalisano, 2011), and evidence suggests that the inclusion of the processing of feared future events could be helpful (Engelhard et al., 2010). Examples of phobias, and their possible target images, are:
  - Dog phobia (e.g., being attacked by a dog)
  - Dental and medical phobias (e.g., extreme pain, being powerless, "bleeding to death")
  - Social phobia (e.g., being rejected or other embarrassing situation)

- *Other psychological disorders*: A fear of future catastrophe will also often be a feature of other psychological disorders such as the following:
  - Body dysmorphic disorder (e.g., a negative remark about appearance)
  - Hypochondriasis (e.g., the end phase of a terminal illness)
  - Psychosis and schizophrenia (e.g., the delusion and fear of being killed)
  - PTSD (fear of situations similar to the trauma)
  - Anorexia nervosa (fear of consequences of eating)

Note: The conditions listed here are examples of those for which the Flashforward Procedure may be utilized, always with the proviso, however, that past traumatic events or other significant experiences should be processed first.

Flashforward Script Notes

How to Use the Flashforward Procedure

In its application, the Flashforward Procedure is identical to the Standard EMDR Protocol, except that the target relates to a feared catastrophic future event (the client's flashforward) rather than to a past one. For example, a client who still fears driving after the trauma of a road traffic accident (RTA), despite having fully processed the traumatic memory, would be asked whether or not he still has a fear of driving, and if so, what future catastrophe he fears the most. For example, he might anticipate his own death in an RTA. This image would be used as a target.

For the most efficacious use of the Flashforward Procedure, it is helpful for the therapist to ask the client to say what she believes will happen to her if she is not able to avoid the fearful situation anymore. To this end, it is important to create a framework that allows and enables the client to think about the impending doom of the worst-case scenario, and to look even beyond this potential catastrophe. These are the steps to create this framework:

Step 1: Identify the catastrophic event

Step 2: Follow the event to its ultimate conclusion

It is important that the therapist follow the worst scenario to its ultimate conclusion, using questions such as the following:

Say, *"What would be the worst thing about that?"*

Repeat until the client gives no new response or says she cannot think of anything worse. Do not assume, for example, that the client's own death is the ultimate catastrophe. *"What would be the worst thing about you dying?"* may bring up more fundamental fears or issues, such as "My family could not cope without me" or "I would be alone."

Step 3: Make a detailed picture of flashforward

The essential elements of a flashforward suitable for treatment with EMDR Therapy are:

- A detailed and still picture
- Contains catastrophic elements of what might happen in the future
- Context specific and conceptually related to client's symptoms
- Intrusive and disturbing

Step 4: Negative cognition (NC) and positive cognition (PC)

These are elicited in the usual way but with reference to the identified flashforward. However, the NC when using the Flashforward Procedure is in essence the (meta)cognition that describes the relationship with the target image as being intrusive and (too) overwhelming to cope with it by the client. Accordingly, it has often appeared most appropriate to suggest the NC "I am powerless" (against the image) and PC "I am in control/I can handle it (the intrusive image)," as standard cognitions.

> *Step 5: Validity of cognition (VOC), emotion, subjective units of disturbance (SUD), and location of body sensation*

These are carried out according to the Standard EMDR Protocol.

> *Step 6: Phases 4 to 8 (desensitization, installation, body scan, closure, and reevaluation)*

These are carried out according to the Standard EMDR Protocol

Cognitive interweaves are utilized in the usual way, and when they become necessary.

The Flashforward Script

Phase 1: Client History

Client history is taken according to the Standard EMDR Protocol.

Phase 2: Preparation

Preparation is done according to the Standard EMDR Protocol, together with an explanation of the Flashforward Procedure and how it will benefit the client.

> Say, *"We have now dealt with all the events from your past that seem to have been feeding into your current problems and these are no longer distressing you. But, it seems that you are still left with some fear and dread of what might happen in the future, which has been left behind, even after all the past events have been dealt with. So, we are now going to focus on this present trigger of the future, and what it is that you are dreading, using the same procedure as we used for the past events."*

Phase 3: Determine the Flashforward

Step 1: Identify the catastrophic event

> Say, *"We need to figure out what kind of image is in your head that makes you scared about a future confrontation with what you fear. What is the worst thing you could imagine happening? Basically we should look for your ultimate doom scenario."*

_____

_____

If necessary, the therapist asks additional questions, for example:

> Say, *"What do you imagine might go wrong if you* _____ (state the concern, such as 'Come across a dog,' 'Have a dental treatment,' 'Climb a tower,' etc.)?"

> Say, *"If you had a terrible nightmare about* _____ (state the concern, such as 'Driving your car to work on a busy road'), *what would the most disturbing picture look like?"*

_____

_____

Step 2: Follow the event to its ultimate conclusion

Say, *"Why would this be so terrible for you?"*

_____

_____

Say, *"What would be the worst thing about that?"*

_____

_____

Repeat as necessary until the client cannot identify anything worse.

Step 3: Make a detailed picture of the flashforward

Image

The therapist might then ask the client to make a still picture of this scene. Ask that the picture be as detailed as possible.

Say, *"Exactly what would* _____ (the flashforward identified earlier) *look like?"*

_____

_____

Or say, *"What can you see in that?"*

_____

_____

If the client still has more than one picture, she is asked to contrast these images, for example, by saying the following:

Say, *"If you were forced to choose, what would be most disturbing for you now: the picture of your dying, or the picture that represents the situation of being unable to care for your family?"*

_____

_____

Negative Cognition

Say, *"What words go best with that picture* _____ (state the flashforward) *that express your negative belief about yourself now?"* or *"When you think of* _____ (state the flashforward), *what negative thought do you have about yourself now?"*

Note: The therapist can suggest, "I am powerless."

_____

_____

Positive Cognition

Say, *"When you bring up the* _____ (state the flashforward), *what would you like to believe about yourself now?"* Or suggest, *"I am in control/I can deal with it/I can handle it."*

_____

_____

Validity of Cognition

Say, *"When you bring up the* _____ (state the flashforward), *how true do those words* _____ (repeat the PC) *feel to you now on a scale of 1 to 7, where 1 feels completely false and 7 feels completely true?"*

1	2	3	4	5	6	7

(completely false)   (completely true)

Emotions

Say, *"When you bring up* _____ (state the flashforward) *and those words* _____ (state the NC), *what emotion do you feel now?"*

_____

_____

Subjective Units of Disturbance

Say, *"On a scale of 0 to 10, where 0 is no disturbance or neutral and 10 is the highest disturbance you can imagine, how disturbing does* _____ (state the flashforward) *feel now?"*

0	1	2	3	4	5	6	7	8	9	10

(no disturbance)   (highest disturbance)

Location of Body Sensation

Say, *"Where do you feel it* (the disturbance) *in your body?"*

_____

_____

Phase 4: Desensitization

Apply the Standard EMDR Protocol in the usual way. During the reprocessing, the therapist should ask the client to do the following:

Say, *"Go with that."*

Or say, *"Notice that"* for subsequent sets of BLS.

To begin, say the following:

Say, *"Now, remember, it is your own brain that is doing the healing and you are the one in control. I will ask you to mentally focus on the target and to follow my fingers (or any other bilateral stimulation, BLS, you are using). Just let whatever happens, happen, and we will talk at the end of the set. Just tell me what comes up, and don't discard anything as unimportant. Any new information that comes to mind is connected in some way. If you want to stop, just raise your hand."*

Then say, *"Bring up the picture and the words* _____ (repeat the NC) *and notice where you feel it in your body. Now follow my fingers with your eyes (or other BLS)."*

Even though the target is a future catastrophe, the client may spontaneously bring up the original trauma even though it had previously, apparently, been fully processed. If this occurs, the therapist should continue to allow the client to go with the past event because the flashforward may have elicited other channels connected to the trauma that had not previously been processed.

As appropriate, the therapist should use cognitive interweaves if these become necessary.

Note: EMDR focused on flashforwards usually goes smoothly and therapists rarely need to use cognitive interweaves.

Phase 5: Installation

Install the PC

Say, *"As you think of the* _____ (state the flashforward), *how true do the words* _____ (state the PC) *feel, from 1 being completely false to 7 being completely true?"*

1	2	3	4	5	6	7

(completely false)   (completely true)

Say, *"Think of the* _____ (state the flashforward) *and hold it together with the words* _____ (repeat the PC). *Go with that."*

Continue this procedure until the VoC is 7.

Phase 6: Body Scan

Say, *"Please close your eyes. As you think of* _____ (state the flashforward), *say to yourself 'I can deal with it.' Then bring your attention to the different parts of your body, starting with your head and working downward. Any place you find any tension, tightness, or unusual sensation, tell me."*

If any sensation is reported, the therapist introduces BLS.

If it is a positive or comfortable sensation, BLS is used to strengthen the positive feelings.

If a sensation of discomfort is reported, this is reprocessed until the discomfort subsides. Finally, the VoC has to be checked.

Say, *"As you think of the incident, how do the words* (restate the PC), *feel from 1 being completely false to 7 being completely true?"*

1   2   3   4   5   6   7

(completely false)   (completely true)

Video Check

Say, *"This time, I'd like you to imagine yourself stepping into the scene of a future confrontation with the object or a situation for which the future template was meant* (e.g., making a trip on an airplane, meeting an unknown person, a dog, a dentist). *Close your eyes and play a movie of this happening, from the beginning until the end. Imagine yourself coping with any challenges that come your way. Notice what you are seeing, thinking, feeling, and experiencing in your body. While playing this movie, let me know if you hit any blocks. If you do, just open your eyes and let me know. If you don't hit any blocks, let me know when you have viewed the whole movie."*

_____

_____

If the client encounters a block and opens her eyes, this is a sign for the therapist to instruct the client as follows:

Say, *"Say to yourself 'I can handle it' and follow my fingers* (or other form of BLS)."

If the client is able to play the movie from start to finish with a sense of confidence and satisfaction, the client is asked to play the movie once more from the beginning to the end, eye movements are introduced, and the PC "I can handle it" is installed. In a sense, this movie is installed as a future template.

Say, *"OK, play the movie one more time from beginning to end and say to yourself 'I can handle it.' Go with that."*

Do this until the movie can be played without any blocks or significant disturbances.

_____

Phase 7: Closure

Say, *"Things may come up or they may not. If they do, great. Write it down and it can be a target for next time. You can use a log to write down triggers, images, thoughts, cognitions, emotions, and sensations; you can rate them on our 0 to 10 scale where 0 is no disturbance or neutral and 10 is the worst disturbance. Please write down the positive experiences, too."*

"If you get any new fantasies, memories, dreams, or situations that disturb you, just take a good snapshot. It isn't necessary to give a lot of detail. Just put down enough to remind you so we can target it next time. The same thing goes for any positive dreams or situations. If negative feelings do come up, try not to make them significant. Remember, it's still just the old stuff. Just write it down for next time. Then use the tape or the Safe Place exercise to let go of as much of the disturbance as possible. Even if nothing comes up, make sure to use the tape every day and give me a call if you need to."

Phase 8: Reevaluation

After application of the Flashforward Procedure, there may still be a need for additional targeting and other strategies to ensure that the treatment goals are met. An evaluation of what still remains to be done should be made at the beginning of the next session. The client is asked about his current symptoms and about his progress. It is advisable to always evaluate in terms of a client's SUD level on the already-processed material.

> Say, *"As you think back on the target that we were working on last time* (mention the flashforward the client had), *on a scale of 0 to 10, where 0 is no disturbance or neutral and 10 is the highest disturbance you can imagine, how disturbing does it feel now?"*
>
> 0   1   2   3   4   5   6   7   8   9   10
>
> (no disturbance)   (highest disturbance)

If the disturbance level has increased above 0, these reverberations have to be targeted or otherwise addressed. The therapist should assess the necessity of teaching the client additional self-control techniques or other relevant exercises that could further enhance his ability to confront the former anxiety-provoking situation in real life.

> Say, *"So, what other resources do you think might be helpful in assisting you to deal with this situation?"*

_____

_____

Summary

The Flashforward Procedure can be extremely effective in rapidly assisting the progress of EMDR Therapy in situations where the processing of past events is not sufficient. Some therapists may be reluctant to use this procedure, as it involves tapping into clients' darkest fears. However, therapists should remind themselves that, for clients, these fears are always present and it is often therapists who are more reluctant to confront such fears than clients are. When clients have been carefully prepared and therapists know their clients well, the Flashforward Procedure can become another valuable tool in the EMDR therapist's toolkit.

References

Böhm, K., & Voderholzer, U. (2010). Use of EMDR in the treatment of obsessive-compulsive disorders: A case series. *Verhaltenstherapie, 20,* 175–181.

de Jongh, A. (2009). EMDR and specific fears: The phobia protocol single event trauma. In M. Luber (Ed.), *Eye movement desensitization and reprocessing: EMDR scripted protocols. Basics and special populations.* (pp. 575–610). New York, NY: Springer.

de Jongh, A., Ernst, R., Marques, L., & Hornsveld, H. (2013). The impact of eye movements and tones on disturbing memories of patients with PTSD and other mental disorders. *Journal of Behavior Therapy and Experimental Psychiatry, 44,* 447–483.

de Jongh, A., & ten Broeke, E. (2007). Treatment of specific phobias with EMDR: Conceptualization and strategies for the selection of appropriate memories. *Journal of EMDR Practice and Research, 1,* 46–57.

de Jongh, A., & ten Broeke, E. (2009). EMDR and the anxiety disorders: Exploring the current status. *Journal of EMDR Practice and Research, 3,* 133–140.

de Jongh, A., ten Broeke, E., & Renssen, M. (1999). Treatment of specific phobias with eye movement desensitization and reprocessing (EMDR): Protocol, empirical status, and conceptual issues. *Journal of Anxiety Disorders, 13,* 69–85.

de Jongh, A., van den Oord, H., & ten Broeke, E. (2002). Efficacy of eye movement desensitization and reprocessing in the treatment of specific phobias: Four single-case studies on dental phobia. *Journal of Clinical Psychology, 58,* 1489–1503.

Doering, S., Ohlmeier, M.-C., de Jongh, A., Hofmann, A., & Bisping, V. (2013). Efficacy of a trauma-focused treatment approach for dental phobia: A randomized clinical trial. *European Journal of Oral Sciences, 121*, 584–593.

Engelhard, I., van den Hout, M., Dek, E., Giele, C., van der Wielen, J., Reijnen, M., & van Roij, B. (2011). Reducing vividness and emotional intensity of recurrent "flashforwards" by taxing working memory: An analogue study. *Journal of Anxiety Disorders, 25*, 599–603.

Engelhard, I., van Uijen, S., & van den Hout, M. (2010). The impact of taxing working memory on negative and positive memories. *European Journal of Psychotraumatology, 1*, 5623. doi:10.3402/ejpt.v1i0.5623

Logie, R., & de Jongh, A. (2014). The flashforward procedure: Confronting the catastrophe. *Journal of EMDR Practice and Research, 8*, 25–32.

Shapiro, F. (2001). *Eye movement desensitization and reprocessing: Basic principles, protocols and procedures* (2nd ed.). New York, NY: Guilford Press.

Triscari, M., Faraci, P., D'Angelo, V., Urso, V., & Catalisano, D. (2011). Two treatments for fear of flying compared: Cognitive behavioral therapy combined with systematic desensitization or eye movement desensitization and reprocessing (EMDR). *Aviation Psychology and Applied Human Factors, 1*, 9–14.

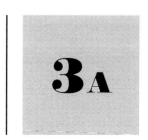

SUMMARY SHEET:
The Flashforward Procedure

Robin Logie and Ad de Jongh
SUMMARY SHEET BY MARILYN LUBER

Name: _____ Diagnosis: _____

Medications: _____

Test Results: _____

☑ Check when task is completed, response has changed, or to indicate symptoms.

Note: This material is meant as a checklist for your response. Please keep in mind that it is only a reminder of different tasks that may or may not apply to your incident.

Definition

The Flashforward Procedure has appeared to be an effective application of Eye Movement Desensitization and Reprocessing (EMDR) Therapy to deal with the second prong ("present") of the three-pronged approach. It is a procedure to address clients' irrational fears and anticipatory anxiety responses, which persist after the core memories of past events have been fully processed. Even though the client's focus is on the future, the fears are experienced in the present, triggered by negative, irrational thoughts with a catastrophic content. To this end, these are considered to be current fears, suitable for processing in the second prong.

Uses for Flashforward Procedure

Anticipatory Fear After Symptoms Fully Processed

Employed once all past traumatic events, relating to the current symptoms in question, have been fully resolved utilizing the Standard EMDR Protocol in the usual way when the client still experiences anticipatory fear of confrontations with certain objects or situations.

Disruptive Feared Event

Use of the Flashforward Procedure might be indicated when a future feared event is so disruptive to normal life that the client is either not sufficiently motivated to consider past events or is incapable of doing so.

Client Skepticism

EMDR Therapy aimed at targeting a client's expected doom scenario or flashforward might be indicated if it is necessary to convince a skeptical client of the benefits of EMDR Therapy by first demonstrating it with some current issue with which the client is preoccupied, and the client is initially unwilling to accept that looking at past events may be the key to unlocking her problems.

Unable to Identify Past Trauma

It may not be possible, with certain clients, to identify any past trauma or negative experience that appear to be at the root of the current symptoms.

Flashforward as Only EMDR Target

In some cases, targeting solely one's irrational fear(s) and/or anticipatory anxiety response(s) by using the Flashforward Procedure is sufficient to effectively alleviate the client's symptoms.

Psychological Conditions Appropriate for Use With Flashforward Procedure

Obsessive-Compulsive Disorder

This disorder relates to preoccupation with, and avoidance of, future events that the client deems to be catastrophic (e.g., being contaminated; house in flames as a consequence of not checking).

Specific Phobias

The fear of future events is also clearly a major component in specific phobias:

- ☐ Dog phobia (e.g., being attacked by a dog)
- ☐ Dental and medical phobias (e.g., extreme pain, being powerless, "bleeding to death")
- ☐ Social phobia (e.g., being rejected or other embarrassing situation)

Other Psychological Disorders

A fear of future catastrophe will also often be a feature of other psychological disorders such as the following:

- ☐ Body dysmorphic disorder (e.g., a negative remark about appearance)
- ☐ Hypochondriasis (e.g., the end phase of a terminal illness)
- ☐ Psychosis and schizophrenia (e.g., the delusion and fear of being killed)
- ☐ Posttraumatic stress disorder (PTSD; fear of situations similar to the trauma)
- ☐ Anorexia nervosa (fear of consequences of eating)

The Flashforward Script

Phase 1: History Taking

Done according to Standard EMDR Protocol.

Phase 2: Preparation

"We have now dealt with all the events from your past that seem to have been feeding into your current problems and these are no longer distressing you. But, it seems that you are still left with some fear and dread of what might happen in the future, which has been left behind, even after all the past events have been dealt with. So, we are now going to focus on this present trigger of the future, and what it is that you are dreading, using the same procedure as we used for the past events."

Phase 3: Determine the Flashforward

Step 1: Identify the Catastrophic Event

> *"We need to figure out what kind of image is in your head that makes you still scared about a future confrontation with what you fear. What is the worst thing you could imagine happening? Basically we should look for your ulti-mate doom scenario."* _____

_____

_____

Step 2: Follow the Event to Its Ultimate Conclusion

> *"Worst thing about it?"* _____

Repeat as necessary until client cannot identify anything worse.

Step 3: Make a Detailed Picture of Flashforward

Use this as target for processing with the Standard EMDR Protocol (SUD = 0; VoC = 7).

Target/Memory/Image:_____

_____

NC: _____

PC: _____

VoC: _____ /7

Emotions: _____

SUD: _____ /10

Sensation: _____

Phase 4: Desensitization

Apply the Standard EMDR Protocol for all targets.

Phase 5: Installation

Install the PC

Original PC: _____   Use Original PC: _____

Use new PC (if new one is better): _____

VoC: _____ /7

Incident + PC + BLS

Phase 6: Body Scan

Unresolved tension/tightness/unusual sensation: _____

_____

Unresolved tension/tightness/unusual sensation + BLS

Strengthen positive sensation using BLS.

If there is more discomfort, reprocess until discomfort subsides + BLS. Then repeat body scan.

VoC: _____ /7

Video Check

"This time, I'd like you to imagine yourself stepping into the future. Close your eyes, and play a movie from the beginning until the end. Imagine yourself coping with any challenges that come your way. Notice what you are seeing, thinking, feeling, and experiencing in your body. While playing this movie, let me know if you hit any blocks. If you do, just open your eyes and let me know. If you don't hit any blocks, let me know when you have viewed the whole movie.

If blocks, say "I can handle it," and BLS. Repeat until whole movie entirely without distress.

VoC: _____ /7

If client can play movie from beginning to end with confidence and satisfaction, play the movie one more time from beginning to end + PC "I can handle it" + BLS: ☐ Yes   ☐ No

Phase 7: Closure

Normal closure: ☐ Yes   ☐ No

Phase 8: Reevaluation

Noticed since last session: _____

_____

Current symptoms: _____

New material: _____

_____

Current SUD of flashforward: ____/10
If disturbance level increased, target it.

New resources needed: ☐ Yes   ☐ No

_____

_____

EMDR Therapy and Obsessive-Compulsive and Related Disorders

Psychiatry's move from *Diagnostic and Statistical Manual of Mental Disorders*, Fourth Edition (*DSM-4*) to the Fifth Edition (*DSM-5*) created a change in the way obsessive-compulsive disorders (OCDs) are coded. They are no longer part of Anxiety Disorders, but instead have their own separate category. The *DSM-5* OCD spectrum includes the following disorders:

- Obsessive-Compulsive Disorder
- Body Dysmorphic Disorder (previously in the Somatoform Disorders category)
- Hoarding Disorder (previously Compulsive Hoarding and listed only as a symptom of OCD and not a diagnostic criterion of OCD)
- Trichotillomania (Hair Pulling Disorder, previously in Impulse-Control Disorders, NOS)
- Excoriation (Skin-Picking) Disorder
- Substance/Medication-Induced Obsessive-Compulsive and Related Disorder
- Obsessive-Compulsive and related disorder due to another medical condition
- Other Specified Obsessive-Compulsive Related Disorders that include Olfactory Reference Syndrome

The chapters in this part highlight four of the disorders along the OCD spectrum: obsessive-compulsive disorder, body dysmorphic disorder, olfactory reference syndrome, and hoarding disorder.

Obsessive-Compulsive Disorder

From the earliest EMDR Network Conferences, Marcia Whisman (1992, 1993, 1994, 1996; Whisman & Keller, 1999) was the first to present her work with OCD patients and explain her model for addressing the key factors that she hypothesized contributed to the development and maintenance of OCD.

De Jongh and ten Broeke (2009), in their review article, "EMDR and the Anxiety Disorders: Exploring the Current Status," in the *Journal of EMDR Practice and Research's Special Section on the 20th Anniversary of EMDR*, concluded the following concerning the state of EMDR and OCD research:

> As research shows that clients with OCD respond relatively well to cognitive-behavioral interventions (i.e., exposure and response prevention and cognitive therapy) EMDR will generally not

play an important role in the treatment of OCD. However, there may be exceptions. For example, there is evidence to suggest that stressful events precipitate this disorder and that in some cases a causal link between severe trauma and the onset of OCD can be identified.... Therefore, it could be argued that if the condition has a direct and known onset and the client's memory of that event is still emotionally charged, it may be helpful to desensitize the memory and to evaluate its effect on the client's symptomatology. However, case reports on the treatment of OCD with EMDR are sparse, and the effects reported in the literature show that EMDR has limited potential to contribute to the treatment of this condition. (Bae, Kim, & Ahn, 2006; Corrigan & Jennett, 2004, p. 137)

In 2009, Böhm introduced his work with eye movement desensitization and reprocessing (EMDR) patients and OCD at the EMDRIA Deutschland Meeting. He discussed his method of interweaving EMDR and Exposure Therapy and Response Prevention work. He followed up this presentation with others (Böhm, 2010, 2012) and a paper published with Voderholzer (2010) on a *case series* that showed EMDR Therapy could be a useful adjunctive method in treating patients with OCD when used with Exposure Therapy and Response Prevention.

Marr's (2012) interest in OCD led him to create two different protocols for four participants with long-standing unremitting OCD. In his experiment, he used two adaptations of Shapiro's phobia protocol (2001). His theoretical perspective is that OCD is a "self-perpetuating disorder with OCD compulsions and obsessions and current triggers reinforcing and maintaining the disorder." Both protocols begin with present triggers (obsessions and compulsions). The difference is that one of the protocols delays the cognitive installation phase while the other uses mental video playback to desensitize the triggers. Participants noticed symptom improvement after 2 to 3 of the 14 to 16 1-hour sessions stipulated. Symptom reduction for the Adapted EMDR Phobia Protocol was 70.4% at posttreatment and 76.1% at follow-up. For the Adapted EMDR Phobia Protocol with Video Playback, symptom reduction was 81.4% at posttreatment and follow-up. In 2014, Keenan, Keenan, Ingham, and Farrell presented a *case series* design with participants who had received cognitive behavioral therapy (CBT) for OCD within the last 5 years but were still experiencing symptoms. They were offered eight sessions of EMDR with 1- and 3-month follow-ups. Targets included past aversive life experiences and intolerance of uncertainty where there were no earlier aversive life experiences. There were significant improvements after the EMDR Therapy intervention based on the psychometric measures and positive behavioral changes.

Over the years, a number of EMDR practitioners have offered case reports of their work with patients who have OCD. Some showed that EMDR Therapy was not promising for treating OCD, as pointed out by de Jongh and ten Broeke (2009; see also Bae et al., 2006; Corrigan & Jennett, 2004), whereas others found that EMDR Therapy—often with adaptations and in combination with exposure and response prevention—was showing positive results for patients with OCD (Bhadlikar, 2014; Crichton, 2014; Grosso, 1996; Kawamura, 2009; Logie, 2014; Marr, 2012; Nisi, 2003; Onofri, 2010; Pinillos, 2012; Rijkeboer & van der Mark, 2011; St. André, 2009, 2010; Sprowls & Marquis, 2012; Strom & Christie, 2001). There is still no clear and consistent manner in which practitioners are creating a workable model for OCD and EMDR Therapy; however, the fact that some of our colleagues are finding ways to work with this group may eventually lead to an effective treatment protocol of OCD with EMDR.

Karsten Böhm is a specialist in OCD, anxiety disorders, and posttraumatic stress disorder (PTSD) and a member of the German National Guideline Commission on the treatment of OCD. His chapter "Obsessive-Compulsive Disorder and EMDR Therapy" explains the importance of doing a thorough diagnostic analysis, determining the obsessions and compulsions in detail so patients are clear about their thoughts and actions, and using assessment instruments. After the diagnosis of OCD, it is helpful to look for other trauma or comorbid diseases, as patients often have experienced many adverse and/or traumatic incidents in their lives; using the timeline (Hofmann & Luber, 2009) can shed light on how patients deal with their OCD. Understanding and helping patients deal with negative emotions is crucial, as well as making sure that they are taking responsibility for their own treatment and their critical internal dialogue. Since obsessions and compulsions are often used to regulate social interactions, checking for deficits in interpersonal skills, conflicts, and connections is important. In this work, Böhm integrates EMDR Therapy into the sanctioned German treatment for OCD (Exposure and Response Prevention, a CBT procedure) so that the patient profits from both procedures. EMDR Therapy is used to increase motivation and affect tolerance, while in vivo work is employed for those who have inner motivation but need to experience success first. He addresses the types of negative cognitions that often occur and writes about a "detail-oriented" interweave that helps clients when they are looping, so often an issue with OCD.

BDD and ORS

In 1997, McGoldrick and Buchanan wrote "Body Dysmorphic Disorder: Seven Cases Treated with Eye Movement Desensitization and Reprocessing," the first published paper addressing BDD and EMDR. They found that six of their seven subjects improved and five had a complete resolution. Often, they found that these patients had traumatic or adverse childhood experiences in their histories that were contributing to their disorder. McGoldrick and Brown, joined by Begum, presented at European conferences as their number of cases grew. They continued to report a high success rate with this population (McGoldrick, 2001; McGoldrick & Begum, 2014; McGoldrick, Brown, & Begum, 2011). In 2010, van Rood and de Roos presented their work on BDD at the European Conference in Hamburg and the following year at a symposium at the European Association for Behavioural and Cognitive Therapy (EABCT) Annual Conference in Iceland (de Roos & van Rood, 2011). They, too, noted that BDD patients often reported traumatic events occurring at the onset of their disorder, as well as intrusive images. They emphasized two ways to target memories for treatment with EMDR: by ordering the significant adverse events on a timeline and processing those that preceded the patient's increase in symptoms; or by selecting the incidents linked to anxious expectations and avoidance behaviors. The results, in their case series, showed that EMDR Therapy was successful with BDD.

The only EMDR-related work on ORS is by McGoldrick, Begum, and Brown. In 2008, they published, "EMDR and Olfactory Reference Syndrome: A Case Series," in the *Journal of EMDR Practice and Research*. As in BDD, they processed adverse life experiences that appeared to cause or trigger their patients' symptomatology, resulting in complete resolution of symptoms in all four cases; their results were maintained at follow-up.

In Scotland, since the 1990s, Keith Brown and Therese McGoldrick have been working with EMDR Therapy and BDD. In their chapter with Millia Begum, "Body Dysmorphic Disorder and Olfactory Reference Syndrome EMDR Protocol," they explore the use of EMDR Therapy with both disorders. They see these disorders as similar in their presentation, symptoms, and treatment response and emphasize that there has been little discussion about trauma as a trigger concerning these disorders. Often, the precipitants were events where the patient was humiliated. They make sure to address the present triggers and future template.

Hoarding Behaviors

When looking for references about EMDR Therapy and hoarding on the Francine Shapiro Library website, there were no citations to match the criteria. Marquis and Sprowls (Chapter 6 in this volume) mention some therapists who use EMDR Therapy as part of a treatment for hoarding (Gomez, 2013; Marich, 2011; Russell & Figley, 2013; Shapiro, 2009), but there were no researchers or clinicians writing or presenting about a specific EMDR protocol for hoarding.

Priscilla Marquis has been working with OCD and its spectrum disorders since 1996 and was certified by the Obsessive Compulsive Foundation to work with patients with this disorder. She also is the OCD Spectrum Disorders treatment group leader at Kaiser in San Francisco. Marquis and Christie Sprowls, an EMDR Trainer and expert in PTSD and anxiety disorders, introduce an EMDR Therapy treatment for hoarding disorder. Their chapter is based on their observations in their clinical practices over many years. They warn that even though EMDR Therapy may have a rapid effect on patients' cognitions and behaviors, decluttering is often slow. They use a modified Phobia Protocol (Shapiro, 2001) and include a number of resources for their patients. They determine an appropriate and desirable goal of treatment and install that desired state as part of the Preparation Phase, as well as teaching self-control techniques and developing a plan of action for decreasing acquisition behaviors. They emphasize the installation of the future template as well as the in vivo practice of discarding.

These chapters in this new section covering Obsessive-Compulsive and Related Disorders represent our authors' exploration into the world of clients with these disorders. The work is challenging. However, with grounding in basic clinical knowledge, and knowledge of EMDR Therapy thorough enough to know when to adapt this structure in the service of clients' needs, there is hope that clients who suffer from these disorders can resolve their issues and function more optimally. Summary sheets accompany each chapter to remind us of the important points in the chapter and to provide a place to incorporate the data of our clients. There is a CD version of this text to use in the field or to enter data.

References

Bae, H., Kim, D., & Ahn, J. (2006, September). [A case series of post-traumatic obsessive compulsive disorder: A six month follow-up evaluation]. *Journal of the Korean Neuropsychiatric Association, 45*(5), 476–480.

Bhadlikar, D. (2014, January). EMDR with obsessive compulsive disorder: An Indian experience. In EMDR in the treatment of fears and phobias/eating disorders/borderline disorder (Derek Farrell, Chair). Presentation at the 2nd EMDR Asia International Conference, Manila, The Philippines.

Böhm, K. (2009, February/May). EMDR in der behandlung von zwangsstörungen [Use of EMDR in the treatment of obsessive-compulsive disorders]. *EMDRIA Deutschland e.V. Rundbrief, 18*, 30–35.

Böhm, K. (2010, June). *EMDR in der behandlung zur zwangsstorung [EMDR in the treatment of obsessive-compulsive disorder].* Presentation at the 11th EMDR Europe Association Conference, Hamburg, Germany.

Böhm, K. (2012, September). *EMDR in der behandlung der zwangsstörung [EMDR in the treatment of obsessive-compulsive disorder].* Presentation at the German Society OCD Conference, Muenster, Germany.

Böhm, K., & Voderholzer, U. (2010, September). EMDR in der behandlung von zwangsstörungen: Eine fallserie [Use of EMDR in the treatment of obsessive-compulsive disorders: A case series]. *Verhaltenstherapie [Behavior Therapy], 20*(3), 175–181. doi:10.1159/000319439

Corrigan, F. M., & Jennett, J. (2004, August). Ephedra alkaloids and brief relapse in EMDR-treated obsessive compulsive disorder. *Acta Psychiatrica Scandinavica, 110*(2), 158. doi:10.1111/j.1600–0047.2004.00368de

Crichton, N. (2014, June). *Understanding and treating resistance in OCD through EMDR.* In EMDR Research Symposium (Derek Farrell, Chair). Symposium presented at the 15th EMDR Europe Association Conference, Edinburgh, Scotland.

de Jongh, A., & ten Broeke, E. (2009). EMDR and the anxiety disorders: Exploring the current status. *Journal of EMDR Practice and Research, 3*(3), 133–140.

de Roos, C., & van Rood, Y. R. (2011, August–September). *Trauma treatment (EMDR) as part of CBT for body dysmorphic disorder. In case conceptualization and treatment of body dysmorphic disorder.* Symposium conducted at the 41st EABCT Annual Congress, Reykjavík, Iceland.

Gomez, A. (Ed.). (2013). *EMDR therapy and adjunct approaches with children: Complex trauma, attachment and dissociation.* New York, NY: Springer.

Grosso, F. C. (1996, June). Children and OCD: Extending the treatment paradigm. *EMDRIA Newsletter, 1*(1), 10–11.

Hofmann, A., & Luber, M. (2009). History taking: The time line. In M. Luber (Ed.), *Eye movement desensitization and reprocessing (EMDR) scripted protocols: Basics and special situations* (pp. 5–10). New York, NY: Springer Publishing Company.

Kawamura, W. (2009, May). [EMDR sessions of a woman with obsessive-compulsive disorder]. *Japanese Journal of EMDR Research and Practice, 1*(1), 44–52.

Keenan, P., Keenan, L., Ingham, C., & Farrell, D. (2014, June). *Treating obsessive compulsive disorder [OCD] using eye movement desensitisation and reprocessing [EMDR]: A case series design.* In EMDR Research Symposium (Derek Farrell, Chair). Symposium presented at the 15th EMDR Europe Association Conference, Edinburgh, Scotland.

Logie, R. (2014, June). *The flash-forward procedure: Confronting the catastrophe.* In EMDR Clinical Practice Symposium (Marilyn Luber, Chair). Symposium presented at the 15th EMDR Europe Association Conference, Edinburgh, Scotland.

Marich, J. (2011). *EMDR made simple: 4 approaches to using EMDR with every client*. Wisconsin: Premier Publishing and Media Eau Claire.

Marr, J. (2012). EMDR treatment of obsessive-compulsive disorder: Preliminary research. *Journal of EMDR Practice and Research, 6*(1), 2–15.

McGoldrick, T. (2001, May). *EMDR treatment of body dysmorphia*. Presentation at the 2nd EMDR Europe Association Conference, London, England.

McGoldrick, T., & Begum, M. (2014, June). *Treatment of olfactory reference syndrome (ORS) and body dysmorphic disorder (BDD) with EMDR*. In EMDR Research Symposium (Derek Farrell, Chair). Symposium presented at the 15th EMDR Europe Association Conference, Edinburgh, Scotland.

McGoldrick, T., Begum, M., & Brown, K. W. (2008). EMDR and olfactory reference syndrome: A case series. *Journal of EMDR Practice and Research, 2*(1), 63–68. doi:10.1891/1933-3196.2.1.63

McGoldrick, T., Brown, K., & Begum, M. (2011, March). *EMDR in the treatment of body dysmorphic disorder & olfactory reference syndrome: A case series*. Symposium conducted at the 9th Annual Conference of the EMDR UK & Ireland, Bristol, UK.

McGoldrick, T., & Buchanan, R. (1997). Body dysmorphic disorder: Seven cases treated with eye movement desensitization and reprocessing. *Behavioural and Cognitive Psychotherapy, 25*(2), 203–207. doi:10.1017/S1352465800018403

Nisi, A. (2003, May). *Non-conventional EMDR protocols in treatment of resistant OCD patients (non or poor responders)*. In Anxiety Disorders. Symposium conducted at the 4th EMDR Europe Association Conference, Rome, Italy.

Onofri, A. (2010). Pensare la mente del padre. Psicoterapia Cognitiva orientata dalla teoria dell'attaccamento e approccio EMDR: Un caso clinico disturbo ossessivo compulsivo [Thinking about the mind of the father. Cognitive theory guided by attachment and EMDR approach: A clinical case of obsessive compulsive disorder]. In L. Onnis (Ed.), *Legami che creano, legami che curano. Attaccamento: una teoria ponte per la psicoterapia* (pp.). Torino, Italy: Bollati Boringhieri.

Pinillos, I. (2012, June). *Aplicaciones y protocolos especiales EMDR segun modelo structural funcional de los trastornos obsesivos compulsivos [Special applications and protocols EMDR according to functional structural model of the compulsive obsessive disorders]*. Poster presented at the 13th EMDR Europe Association Conference, Madrid, Spain.

Rijkeboer, M., & van der Mark, W. (2011, April). *Therapieresistente dwang: Hoe EMDR een uitkomst kan bieden bij OCD" [Therapy resistant coercion: How EMDR can provide a solution to OCD]*. Presentation at the 5th Vereniging EMDR Nederland Conference, Nijmegen, The Netherlands.

Russell, M., & Figley, C. (2013). *Treating traumatic stress injuries in military personnel: An EMDR practitioner's guide* (Routledge Psychosocial Stress Series). New York, NY: Routledge.

Shapiro, F. (2001). *Eye movement desensitization and reprocessing: Basic principles, protocols and procedures* (2nd ed.). New York, NY: Guilford Press.

Shapiro, R. (Ed.). (2009). *EMDR solutions II, for depression, eating disorders, performance and more*. New York, NY: W.W. Norton.

Sprowls, C., & Marquis, P. (2012, June). *Treatment of OCD [Tratamiento del TOC]*. Presentation at the annual meeting of EMDR Europe Association, Madrid, Spain.

St. André, E. (2009, August). *EMDR and OCD*. Presentation at the 14th EMDR International Association Conference, Atlanta, GA.

St. André, É. (2010, April/May). *Use of EMDR in the treatment of obsessive compulsive disorder: A case study*. Presentation at the annual meeting of EMDR Canada, Toronto, ON.

Strom, I., & Christie, H. (2001, May). *Possible EMDR targets when working with children diagnosed with OCD: A case history*. Poster presented at the 2nd EMDR Europe Association Conference, London, England.

van Rood, Y., & de Roos, C. (2010, June). *EMDR in the treatment of body dysmorphic disorder*. Presentation at the 11th EMDR Europe Association Conference, Hamburg, Germany.

Whisman, M. (1992, April). *Obsessive compulsive disorder*. Presentation at the EMDR Network Conference, Sunnyvale, CA.

Whisman, M. (1993, March). *OCD and EMD/R*. Presentation at the EMDR Network Conference, Sunnyvale, CA.

Whisman, M. (1994, March). *Obsessive compulsive disorder*. Presentation at the EMDR Network Conference, Sunnyvale, CA.

Whisman, M. (1996, June). *EMDR in the treatment of panic, phobia, and obsessive compulsive disorders*. Presentation at the 1st EMDR International Association Conference, Denver, CO.

Whisman, M., & Keller, M. (1999, June). *Integrating EMDR in the treatment of obsessive compulsive disorder*. Presentation at the 4th EMDR International Association Conference, Las Vegas, NV.

Obsessive-Compulsive Disorder and EMDR Therapy

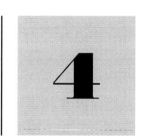

Karsten Böhm

Introduction

Obsessive-compulsive disorder (OCD) is a serious, intrusive, and distressing disorder for patients. According to the *Diagnostic and Statistical Manual*, 5th edition (*DSM-5*) by the American Psychiatric Association (APA, 2013), OCD is defined as obsessions and/or compulsions.

- *Obsessions*: Thoughts, mental images, or ideas that keep coming back and are intrusive and unwanted, for example, "I could have been affected by a serious illness," after touching door handles or shaking hands.
- *Compulsions*: The individual feels driven to repeat behaviors and mental acts as a reaction to an obsession or rules that must be used strictly to avoid or decrease distress or some feared situation; for example, washing hands in a ritualized fashion after touching a door handle or shaking hands.

Obsessions and compulsions take a considerable amount of time each day (defined by more than 1 hour per day). OCD occurs mainly in late adolescence and young adulthood and usually becomes chronic if untreated. Prevalence rates worldwide range between 1% and 2% (Ruscio, Stein, Chiu, & Kessler, 2010; Voderholzer, Schlegl, & Külz, 2011). Traumatic life experiences can be an explanation for the development of acute and chronic OCD, as 82% of therapy-resistant OCD patients experienced at least one trauma and 50% meet the criteria of posttraumatic stress disorder (PTSD; Gershuny, Baer, Parker, Gentes, Infield, & Jenike, 2007).

The Standard Treatment for OCD

Current therapy guidelines consider both exposure and response prevention (ERP) and cognitive therapy as standard treatment for OCD (APA, 2007; Hohagan et al., 2015). These therapies integrate "in vivo desensitization" as a main factor for effectiveness and as one element in the therapy process (APA, 2007; National Collaborating Centre for Mental Health [NCCMH], 2006), which is essential in the treatment of patients with OCD (NCCMH, 2006). In ERP, exercises are done mainly during the sessions, whereas cognitive therapies use in vivo exercises as homework. The descriptions of these different types of in vivo desensitization are as follows:

- *Exposure*: to confront the patient with cues that trigger obsessive thoughts (i.e., words, situations, or images)

- *Response prevention*: to tell the patient *not to* do the behavior, which is meant to prevent feared consequences from occurring

Patients with OCD often experience this standard treatment as arduous and distressing and tend to be less motivated or do not complete it. It is estimated that 15% to 40% of the patients do not benefit significantly from this standard treatment (NCCMH, 2006). One reason could be that there are a high number of connections between adverse and/or traumatic life events and OCD (Fricke, Köhler, & Moritz, 2007; Gershuny, Baer, Wilson, Radomsky, & Jenike, 2003; Gershuny et al., 2007), which should be focused on during therapy to get integration at the emotional level.

EMDR Therapy and OCD

Within the eye movement desensitization and reprocessing (EMDR) assessment, the activation of feeling during bilateral stimulation (BLS) is present. When eliciting the steps of the assessment, the goal is to activate the emotion and sensation related to the issue. EMDR is, of course, much more and although the emotional part is focused on here, the whole EMDR process is used and necessary to work with OCD patients. According to Gershuny, Baer, Parker, Gentes, Infield, and Jenike (2007), it is helpful to assist OCD patients to improve their regulation of emotions by first reducing the emotional distress of critical life events. With this in mind, EMDR Therapy can be used to target the obsession itself, and/or to overcome a trauma that is connected to the compulsions and/or obsessions. By working with earlier incidents connected to the obsessions and compulsions, overall emotional distress and arousal are reduced.

EMDR Therapy for OCD patients mainly follows the Standard EMDR Protocol and Procedures, including the eight phases and the use of BLS (i.e., eye movements). Modifications will be described in more detail in the course of this chapter. Further specific goals when treating OCD are the following:

- Unlock the nervous system so that the traumatic experience can be processed adequately
- Enable OCD patients to observe precisely and experience their inner processes
- Support the understanding and acceptance of connections between the obsessions and the emotional distress

Preliminary studies show that EMDR Therapy could be good supplementary therapy in the standard treatments for OCD (Bekkers, 1999; Böhm & Voderholzer, 2010).

EMDR Therapy and the Standard Treatment for OCD

For optimal progress in the treatment of OCD, both in vivo desensitization and work on the earlier incidents connected to the OCD with EMDR Therapy should be targeted. Due to the focus on practical exercises in the standard treatments, patients learn to leave the compulsions undone and to resist the compulsive performance of rituals in real-life situations. With the help of EMDR Therapy, the emotional aspects of issues can be integrated better, so that patients are able to transfer their emotional learning to everyday life and to tolerate their emotional distress. Therefore, a combination of EMDR Therapy and the standard treatment for OCD is indicated (Böhm & Voderholzer, 2010). Current results indicate that a combination of both methods leads to significant long-term reduction of OCD-related symptoms. In comparison to ERP therapy alone, combined EMDR Therapy and ERP therapy-related studies show lower dropout rates and higher motivation in patients (Bekkers, 1999; Böhm & Voderholzer, 2010).

There is a complementary aspect to the different forms of therapies. Even though both organize distress-related stimuli in a hierarchical manner, EMDR Therapy usually starts with the most fearful and distressing mental image (Hofmann, 2009). In contrast, standard behavioral treatments usually start with exposure to situations that cause moderate anxiety (40–60%). The patient then subsequently works up to situations that cause greater anxiety (hierarchy of fearful situations).

Sequencing Standard OCD Treatment With EMDR Therapy

The combination of in vivo desensitization with EMDR Therapy can be done in different ways. The research standard (Bekkers, 1999; Böhm & Voderholzer, 2010) is to alternate usage. In vivo desensitization and EMDR Therapy are not combined in one session. Each modality requires its own session and preparation. As one of the most important goals to achieve is the patient's motivation to take the risk of leaving the compulsion undone, the chronological sequence of the therapies is important. Our clinical experience shows that personality styles can be guidance for this decision. The two observed personality styles relevant to patients with OCD are the anxious and fearful and the narcissistic style:

- *Anxious and fearful personality style*: They often lack the motivation for risk-taking. In this case it is important to *reduce emotional distress first*, which can best be achieved with EMDR Therapy. Improving the emotional regulation strategies enables these OCD patients to address issues with in vivo work as the second step.
- *Narcissistic personality style*: Patients who already have some sort of inner motivation to take a risk, and need to experience success, benefit from a therapy addressing in vivo work first; for example, ERP or cognitive therapy (Böhm, 2011). The regulation of emotions through EMDR Therapy is focused on as the second step.

In the continued therapy process, EMDR Therapy and in vivo desensitization are used in an alternating way for all patients. It is recommended that the treatment of OCD include both the standard treatment and EMDR Therapy.

OCD and EMDR Therapy Script Notes

During the use of EMDR Therapy, the treatment of OCD follows the Standard EMDR Protocol. Nevertheless, the eight phases include some adaptations. In Phase 1, our goal is to take a thorough client history about our patient's medical and personal factors, such as ability to cope with negative emotions and motivation for therapy.

There are a number of important elements in Phase 1.

Determine the Type of OCD (Obsessions and/or Compulsions) and Its Severity

The first step is a thorough diagnostic analysis, following the criteria of *DSM-5* (300.3; APA, 2013), to see if the patient fulfills the criteria for the diagnosis of OCD. For EMDR Therapy, the therapist must be able to differentiate between obsessions and compulsions, as the focus is on the obsessions and not on the compulsions as targets (the discussion of target selection in Phase 2 gives more details).

Obsessions include the following types of thoughts:

- Repetitive thoughts, impulses or mental pictures that are experienced as unwanted and disturbing; they produce fear and despair in most individuals
- Trying to overlook, repress, or neutralize these thoughts, impulses, or mental pictures with other ideas of actions

Compulsions include the following types of behaviors and mental acts:

- Driven to execute recurrent behaviors (hand washing, arraying, checking) and mental acts (praying, counting, replicating words) as a reaction to an obsession or rules, which must be performed perfectly
- Performances or mental acts are intended to avoid or decrease distress or some feared situation; however, these performances or mental acts are not an accurate, appropriate, or effective response to the distress or feared situation and do not neutralize or prevent them

Determine the Obsessions and Compulsions in Detail

It is helpful to compile a hierarchy of situations in which obsessions and compulsions come up. It is important to differentiate between obsessions and compulsions, so that the patient's compulsion procedure becomes clearer. *Obsessions cause inner distress* and are unwanted and intrusive, whereas *compulsions are behaviors or thoughts* that reduce, more or less consciously, this distress. Therefore, compulsions are dysfunctional behaviors that result in the strengthening of the obsession(s). Phase 1 should be used to make the distinction between compulsions and obsessions clearer to the patient and the therapist.

Identify Possible Traumas and Comorbid Diseases

After the diagnosis of OCD, explore and look for possible traumas and other comorbid diseases. Patients suffering from OCD often report that they have experienced traumatic life events that can be, but do not necessarily have to be, linked to their OCD. It is helpful to ask questions such as: Do you suffer from any other symptoms or problems? Or: Did your obsession and/or compulsion start with a traumatic event? Using a timeline (Hofmann & Luber, 2009) can give a lot of information that is necessary for the next phases in EMDR. In this way, it is possible to begin the process of comprehending how the patient tries to deal with OCD.

Usually, it is helpful to use a battery of tests such as the Yale–Brown Obsessive Compulsive Scale (Y-BOCS) to quantify the severity of OCD (before and after treatment), and Beck's Depression Inventory (BDI-II) and the Posttraumatic Stress Diagnostic Scale (PDS; Böhm & Voderholzer, 2010) to get more information about OCD and comorbid symptoms and diseases.

It is important to test also for dissociation using the Dissociative Experience Scale II (DES II), as this could change the chronological order of the EMDR Protocol. Generally, in OCD, the use of dissociation is low (Maier, Kuelz, & Voderholzer, 2009), but if it is high, it is important to look for trauma-related lifetime events.

Note: Contraindications to the use of EMDR with OCD patients are the following: high levels of dissociation, a diagnosis of psychosis, critical physical diseases, or severe personality disorders.

Identify Affects Regulation Ability

Since difficulty with emotional self-regulation often is central to the underpinnings of OCD thoughts and behaviors, it is important to address this material in therapy. The typical *emotions* that are expressed by clients with OCD are anxiety, disgust, shame, guilt, failure, loneliness, inner emptiness, boredom, and anger. It is helpful to understand how patients deal with these negative emotions.

Note: Not every OCD patient feels fear; specifically, those patients experiencing disgust, as these two emotions are mutually exclusive. Most OCD patients have major difficulties in dealing with emotions and the use of obsessions and compulsions seems to be one way of avoiding or handling them.

Patients tend to delegate responsibility (responsibility for both intrapsychic and interpersonal situations) in order to obtain a feeling of intrapsychic stability. As a result of delegating responsibility, patients are unable to confront their own negative emotions and their own earlier incidents connected to the obsessions and compulsions. This difficulty creates a blockage/barrier to patients trying new behaviors. Therefore, it is important to make learning how to assume responsibility for their own therapeutic process part of the therapeutic process for patients.

Some OCD patients tend to live by high moral standards. It is important to question and challenge these standards, because they often compensate for a general lack of self-worth by giving the patient a sense of purpose and control, but in a dysfunctional way. In the early stages of treatment, it is helpful to challenge these high standards, as they are—for the most part—unattainable. The aim in challenging these unrelenting standards is to help patients attend to their internal dialogue by questioning it and taking responsibility for it.

In this part of the treatment, it is also necessary to look for possible deficits in interpersonal skills, conflicts, and connections. Obsessions and compulsions can be used to regulate social interactions in the following ways:

- Controlling closeness and distance
- Finding an outlet for suppressed aggression against others
- Dealing with conflict and its resolution
- Handling social deficits and difficulties
- Accomplishing something that can be admired by others

If this is the case, it is important to consider improving existing social skills. For the following therapy process and the therapeutic relationship, it is helpful to understand some of the dynamics of these conflicts.

Identify Motivation for Treatment

It is helpful in Phase 1 to clarify the motivation of patients for coming into treatment at this time, the type and intensity of suffering, and if there are current social situations that impact the OCD or vice versa.

In addition, to support the motivation for treatment, it is essential to build a supportive therapeutic relationship in which patients can discuss their difficulties and show their feelings. This is very important for the following treatment process.

Determine a Treatment Plan

The second part of Phase 1 is to work out the treatment plan. This plan should be developed with the patient and, of course, can be changed during the treatment, if necessary. Because OCD is a disease that includes repetitive actions such as recurrent thoughts or repetitive behaviors, the treatment plan always includes both EMDR Therapy and exposure therapy concerning obsessions in difficult situations (such as using a faucet after touching a doorknob in washing OCD).

The usual sequence in using EMDR Therapy and in vivo desensitization is the following:

- Treatment Plan A: Patients who already have some sort of inner motivation to take a risk, and who need to experience success, benefit from a therapy addressing in vivo work first, for example, ERP or cognitive therapy (Böhm, 2011). The regulation of the emotions through EMDR Therapy is focused on as the second step.
- Treatment Plan B: The exception is with patients who do not have any real goals in their lives and do not know what they are "fighting" for. With these patients, start with a longer period of EMDR Therapy sessions focusing on building up goals and the willingness to take risks to reach them. Human beings only take risks in their lives when their goal(s) is/are compelling. If the only goal is to suffer less, more often than not OCD patients will choose their OCD. Only if they know what they are fighting for will they face and "fight" in these difficult circumstances. Improving their emotional regulation strategies enables these OCD patients to address issues with in vivo work as the second step.

Note: In most cases, Treatment Plan A is used. Treatment Plan B is indicated if patients lack goals and self-confidence. Make sure treatment plans include in vivo desensitization after working with EMDR Therapy.

Phase 2/Preparation entails detailed preparation for the use of EMDR Therapy and reaffirmation that the patient is stable enough to work with EMDR Therapy.

- *Step 1: Check for stabilization*
  - The stabilization of OCD patients is usually easier than with trauma patients and can therefore be quite short. Nevertheless, it is important to make sure that the social surroundings are not changing too much during treatment, as that would provide patients with an excuse for not working on their OCD. Install the imaginary "safe place" and work on resources, when needed, as is done with trauma patients.
- *Step 2: Apply psychoeducation*
  - Another step, in this second phase, is to help patients understand what the reasons are for using EMDR Therapy and in vivo desensitization and what the protocols entail. This psychoeducation is very important for OCD patients so that they can maintain a feeling of control and to support their being receptive to the rest of the work.
  - In explaining EMDR Therapy, it is helpful to make clear that the patient will first work on the most emotionally charged image and/or real-life event. In order to familiarize the patient with the procedure and especially with the BLS, it can be helpful to show the BLS without content. Beginning with this small practical exercise gives the patient a feeling of safety and control.
- *Step 3: Make the target selection now*
  - Following stabilization and psychoeducation, the third step includes informing patients about the specifics of working with EMDR Therapy. In Phase 1, the sequence of working with different modalities and EMDR Therapy was explained. Now, it is time to decide which target will be used for EMDR Therapy. The target selection occurs after the stabilization and psychoeducation steps, as the knowledge gained from these preparations assists in picking the best target. The target selection is based on activating patients' emotional charge concerning the image or the experience (Böhm, 2011). The therapist and the patient choose a real-life situation or a mental image that activates the patient's emotions; that is, the target with the highest subjective units of disturbance (SUDs) is used here. A helpful question might be: "What is the mental image or situation that brings up the most emotion and sensation for you?"
  Different types of targets can be used with OCD patients, such as the following:
  ☐ *Traumatic memory*: Patients with OCD often report that they experienced traumatic life events that can, but do not have to, be linked to their OCD. The specific traumatic memory can be used as a target.
  ☐ *Worst case scenario/flashforward*: Another target could be the worst scenario that could occur when the patient is in an *obsessive situation* and nothing can be used to handle the emotions, including compulsive behavior. It is helpful to ask for short- and long-term consequences. The picture/catastrophe is the patient's flashforward. These consequences can extend to after-death preoccupations, such as, "God will punish me for that." For example, the patient might be asked about the potential consequences of not engaging in compulsive washing for a contamination fear. The patient might also imagine an anticipated disastrous event or even facing death scenarios, such as, "What will happen afterward? What will happen after death?" It is helpful to use the worst part of that sequence as the target in Phase 3.
  ☐ *Automatic and intrusive mental images*: Special kinds of worst-case scenarios are automatic and intrusive mental images. They can occur without obsessive thoughts and can cause severe distress. Often, they are connected to aggressive obsessions, such as an image of "how I am going to stab my baby to death." The image could be a future template, a flashforward, an occurrence in the past, or a trigger in the present.
  ☐ *Imaginary blocking of compulsive action*: This is a type of cognitive interweave where patients are asked to imagine that the compulsive action *cannot* be

executed. For example, the patient imagines an object or situation that triggers obsessions that arouse severe anxiety. The therapist then asks the patient to stay in contact with the obsession trigger and an external event that prevents engaging in the ritual behaviors (e.g., the patient cannot engage in hand-washing rituals as the water tap is not working). The worst part of that scenery is used as the target in Phase 3. This kind of target is rarely used because the other types of targets usually have higher SUDs.

☐ Imaginary trigger situation of obsession: The obsessive trigger situation or stimulus itself is imagined here. The image can be a representation of a past memory or an anticipated event as a future template. Patients are therefore asked to imagine a real-life situation that triggers their obsession and arouses their distress and anxiety. Patients are then asked to resist the compulsion to perform rituals. The most difficult picture would be used in Phase 3.

☐ Real trigger situation: Trigger situations can also be produced in real situations with real stimuli. As a result, patients experience the urgent need to neutralize the obsession. The resulting pressure (SUD) can be used as a way to access the target for Phase 3. Patients who suffer from contamination fears, for instance, may touch the door handle as a trigger.

Note: Response prevention and standard exposure are not used here.

In Phase 3: Assessment, the treatment plan (A or B) is implemented. In vivo desensitization should be implemented as described earlier (Treatment Plan in Phase 1 and 2: A or B). In Phase 3, the focus is on the EMDR Therapy process. While working with in vivo desensitization, make sure that patients practice their reactions in real trigger situations without using compulsive behaviors or avoidance. Even during the EMDR phase of treatment, it is necessary to verify that the patients continue with the in vivo desensitization on their own.

For patients with OCD, the negative cognition (NC) is a representation of the underlying central obsessive thought. It is important that this obsessive thought be generalizable. Patients often report obsessive thoughts that are too specific, such as "the stove is still on." In this case, the therapist needs to help patients verbalize the underlying and generalizable obsessive thought, such as "I am dangerous."

When working with OCD patients, the therapist will encounter two main categories of NCs concerning safety: "I am dangerous" (e.g., I will stab my child) or "I am in danger" (e.g., The bacteria will kill me); some patients have both. If the latter is the case, use the stronger one or go for the self-confidence issue ("I am worthless") or the control domain ("I have no control").

Develop the positive cognition (PC) at the same level as the NC but with a positive resolution. It is essential that the PCs be beliefs and not just assumptions or descriptions. In this way, the therapist assists the patient in finding a complementary inner conviction/resource.

In Phase 4: Desensitization for patients with OCD, the Standard EMDR Protocol is used to process all targets. If there are no blockages, follow the Standard EMDR Protocol. When beginning EMDR Therapy processing, many patients with OCD shut down and the process stops. When this occurs, it is helpful to understand what could be going on for the patient. Usually, it has to do with the need to please and/or "do everything right."

Patients with OCD need to "do everything right." They want to be good, hardworking patients who follow the therapy process perfectly. Nonetheless, beginning EMDR Therapy processing creates pressure not to fail and all the attention is directed to that fear, resulting in the opposite of what patients want to achieve, as in the following:

- Unable to "just go along with the process"
- Feeling pressure "to get it right," resulting in their jumping from one mental image to the next but getting nowhere ("looping")

As a consequence, often the desensitization process is long, ineffective, and, finally, results in or leads to mental blockage. In this case, a special interweave is used as an intervention to jumpstart the process that is emotionally driven.

If the therapist perceives that patients are unable to get out of the "do everything right" loop quickly, it is helpful to encourage them to stay with the description of the target picture and not talk about thoughts, emotions, or bodily sensations; this is called *the "detail-oriented" interweave*. While focusing on the description—and neglecting everything else—the therapeutic process is simplified. Patients experience the description of a picture as simple and doable, even in situations when their arousal and distress are very high. The mental blockage can be resolved and the patients get the feeling that they can be successful at EMDR Therapy and fulfill therapeutic demands ("I can do this"). This motivates and enables them to engage in the EMDR Therapy processing (Böhm, 2011). However, if this does not help move the process along, it is helpful to ask patients to orient themselves in present time by describing a picture in the room in detail, such as a picture on the wall in the office, and then go back to the previous process with the target.

By applying this detail-oriented interweave, the therapist interrupts patients during the OCD type of looping, where the patient has been jumping from one aspect to another and a real chain of associations has not started yet. Experience with OCD patients shows that looping does not have a positive effect; if continued, the result is usually that patients feel guilty, a feeling they are familiar with in real life. It is helpful to do what is possible to not recreate the same experience again during the EMDR process, but rather to create an EMDR experience that helps patients reduce distress and fear.

By being both emphatic and active, the therapist aims to facilitate patients' interweaves until they recollect the mental target without disturbances. The therapist makes sure that patients follow the task of just describing the picture. In order to support EMDR reprocessing, the therapist has to simplify the therapeutic process by being direct. Furthermore, the therapist interrupts patients as soon as they jump to another mental image again. The detail-oriented interweave appears to stimulate the blocked information processing system and the patients learn to follow their own processing path, which ensures a feeling of self-healing.

Phases 5 and 6 are according to the Standard EMDR Protocol.

In Phase 7: There should be closure at the end of each session. The therapist should think about the treatment plan and possible changes for the next session and choose the next target with the patient.

Experience shows that beginning treatment with in vivo desensitization, followed by EMDR Therapy, is most effective. Keep in mind that EMDR Therapy for patients suffering from OCD aims to improve their emotional regulation. Improving their emotional regulation strategies can enable them to build up their window of tolerance to address issues during in vivo desensitization. The reduction of OCD symptoms will be recognized in daily life situations.

OCD and EMDR Therapy Protocol Script

Phase 1: Client History

To find out about obsessions, ask the following:

Say, *"Do you have thoughts/mental images or ideas that are repetitive/or you keep thinking about?"*

If not, go to the following material on compulsions.

_____

_____

If so, say, *"Tell me about it."*

_____

_____

To find out about the severity:

Say, *"How much time during the day do you spend approximately on the _____ (state the obsession(s)) that you mentioned?"*

_____

_____

To find out about compulsions, say the following:

Say, *"What compulsions or repeated behavior/thoughts are you experiencing?"*

_____

_____

If the patient reveals compulsion(s) say, *"Tell me about it."*

_____

_____

Ask if it makes them feel safer:

Say, *"Do they make you feel any safer?"*

_____

_____

To find out about the severity:

Say, *"How much time during the day do you spend approximately on the _____ (state the relevant compulsion(s)) that you mentioned?"*

_____

_____

Determine the Obsessions and Compulsions in Detail

Say, *"It is important to distinguish between your obsessions and compulsions (if a patient has both). What exactly are your obsessions and what are your compulsions?"*

_____

_____

_____

Say, *"In which situations do your obsessions and/or compulsions occur?"*

_____

_____

Say, *"Describe the situation and related objects."*

_____

_____

Say, *"Please put these situations in an order that shows the severity between zero and a hundred."*

_____

_____

_____

_____

_____

_____

Identify Possible Traumas and Comorbid Diseases

Say, *"Do you suffer from any other symptoms or problems?"*

_____

_____

If so, say, *"Tell me about it."*

_____

_____

Say, *"Did your* _____ (state the relevant obsession and/or compulsion(s)) *start with a traumatic event or did you have any traumatic experience in your lifetime?"*

_____

_____

Say, *"How have you been dealing with your obsession(s) and or compulsion(s)?"*

_____

_____

Determine the Timeline (Hofmann & Luber, 2009)

Say, *"Today, I am going to ask you to remember the best and the worst memories connected with the obsessive thoughts or compulsive behaviors you have had and we will put them into this chart. We can start with about five and if there are more or less, that is fine. Where would you like to start?"*

_____

_____

Say, *"What is the first* _____ (worst or best) *memory that you can re-member throughout the whole timeline of your life? You do not have to go into all of the details because we will do that later."*

_____

_____

Say, *"How old were you when you had that* _____ *(worst or best) experience?"*

_____

_____

Only ask for the SUD scale for the worst memories.

Say, *"On a scale of 0 to 10, where 0 is no disturbance or neutral, and 10 is the highest disturbance you can imagine, how disturbing does it feel now?"*

0	1	2	3	4	5	6	7	8	9	10

(no disturbance)   (highest disturbance)

Create a Positive and Negative Memories Map with the client.

Say, *"Now that we have talked about the memories that are the most important to you in your life, let's create a map. We can put the positive or best memories on top of the 'Age' line and we can put the negative or worst ones memories under the 'Age' line. I have found it very helpful to see the important events in a person's life along the timeline. Where would you like to start?"*

_____

_____

Say, *"Do you have any thoughts about the timeline of your life now that we can see it? What do you think about what has happened in your life?"*

_____

_____

Say, *"Are there any particular themes that seem clearer to you now that you can 'see' the important memories of your life in front of you. Or, does anything of importance jump out to you?"*

_____

_____

Identify Affects Regulation Ability

Say, *"What emotions do you experience typically when you are experiencing* _____ *(state the obsession(s) and/or compulsions)?"*

_____

_____

Say, *"How do you handle negative emotions in general?"*

_____

_____

Say, *"To what or to whom do you attribute these negative emotions that you experience?"*

_____

_____

Say, *"How do you handle negative emotions in an OCD-triggered situation?"*

_____

_____

Note: The content of obsessions often has to do with issues of aggression, religion/blasphemy, and sexuality. The higher the moral standard, the higher the distress caused by the thought.

Say, *"Tell me about your views regarding aggression, religion/blasphemy, and sexuality. What kind of moral standards do you have concerning* _____ (state patient's obsessive thought)*?"*

_____

_____

If they are high, say, *"Tell me about it."*

_____

_____

Say, *"Would you consider learning how to modify these very high standards that you have?"*

_____

_____

Say, *"How do your obsessions and compulsions affect your social interactions?"*

_____

_____

Say, *"Are they helpful in assisting your handling of social situations and/or making you feel more powerful?"*

_____

_____

Identify Motivation for Treatment

Say, *"What are the consequences of your obsessive thoughts and compulsive behaviors? Please think about long- and short-term consequences, either positive or negative."*

_____

_____

Say, *"How does your* _____ (state the obsession or compulsion) *impact your daily living?"*

_____

_____

Say, *"What is your motivation for this therapy?"*

_____

_____

Say, *"How has your OCD affected you?"*

_____

_____

Say, *"How much are you suffering because of your OCD?"*

_____

_____

Say, *"How does your OCD affect your social interactions?"*

_____

_____

Say, *"Are others affected by your OCD?"*

_____

_____

Say, *"If you no longer had OCD, how would your life be different?"*

_____

_____

Say, *"Do you have any concerns about our therapeutic relationship?"*

_____

_____

Say, *"What are your goals for treatment? Please tell them to me in detail."*

_____

_____

Determine a Treatment Plan

Say, *"Based on what we talked about concerning your OCD, let's make a plan together and figure out how we will work together to address your OCD. Our goal should be a long-term reduction of your* _____ (state obsession and/or compulsion behaviors). *For this it is necessary to combine work on your emotions and life events using EMDR Therapy, and on the behavior itself, using in vivo desensitization."*

If using Treatment A, say the following:

A. Say, *"To build the best treatment plan for you, I would suggest we start with an exercise called in vivo desensitization. This means that you face a trigger situation or object and do not react by using your compulsive behaviors or avoidance. I would like to start with something that is of a medium-sized difficulty. After we have done these exercises, we will use EMDR to process your emotions and conflicts that are underlying your OCD. Does this make sense to you?"*

_____

_____

Say, *"Do you have any questions about it?"*

_____

_____

If using Treatment B, say the following:

B. Say, *"To build the best treatment plan for you, I would suggest starting with EMDR sessions to help us find out more about your goals and emotions. With EMDR, it is helpful to start with the most difficult situations we discussed and then we will focus on in vivo desensitization. When using in vivo desensitization, you will face a trigger situation or object and not react by using your compulsive behaviors or avoidance. Does this sequence make sense to you?"*

_____

_____

Say, *"Do you have any questions about it?"*

_____

_____

Note: In most cases, Treatment Plan A is used. Treatment Plan B is indicated if your patient lacks goals and self-confidence. Make sure that your treatment plan includes in vivo desensitization after working with EMDR.

Phase 2: Preparation Phase

Step 1: Check for stabilization

Say, *"Please imagine a safe place. Tell me about it."*

_____

_____

Step 2: Apply psychoeducation and EMDR

Say, *"Throughout EMDR processing, we are going to stop and examine the target from time to time. You can control the situation at any time by putting your hand up to let me know that you want to stop. I will also ask you to take responsibility for yourself by letting me know about any feelings or images that come up when we stop. I need brief, precise feedback from you, best in one or two sentences. I will ask you what you are experiencing in that particular moment—sometimes you will feel a change, sometimes you will not. There are no 'supposed to's.' Try, as accurately as possible, to describe what you are experiencing in that moment, but without evaluating it. It is important that you allow whatever is happening to happen. Then we will use bilateral stimulation for a little while, and after that we will talk about it. I want you to feel comfortable. If you feel any discomfort, you are to raise your hand as a stop signal at any time. Before we actually start, let's try an exercise that gives you an example of how EMDR will work."*

Step 3: Make the target selection now

Note: Doing the target selection in Phase 2 instead of in Phase 1 is necessary because, with OCD patients, extended information gathering and preparation are necessary.

Say, *"Based on our work, what are the most difficult situations or images you have? They can be in the past, present, or future, related to your OCD or not. Tell me about them."*

_____

_____

The following types of targets can be elicited from patients with OCD:

- Traumatic memory:

Say, *"Where and when did the* _____ (state the obsession(s)) *first occur?"*

_____

_____

Say, *"Based on the timeline you made, it is helpful to look at the worst incidents in your life. What has the highest SUD for you?"*

_____

_____

Say, *"On a scale from 0 to 10, how strong was the desire to follow that* _____ (state the target)*?"*

0   1   2   3   4   5   6   7   8   9   10

(no desire)   (highest desire)

- Worst case scenario/flashforward:

Say, *"What is the worst that could happen, if you don't use compulsive behaviors or avoidance in an obsessive situation? Tell me in detail."*

_____

_____

Say, *"OK, if this is the worst thing that could happen, what would happen next?"*

_____

_____

Say, *"OK. What do you think will happen with it, even after death?"*

_____

_____

Say, *"On a scale from 0 to 10, how strong was the desire to follow that* _____
(state the target)?"

0	1	2	3	4	5	6	7	8	9	10

(no desire)   (highest desire)

- Disastrous obsessive mental images:

Say, *"What is the worst image or mental picture you had concerning your obsessive thoughts? Tell me in detail."*

_____

_____

Say, *"On a scale from 0 to 10, how strong was the desire to follow that* _____
(state the target)?"

0	1	2	3	4	5	6	7	8	9	10

(no desire)   (highest desire)

- Imaginary blocking compulsive action:

Say, *"Please imagine being in a trigger situation for your OCD, but the use of the compulsion is not possible. Let's find an example for that. Do you have one?"*

_____

_____

Say, *"Which picture is the most difficult one in this scene?"*

_____

_____

Say, *"On a scale from 0 to 10, how strong was the desire to follow that* _____
(state the target)?"

0	1	2	3	4	5	6	7	8	9	10

(no desire)   (highest desire)

- Imaginary trigger situation:

Say, *"What is the worst obsessive trigger situation or object to you that arouses your distress and anxiety? It can be something that happened in your past, or could be imagined in the future. Tell me in detail."*

_____

_____

Say, *"Please imagine resisting your compulsion to* _____ *(state the ritual used)."*

_____

_____

Say, *"What would be the worst picture you can imagine associated with this situation?"*

_____

_____

Say, *"On a scale from 0 to 10, how strong was the desire to follow that* _____ *(state the target)?"*

0	1	2	3	4	5	6	7	8	9	10

(no desire)   (highest desire)

• Real trigger situation:

Say, *"Do you have a trigger situation or object that you can see in the office? In other words, something that triggers your OCD, which is around here? Tell me in detail."*

_____

_____

Say, *"On a scale from 0 to 10, how strong was the desire to follow that* _____ *(state the target)?"*

0	1	2	3	4	5	6	7	8	9	10

(no desire)   (highest desire)

The target image for the EMDR process is the one that arouses the patients' anxiety and distress the most and triggers their obsessions and/or compulsions.

Say, *"What image represents the most disturbing part of* _____ *(state the issue)?"*

_____

_____

Say, *"Is it OK to begin working with this target?"* (Make sure to get consent.)

_____

_____

In general, while working with patients suffering from OCD, it is indispensable to emphasize that although they need a certain amount of control, they also need to take responsibility for their own actions.

Say, *"To help you achieve your goal to decrease and/or eliminate your OCD, it is very important that you learn to manage the images, thoughts, emotions, sensations, forgotten traumatic events, or distressing moments that will come up. Would you be willing to take on this responsibility?"*

_____

_____

If no, say, *"Let's work on that. What would you need to take on that risk?"*

_____

_____

Phase 3: Assessment

In vivo desensitization should be implemented as described earlier (Treatment Plan in Phase 1: A or B).

Say, *"Before we start using EMDR today, which exercises did you do between the sessions? Tell me about them."*

_____

_____

Target Selection

In Phase 3, follow the Standard EMDR Protocol with the target chosen in Phase 1 or 2. It is the real-life situation or mental image that arouses the patient's distress the most, has the highest SUD, and triggers the patient's obsessive thoughts and/or compulsive behaviors.

Say, *"What picture represents the most disturbing part of this target?"*

_____

_____

Obtaining NC and PC

For patients with OCD, the NC is a representation of the underlying central obsessive thought. It is important that this obsessive thought be generalizable. Patients often report obsessive thoughts that are too specific, such as "the stove is still on." In this case, the therapist needs to help the patient verbalize the underlying and generalizable obsessive thought, such as "I am dangerous."

When working with OCD patients, the therapist will encounter two main categories of NCs concerning safety: "I am dangerous" (e.g., I will stab my child) or "I am in danger" (e.g., The bacteria will kill me); some patients have both. If it is the latter, take the stronger one or go for the self-confidence issue ("I am worthless") or the control domain ("I have no control").

NEGATIVE COGNITION

Say, *"What words best go with the picture that express your negative belief about yourself now?"*

_____

_____

POSITIVE COGNITION

> Say, *"When you bring up the picture of the target, what would you like to believe about yourself instead?"*

_____

_____

Validity of Cognition

> Say, *"When you bring up this picture, how true do those words* _____ (repeat the PC) *feel to you now on a scale of 1 to 7, where 1 feels completely false and 7 feels completely true?"*

_____

_____

1	2	3	4	5	6	7
(completely false)				(completely true)		

Sometimes, it is necessary to explain further.

> Say, *"Remember, sometimes we know something with our head, but it feels differently in our gut. In this case, what is the gut-level feeling of the truth of* _____ (state the PC), *from 1 (completely false) to 7 (completely true)?"*

_____

_____

1	2	3	4	5	6	7
(completely false)				(completely true)		

Emotions

At this point, emotions are just briefly mentioned but not further explored.

> Say, *"When you bring up the picture or* _____ (state the issue) *and those words* _____ (state the NC), *what emotion do you feel now?"*

_____

_____

Subjective Units of Disturbance

> Say, *"On a scale of 0 to 10, where 0 is no disturbance or neutral and 10 is the highest disturbance you can imagine, how disturbing does it feel now?"*

0	1	2	3	4	5	6	7	8	9	10
(no disturbance)							(highest disturbance)			

Location of Body Sensation

Bodily sensations are perceived but not further explored.

Say, *"Where do you feel it* (the disturbance) *in your body?"*

_____

_____

Phase 4: Desensitization Phase

During the Desensitization Phase for patients with OCD, the Standard EMDR Protocol is used to process all targets.

> Say, *"Now, remember, it is your own brain that is doing the healing and you are the one in control. I will ask you to mentally focus on the target and to follow my fingers* (or any other BLS you are using). *Just let whatever happens, happen, and we will talk at the end of the set. Just tell me what comes up, and don't discard anything as unimportant. Any new information that comes to mind is connected in some way. If you want to stop, just raise your hand."*

> Then say, *"Bring up the picture and the words _____* (repeat the NC) *and notice where you feel it in your body. Now follow my fingers with your eyes* (or other BLS)."

If there are blockages, a few changes might be necessary, especially when working with patients who have an excessive need to please. Use the "detail-oriented" interweave.

If the detail-oriented interweave is needed, say the following:

Note: It is important that the therapist get the patient's consent for this exercise, as it gives a feeling of control and safety.

> Say, *"Before we go on, let's try something different. Would that be OK with you?"*

_____

_____

> Say, *"Look at the picture that is your target for today. Please describe the picture in detail."*

_____

_____

> Say, *"I want you to focus on that picture. Each time I ask you to tell me 'what is there,' please just tell me what you see in that picture. Even if the picture disappeared during the bilateral stimulation, please go back to it and just tell me what you see. Please do not focus on your emotions, thoughts, or body sensations. Just tell me in one or two sentences about what you see in your picture. Is that clear to you?"*

_____

_____

continued

If no, say, *"Look at the picture on that wall. Describe the picture in detail, please!"* (Make sure there is no interpretation with it, just a pure description of the picture.)

_____

_____

If so, say, *"Now, could you do the same with the picture we want to work with? When you go back to the original incident, what appears?"*

_____

_____

To continue with the BLS, say, *"Concentrate on that picture. OK, have you got it? Go with that."*

_____

_____

If the patient concentrates on the picture, say, *"Go with that."*

_____

_____

If the patient talks about any other aspect, say, *"Please go back to the picture; what do you see?"*

_____

_____

As soon as the therapist notices that the patient is back into the EMDR reprocessing, the therapist continues with the standard process of desensitization (Böhm, 2011). The patient will show that she is back into EMDR reprocessing by a concentrated focus on the bilateral stimulation, as well as following her internal process without disturbance.

Use sets of eye movements or other BLS until the SUD is 0.

Say, *"On a scale of 0 to 10, where 0 is no disturbance or neutral and 10 is the highest disturbance you can imagine, how disturbing does it feel now?"*

0   1   2   3   4   5   6   7   8   9   10

(no disturbance)   (highest disturbance)

Phase 5: Installation

Install PC

Say, *"Do the words* _____ (repeat the PC) *still fit, or is there another positive statement that feels better?"* (Check first if the positive thought is still valid.)

_____

_____

Say, *"As you think of the incident, how do the words _____ (repeat the PC) feel to you now on a scale of 1 to 7, where 1 feels completely false and 7 feels completely true?"*

    1   2   3   4   5   6   7

(completely false)   (completely true)

Say, *"Think of the event and hold it together with the words _____ (repeat the PC). Go with that."*

_____

_____

Continue until the goal of a Validity of Cognition (VoC) of 7 is reached.

Phase 6: Body Scan

Say, *"Close your eyes and keep in mind the original memory and the positive cognition. Then bring your attention to the different parts of your body, starting with your head and working downward. Any place you find any tension, tightness, or unusual sensation, tell me."*

_____

_____

If any sensation is reported, the therapist introduces BLS. Positive or comfortable sensations are strengthened by slow BLS, whereas negative sensations are dealt with by fast BLS.

Say, *"How is the sensation now?"*

_____

_____

Continue until any negative sensations have disappeared.

Phase 7: Closure

Say, *"What changes do you feel? What have you learned today?"*

_____

_____

Say, *"Things may come up or they may not. If they do, great. Write it down and it can be a target for next time. You can use a log to write down triggers, images, thoughts or cognitions, emotions, and sensations. You can rate them on our 0 to 10 scale where 0 is no disturbance or neutral and 10 is the worst disturbance. Please write down the positive experiences, too."*

"If you get any new memories, dreams, or situations that disturb you, just take a good snapshot. It isn't necessary to give a lot of detail. Just put down enough to remind you so we can target it next time. The same thing goes for any positive dreams or situations. If negative feelings do come up, try not to make them significant. Remember, it's still just the old stuff. Just write it down for next time. Then use the Safe Place exercise to let go of as much of the disturbance as possible. Even if nothing comes up, make sure to use your in vivo exercises every day and give me a call if you need to."

Treatment Plan Including Exposures to Triggers in Daily Life

At the end of each session, the therapist should think about the treatment plan and possible changes for the next session. Work with the target from the last session until it is fully processed or choose the next target if the last one was completed.

> Say, *"How are you doing and how do you think we did during the EMDR reprocessing?"*

_____

_____

> Say, *"We are finished with today's target. Is there a new one that we should continue with next time?"*

_____

_____

Furthermore, the therapist should think about and decide on the right time to combine EMDR and in vivo desensitization. Keep in mind that EMDR for patients suffering from OCD aims to improve their emotional regulation. Improving their emotional regulation strategies can enable them to build up their window of tolerance to address issues during in vivo desensitization. The reduction of OCD symptoms will be recognized in daily life situations.

When the SUDs of the EMDR targets = 0, introduce the following:

> Say, *"Great, now you have found out a lot about your emotions and related life events with the processing that we did today. You can handle them better. I want you now to notice whether this helps you in fighting against your OCD in your daily life. Therefore, I want to ask you if you would be willing to expose yourself to difficult situations or objects between this session and the next session. Would you be willing to do that?"*

_____

_____

If the exposure seems to be too difficult to be done by the patient alone, say the following:

> Say, *"I would like to use our next sessions to assist you in exposing yourself to a difficult situation that triggers your obsessive thinking. Would you be willing for us to do that together?"*

_____

_____

> Say, *"What are the triggers that most strongly activate your obsessive thinking and/or compulsive behaviors? Let's choose one for you to work on at home."* (Use the hierarchy of OCD situations made in Phase 1.)

_____

_____

> Say, *"How big is the urge to follow your _____ (state the appropriate obsession(s) and/or compulsion(s)) now on a scale of 0 to 10, where 0 is no disturbance or neutral and 10 is the highest disturbance you can imagine, how disturbing does it feel now?"*

0	1	2	3	4	5	6	7	8	9	10

(no disturbance)   (highest disturbance)

Say, *"Have you noticed any improvements?"*

_____

_____

Phase 8: Reevaluation

In this phase the therapist and patient evaluate the last session. It is also important to check on homework, for example, logs.

Say, *"Focus on the target of our last session _____ (mention the target). On a scale of 0 to 10, where 0 is no disturbance or neutral and 10 is the highest disturbance you can imagine, how disturbing does it feel now?"*

0	1	2	3	4	5	6	7	8	9	10

(no disturbance)   (highest disturbance)

Say, *"Is there something you have noticed over the period of time since your last session?"*

_____

_____

Say, *"After successfully dealing with the last target, what target do you want to work on next?"*

_____

_____

Say, *"Let's have a look at your log and exercises. What have you worked on and written since our last session?"*

_____

_____

Continue to work with each target until SUDs = 0 and VoC = 7. Also, include present triggers and future templates, as well as any other experiences that emerge during the reprocessing or in between sessions from the past.

Summary

EMDR Therapy can be used successfully for the treatment of OCD patients. The treatment plan requires a deep understanding and knowledge of obsessions and compulsions as well as EMDR Therapy. To be effective, the EMDR Therapy protocol should be adapted in the way described here. Otherwise, these patients—with their need to feel in control—feel out of control and show blockages, which make the EMDR Therapy process ineffective. At the end of the described treatment, patients have worked both on their obsessions and compulsions as well as on their affect regulation. The combination of in vivo desensitization with EMDR Therapy is strongly recommended to obtain a long-lasting and effective therapy outcome.

References

American Psychiatric Association (APA). (2007). Practice guideline for the treatment of patients with obsessive-compulsive disorder. *American Journal Psychiatry, 164*, 1–56.

American Psychiatric Association (APA). (2013). *Diagnostic and statistical manual of mental disorders: Fifth edition: DSM-5*. Washington, DC: Author.

Bekkers, A. F. M. I. (1999). Enige ervaringen met EMDR bij dwang. In W. P. Haaijman, Ph. H. J. Diepstraten, & R. E. O. van Schevikhoven (Eds.), *Ongewoon en anders*. 25 jaar kliniek Overwaal te Lent. Nederlands: Boekwinkeltjes.

Böhm, K. (2011). Die Therapiemethode EMDR bei Zwängen. *Z-aktuell, 4*, 6–7.

Böhm, K., & Voderholzer, U. (2010). Use of EMDR in the treatment of obsessive-compulsive disorders: A case series. *Verhaltenstherapie, 20*, 175–181. doi:10.1159/000319439

Fricke, S., Köhler, S., & Moritz, S. (2007). Frühe interpersonale Traumatisierung bei Zwangserkrankungen: Eine Pilotstudie. *Verhaltenstherapie, 17*(4), 243–250.

Gershuny, B. S., Baer, L., Parker, H., Gentes, E. L., Infield, A. L., & Jenike, M. A. (2007). Trauma and posttraumatic stress disorder in treatment-resistant obsessive-compulsive disorder. *Depress Anxiety* Feb 22 [Epub ahead of print]. doi:10.1002/da.20284

Gershuny, B. S., Baer, L., Wilson, K. A., Radomsky, A. S., & Jenike, M. A. (2003). Connections among symptoms of obsessive-compulsive disorder and posttraumatic stress disorder: A case series. *Behavior Research Therapy, 41*, 1029–1041.

Hofmann, A. (2009). *EMDR: Therapie psychotraumatischer Belastungsstörung*. Stuttgart: Thieme.

Hofmann, A., & Luber, M. (2009). History talking: The time line. In M. Luber (Ed.), *Eye movement desensitization and reprocessing (EMDR) scripted protocols: Basics and special populations*. New York, NY: Springer.

Hohagen, F., Wahl-Kordon A., Lotz-Rambaldi, W., & Muche-Borowski, C. (2015). Deutschen Gesellschaft für Psychiatrie und Psychotherapie, Psychosomatik und Nervenheilkunde (DGPPN) *S3-Leitlinie Zwangsstörungen*. AWMF Number 038-017. Heidelberg, Germany: Springer.

Maier, S., Kuelz, A. K., & Voderholzer, U. (2009). Traumatisierung und Dissoziationsneigung bei Zwangserkrankten: Ein Überblick. *Verhaltenstherapie, 19*, 219–227. doi:10.1159/000247333

National Collaborating Centre for Mental Health (NCCMH). (2006). *Obsessive-compulsive disorder: Core interventions in the treatment of obsessive-compulsive disorder and body dysmorphic disorder* (National Clinical Practice Guideline Number 31). Leicester, England: British Psychological Society & The Royal College of Psychiatrists.

Ruscio, A. M., Stein, D. J., Chiu, W. T., & Kessler, R. C. (2010). The epidemiology of obsessive-compulsive disorder in the National Comorbidity Survey Replication. *Molecular Psychiatry, 15*(1), 53–63.

Voderholzer, U., Schlegl, S., & Külz, A. K. (2011). Epidemiology and health care situation of obsessive-compulsive disorders. *Nervenarzt, 82*(3), 273–274.

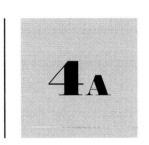

SUMMARY SHEET:
Obsessive-Compulsive Disorder and EMDR Therapy

Karsten Böhm
SUMMARY SHEET BY MARILYN LUBER

Name: _____ Diagnosis: _____

☑ Check when task is completed, response has changed, or to indicate symptoms or diagnosis.

Note: This material is meant as a checklist for your response. Please keep in mind that it is only a reminder of different tasks that may or may not apply to your client.

Introduction

DSM-5 Criteria Obsessive-Compulsive Disorder

☐ *Obsessions*: Thoughts, mental images, or ideas that keep coming back and are intrusive and unwanted; for example, "I could have been affected by a serious illness" after touching door handles or shaking hands.

☐ *Compulsions*: The individual feels driven to repeat behaviors and mental acts as a reaction to an obsession or rules that must be used strictly to avoid or decrease distress or some feared situation; for example, washing hands in a ritualized fashion after touching a door handle or shaking hands.

The Standard Treatment for OCD

Current therapy guidelines consider both exposure and response prevention (ERP) and cognitive therapy as standard treatment for obsessive-compulsive disorder (OCD; DGPPN, 2013; American Psychiatric Association [APA], 2007).

☐ *Exposure*: To confront the patient with cues that trigger obsessive thoughts (i.e., words, situations, or images)

☐ *Response prevention*: To tell the patient *not to* do the behavior, which is meant to prevent feared consequences from occurring; 15% to 40% of patients do not benefit significantly from this standard treatment (NCCMH, 2006)

EMDR Therapy and the Standard Treatment for OCD

Standard treatments—patients learn to leave the compulsions undone and to resist the compulsive performance of rituals in real-life situations. Starts with moderate anxiety.

Eye movement desensitization and reprocessing (EMDR) Therapy—the emotional aspects of the issues can be integrated better, so that patients are able to transfer their emotional learning to everyday life and to tolerate their emotional distress. Starts with most distressing.

Sequencing Standard OCD Treatment With EMDR Therapy

Sequencing depends on personality style:

☐ *Anxious and fearful personality style:* They often lack the motivation for risk-taking. In this case, it is important to *reduce emotional distress first*, which can best be achieved with EMDR Therapy. Improving the emotional regulation strategies enables these OCD patients to address issues with in vivo work as the second step.

☐ *Narcissistic personality style*: Patients who already have some sort of inner motivation to take a risk, and need to experience success, benefit from a therapy addressing in vivo work first, for example, ERP or cognitive therapy (Böhm, 2011). The regulation of the emotions through EMDR Therapy is focused on as the second step.

Obsessive-Compulsive Disorder and EMDR Therapy Script Notes

Determine the Type of OCD (Obsessions and/or Compulsions) and Its Severity

The first step is a thorough diagnostic analysis, following the criteria of *DSM-5* (300.3; APA, 2013), to see if the patient fulfills the criteria for the diagnosis of OCD. For EMDR Therapy, the therapist must be able to differentiate between obsessions and compulsions, as the focus is on the obsessions and not on the compulsions as targets (the discussion of target selection in Phase 2 gives more details).

Obsessions include the following types of thoughts:

☐ Repetitive thoughts, impulses or mental pictures that are experienced as unwanted and disturbing; they produce fear and despair in most individuals
☐ Trying to overlook, repress, or neutralize these thoughts, impulses, or mental pictures with other ideas of actions

Compulsions include the following types of behaviors and mental acts:

☐ Driven to execute recurrent behaviors (hand washing, arraying, checking) and mental acts (praying, counting, replicating words) as a reaction to an obsession or rules, which must be performed perfectly
☐ Performances or mental acts are intended to avoid or decrease distress or some feared situation; however, these performances or mental acts are not an accurate, appropriate, or effective response to the distress or feared situation and do not neutralize or prevent them

Determine the Obsessions and Compulsions in Detail

Identify Possible Traumas and Comorbid Diseases

Testing:

☐ Yale–Brown Obsessive Compulsive Scale (Y-BOCS)
☐ Beck Depression Inventory II (BDI-II)
☐ Posttraumatic Stress Diagnostic Scale (PDS)

Contraindications for the use of EMDR for OCD:

- ☐ High levels of dissociation
- ☐ Psychosis diagnosis
- ☐ Critical physical diseases
- ☐ Severe personality disorders

Identify Affect Regulation Ability

Typical Emotions: ☐ Anxiety   ☐ Disgust   ☐ Shame   ☐ Guilt   ☐ Failure   ☐ Loneliness
☐ Inner Emptiness   ☐ Boredom   ☐ Anger
Delegates responsibility away from self for   ☐ Intrapsychic and   ☐ Interpersonal
situations

Obsessions and compulsions can be used to regulate social interactions
- ☐ Controlling closeness and distance
- ☐ Finding an outlet for suppressed aggression against others
- ☐ Dealing with conflict and its resolution
- ☐ Handling social deficits and difficulties
- ☐ Accomplishing something that can be admired by others

Identify Motivation for Treatment

Determine a Treatment Plan

The usual sequence in using EMDR Therapy and in vivo desensitization is the following:

- ☐ Treatment Plan A: Start with in vivo desensitization and then alternate to EMDR Therapy. Patients tend to avoid in vivo desensitization, so by using EMDR Therapy for a longer period of time, patients get used to avoiding in vivo desensitization and will not easily agree to it later in therapy. Findings show (Bekkers, 1999; Böhm & Voderholzer, 2010) that EMDR Therapy alone is not successful in most OCD patients.
- ☐ Treatment Plan B: The exception is with patients who do not have any real goals in their lives and do not know what they are "fighting" for. With these patients, start with a longer period of EMDR sessions focusing on building up goals and the willingness to take risks to reach them. Human beings only take risks in their lives when their goal(s) is/are compelling. If the only goal is to suffer less, more often than not, OCD patients will choose their OCD. Only if they know what they are fighting for will they face and "fight" in these difficult circumstances.

OCD and EMDR Therapy Protocol Script

Phase 1: Client History

Obsessions

Detail: _____

_____

_____

Severity: _____

Description of situations in which obsessions occur: _____

_____

_____

Compulsions

Detail: _____

_____

Feel safer after: □ Yes   □ No

Severity: _____

Description of situations in which obsessions occur: _____

_____

_____

Hierarchy of obsessions and compulsions (0 to 100) showing the severity

_____

_____

_____

Other comorbid diseases: _____

_____

Determine the Timeline (Hofmann & Luber, 2009)

"Let's draw a timeline of your panic history and traumatic experiences until now. The horizontal line represents the time, and the vertical line the severity of the symptoms."

Identify Affect Regulation Ability

Typical Emotions: □ Anxiety   □ Disgust   □ Shame   □ Guilt   □ Failure   □ Loneliness
□ Inner Emptiness   □ Boredom   □ Anger

Handling negative emotions in OCD-triggered situations: _____

_____

_____

Views regarding aggression, religion/blasphemy, and sexuality: _____

_____

_____

Affect on social interactions: _____

_____

Identify Motivation for Treatment

Consequence of OCD: _____

_____

Impact on daily living: _____

_____

Therapy motivation: _____

_____

Suffering caused by OCD: _____

_____

Impact on social interactions: _____

_____

Life if no OCD: _____

_____

Goals for treatment: _____

_____

Determine a Treatment Plan

☐ TREATMENT A

☐ TREATMENT B

Phase 2: Preparation

Step 1: Check for Stabilization

Safe Place   ☐ Yes ☐ No   Describe: _____

_____

Other resource(s)   ☐ Yes ☐ No   Describe: _____

_____

Step 2: Apply Psychoeducation

OCD

EMDR

Step 3: Make the Target Selection Now

☐ Traumatic memory   SUDs: _____ /10

Target/Memory/Image: _____

_____

☐ Worst-case scenario/Flashforward   SUDs: _____ /10

Target/Memory/Image: _____

_____

☐ Disastrous obsessive mental images   SUDs: _____ /10

Target/Memory/Image:_____

_____

☐ Imaginary blocking compulsive action   SUDs: _____ /10

Target/Memory/Image: _____

_____

☐ Imaginary trigger situation   SUDs: _____ /10

Target/Memory/Image: _____

_____

☐ Real trigger situation   SUDs: _____ /10

Target/Memory/Image: _____

_____

Phase 3: Assessment

Past Memories

Target Selection

Target/Memory/Image: _____

_____

Obtaining Negative and Positive Cognitions

NC: _____

PC: _____

VoC: _____ /7

Emotions: _____

SUDs: _____ /10

Sensation: _____

Phase 4: Desensitization

"Now, remember, it is your own brain that is doing the healing and you are the one in control. I will ask you to mentally focus on the target and to follow my fingers (or any other BLS you are using). *Just let whatever happens, happen, and we will talk at the end of the*

set. Just tell me what comes up, and don't discard anything as unimportant. Any new information that comes to mind is connected in some way. If you want to stop, just raise your hand. Bring up the picture and the words _____ (repeat the NC) and notice where you feel it in your body. Now follow my fingers with your eyes (or other BLS)."

Detail-Oriented Interweave

- ☐ If there are blockages, a few changes might be necessary, especially when working with patients who have an excessive need to please. Use the detail-oriented interweave.
  Describe picture/target in detail + BLS. Only focus on picture and not emotions, thoughts, or body sensations. Report details of picture until can return to Standard EMDR Protocol.
- ☐ If can't go into detail on target, use something in office to practice and then follow above.

Phase 5: Installation

PC: ☐ Completed

New PC (if new one is better): _____

VoC: _____ /7

Incident + PC + BLS

Phase 6: Body Scan

"Close your eyes and keep in mind the experience (e.g., an urge to perform a compulsion) that you will have in the future. Then bring your attention to the different parts of your body, starting with your head and working downward. Any place you find any tension, tightness, or unusual sensation, tell me."

If positive, add BLS.

If negative/discomfort, reprocess until discomfort subsides.

Check VoC: _____ /10

Phase 7: Closure

Changes you feel: _____

_____

Explain expectations between sessions:

> *"Things may come up or they may not. If they do, great. Write it down and it can be a target for next time. If you get any new memories, dreams, or situations that disturb you, just take a good snapshot. It isn't necessary to give a lot of detail. Just put down enough to remind you so we can target it next time. The same thing goes for any positive dreams or situations. If negative feelings do come up, try not to make them significant. Remember, it's still just the old stuff. Just write it down for next time."*

Treatment Plan Including Exposures to Triggers in Daily Life

Target finished: ☐ Yes   ☐ No

New target: ☐ Yes   ☐ No

Describe: _____

_____

Exposure to difficult situations or objects between sessions: ☐ Yes   ☐ No"

If yes: *"Great, now you have found out a lot about your emotions and related life events with the processing that we did today. You can handle them better. I want you, now, to notice whether this helps you in fighting against your OCD in your daily life. Therefore, I want to ask you if you would be willing to expose yourself to difficult situations or objects between this session and the next session. Would you be willing to do that?"*

If no: *"I would like to use our next sessions to assist you in exposing yourself to a difficult situation that triggers your obsessive thinking. Would you be willing for us to do that together?"*

                                                                                ☐ Yes   ☐ No

Triggers activating obsessive thinking or compulsive behavior:

_____

_____

Urge to follow obsession and/or compulsions now: _____ /10

Improvements   ☐ Yes   ☐ No

Describe: _____

_____

Present Triggers

Phase 8: Reevaluation

Last target: _____ /10

Log/Noticed: _____

_____

References

American Psychiatric Association. (2007). Practice guideline for the treatment of patients with obsessive-compulsive disorder. *American Journal of Psychiatry, 164*, 1–56.

American Psychiatric Association. (2013). *Diagnostic and statistical manual of mental disorders: Fifth edition: DSM-5*. Washington, DC: Author.

Bekkers, A. F. M. I. (1999). Enige ervaringen met EMDR bij dwang. In W. P. Haaijman, Ph. H. J. Diepstraten, & R. E. O. van Schevikhoven (Eds.), *Ongewoon en anders*. 25 jaar kliniek Overwaal te Lent. The Netherlands: Boekwinkeltjes.

Böhm, K. (2011). Die Therapiemethode EMDR bei Zwängen. *Z-aktuell, 4*, 6–7.

Böhm, K., & Voderholzer, U. (2010). Use of EMDR in the treatment of obsessive-compulsive disorders: A case series. *Verhaltenstherapie, 20*, 175–181. doi:10.1159/000319439

Deutsche Gesellschaft für Psychiatrie und Psychotherapie, Psychosomatik und Nervenheilkunde (DGPPN): Hohagen, F., Wahl-Kordon A., Lotz-Rambaldi, W., & Muche-Borowski, C. (2015). *S3-Leitlinie Zwangsstörungen. AWMF Number 038–017*. Heidelberg, Germany: Springer.

Hofmann, A., & Luber, M. (2009). History talking: The time line. In M. Luber (Ed.), *Eye movement desensitization and reprocessing (EMDR) scripted protocols: Basics and special populations.* New York, NY: Springer.

National Collaborating Centre for Mental Health (NCCMH). (2006). *Obsessive-compulsive disorder: Core interventions in the treatment of obsessive-compulsive disorder and body dysmorphic disorder* (National Clinical Practice Guideline Number 31). Leicester, England: British Psychological Society & The Royal College of Psychiatrists.

Body Dysmorphic Disorder and Olfactory Reference Syndrome EMDR Therapy Protocol

Therese McGoldrick, Millia Begum, and Keith Brown

Introduction

The features of body dysmorphic disorder (BDD) and olfactory reference syndrome (ORS) have been described for more than a century, but both disorders have proven resistant to easy classification. Both conditions share similarities in onset, demographics, symptom profile, and response to treatment. Both also have a high rate of attempted suicide (Munro, 1982; Phillips, Coles, et al., 2005). There has been considerable discussion about their phenomenology, but little attention has been paid to the possibility of traumatic precipitants.

BDD is a relatively common, severe, and frequently underdiagnosed disorder (Conroy et al., 2008; Phillips, Didie et al., 2008). In 1891, BDD was first described by Morselli (1891) and further elaborated on by Janet (1903), then Kraepelin (1909–1915). In 1959, Freud described one of his patients as the "Wolf-Man." Later, Brunswick (1971) did a further analysis on the Wolf-Man and described in detail his preoccupation and related extreme distress regarding his nose.

The core feature in BDD is *a preoccupation with an imagined defect in appearance causing clinically significant distress or impairment without or with minimal evidence to support the belief*. The most commonly occurring preoccupations are with the skin, hair, and nose, and it is known that sufferers are frequently comorbid with other conditions, most commonly mood disorders, psychotic disorders, substance misuse, and personality disorders (Phillips, Mernard et al., 2005). The disorder is seriously debilitating, with checking, avoidance, and camouflage behaviors taking up to several hours per day and affecting all areas of the sufferer's life, often causing hospitalization and suicide. Almost 40% of these patients hold their beliefs with delusional intensity (American Psychiatric Association, 2013; Philips, McElroy, Keck, Hudson, & Pope, 1993).

ORS was first described as a hallucination of smell (Potts, 1891), and investigated extensively by Pryse-Philips (1971), who coined the term to differentiate between the olfactory symptoms seen in this condition from similar symptoms that may be present in schizophrenia, severe depression, and temporal lobe epilepsy. It has been explored in the literature under various terms, including bromidrosiphobia (Sutton, 1919), chronic olfactory paranoid syndrome (Videbech, 1966), monosymptomatic hypochondriasis (Bishop, 1980), and monosymptomatic hypochondriacal psychosis (Munro, 1982). The core feature of ORS is *a belief that the person emits strong foul body odor despite lack of physical evidence for the same*. As with BDD, there is associated clinically significant distress, and moderate to extreme and incapacitating impairment in social, occupational, or other important areas of functioning, with a high proportion experiencing psychiatric hospitalization.

The psychological origins and the nature of these rigidly held beliefs in BDD or ORS are not well understood. Whether these beliefs come under either anxiety or obsessional disorders (Stein, Le Roux, Bouwer, & van Heerden, 1998) or perhaps even a delusional disorder or simply a disorder of overvalued ideas (McKenna, 1984) is still debated. BDD now comes under the category of Hypochondriasis in (*International Classification of Diseases 10* (ICD-10; WHO, 1994) and Obsessive-Compulsive and Related Disorders in the *Diagnostic and Statistical Manual of Mental Disorders* (*DSM-5*; American Psychiatric Association, 2013). Presently, ORS comes under the "unspecified" category in *DSM-5* and is classed as a delusional disorder in ICD-10.

Diagnostic Criteria for Body Dysmorphic Disorder and Olfactory Reference Syndrome

Body Dysmorphic Disorder (BDD) is characterized by a constant worry about one or more self-perceived defects or imperfections concerning physical appearance that are not visible or appear insubstantial to others. During BDD, repetitive behaviors occur (such as mirror checking, skin picking) or mental acts (comparision of behavior with others). This fixation can cause distress ranging to impairment in professional, social, or others areas of functioning. The preoccupation with appearance is not explained by concerns with weight in those who meet the criteria for eating disorder. If the person is overfocused on a body that is perceived as too small or not muscular enough, use the specifier, "With muscle dysmorphia." It is also helpful to specify the degree of insight concerning beliefs about BDD: with good or fair insight; with poor insight; with absent insight/delusional beliefs.

Olfactory Reference Syndrome (ORS) is under the category of "Other Specified Obsessive-Compulsive and Related Disorder" and has to do with the conviction that the body or its functions are offensive to others and focuses on the affected individual's embarrassment.

Research

The research studies are limited in both these conditions and may be a consequence of those affected not believing that their illness may be related to psychological origins and instead approaching physicians, dermatologists, dentists, surgeons, and various other health professionals. The prevalence of BDD is 0.7% to 1.1% in community samples, 2% to 13% of nonclinical student samples, and 13% to 16% of psychiatric inpatients (Conroy et al., 2008; Phillips, 1991). The prevalence of ORS is not known. A recent world systematic review of the literature of over a century identified only 84 patients who strictly met all criteria for ORS, excluding other major mental disorders or substance misuse or ongoing medical conditions (Begum & McKenna, 2010).

Clients with these fixed beliefs of flaws in appearance or personal body odor are considered to have poor prognosis in general. Treatment options have been nonspecific, with clinicians using a range of pharmacological and psychological interventions without any clear formulation or etiological exploration. For BDD, the most recent Cochrane review (Ipser, 2009) found that serotonin-specific reuptake inhibitors (SSRIs) such as fluoxetine, the tricyclic clomipramine, or cognitive behavioral therapy (CBT) may be effective. The number of CBT sessions ranged from 12 to 20.

The response to treatment in ORS is even less well studied. Interventions have been wide-ranging and nonspecific. Failure has been reported with electroconvulsive therapy, hypoglycemic coma, psychosurgery, and many neuroleptics (Videbech, 1966). Success has been described with the neuroleptic pimozide (Munro, 1988) and in two cases with SSRIs (Stein et al., 1998). Limited success has been reported with behavioral and psychodynamic psychotherapy (Beary & Cobb, 1981; Brosig, Kupfer, Niemeier, & Gieler, 2001; Marks & Misham, 1998).

Until recently, little significance has been attached to the etiology of these conditions, although a number of researchers have identified an association between distressing early experiences and BDD (Buhlmann, Cook, Fama, & Wilhelm, 2007; Osman, Cooper, Hackmann, & Veale, 2004).

Similarly, precipitating events, some traumatic in nature, were noted in almost half of the ORS clients (Begum & McKenna, 2010). As early as 1900, Wernicke noted that disorders with overvalued ideas "often dated from experiences that at the time aroused strong feelings" (cited in McKenna, 1984), and, in his seminal paper, Pryse-Philips (1971) describes such an event in one of the case studies. However, no clinical significance has been attached to these observations in either BDD or ORS, nor were the noted events ever the target of a clinical intervention.

In 1997, the first paper was published describing the use of Eye Movement Desensitization and Reprocessing (EMDR) Therapy in seven cases of BDD to target these precipitating events, with full remission in six. The one failure had no precipitating event (Brown, McGoldrick, & Buchanan, 1997). This was followed by a case series of four ORS subjects, all of whom had complete remission following EMDR Therapy that targeted the precipitating event (McGoldrick, Begum, & Brown, 2008). The number of sessions in each condition ranged from one to five. In all of these cases, the precipitating event was of a shaming or humiliating nature, most commonly experienced in adolescence, and the condition had been endured from 3 to 40 years, with many unsuccessful psychiatric and psychotherapeutic interventions. The authors offer a hypothesis based on the Adaptive Information Processing (AIP) model to explain the phenomenology of ORS and BDD and therefore predict successful outcomes with EMDR Therapy. They suggest that BDD and ORS can be among the many pathologies that can develop as a consequence of the insufficiently processed, disturbing experiences from earlier life events (Shapiro, 2001).

BDD and ORS EMDR Therapy Protocol Script Notes

Both BDD and ORS can be conceptualized using the AIP model, as hypothesized by Shapiro (2001). This posits that adverse life experiences, including trauma, are the actual genesis of many disorders and can be reprocessed adaptively through focused treatment with EMDR Therapy. In the cases of ORS and BDD, the therapist is looking for any past experiences, probably of a shaming or humiliating nature, usually but not exclusively occurring in early adolescence, that link to the present dysfunction.

There are some differences between working with clients who have BDD and ORS as compared to those with trauma-related conditions.

- *No obvious history of trauma:* Clients do not generally present with a history of trauma in the first instance. They have usually spent some considerable time and money on dermatologists, cosmetic surgeons, and other forms of medical intervention. Because the perceived defect believed to be present is seen as true, these clients may be resentful or baffled as to why they have been referred for psychological assessment and thus they require particular tact and understanding. Although it may seem obvious, the therapist should ascertain whether they have grounds for their beliefs. If this involves an intimate body part, it may be necessary to get consent to get some confirmation or otherwise from their medical practitioner. *Clinician stance*: If it is clearly a case of BDD or ORS, then particular sensitivity and honesty are needed. The clients need to know that you acknowledge their conviction but that you do not share it. It is helpful both to explain the nature of the disorder and to link the genesis to the AIP model early on to form a good therapeutic relationship and to elicit whether the clients can identify such events. Although our experience is that these shaming precipitants mostly occur in early adolescence, they can occur earlier in BDD clients, and/or in adulthood, following injury or surgery that has impacted the perception of appearance. Childhood sexual abuse experiences can also contribute to ORS if a strong odor was present at the time (for example, the presence of the smell of alcohol and/or an unwashed body). If adverse related experiences are not easily accessible, using a Float-Back or affect bridge will be helpful.
- *Humiliating or shaming experience(s)*: Trauma(s) that are linked to the onset of these beliefs may not appear particularly severe, being usually of a humiliating or shaming

nature. The sensitizing event may be so far in the past that it may not be easily available to the client. Or, clients may not attach emotional significance to the incidents that they may have experienced that preceded the onset of the belief. Again, a Float-Back or affect bridge may be helpful.

Note: If a major trauma is involved, the connection may not be recognized or even believed. In such cases, the major trauma should be targeted first. An example is one of the cases that follows, in which the connection between the gang rape and the belief of having a foul odor was not believed until symptom relief following processing of the trauma.

These are examples of categories of precipitating events.

Unpleasant odor:
- Client was accused of poor personal hygiene by classmates after opening her bag to get her gym kit out and the room was engulfed by a smell of rotting fish left there since a cancelled cookery class 3 days earlier
- During a gang rape, one of the perpetrators inserted fingers into the subject's vagina and invited the others to smell the fingers, whereupon they all jeered that she smelled like a fish
- Client smelled the overpowering odor of her childhood abuser as an olfactory flashback and experienced it as coming from herself

Humiliating comment(s) about body part(s):
- Client was the subject of a humorous remark regarding a receding hairline, causing great hilarity among friends
- Client overheard disparaging remarks made by colleague that he had a "head like Hercule Poirot"
- Client was subjected to offensive remarks on her appearance when she was wearing a dental brace
- Client was repeatedly teased by group of male peers about her nose, which was slightly large
- Relative commented disparagingly about client's underarm hair
- Humiliating episode in lounge bar where a man informed client, who had recently given birth and was out for her first social occasion, "your tits have more wrinkles than my granny's face" (*tits* is a derogatory Scottish colloquialism for breasts)
- Client was bullied in showers at school regarding then-underdeveloped genitalia

Humiliating comment about body related to action person did
- Loudly accused by mother of breaking wind in a small packed church (it was a male person in the pew in front)

Case Conceptualization and Treatment Planning

Use the 3-Pronged Protocol to identify these memories.

Past Memories

Look for the *earliest memory* related to the current belief about the self; this is usually of a shaming or humiliating nature. It is recommended that a *Float-Back* or *affect bridge* always be used with this population, as the actual event may be decades ago and there may be no recognition of the event itself or the significance.

As well as the touchstone event, look for *ancillary situations* in which the person thought others were behaving as if the defect/odor were present and he or she reexperienced shame and humiliation, as these may also have to be targeted.

In ORS, there may have been a time when the person did smell, perhaps due to childhood neglect, and this can be reexperienced as an olfactory intrusion/flashback in adulthood. This can still be successfully targeted, as now the client is not smelling and the intrusion disappears following successful treatment. Similarly, with BDD there may be a time when a defect was present, such as severe acne, but the client believes and behaves in the present as if the defect were still there.

When working with these populations, please bear in mind that there may be a number of significant events, particularly in cases of bullying and teasing.

Present Triggers

- *BDD*: The present triggers may include social situations and any events requiring exposure to others. Clients are particularly sensitive to what they identify as disgust or revulsion in others' expressions. There are often numerous avoidance behaviors and excessive checking and camouflage behaviors, such as mirror gazing, reassurance seeking, overuse of cosmetics, and pursuing dermatological treatment or cosmetic surgery.
- *ORS*: The present triggers may include excessive washing and showering behaviors; excessive use of deodorants, mouthwash, and perfumes; repeated investigations of the source of the perceived odor; excessive changes of clothing; and avoidance of social and intimate situations.

Future Template

The future template will generally involve the following types of events:

- Being confident in social/intimate situations
- Getting through the day without checking behaviors
- Not using a previous coping mechanism, for instance, wearing a nose splint to cover a perceived deformity, not showering four times daily

BDD and ORS EMDR Therapy Protocol Script

Phase 1: History Taking

Most of these questions apply to either disorder and will supplement your usual history taking.

Past

Say, *"I understand you have been referred here because of your concerns about* _____ (state perceived defect/odor). *Can you tell me a bit about that?"*

_____

_____

Say, *"Is there anything you do to disguise/correct perceived* _____ (state defect/odor)?"

_____

_____

Say, *"Is there anything you avoid doing because of perceived* _____ (state defect/odor)?"

_____

_____

Say, *"When did you first start believing* _____ (state the belief) *about yourself? Was there anything significant going on in your life at the time?"*

_____

_____

Say, *"Have you spent considerable time, energy, and money on dermatologists, cosmetic surgeons, and other forms of medical intervention?"*

_____

_____

Say, *"Do you have any thoughts or feelings about being referred here for a psychological assessment?"*

_____

_____

Say, *"Do you have any intrusive imagery related to* _____ (state perceived defect)*?"*

_____

_____

Say, *"What is the proof to you that your perception is accurate?"*

_____

_____

Say, *"Do you often do repetitive types of behaviors concerning your* _____ (state perceived defect/odor)*? Any checking or excessive personal hygiene grooming?"*

_____

_____

Say, *"How much time would you spend on this on a daily basis?"*

_____

_____

Say, *"Do you often compare yourself to others concerning physical appearance?"*

_____

_____

Say, *"Do you sometimes feel that your body build is too small or insufficiently muscular?"*

_____

_____

Say, *"Has there been anything that has helped you in handling this problem?"*

_____

_____

Say, *"What have you tried and has not worked concerning your problem?"*

_____

_____

Say, *"Have you had any distressing early experiences that you think might be related to _____ (state the specific defect)?"*

Say, *"Have you any memories of being bullied as a child/teenager—even a minor incident?"*

_____

_____

Say, *"Has anyone ever humiliated or shamed you in adolescence or earlier—even a minor incident?"*

_____

_____

Say, *"Have you ever overheard anyone humiliating or shaming you in adolescence or earlier—even a minor incident?"*

_____

_____

Say, *"Has any partner ever commented disparagingly on your appearance?"*

_____

_____

Say, *"Has anything happened to you that altered your appearance in any way—accident, injury, surgeries?"*

_____

_____

Say, *"Would your friends/family share your belief?"*

_____

_____

Say, *"On a scale of 0 to 10, where 0 is do not believe it at all and 10 is completely believe it, how much do you believe _____ (state perceived defect) to be present now?"*

0	1	2	3	4	5	6	7	8	9	10

(no belief)   (complete belief)

Say, *"On a percentage scale where 0% is no time at all and 100% is all the time, roughly what percent of your day would be preoccupied with _____ (state perceived defect)?"*

0   10%   20%   30%   40%   50%   60%   70%   80%   90%   100%

Say, *"Would your friends/family share your belief about yourself?"*

_____

_____

Say, *"On a scale of 0 to 10, where 0 is no disturbance or neutral and 10 is the highest disturbance you can imagine, how distressing is _____ (state perceived defect/odor) to be present now?"*

0   1   2   3   4   5   6   7   8   9   10

(no disturbance)   (highest disturbance)

Present

Say, *"How does _____ (state perceived defect/odor) affect your life now?"*

_____

_____

Say, *"What do you do presently to cope with _____ (state perceived defect/odor)?"*

_____

_____

Say, *"Are there things you avoid because of _____ (state perceived defect/odor)?"*

_____

_____

Say, *"Is there anything that makes _____ (state perceived defect/odor) more/less distressing?"*

_____

_____

Future

Say, *"What would you like to be able to do in the future if you didn't have this problem?"*

_____

_____

Say, *"What would demonstrate to you that you had got over this problem?"*

_____

_____

For those interested in research or formal measures, here are some measures:

- Body Dysmorphic Disorder Questionnaire (BDDQ; Phillips, 2005). This is a self-report measure.
- Yale–Brown Obsessive Compulsive Scale Modified for BDD (BDD-YBOCS; Phillips, 2005; Phillips, Hollander, Rasmussen, Aronowitz, DeCaria, & Goodman, 1997). This is a clinician-administered measure.
- The Brown Assessment of Beliefs Scale: reliability and validity (Eisen, Philips, & Baer, 1998). This measures the delusional intensity with which a belief is held.

Phase 2: Preparation

Explanation of BDD/ORS

It is helpful both to explain the nature of the disorder and to link the genesis to the AIP model early on to form a good therapeutic relationship and to elicit whether the client can identify such events. The authors have found the *DSM-5* criteria and the following reviews to be particularly useful to help in formulating an explanation of each disorder at different levels of simplicity/complexity depending on the presenting client and in furthering the therapist's own understanding.

For ORS: "Olfactory Reference Syndrome: Issues for *DSM-5*" (Feusner, Philips, & Stein, 2010).

For BDD: "Review: Body Dysmorphic Disorder" (Veale et al., 2003).

Explanation of AIP model

The authors recommend "Getting Past Your Past" (Shapiro, 2012) to clients to help them understand the AIP model and ORS, as Shapiro includes a description of an ORS client as one of her examples (pp. 167–168). A simple way of introducing the AIP model is as follows:

> Say, *"It is our experience that most clients who present difficulties similar to yours have had an unpleasant related experience or experiences in the past that conditioned the belief that is held in the present. It is usually something humiliating or shameful that caused considerable distress at the time. It may be so long ago that it is difficult to remember. It is usually something around early adolescence, but it could be earlier or later. We find that if we target these experiences with EMDR Therapy, then clients have considerable relief from their problem. Can you think of anything that seems related? If not, we have a very useful technique to help you with that. It is called the Float-Back. What we do is ask you to remember the last time you experienced _____ (state perceived belief), to bring up a picture of it and a negative belief, to notice what emotion is associated with that now and where you feel it in your body, and to let your mind go back in time to see if it connects with anything in your past. We can also do it without the negative belief, in which case it is called an affect scan. How would you be with trying one of these at our next session before we start your treatment?"*

Explanation of EMDR Therapy

> Say, *"When a negative and distressing event, occurs, it seems to get locked in the nervous system with the original picture, sounds, thoughts, and feelings. The eye movements we use in EMDR seem to unlock the nervous system and*

allow the brain to process the experience. These eye movements may help to process the unconscious material. It is important to remember that it is your own brain that will be doing the healing and that you are the one in control."

Creating a Safe, Calm, or Secure Place Script

Note: You must not proceed to the desensitization phase without establishing that your client can self-soothe.

Image (Actual or Imaginary Place)

Ask the client to find a place with positive associations where he or she feels safe, comfortable, peaceful, or calm. (Avoid images containing close family members, as they usually have both positive and negative associations.)

> Say, *"I'd like you to think about some place you have been or imagine being that feels very safe or calm. Perhaps, being on the beach or sitting by a mountain stream."*

> (Pause)

> Say, *"Where would you be?"*

_____

If the client finds it difficult to imagine a peaceful and safe place, spend more time on developing one, if necessary creating an imaginary one. Identify an image that the client can easily evoke and that creates a personal feeling of calm and safety.

> Say, *"If you could imagine a place that for you is safe, calm, or secure, what would that place be? Describe it to me. Tell me what you see, what you smell, what you feel. Tell me about anything you need to make that place secure for you."*

Note: It is essential that the clinician write down the details of the image in order to be able to take the client to the Safe Place at the end of an incomplete session.

_____

_____

Emotions and Sensations

Ask the client to focus on the image, to feel the positive emotions, and to identify the location of the pleasing physical sensation.

> Say, *"As you think of that safe* (or calm) *place, notice what you see, hear, and feel right now."*

> (Pause)

> Say, *"What do you notice?"*

_____

_____

Enhancement

Ask the client to describe any sounds, pleasant smells, and/or sensations associated with the image.

Say, *"Focus on your safe* (or calm) *place, its sights, sounds, smells, and body sensations. Tell me more about what you are noticing."*

_____

_____

Bilateral Stimulation

Say, *"Bring up the image of that place. Concentrate on where you feel the pleasant sensations in your body and allow yourself to enjoy them. Now concentrate on those sensations and follow my fingers* (or whatever bilateral stimulation or BLS you use)*."*

Use 4 to 8 short sets of tapping or *slow* eye movements.

Say, *"How do you feel now?"*

_____

_____

Repeat several times if the process has enhanced the client's positive feelings and sensations.
If positive, say, *"Focus on that."*
Repeat BLS.

Say, *"What do you notice now?"*

_____

_____

At the end of each set ask the client:

Say, *"Does that positive feeling feel as good, better, or less good?"*

Continue to do short sets of tapping or EMs as long as the positive effect enhances. If the client's positive emotions have not increased, try alternative directions of eye movements until improvement is reported.

Cue Word

The client is then asked to identify a single word or phrase that fits the Safe Place (e.g., "relax," "safe," "beach," "in control"). The client is then asked to bring up the image while repeating the "cue word" to himself or herself.

Say, *"Is there a word or phrase that represents your safe* (or calm) *place?"*

_____

_____

Then say, *"Think of* _____ (cue word) *and notice the positive feelings you have when you think of that word. Now concentrate on those sensations and the cue word and follow* _____ (state BLS using)*."*

Use short sets (4 to 6) of BLS with any positive responses.

Say, *"How do you feel now?"*

_____

_____

Say, *"Does that word fit/resonate?"*

_____

_____

Repeat several times. Enhance positive feelings with BLS several times.

Self-Cuing

The client is asked to repeat the procedure on his own, bringing up the image and the cue word and experiencing the positive feelings (emotionally and physically) without any eye movements.

Say, *"Now I'd like you to say that word _____ (cue word) and notice how you feel."*

_____

_____

Note: If at any time, during this process, the client experiences negative emotion, discard the memory and find another. Do not try to fix it.

The next two steps (cuing with disturbance and self-cuing with disturbance) are only used once clients demonstrate that they can go to the Safe Place with ease. The next two steps are important, as they test the clients' readiness to proceed with EDMR. If clients are unable to complete these final steps, it indicates that you need to spend more time with preparation.

Cuing With Disturbance

Ask the client to bring up a *minor* concern or problem and notice the accompanying negative feelings.

Say, *"Now imagine a minor annoyance and how it feels."*

(Pause)

The client is guided through the Safe Place exercise until he can reconnect with positive feelings. Cuing with disturbance is now achieved.

Say, *"Now bring up your safe* (or calm) *place and notice any shifts in your body."*

_____

_____

Do BLS.
Guide the client through the process until he is able to experience the positive emotions and sensations. Repeat as often as necessary.

Cuing achieved?   ☐ Yes   ☐ No

Self-Cuing With Disturbance (Do Not Use Eye Movements)

The client brings up another minor disturbance or concern and reconnects with the positive image and cue word, this time without the clinician's assistance, until the client can reexperience the positive affect of the Safe Place.

Say, *"Now I'd like you to think of another mildly annoying incident and bring up your safe* (or calm) *place by yourself again, especially noticing any changes in your body when you have gone to your safe* (or calm) *place."*

_____

_____

Self-cuing independently achieved? ☐ Yes ☐ No

Practice

Say, *"I'd like you to practice using your safe place, between now and our next session, at any time you feel a little annoyed. Keep track of how things go and we'll talk about it next time we meet. Do you have any questions before we stop?"*

_____

_____

Phase 3: Assessment

Say, *"First of all, as explained in the previous session, we are going to look for a previous experience that is linked to your current problem and see if we can find the earliest representation that you have of it."*

_____

_____

Say, *"Can you give me a recent example of when you experienced this problem?"*

_____

_____

Say, *"What picture represents the worst part of this recent memory?"*

_____

_____

Say, *"What words go best with that picture which represent your negative belief about yourself now?"*

_____

_____

Say, *"Please bring up that image of* _____ (state the image) *and those words* _____ (state the words). *Notice what feelings are coming up for you now and where you are feeling them in your body.*

"As you notice those feelings and that negative thought _____ (repeat NC), *are they familiar? Just let those feelings and that thought float back to a time earlier in your life; don't search for anything, just let your mind float. Take as long as it takes: you may land somewhere, you may not. Just let me know the earliest memory that comes to mind when you had similar thoughts and feelings."*

_____

_____

Remind the client that this is not a cognitive exercise; "just follow your feelings."

Say, *"If you can, allow yourself to follow your feelings."*

Say, *"Does this early touchstone memory seem related in some way to the present concern?"*

_____

_____

Or say, *"Does this touchstone memory seem to be the earliest time that you experienced this problem?"*

_____

_____

If the client answers no to either of these questions, continue Float-Back until you find an early memory that does fit.

If the client cannot identify a negative belief (unlikely in these conditions) but has significant affect, use the *affect bridge*; this is as above but without the NC.

Say, *"Please bring up that image of _____ (state the image). Notice what feelings are coming up for you now and where you are feeling them in your body.*

As you notice those feelings, are they familiar? Just let those feelings float back to a time earlier in your life; don't search for anything, just let your mind float. Take as long as it takes: you may land somewhere, you may not. Just let me know the earliest memory that comes to mind when you had similar feelings."

_____

The clinician then proceeds to the Standard EMDR Protocol.

Picture

Say, *"What picture represents the entire _____ (state the issue)?"*

_____

_____

Say, *"What picture represents the most traumatic part of _____ (state the issue)?"*

_____

_____

Negative Cognition

In this group, NCs are in the responsibility/self-defectiveness domain. The most common NCs encountered clinically are the following:

For BDD: "I am ugly," "I am defective," "I am repulsive," or "I am deformed."

For ORS: "I smell (obviously)!" "I am repulsive," or "I am disgusting."

Say, *"What words best go with the picture that express your negative belief about yourself now?"*

_____

_____

Positive Cognition

Note: Depending on how strongly the NC is held, PCs can range from a statement that is the opposite of any of the above or may be much more tentative. Rather than an "I am" statement, it may start something like, "I can begin to believe (desired state)." This generally changes during processing and a more empowering statement can be substituted.

Common PCs developed in both groups are the following: "I am normal," "I am acceptable," or "I am OK as I am."

Say, *"When you bring up that picture or* _____ (state the issue), *what would you like to believe about yourself now?"*

_____

_____

Note: Depending on how strongly the NC is held, PCs can range from a statement that is the opposite of any of the above or may be much more tentative. Rather than an "I am" statement, it may start something like, "I can begin to believe (desired state)." This generally changes during processing and a more empowering statement can be substituted.

Common PCs developed in both groups are the following: "I am normal," "I am acceptable," or "I am OK as I am."

Validity of Cognition

Say, *"When you think of* _____ (state the issue, or picture), *how true do those words* _____ (repeat the PC) *feel to you now on a scale of 1 to 7, where 1 feels completely false and 7 feels completely true?"*

1	2	3	4	5	6	7

(completely false)   (completely true)

Sometimes it is necessary to explain further.

Say, *"Remember, sometimes we know something with our head, but it feels differently in our gut. In this case, what is the gut-level feeling of the truth of* _____ (state the PC), *from 1* (completely false) *to 7 (completely true)?"*

1	2	3	4	5	6	7

(completely false)   (completely true)

Emotions

This is usually shame, embarrassment, or humiliation.

Say, *"When you bring up the picture or* _____ (state the issue) *and those words* _____ (state the NC), *what emotion do you feel now?"*

_____

_____

Subjective Units of Disturbance

Say, *"On a scale of 0 to 10, where 0 is no disturbance or neutral and 10 is the highest disturbance you can imagine, how disturbing does it feel now?"*

0	1	2	3	4	5	6	7	8	9	10

(no disturbance)   (highest disturbance)

Location of Body Sensation

Say, *"Where do you feel it* (the disturbance) *in your body?"*

_____

_____

Say, *"Now, remember, it is your own brain that is doing the healing and you are the one in control. I will ask you to mentally focus on the target and to follow my fingers* (or any other BLS you are using). *Just let whatever happens, happen, and we will talk at the end of the set. Just tell me what comes up, and don't discard anything as unimportant. Any new information that comes to mind is connected in some way. If you want to stop, just raise your hand."*

Then say, *"Bring up the picture and the words* _____ (repeat the NC) *and notice where you feel it in your body. Now follow my fingers with your eyes* (or other BLS)."

Phase 4: Desensitization

The work in Phase 4 follows the Standard EMDR Protocol. To begin, say the following:

Say, *"Now, remember, it is your own brain that is doing the healing and you are the one in control. I will ask you to mentally focus on the target and to _____* (state BLS you are using). *Just let whatever happens, happen, and we will talk at the end of the set. Just tell me what comes up, and don't discard anything as unimportant. Any new information that comes to mind is connected in some way. If you want to stop, just raise your hand."*

Then say, *"Bring up the picture and the words* _____ (repeat the NC) *and notice where you feel it in your body. Now follow* _____ (state BLS)."

_____

_____

This procedure is to be repeated until the SUDs = 0. Then the PC is installed. Each traumatic event associated with the problem that is not reprocessed during the normal course of the first target must be processed using the above protocol until the SUDs reach an ecological 1 or 0 and the PC is installed.

Phase 5: Installation

Say, *"How does* _____ (repeat the PC) *sound?"*

_____

_____

Say, *"Do the words _____ (repeat the PC) still fit, or is there another positive statement that feels better?"*

_____

_____

If the client accepts the original PC, the clinician should ask for a VoC rating to see if it has improved:

Say, *"As you think of the incident, how do the words feel, from 1 (completely false) to 7 (completely true)?"*

1	2	3	4	5	6	7

(completely false)   (completely true)

Say, *"Think of the event and hold it together with the words _____ (repeat the PC)."*

Do a long set of BLS to see if there is more processing to be done.

Phase 6: Body Scan

Say, *"Close your eyes and keep in mind the original memory and the positive cognition. Then bring your attention to the different parts of your body, starting with your head and working downward. Any place you find any tension, tightness, or unusual sensation, tell me."*

_____

_____

Phase 7: Closure

Say, *"Things may come up or they may not. If they do, great. Write it down and it can be a target for next time. You can use a log to write down triggers, images, thoughts or cognitions, emotions, and sensations; you can rate them on our 0 to 10 scale where 0 is no disturbance or neutral and 10 is the worst disturbance. Please write down the positive experiences, too."*

"If you get any new memories, dreams, or situations that disturb you, just take a good snapshot. It isn't necessary to give a lot of detail. Just put down enough to remind you so we can target it next time. The same thing goes for any positive dreams or situations. If negative feelings do come up, try not to make them significant. Remember, it's still just the old stuff. Just write it down for next time. Then use the tape or the Safe Place exercise to let go of as much of the disturbance as possible. Even if nothing comes up, make sure to use the tape every day and give me a call if you need to."

Phase 8: Reevaluation

It is important to pay attention to the following questions when the client returns after doing EMDR work.

Say, *"When you think of whatever is left of the problem that we worked on last time, how disturbing is it now, on a scale of 0 to 10 where 0 is no disturbance or neutral and 10 is the highest disturbance you can imagine?"*

0	1	2	3	4	5	6	7	8	9	10

(no disturbance)   (highest disturbance)

Say, *"Have you noticed any other material associated with the original memory since the last session?"*

_____

_____

_____

Say, *"Have all the necessary targets been reprocessed so that you can feel at peace with the past, empowered in the present, and able to make choices for the future?"*

_____

_____

_____

Say, *"Has the work that we have done with EMDR helped you be more adaptive in your day-to-day life?"*

_____

_____

_____

Present Stimuli That Trigger the Disturbing Memory or Reaction

List the situations that still elicit the symptom(s). Although these often resolve once the index trauma and ancillary events have been treated, it is essential to check which of those stimuli elicited the symptoms if conceptualization remains.

Say, *"What are the situations, events, or stimuli that trigger your belief _____ (state the belief)? Let's process these situations, events, or stimuli triggers one by one."*

Situations, Events, or Stimuli Trigger List

_____

_____

_____

_____

_____

Target or Memory

Say, *"What situation, event, or stimulus that triggers would you like to use as a target today?"*

_____

_____

Picture

Say, *"What picture represents the* _____ (state the situation, event, or stimulus) *that triggers you?"*

_____

_____

If there are many choices or if the client becomes confused, the clinician assists by asking the following:

Say, *"What picture represents the most traumatic part of the* _____ (state the situation, event, or stimulus) *that triggers you?"*

_____

_____

When a picture is unavailable, the clinician merely invites the client to do the following:

Say, *"Think of the* _____ (state the situation, event, or stimulus) *that triggers you."*

_____

_____

Negative Cognition

Say, *"What words best go with the picture that express your negative belief about yourself now?"*

_____

_____

Positive Cognition

Say, *"When you bring up that picture or the* _____ (state the situation, event, or stimulus) *that triggers you, what would you like to believe about yourself now?"*

_____

_____

Validity of Cognition

Say, *"When you think of the* _____ (state the triggering situation, event, stimulus, or picture), *how true do those words* _____ (repeat the PC) *feel to you now on a scale of 1 to 7, where 1 feels completely false and 7 feels completely true?"*

   1   2   3   4   5   6   7

(completely false)   (completely true)

Sometimes it is necessary to explain further.

Say, *"Remember, sometimes we know something with our head, but it feels differently in our gut. In this case, what is the gut-level feeling of the truth of _____* (state the PC), *from 1 (completely false) to 7 (completely true)?"*

1	2	3	4	5	6	7

(completely false)   (completely true)

Emotions

Say, *"When you bring up the picture* (or state the situation, event, or stimulus) *that triggers you and those words _____* (state the NC), *what emotion do you feel now?"*

_____

_____

Subjective Units of Disturbance

Say, *"On a scale of 0 to 10, where 0 is no disturbance or neutral and 10 is the highest disturbance you can imagine, how disturbing does it feel now?"*

0	1	2	3	4	5	6	7	8	9	10

(no disturbance)   (highest disturbance)

Location of Body Sensation

Say, *"Where do you feel it* (the disturbance) *in your body?"*

_____

_____

Continue with Phases 4 through 7 for the situation, event, or stimulus that triggers the client, either the same one or any others.

Future Template

In this population, the future template is generally about behaving confidently in a social situation or not using the previous coping strategy; for example, in cases of BDD, perhaps not using excessive cosmetics or other means to disguise the perceived deformity. In cases of ORS, it may be resisting the impulse to shower or change underclothing several times a day.

Incorporate a Detailed Template for a Trauma-Free Future Action (Shapiro, 2006)

Say, *"I would like you to imagine yourself coping effectively with _____* (state the goal) *in the future. With the positive belief _____* (state the positive belief) *and your new sense of _____* (state the quality, i.e., strength, clarity, confidence, calm), *imagine stepping into this scene. Notice what you see and how you are handling the situation. Notice what you are thinking, feeling, and experiencing in your body."*

_____

_____

Again, here is an opportunity to catch any disturbance that may have been missed.

Say, *"Are there any blocks, anxieties, or fears that arise as you think about this future scene?"*

_____

_____

If yes, say the following:

Say, *"Then focus on these blocks and follow my fingers* (or any other BLS)*."*

Say, *"What do you get now?"*

_____

_____

If the blocks do not resolve quickly, evaluate if the client needs any new information, resources, or skills to be able to comfortably visualize the future coping scene. Introduce needed information or skills.

Say, *"What would you need to feel confident in handling the situation?"*

_____

_____

Or say, *"What is missing from your handling of this situation?"*

_____

_____

If the block still does not resolve and the client is unable to visualize the future scene with confidence and clarity, use direct questions, the affect scan, or the Float-Back Technique to identify old targets related to blocks, anxieties, or fears. Remember, the point of the 3-Pronged Protocol is not only to reinforce positive feelings and behavior in the future, but also to catch any unresolved material that may be getting in the way of an adaptive resolution of the issue(s) again. Use the Standard EMDR Protocol to address these targets before proceeding with the template (see the worksheets in Appendix A).

If there are no apparent blocks and the client is able to visualize the future scene with confidence and clarity, say the following:

Say, *"Please focus on the image, the positive belief, and the sensations associated with this future scene and follow my fingers* (or any other BLS)*."*

_____

_____

Process and reinforce the positive associations with BLS. Do several sets until the future template is sufficiently strengthened.

Say, *"Go with that."*

Then say, *"Close your eyes and keep in mind the image of the future and the positive cognition. Then bring your attention to the different parts of your · body, starting with your head and working downward. Any place you find any tension, tightness, or unusual sensation, tell me."*

_____

_____

If any sensation is reported, do BLS.

Say, *"Go with that."*

_____

_____

If it is a positive or comfortable sensation, do BLS to strengthen the positive feelings.

Say, *"Go with that."*

_____

_____

If a sensation of discomfort is reported, reprocess until the discomfort subsides.

Say, *"Go with that."*

_____

_____

When the discomfort subsides, check the VoC.

Say, *"When you think of the incident* (or picture), *how true do those words* _____ (repeat the PC) *feel to you now on a scale of 1 to 7, where 1 feels completely false and 7 feels completely true?"*

1	2	3	4	5	6	7

(completely false)   (completely true)

Continue to use BLS until reaching VoC = 7 or there is an ecological resolution. When the image as future template is clear and the PC is true, move on to the movie as future template.

Movie as Future Template or Imaginal Rehearsing

During this next level of future template installation, clients are asked to move from imagining this one scene or snapshot to imagining a movie about coping in the future that has a beginning, middle, and end. Encourage clients to imagine themselves coping effectively in the face of specific challenges, triggers, or snafus. Therapists can make some suggestions of things in order to help inoculate clients with future problems. It is helpful to use this type of future template after clients have received needed education concerning social skills and customs, assertiveness, and any other newly learned skills.

Say, *"This time I'd like you to close your eyes and play a movie, imagining yourself coping effectively with* _____ (state where client will be) *in the future. With the new positive belief* _____ (state positive belief) *and your new sense of* _____ (strength, clarity, confidence, calm), *imagine stepping into the future. Imagine yourself coping with ANY challenges that come your way. Make sure that this movie has a beginning, middle, and end. Notice what you are seeing, thinking, feeling, and experiencing in your body. Let me know if you hit any blocks. If you do, just open your eyes and let me know. If you don't hit any blocks, let me know when you have viewed the whole movie."*

_____

_____

...

If the client hits blocks, address as before with BLS until the disturbance dissipates.

Say, *"Go with that."*

_____

_____

If the material does not shift, use interweaves, new skills, information, resources, direct questions, and any other ways to help clients access information that will allow them to move on. If these options are not successful, it usually means that there is earlier material still unprocessed; the Float-Back and affect scan are helpful in these cases to access the material that keeps clients stuck.

If clients are able to play the movie from start to finish with a sense of confidence and satisfaction, ask them to play the movie one more time from beginning to end and introduce BLS.

Say, *"OK, play the movie one more time from beginning to end. Go with that."*

Use BLS.

In a sense you are installing this movie as a future template.

After clients have fully processed their issue(s), they might want to work on other positive templates for the future in other areas of their lives using the same type of future templates.

Summary

In summary, both BDD and ORS can be conceptualized using the AIP model. If the genesis can be established as an earlier shaming or humiliating event, usually in early adolescence but possibly earlier, EMDR Therapy can be successfully used to desensitize the event and allow AIP. Although many authors (previously cited) have identified such events as a precursor to the development of these conditions, to our knowledge these events have never been a target of therapeutic intervention. In our experience, successfully targeting these events has led to complete remission in all such cases.

References

American Psychiatric Association. (2013). *Diagnostic and statistical manual of mental disorders* (5th ed.). Washington, DC: Author.

Beary, M. D., & Cobb, J. P. (1981). Solitary psychosis: Three cases of monosymptomatic delusion of alimentary stench treated with behavioural psychotherapy. *British Journal of Psychiatry, 138*, 64–66.

Begum, M., & McKenna, P. J. (2010). Olfactory reference syndrome: A systematic review of the world literature. *Psychological Medicine, 9*, 1–9.

Bishop, E. R. (1980). Monosymptomatic hypochondriasis. *Psychosomatics, 21*, 731–747.

Brosig, B., Kupfer, J., Niemeier, V., & Gieler, U. (2001). Delusional bromidrosis in psychiatry—A case study. *Dermatology and Psychosomatics, 2*, 203–207.

Brown, K. W., McGoldrick, T., & Buchanan, R. (1997). Body dysmorphic disorder: Seven cases treated with eye movement desensitization and reprocessing. *Behavioural & Cognitive Psychotherapy, 25*, 203–207.

Brunswick, R. M. (1971). Pertaining to the wolf man: A supplement to Freud's "The history of an infantile neurosis." *Rev Psicoanal, 35*, 5–46.

Buhlmann, U., Cook, L. M., Fama, J. M., & Wilhelm, S. (2007). Perceived teasing experiences in body dysmorphic disorder. *Body Image, 4*(4), 381–385.

Conroy, M., Menard, W., Fleming-Ives, K., Modha, P., Cerullo, H., & Phillips, K. A. (2008). Prevalence and clinical characteristics of body dysmorphic disorder in an adult inpatient setting. *General Hospital Psychiatry, 30*(1), 67–72.

Eisen, J. L., Philips, K. A., & Baer, L. (1998). The Brown Assessment of Beliefs Scale: Reliability and validity. *American Journal of Psychiatry, 155*, 102–108.

Feusner, D., Philips, K. A., & Stein, D. J (2010). Olfactory reference syndrome: Issues for DSM-5. *Depression and Anxiety, 27*(6), 592–599.

Freud, S. (1959). *Three case histories: The wolfman, the ratman and the psychotic doctor.* London, England: Screber.

Isper, J. C., Sander, C., & Stein, D. J. (2009, Jan 21). Phramacotherapy and psychotherapy for body dysmorphic disorder. *Cochrane Database Syst Rev.* (1):CD005332. doi:10.1002/14651858.CD005332.pub2.

Janet, P. (1903). *Les obsessions et la psychasthenie.* Paris, France: Felix Alcan.

Kraepelin, E. (1909-1915). *Psychiatrie* (8th ed., vol. 4). Leipzig, Germany: Barth.

Marks, I. M., & Misham, J. (1998). Dysmorphophobic avoidance with disturbed bodily perception: A pilot study of exposure therapy. *British Journal of Psychiatry, 152,* 494–499.

McGoldrick, T., Begum, M., & Brown, K. W. (2008). EMDR and olfactory reference syndrome: A case series. *Journal of EMDR Practice and Research, 2,* 63–68.

McKenna, P. J. (1984). Disorders with overvalued ideas. *British Journal of Psychiatry, 145,* 579–585.

Morselli, E. (1891). Sulla dismorfofobia e sulla tafefobia: Due forme non per anco descritte di Pazzia con idee fisse. *Boll R Accad Genova, 6,* 110–119.

Munro, A. (1982). *Delusional hypochondriasis: A description of monosymptomatic hypochondriacal psychosis* (Monograph Series 5). Toronto, Canada: Clarke Institute of Psychiatry.

Munro, A. (1988). Monosymptomatic hypochondriacal psychosis. *British Journal of Psychiatry, 153*(suppl. 2), 37–40.

Osman, S., Cooper, M., Hackmann, A., & Veale, D. (2004). Spontaneously occurring images and early memories in people with body dysmorphic disorder. *Memory, 12*(4), 428–436.

Phillips, K. A. (1991). Body dysmorphic disorder: The distress of imagined ugliness. *American Journal of Psychiatry, 148,* 1138–1149.

Phillips, K. A. (2005). *The broken mirror: Understanding and treating body dysmorphic disorder* (rev. and expanded ed.). New York, NY: Oxford University Press.

Phillips, K. A., Coles, M. E., Menard, W., Yen, S., Fay, C., & Weisberg, R. B. (2005). Suicidal ideation and suicide attempts in body dysmorphic disorder. *Journal of Clinical Psychiatry, 66*(6), 717–725.

Phillips, K. A., Didie, E. R., Feusner, J., & Wilhelm, S. (2008). Body dysmorphic disorder: Treating an underrecognized disorder. *American Journal of Psychiatry, 165*(9), 1111–1118.

Phillips, K. A., Hollander, E., Rasmussen, S. A., Aronowitz, B. R., DeCaria, C., & Goodman, W. K. (1997). A severity rating scale for body dysmorphic disorder: Development, reliability, and validity of a modified version of the Yale-Brown Obsessive Compulsive Scale. *Psychopharmacology Bulletin, 33,* 17–22.

Phillips, K. A., McElroy, S. L., Keck, P. E., Jr., Hudson, J. I., & Pope, H. G., Jr. (1994). A comparison of delusional and nondelusional body dysmorphic disorder in 100 cases. *Psychopharmacology Bulletin, 30,* 179–186.

Phillips, K. A., McElroy, S. L., Keck, P. E., Jr., Pope, H. G., Jr., & Hudson, J. I. (1993). Body dysmorphic disorder: 30 cases of imagined ugliness. *American Journal of Psychiatry, 150,* 302–308.

Phillips, K. A., Menard, W., Fay, C., & Weisberg, R. (2005). Demographic characteristics, phenomenology, comorbidity, and family history in 200 individuals with body dysmorphic disorder. *Psychosomatics, 46,* 317–325.

Potts, C. S. (1891). Two cases of hallucination of smell. *University of Pennsylvania Medical Magazine,* p. 226.

Pryse-Phillips, W. (1971). An olfactory reference syndrome. *Acta Psychiatrica Scandinavica, 47*(4), 484–509.

Shapiro, F. (2001). *Eye movement desensitization and reprocessing: Basic principles, protocols and procedures* (2nd ed.). New York, NY: Guilford Press.

Stein, D. J., Le Roux, L., Bouwer, C., & van Heerden, B. (1998). Is olfactory reference syndrome an obsessive-compulsive spectrum disorder? Two cases and a discussion. *Journal of Neuropsychiatry and Clinical Neurosciences, 10*(1), 96–99.

Sutton, R. L. (1919). Bromidrosiphobia. *Journal of the American Medical Association, 72,* 1267–1268.

Veale, D., Kinderman, P., Riley, S. & Lambrou, C. (2003, June). Self-discrepancy in body dysmorphic disorder. *Br J Clin Psychol. 42*(Pt2), 157–169.

Videbech, T. (1966). Chronic olfactory paranoid syndromes. *Acta Psychiatrica Scandinavica, 42,* 183–213.

World Health Organization. (1994). *ICD 10.* Geneva, Switzerland: Elsevier Limited.

Therese McGoldrick, Millia Begum, and Keith Brown
SUMMARY SHEET BY MARILYN LUBER

Name: _____ Diagnosis: _____

☑ Check when task is completed, response has changed, or to indicate symptoms or diagnosis.

Note: This material is meant as a checklist for your response. Please keep in mind that it is only a reminder of different tasks that may or may not apply to your client.

BDD and ORS EMDR Therapy Protocol Script Notes

Differences between trauma-related conditions and BDD and ORS cases:

- ☐ No obvious history of trauma
- ☐ Perceive defect as true
- ☐ Traumas may not appear severe at onset
- ☐ Usually to do with humiliation or shaming
- ☐ Target major trauma first, as often clients do not make the connection between the event and the defect/odor

Categories of precipitating events:

- ☐ Unpleasant odor
- ☐ Humiliating comment(s) about body part(s)
- ☐ Humiliating comment about body related to action person did

Case Conceptualization and Treatment Planning

Past

- ☐ Look for earliest memory—usually shaming/humiliating
- ☐ Float-Back/affect bridge
- ☐ Look for ancillary situations—others behaving as if defect/odor were present
- ☐ In ORS: target the olfactory intrusion/flashback
- ☐ Usually a number of significant events

Present

- ☐ Social situations
- ☐ Any event requiring exposure to others
- ☐ Disgust or revulsion in other's expressions

Future

- ☐ Social interaction situations
- ☐ Getting through the day without checking behaviors
- ☐ Not using a previous coping mechanism, for instance, not wearing a nose splint to cover a perceived deformity, not showering four times daily

BDD and ORS EMDR Therapy Protocol Script

Phase 1: Client History

Past

Perceived defect/odor: _____

Avoid because of defect/odor: _____

_____

_____

When started to believe: _____

_____

Much money spent on doctors and medical intervention: _____

When first started believing _____ (belief)? _____

Feelings about being here?   ☐ Yes   ☐ No

Describe: _____

Intrusive imagery related to defect/odor?   ☐ Yes   ☐ No

Describe: _____

Proof of accuracy of perception: _____

_____

_____

Repetitive behaviors concerning defect/odor: _____

_____

_____

Compare self to others re physical appearance: ☐ Yes   ☐ No

Describe: _____

Anything that helps? _____

_____

What was tried but didn't work: _____

_____

_____

Distressing early experiences related to defect/odor: _____

Avoid because of defect/odor: _____

_____

_____

Experienced bullying: _____

Shamed or humiliated as adolescent or younger: _____

Partner commented disparagingly about appearance: ☐ Yes   ☐ No

Describe: _____

Anything altered your appearance?   ☐ Yes   ☐ No

Describe: _____

Friends/family sharing belief?   ☐ Yes   ☐ No

Describe: _____

How present is _____ (defect/odor) now? _____ /10

Percent of day preoccupied with _____ (defect/odor)? _____%

Present Triggers

Effect on life of _____ (defect/odor): _____

_____

What you do to cope with _____ (perceived defect/odor): _____

_____

What you avoid because of it: _____

_____

Anything that makes it more or less distressing: _____

_____

Future

What you would do if no problem: _____

_____

How you would know you had gotten over this problem: _____

_____

Phase 2: Preparation

☐ Explain BDD/ORS:

  ☐ *For ORS*: "Olfactory Reference Syndrome: Issues for *DSM-5*" (Feusner, Philips, & Stein, 2010).

  ☐ *For BDD*: "Review: Body Dysmorphic Disorder" (Veale et al., 2003).

☐ Explanation of AIP model: *"It is our experience that most clients who present difficulties similar to yours have had an unpleasant related experience or experiences in the past that conditioned in the belief that is held in the present. It is usually something humiliating or shameful that caused considerable distress at the time. It may be so long ago that it is difficult to remember. It is usually something around early adolescence, but it could be earlier or later. We find that if we target these experiences with EMDR Therapy, then clients have considerable relief from their problem. Can you think of anything that seems related? If not, we have a very useful technique to help you with that. It is called the Float-Back. What we do is ask you to remember the last time you experienced* _____ (state perceived belief), *to bring up a picture of it and a negative belief, to notice what emotion is associated with that now and where you feel it in your body, and to let your mind go back in time to see if it connects with anything in your past. We can also do it without the negative belief, in which case it is called an affect scan. How would you be with trying one of these at our next session before we start your treatment?"*

☐ Explain EMDR Therapy: *"When a negative and distressing event occurs, it seems to get locked in the nervous system with the original picture, sounds, thoughts, and feelings. The eye movements we use in EMDR seem to unlock the nervous system and allow the brain to process the experience. Those eye movements may help to process the unconscious material. It is important to remember that it is your own brain that will be doing the healing and that you are the one in control."*

☐ Safe Place

Phase 3: Assessment

Recent example of problem: _____

Picture of worst part: _____

Negative Cognition

"Please bring up that image of _____ (state the image) *and those words* _____ (state the words of the NC). *Notice what feelings are coming up for you now and where you are feeling them in your body. As you notice those feelings and that negative thought* _____ (repeat NC), *are they familiar? Just let those feelings and that thought float back to a time earlier in your life; don't search for anything, just let your mind float. Take as long as it takes: you may land somewhere, you may not. Just let me know the earliest memory that comes to mind when you had similar thoughts and feelings."*

_____

_____

Memory related to present concern?   ☐ Yes   ☐ No

Affect bridge: *"Please bring up that image of* _____ (state the image). *Notice what feelings are coming up for you now and where you are feeling them in your body. As you notice those feelings, are they familiar? Just let those feelings float back to a time earlier in your life; don't search for anything, just let your mind float. Take as long as it takes: you may land somewhere, you may*

not. Just let me know the earliest memory that comes to mind when you had
similar feelings." _____

_____

_____

Target selection (touchstone event): _____

Incident: _____

Picture: _____

NC: _____

For BDD: "I am ugly," "I am defective," "I am repulsive," or "I am deformed."

For ORS: "I smell (obviously)!" "I am repulsive," or "I am disgusting."

PC: _____

Common PCs developed in both groups are the following: "I am normal," "I am acceptable," or "I am OK as I am."

VoC: _____ /7

Emotions: _____

SUD: _____ /10

Location of body sensation: _____

Phase 4: Desensitization

Introduce according to EMDR Standard Protocol.
If SUD = 1 or more, continue processing.
If SUD continues to be 0 after 2 sets of BLS, go to the installation phase.

Phase 5: Installation

PC: _____   □ Completed

New PC (if new one is better):

VoC: _____ /7

Incident + PC + BLS

Continue installation with BLS until material becomes increasingly adaptive. If VoC = 6 or less, check and see if there is a limiting belief:

"Which thoughts or concerns prevent you from feeling those words as completely true?"

_____

Note: If the limiting belief is not resolved quickly, explore to see whether there are any other limiting beliefs or unidentified/unprocessed memory(ies)/networks that are causing this difficulty.

The session is then considered incomplete; therefore, return to the incomplete target and continue the installation process in the next session.

Phase Completed   □ Yes   □ No

Phase 6: Body Scan   ☐ Completed

"Close your eyes, and keep in mind the original memory and the words _____ (state the positive belief). Then bring your attention to different parts of your body, starting with your head and working downward. Any place you find any tension, tightness, or any unusual feeling, let me know."

Note: If the client reports any negative feeling, do a set of BLS until it disappears. If the client reports positive feelings, continue with BLS in order to strengthen them.

Phase 7: Closure   ☐ Completed

"Things may come up or they may not. If they do, great. Write it down and it can be a target for next time. You can use a log to write down triggers, images, thoughts or cognitions, emotions, and sensations; you can rate them on our 0 to 10 scale where 0 is no disturbance or neutral and 10 is the worst disturbance. Please write down the positive experiences, too."

"If you get any new memories, dreams, or situations that disturb you, just take a good snapshot. It isn't necessary to give a lot of detail. Just put down enough to remind you so we can target it next time. The same thing goes for any positive dreams or situations. If negative feelings do come up, try not to make them significant. Remember, it's still just the old stuff. Just write it down for next time. Then use the tape or the Safe Place exercise to let go of as much of the disturbance as possible. Even if nothing comes up, make sure to use the tape every day and give me a call if you need to."

Present Triggers

List of Triggers

Trigger 1:

Worst incident: _____

_____

Trigger 2:

Worst incident: _____

_____

Trigger 3:

Worst incident: _____

_____

Trigger 4:

Worst incident: _____

_____

Trigger 5:

Worst incident: _____

_____

Future Template

Incorporate a detailed template for dealing adaptively with an appropriate future situation (e.g., coping with a similar situation, or coping with present triggers/reminders, see above).

Image of coping effectively with/or in goal in future: _____

_____

PC: _____

New quality/attribute needed: _____

What you see as handling the situation: _____

Thinking, feeling, and experiencing in body: _____

+ BLS

VoC (able to handle the situation): _____ /7

Install until VoC = 7.

If VoC continues to be > 7, there are more targets to be identified and addressed with the Standard EMDR Protocol.

Blocks/anxieties/fears in future scene: _____

1. _____

2. _____

3. _____

Do BLS. If they do not resolve, ask for other qualities needed to handle the situation.

Other new information, resources, or skills to comfortably visualize coping in the future:

1. _____

2. _____

3. _____

If blocks are not resolved, identify unprocessed material and process with Standard EMDR Protocol:

1. _____

2. _____

3. _____

Target/Memory/Image: _____

_____

NC: _____

PC: _____

VoC: _____ /7

Emotions: _____

SUD: _____ /10

Sensation: _____

If there are no blocks, move on.

Future Image + PC + Sensations associated with future scenes + BLS

Do a body scan. (Close eyes + Image of Future + PC + Attention to Different Parts of Your Body + Report Tension/Tightness/Unusual Sensation). _____

If there is a sensation, process until the sensation subsides and the VoC = 7/ecological resolution and move on to the movie as a future template.

VoC: _____ /7

Image as future template: ☐ Completed

MOVIE AS FUTURE TEMPLATE OR IMAGINAL REHEARSING

Close eyes and play a movie adaptively coping with a difficult situation with a beginning, middle, and end.

Coping effectively with problem/in the location: _____

PC: _____

New quality/attribute: _____

Step into the future and imagine coping with ANY challenges. Movie has a beginning, middle, and end.

Thinking, feeling, and experiencing in body: _____

Blocks/anxieties/fears in future scene:

1. _____

2. _____

3. _____

If blocks, use BLS until disturbance dissipates or check for other qualities/resources needed. Other qualities/resources needed:

1. _____

2. _____

3. _____

If blocks are not resolved, identify unprocessed material and process with Standard EMDR Protocol:

1. _____

2. _____

3. _____

Target/Memory/Image: _____

_____

_____

NC: _____

PC: _____

VoC: _____ /7

Emotions: _____

SUD: _____ /10

Sensation: _____

If client can play movie from beginning to end with confidence and satisfaction, play the movie one more time from beginning to end + BLS: □ Completed

Movie as future template: □ Completed

References

Feusner, D., Philips, K. A., & Stein, D. J (2010). Olfactory reference syndrome: Issues for DSM-5. *Depression and Anxiety, 27*(6), 592–599.

Veale, D., Kinderman, P., Riley, S., & Lambrou, C. (2003, June). Self-discrepancy in body dysmorphic disorder. *British Journal of Clinical Psychology, 42*(Pt2), 157–169.

EMDR Therapy and Hoarding: The Hoarding Protocol

6

Priscilla Marquis and Christie Sprowls

Introduction

Compulsive hoarding is described as acquiring a large number of possessions and failing to discard them. These possessions create significant clutter in the environment and can preclude normal activities in the living spaces for which those spaces are designed. Hoarding creates significant distress and impairment in functioning for the individual and frequently their family members (Frost & Steketee, 2013).

Compulsive hoarding has recently become a separate diagnosis in the *Diagnostic and Statistical Manual of Mental Disorders* (*DSM-5*, Hoarding Disorder; American Psychiatric Association [APA], 2013) under the category of obsessive-compulsive disorder (OCD) and related disorders. It was placed there because research has not provided evidence that hoarding is *not* a symptom or subtype of OCD as previously thought (Frost & Steketee, 2013; Frost, Steketee, & Tolin, 2011; Mataix-Cols, Billotti, Fernandez de la Cruz, & Nordsletten, 2013). Many aspects of compulsive hoarding are still not fully understood.

Individuals with Hoarding Disorder may have comorbid attention deficit hyperactivity disorder (ADHD), OCD, depression, general anxiety disorder (GAD), social anxiety disorder (SAD), or problems with their executive functioning. Timpano et al. (2011) determined that 5.8% of the population suffers from compulsive hoarding. Research into the treatment of hoarding is relatively recent and most treatment has focused on cognitive behavioral treatment (CBT). Frost and Steketee (2013) presented a protocol for the treatment of Hoarding Disorder utilizing a combination treatment: education, motivational enhancement, goal setting, organizing skills training, decision-making skills training, practice resisting acquisition, and CBT to address dysfunctional beliefs, because they report that CBT alone has had limited utility in treating the disorder.

While many Eye Movement Desensitization and Reprocessing (EMDR) experts mention using EMDR Therapy as part of the treatment for hoarding (Gomez, 2013; Marich, 2011; Russell & Figley, 2013; Shapiro, 2009), the authors are unaware of any research or protocols used specifically for hoarding. The goal of this script is to provide guidance and focus for individuals who wish to use EMDR Therapy as a treatment for Hoarding Disorder. This script has been applied in clinical practice. It is important to note that individuals suffering from Hoarding Disorder typically have taken years to come to treatment. While EMDR Therapy may have a rapid impact on the behaviors and cognitions that constitute hoarding, the processing of completely decluttering their environment is often slow.

Criteria for Hoarding (APA, 2013)

Determine to what extent the client fulfills *DSM-5* criteria for Hoarding Disorder. The specific criteria can be found in the *DSM-5* (APA, 2013).

Among the criteria are:

1. Ongoing trouble with discarding or parting with possessions, regardless of their value.
2. The difficulty is due to the person feeling a need to save the items and distress when he or she discards them.
3. Difficulty with discarding items causes the accumulation of possessions that cause significant clutter and impacts on the intended use of living areas. If the person with hoarding does not have cluttered living areas it is only due to interventions of others (e.g., family members, house cleaners, or authorities).
4. Hoarding causes significant distress or impairment in social, occupational, or other key areas of functioning (including maintaining a safe environment for the person and others).
5. Hoarding is not due to another medical condition (e.g., brain injury, neurodegenerative disease or Prader–Willi syndrome.
6. Another psychiatric disorder (e.g., obsessions in OCD, decreased energy in Major Depressive Disorder, delusions in psychotic disorders, cognitive deficits in Major Neurocognitive Disorder, or restricted range of interests in Autism Spectrum Disorder) does not account more accurately for the presenting symptoms of hoarding.

Note if: The individual with hoarding has the following:

- Excessive acquisition when items are not needed or when there is no available space.
- Good or fair insight: The person recognizes that hoarding-related beliefs and behaviors are a problem.
- With poor insight: The individual believes most of the time that hoarding-related beliefs and behaviors are not problematic despite evidence to the contrary.
- With lack of insight or delusional beliefs: The person with hoarding is certain that hoarding-related beliefs and behaviors are not an issue despite proof that they are a problem.

Approximately 80% to 90% of individuals with Hoarding Disorder show excessive acquisition, for example. excessive buying or acquisition of free items. Some individuals may not report excessive acquisition at first, yet it may be revealed later during treatment. Individuals with Hoarding Disorder usually experience upset if they cannot acquire items (APA, 2013).

Adaptive Information Processing Model

It is important to conceptualize the EMDR treatment for Hoarding Disorder within the Adaptive Information Processing (AIP) framework. The individual's past experiences of hoarding and cluttering are like small traumas that remain unprocessed in the individual's information processing system, causing continual upset. Each time the person acquires new items, is unable to discard items, is upset by seeing stacks of items, or feels shame about the condition of her home, it is like a small trauma for that individual. Individuals with Hoarding Disorder avoid facing the anxiety of not acquiring an item or of discarding an item, much the way an individual with posttraumatic stress disorder (PTSD) avoids reminders of the trauma. With EMDR Therapy, reprocessing of the targets related to the Hoarding Disorder allows the individual to face the experience of not acquiring or of discarding without activating the negative network associated with Hoarding Disorder. This allows these persons to make permanent changes in their information processing related to hoarding, which will ultimately result in decreasing clutter and help them to achieve their desired goals.

The EMDR Therapy Hoarding Disorder Protocol Summary

The following is the Phobia Protocol Summary (Shapiro, 2001, p. 228) modified to apply to Hoarding Disorder. Use the Standard EMDR Protocol for targets elicited below.

1. Teach self-control procedures to handle the "fear of fear."

   Past Memories
2. Target and reprocess the following:
   a. Antecedent or ancillary events that contribute to the hoarding.
   b. First time hoarding was experienced.
   c. Most disturbing experiences related to hoarding.
   d. Most recent time it was experienced.

   Present Triggers
   e. Any associated present stimuli, including in vivo practice of discarding with patient in session.
   f. The physical sensations or other manifestations of fear, including hyperventilation.

   Future Template
3. Incorporate a positive template for fear-free future action.
4. Arrange contract for action.
5. Run mental videotape of full sequence and reprocess disturbance, imagining discarding objects and limiting acquisition behaviors.
6. Complete reprocessing of targets revealed between sessions.

The EMDR Therapy Hoarding Disorder Protocol Script Notes

During Phase 2: Preparation, it is important for the hoarding client to develop resources and gain information relevant to this disorder and EMDR Therapy.

- *Determine an appropriate and desirable goal of treatment; install desired state:* Often, it is difficult for individuals to work on their hoarding because it causes significant distress to discard items. One difficulty common to hoarding behaviors is the executive functioning skill of organizing and planning. Often, treatment of Hoarding Disorder fails because the individual is overwhelmed by the clutter and does not know where to begin. To address this distress, it is helpful to use the installation of a desired state (Popky, 2009):
  - Identify a *specific, positive, goal* that is *easy to achieve.*
  - Utilize a small area that can be easily decluttered in a short amount of time to help build mastery and self-efficacy for the client.
  - Imagine cleaning a small area of the kitchen counter, a coffee table, or an area of the bed.
  - Imagine this area free from clutter and available for its intended use.
  - Install the area free of clutter using short sets of bilateral stimulation (BLS; six to eight sets of BLS).
  - Imagine using this space to do a desired activity or seeing himself proudly showing someone this area.
  - Refocus on this desired state and continue enhancing using short sets of BLS until the individual can picture the target goal with positive emotion free from distress.

Note: Remember that during the preparation phase, we used the installation of the desired state to help pave the way for the processing of targets. It may be necessary to revisit the desired state frequently throughout treatment to help the individual decrease shame and maintain motivation for the difficult work of discarding. The desired state should be paired with BLS.

- *The Safe Place exercise:* Additionally, the use of the Safe Place exercise can be an important self-control technique for every client. Typically, the Safe Place is taught during one of the first sessions and clients are encouraged to practice the Safe Place exercise daily. This exercise can be found in Francine Shapiro's book, *Eye Movement Desensitization and Reprocessing: Basic Principles, Protocols and Procedures* (2nd ed., 2001) and scripted in Luber's *Eye Movement Desensitization and Reprocessing: Basics and Special Situations* (2009, pp. 67–70).
- *Rapport:* The reprocessing work should not start until rapport has been established and the therapist has explained the EMDR approach to the client. Rapport is particularly important for individuals who suffer from Hoarding Disorder, as they are often quite ashamed of their problem with clutter. It is important to give a basic explanation of EMDR tailored to the individual's level of education and psychological sophistication (Shapiro, 2001).
- *Clarify expectations*: For hoarding, preparation should include information about the course of treatment. It is important for both client and clinician to have appropriate expectations. Typically, by the time individuals come for treatment, they have been hoarding for many years and their living space and storage areas are extremely cluttered. It is helpful to encourage clients to understand that "Rome was not built in a day" and that the course of treatment progress may be slow but it will be permanent. Usually, in the initial phase of treatment, the focus is on decreasing acquisition behaviors. Then, the focus turns to discarding hoarded items.
  Note: Doing "clean-outs" where someone comes in and discards all hoarded items is generally not effective. Typically, a clean-out will cause the client to simply continue with previous acquisition behaviors and eventually the home will reach the same level of clutter.

During Phase 1: History Taking, or the assessment phase, the target selection and case conceptualization include a number of important ideas to keep in mind for this population:

- *Targeting*: Remember, the first target is typically the first time the individual started acquiring or hoarding; then the worst time; followed by the most recent time. After these targets, the clinician will help the client to target present stimuli or triggers such as urges to acquire or fear of discarding. However, some individuals may have an ancillary or antecedent memory that occurred prior to starting hoarding that should be targeted first, if possible. For example, a client may identify the memory of a loved one throwing away a treasured item, and realize that he later began hoarding related to this specific incident. For some individuals with hoarding, the initial target may actually be imagining some area of their home that is very cluttered or embarrassing.
- *Current triggers*: Triggers are important to address and may include urges to acquire objects, such as passing by certain stores, newspaper stands, or going to internet websites. Another common trigger is seeing stacks of items or clutter in the home that may prevent the client from doing daily activities. For individuals with hoarding, it may also be necessary to spend more time processing present stimuli. The individual can become triggered simply by being in the home environment, viewing stacks of hoarded items, seeing unpaid bills that are mixed in with uncluttered items, or being unable to use parts of the home for the intended purpose (such as being unable to sleep in a bed or being unable to turn on the heat). These triggers should be addressed with BLS using the full EMDR protocol.
  Note: Often, when a loved one who had a hoarding disorder dies, the individual who inherits that person's belongings develops a hoarding disorder as well. This

is a common antecedent to exacerbating a hoarding disorder. Also, it is helpful to understand that the main emotions individuals with this disorder experience related to sorting, discarding, and/or acquiring often are fear and/or shame.

During Phase 3: Assessment, obtaining the negative cognition (NC) and the positive cognition (PC) for patients with hoarding behaviors is essential. This is individualized and depends on the client and the characteristics of the target event. An NC should meet these criteria:

- Related to the target
- In present time
- Current irrational belief about the past experience, not a description of what happened at the time of event
- An irrational, negative self-referencing belief

Often with hoarding, individuals may have certain typical NCs and PCs depending on whether they are focused on acquiring or discarding behaviors.
For acquiring behaviors, the following cognitions are representative:

Negative Cognition	Positive Cognition
I am powerless	I am in control
I am unlovable (without desired object)	I am loveable
I am in danger	I am safe in the world

For discarding behaviors, the following cognitions are representative:

Negative Cognition	Positive Cognition
I am out of control	I am in control
I am worthless (without it)	I am loveable and worthwhile
I am in danger	I am safe now

Note: If there are ancillary memories related to hoarding, the NC and PC of these targets might have different cognitive domains (responsibility, safety, and/or choices) from the cognitions related to hoarding targets. For example, an individual may have a memory of a plumber who came to fix the shower. He experienced extreme shame when the plumber saw his severely hoarded apartment and chose the NC "I am worthless." The shame could be related to an ancillary memory of a parent's hoarding behavior that resulted in the NC: "I am unloveable."

Use the Standard EMDR Protocol to process targets relating to hoarding behaviors using the order of ancillary memory, first memory, worst memory, most recent memory, current triggers, and future issues.

When using the future template, if all targets are reprocessed and the body scan is clear, it is helpful for clients to process future situations where they will have to decrease acquisition behaviors or will have to discard hoarded items.

- *End-of-session use*: It may not be possible to reprocess all targets in one session. It is helpful, therefore, to install the future template at the end of each session, to help the client maintain motivation to continue the difficult work of decreasing acquisition behaviors and discarding.
- *Desired state*: In addition, individuals with Hoarding Disorder can get discouraged about persevering with discarding, as progress can seem slow. It can be helpful

during the installation of the future template to have the individual go back to the desired state *first*, then she can imagine working on discarding and imagining how wonderful it would feel to have a table with space to do art projects, or to have the entire bed available for sleeping.

- *Challenges client is facing*: Remember that working with the future template is an opportunity to be creative. Think through the challenges that the client will be facing in the coming week and incorporate them into the future template. Have the client imagine going through the week with the PC in mind, meeting the challenges of decreasing acquisition behaviors, discarding items, and maintaining appropriate self-caring behaviors.
  Note: Individuals with Hoarding Disorder often spend all of the time avoiding discarding and feeling depressed and guilty about it. The focus of treatment is to help the individual take back his life while slowly discarding hoarded items.
- *Specific goals*: For individuals with hoarding behaviors, it may be helpful to have the clinician assist the client with specific goals for the week. For example, if an individual is going to the thrift store daily to acquire new items, the future template could include having the client imagine only going one day that week or perhaps going with a list of questions and reading them before purchasing an item. If clients are working on discarding magazines, the clinician could have them imagine addressing a stack of magazines, holding in mind the PC ("I am in control") while confidently discarding the magazines. Individuals with Hoarding Disorder tend to be very avoidant of distressing stimuli and to have difficulty with planning, organizing, and recognizing salient stimuli. Have the client imagine the future and add the BLS. The BLS continues as long as the client reports positive insights and increased coping or confidence. The future template is successful when the client is able to picture the distressing situation with positive coping strategies and as little distress as possible. Remember that creativity and specificity to the situation are important for the future template.

In vivo practice of discarding helps clients who have Hoarding Disorder to have decreased avoidance and learn skills for discarding.

- *Slow going:* Individuals with hoarding often go very slowly when discarding to avoid making a mistake and doubt their ability to choose what to discard correctly.
- *In vivo practice–office*: Have the client bring in some hoarded items.
- *In vivo practice–home*: Alternatively, some clinicians work in the individual's home, helping her to practice discarding. Respect of the individual and the home is important, no matter how cluttered the home or apparently useless the items. Individuals with hoarding are often very ashamed of their clutter and their disorder.
- *Goal*: Part of the goal of the practice of discarding is to speed up the process and have clients face the fear that they may discard something incorrectly.
- *Practice*: It can be helpful to intentionally discard a useful item. BLS can be added to help the client with the level of distress. The clinician will assist the client in going through the stack of hoarded items. If he gets stuck, the clinician can add BLS to decrease distress.
- *Therapist attitude:* It is important for the clinician to remain positive but firm during this practice exercise.
- *Future template:* When finished, the clinician can use a future template to install the experience of discarding.
- *Homework:* The client should be encouraged to continue to practice at home. When you discuss specific homework with the client, keep the goal in mind: to work on decreasing acquiring, or discarding items for the week. It is important that the homework be time limited and that the client spend no more than 45 minutes per day (less is preferable) on hoarding homework.

Typically clients are seen at least weekly for EMDR Therapy. The treatment of Hoarding Disorder is likely to be slow, given that it has taken many years for these individuals' spaces to become cluttered and as a result it may take time to become uncluttered. It is important to remind clients that they may relapse on acquisition behaviors or have increased difficulty with discarding. It is important to remind clients that these setbacks are merely feedback and can be used as targets for subsequent sessions.

A *reevaluation* of the work that still remains to be done should be made at the beginning of each session. The client is asked about his current symptoms and about his progress in terms of success in carrying out his homework. It is important to reevaluate the client's subjective units of disturbance (SUD) level on the material that he was processing in the previous session. If the disturbance level has increased, it is important to retarget the event or issue. The therapist should assess the necessity of teaching the client additional self-control and relaxation techniques, as appropriate. With hoarding, clients may need help in decluttering or the assistance of a professional organizer. After processing through the Hoarding Disorder Protocol, there may be a need for additional targeting, particularly of ancillary present stimuli and other strategies necessary to ensure that the treatment goals are met.

Practice and positive reinforcement for success are essential. Individuals with Hoarding Disorder have often spent many years feeling inadequate and ineffectual. Remind clients frequently about their gains, however small. It is important to encourage hope and motivation for treatment, as they may see only the large amount of work that they have ahead of them.

It may have taken many years for individuals with hoarding behaviors to clutter their living spaces. Behavioral and cognitive change in hoarding may be quite rapid. The individual may drastically decrease or stop acquiring soon after beginning treatment. She may have changes in cognition and start discarding. EMDR Therapy can help clients to have a paradigm shift in the way they view their possessions. Many have been terrified to discard or stop acquiring. However, actual decluttering of their environment may be slow but permanent. Because individuals with Hoarding Disorder have difficulty with executive functioning skills of prioritization, organization, and staying focused, this can impact their ability to discard rapidly. It is important for the clinician to keep this in mind so that individuals do not become discouraged with treatment. The analogy of dieting is helpful. Rather than going on a hoarding diet, the goal is to make slow, permanent, lifelong changes.

The EMDR Therapy Hoarding Protocol Script

Phase 1: History Taking

Types of Hoarding and Severity

Determine the types of hoarding that occur and its severity.

Say, *"What sorts of items are you collecting, cluttering, or hoarding?"*

_____

_____

Say, *"Do you feel the need to continue acquiring these items?"*

_____

_____

Say, *"Do you have difficulty discarding them?"*

_____

_____

Say, *"Are there certain types of repetitive patterns that you have for acquiring items, such as daily online shopping or going to certain stores frequently?"*

_____

_____

Say, *"Are there areas in your house that you can't use for the intended purpose (such as not being able to use your bed for sleeping or your desk for writing)?"*

_____

_____

Say, *"How much distress is associated with discarding items? Are there certain categories of items that cause more distress than others?"*

_____

_____

Say, *"Do you feel that the amount of items that you have in your home or storage areas is excessive and causes you difficulty with your ability to live your life the way you want to live it?"*

_____

_____

Determine to What Extent the Client Fulfills Criteria for Hoarding Behavior (APA, 2013)

☐ Ongoing trouble with discarding or parting with possessions, regardless of their value.

☐ The difficulty is due to the person feeling a need to save the items and distress when he or she discards them.

☐ Difficulty with discarding items causes the accumulation of possessions that cause significant clutter and impacts on the intended use of living areas. If the person with hoarding does not have cluttered living areas it is only due to interventions of others (e.g., family members, house cleaners, or authorities).

☐ Hoarding causes significant distress or impairment in social, occupational, or other key areas of functioning (including maintaining safe environment for the person and others).

☐ Hoarding is not due to another medical condition (e.g., brain injury, neurodegenerative disease or Prader–Willi syndrome).

☐ Another psychiatric disorder (e.g., obsessions in OCD, decreased energy in Major Depressive Disorder, delusions in psychotic disorders, cognitive deficits in Major Neurocognitive Disorders, or restricted range of interests in Autism Spectrum Disorder) does not account more accurately for the presenting symptoms of hoarding.

Note if: The individual with hoarding has the following:

☐ Excessive acquisition when items are not needed or when there is no available space.

☐ Good or fair insight: The person recognizes that hoarding-related beliefs and behaviors are a problem.

☐ With poor insight: The individual believes most of the time that hoarding-related beliefs and behaviors are not problematic despite evidence to the contrary.

☐ With lack of insight or delusional beliefs: The person with hoarding is certain that hoarding-related beliefs and behaviors are not an issue despite proof that they are a problem.

Identify the Targets

EARLIER (ANCILLARY) EXPERIENCE

Check whether there were any ancillary experiences that contributed to the development of the Hoarding Disorder. What experiences laid the groundwork for this problem? What was happening at the time the individual began acquiring or had difficulty discarding for the first time?

Say, *"What else was happening around the time that this problem began?"*

_____

_____

FIRST TIME/TOUCHSTONE HOARDING EVENT

Say, *"What is the first time that you felt compelled to acquire or the first time that you felt distress when you discarded an object or objects? Or, in other words, when did the problem with hoarding and cluttering begin?"*

_____

_____

Or say, *"When did you notice this fear for the first time?"*

_____

_____

Or say, *"What incident caused you to start hoarding?"*

_____

_____

WORST EXPERIENCE OF HOARDING

Identify the worst experience of hoarding behavior.

Say, *"What is the worst or most distressing experience of your hoarding and cluttering?"*

_____

_____

MOST RECENT HOARDING EXPERIENCE

Identify the most recent experience of hoarding.

Say, *"When was the most recent time you experienced distress about your hoarding, acquiring, cluttering, or attempting to discard items?"*

_____

_____

OTHER RELEVANT EXPERIENCES OF HOARDING

Identify other relevant experiences of hoarding.

>   Say, *"What other past experiences might be important in relation to acquiring objects, hoarding, or anxiety about discarding objects?"*

_____

_____

PRESENT TRIGGERS

Identify any associated present stimuli.

>   Say, *"What triggers you to acquire or hoard objects?"*

_____

_____

>   Say, *"What triggers your anxiety about discarding objects?"*

_____

_____

Identify any other physical sensations or manifestations concerning hoarding behaviors.

>   Say, *"What physical sensations do you have that come up about acquiring objects, hoarding, or discarding objects?"*

_____

_____

FUTURE TEMPLATE

Identify the future concerns.

>   Say, *"What are your future concerns or anxieties about acquiring objects, hoarding, or discarding objects?"*

_____

_____

Phase 2: Preparation

EMDR Therapy Explanation

Explain EMDR Therapy to the client.

>   Say, *"When a trauma occurs, it seems to get locked in the nervous system with the original picture, sounds, thoughts, and feelings. Hoarding can be like having many small traumas occurring repeatedly each day. Each time we see something we want to acquire but shouldn't, or see items we want to discard but haven't, these are like small traumas. The eye movements we use in EMDR seem to unlock the nervous system and allow the brain to process the experience. That may be what is happening in REM or dream sleep: the eye movements may help to process the unconscious material. It is important to remember that it is your own brain that will be doing the healing and that you are the one in control."*

Determine an Appropriate and Desirable Goal of Treatment, Install Desired State

Help the individual identify a specific, positive goal that is easy to achieve.

> Say, *"See a small part of your home, such as a corner of the coffee table, cleared off and uncluttered* (or whatever is appropriate to your client). *Really see it, imagining how good it would look. Imagining how you would feel about yourself and your home when you accomplish this. Imagine it in Technicolor, seeing it brightly. Imagine using it to set your coffee cup on or putting up your feet on it."*

Add BLS in short sets (6 to 8 sets of eye movements).

> Say, *"What do you notice now?"*

_____

_____

If positive, add BLS.

If negative, refocus on desired state. Continue, repeating until client achieves positive enhancement and can picture the target goal with positive emotion free from distress.

Self-Control Techniques

Often, when individuals with Hoarding Disorder imagine discarding items or delaying acquiring items, they experience high levels of anxiety. It is helpful to teach clients self-control procedures, and practice this skill with them before beginning EMDR processing.

> Say, *"Self-control techniques can be helpful in managing your anxiety between sessions. The more you practice, the better you get at doing these techniques, making them more effective. Let's practice some of these techniques."*

ABDOMINAL BREATHING

> Say, *"I would like to teach you about abdominal breathing. Sit quietly with room for your abdomen to expand. Do gentle and even abdominal breathing, exhaling all of the way. See if you can make your exhale longer than your inhale. As you breathe in think: 'One.' As you breathe out think: 'Nothing.' Just focus on the breathing. If you get distracted, this is normal. Just gently refocus on the breathing, thinking the words: 'One' and 'Nothing.'"*

Encourage clients to practice this exercise for 5 minutes, twice per day, at first. They can do 5 minutes in the morning and 5 minutes in the evening. Gradually, they can increase their practice.

> Say, *"It is helpful to practice this exercise for 5 minutes, twice per day, at first. You might try 5 minutes in the morning and then 5 minutes in the evening. Gradually you can increase your practice to 20 to 30 minutes per day or more."*

PROGRESSIVE MUSCLE RELAXATION

> Say, *"I would like to introduce you to Progressive Muscle Relaxation. Clench your fists with your arms extended for 10 seconds, then release. Repeat, simply noticing the tension and release.*
>
> *Extend your arms with fingers up, hands stretched back at the wrists, for 10 seconds, then release and repeat, simply noticing the tension and release.*
>
> *Clench your fists, with your arms doubled up, for 10 seconds, then release. Repeat, simply noticing the tension and release.*
>
> *Now relax your arms and leave them resting comfortably.*

> *Lift eyebrows, wrinkling forehead, for 10 seconds and release. Then repeat, simply noticing the tension and release.*
>
> *Close your eyes tightly for 10 seconds, then release. Repeat, simply noticing the tension and release.*
>
> *Smile widely for 10 seconds and release, letting your jaw hang slack. Repeat, simply noticing the tension and release.*
>
> *Press your lips together for 10 seconds and release. Repeat, simply noticing the tension and release. Press your tongue on the roof of your mouth for 10 seconds and release. Repeat, simply noticing the tension and release.*
>
> *Open your jaw wide for 10 seconds and release. Repeat, simply noticing the tension and release. Gently tilt your head to one side for 10 seconds, then tilt head forward for 10 seconds, then to the other side for 10 seconds. Repeat, simply noticing the tension and release.*
>
> *Lift your shoulders up toward your ears for 10 seconds and release. Repeat, simply noticing the tension and release.*
>
> *Lean back slightly, to engage your back muscles (gently), for 10 seconds and release. Repeat, simply noticing the tension and release.*
>
> *Press your stomach muscles back toward your back for 10 seconds and release. Repeat, simply noticing the tension and release.*
>
> *Press your heels into the floor for 10 seconds and release. Repeat, simply noticing the tension and release.*
>
> *Lift your feet up, with your toes toward the ceiling for 10 seconds and then release. Repeat, simply noticing the tension and release.*
>
> *Lift up your heels for 10 seconds and then release. Repeat, simply noticing the tension and release. Lift up your toes for 10 seconds then release. Repeat, simply noticing the tension and release.*
>
> *Now scan your entire body from the top of your head to the tips of your toes, releasing any residual tension."*

Typically it is helpful to practice 10 to 15 minutes per day and increase this to up to an hour.

THE SAFE PLACE

Teach the Safe Place exercise. This exercise can be found in *Eye Movement Desensitization and Reprocessing (EMDR), Second Edition: Basic Principles, Protocols and Procedures* (Shapiro, 2001), and scripted in *Eye Movement Desensitization and Reprocessing (EMDR) Scripted Protocols: Basics and Special Situations* (Luber, 2009).

Course of Treatment

For hoarding, preparation should include information about the course of treatment with appropriate expectations.

> Say, *"It may have taken you many years for your living space to get cluttered up. It will take time to get uncluttered. We are making permanent changes in behaviors that will result in an uncluttered life. The progress will be slow but steady and permanent."*

Decreasing Acquisition Behaviors

With Hoarding Disorder, decreasing acquisition behaviors is done as part of the preparation phase; however, if the individual has difficulty in decreasing acquisition behaviors, this may have to be paired with BLS to increase the assimilation of new behaviors.

Usually, in the initial phase of treatment, the focus is on decreasing acquisition behaviors. Then, the focus turns to discarding hoarded items.

Say, *"We are going to focus on helping you to decrease acquisition behaviors first. Then we will work on helping you to learn how to discard your hoarded items. The progress may be slow, but will be permanent. Just like crash diets that do not work for people who want to lose weight, trying to discard all your hoarded items at once will not be effective. People who do this 'all or nothing' approach often feel overwhelmed, discouraged, and depressed. Rome wasn't built in a day. We want to focus on decluttering a little every day, then move on, living your life, doing things to take care of yourself and doing pleasant activities. Often a 5 minute tornado is helpful where you spend 5 minutes going through items, saying, 'Keep. Throw away. Keep. Throw away.' Then, discard the items and reward yourself for a job well done!"*

Say, *"Often people with a hoarding disorder find it helpful to ask themselves the following questions when trying to determine whether to acquire or discard an item:*

- *Do I really need it?*
- *Is keeping it going to help me with my long-term goals* (i.e., having an uncluttered life, improving my relationship, having time and space to do art, etc.)*?*
- *Do I have an immediate plan for its use?*

Note: Typically clients with hoarding will never get to their projects. They have many plans to complete projects but with their level of clutter, they do not have time or space to complete them.

- *Do I have a place to put it?*
- *Do I already have one?*
- *Do I have time to do it?*
- *How many does one need?*
- *Is this available online?"*

Say, *"You can use this list of questions when going shopping or use this list when trying to decide whether to acquire or discard an object."*

Phase 3: Assessment

Past Memories: Target Selection

Select a target image of the memory. As mentioned in the notes, typically the first target is the first distressing event associated with hoarding. Targets are selected during the assessment phase. Remembering the case conceptualization, we always work from the past, to the present, to the future. Use the Phobia Protocol: Ancillary Events, First Time, Worst Time, Most Recent Time, Present Triggers, and then the Future.

ANCILLARY OR ANTECEDENT EVENTS CONTRIBUTING TO HOARDING BEHAVIORS

Incident

Say, *"The memory that we will start with today is* _____ (select the incident from the treatment plan).*"*

_____

_____

Picture

Say, *"What picture represents the most disturbing part of this incident now?"*

_____

_____

Negative Cognition

Note: Often NCs and PCs vary according to whether they are connected to acquiring or discarding behaviors. If there are ancillary memories to the memories related to the hoarding, the NC and PC of these targets may have different cognitive domains from the cognitions related to hoarding targets.

Say, *"What words best go with the picture that express your negative belief about yourself now?"*

_____

_____

Positive Cognition

Say, *"When you bring up the picture of the incident, what would you like to believe about yourself now?"*

_____

_____

Validity of Cognition

Say, *"When you bring up the picture of the incident, how true do those words _____ (repeat the PC) feel to you now on a scale of 1 to 7, where 1 feels completely false and 7 feels completely true?"*

_____

_____

1	2	3	4	5	6	7

(completely false)   (completely true)

Emotions

Say, *"When you bring up the picture* (or incident) *and those words* _____ (state the NC), *what emotion do you feel now?"*

_____

_____

Subjective Units of Disturbance

Say, *"On a scale of 0 to 10, where 0 is no disturbance or neutral and 10 is the highest disturbance you can imagine, how disturbing does it feel now?"*

0	1	2	3	4	5	6	7	8	9	10

(no disturbance)   (highest disturbance)

Location of Body Sensations

Say, *"Where do you feel it* (the disturbance) *in your body?"*

_____

_____

FIRST TIME HOARDING BEHAVIOR EXPERIENCED

Incident

Say, *"The memory that we will start with today is* _____ (select the incident from the treatment plan)*."*

_____

_____

Picture

Say, *"What picture represents the most disturbing part of this incident now?"*

_____

_____

Negative Cognition

Say, *"What words best go with the picture that express your negative belief about yourself now?"*

_____

_____

Positive Cognition

Say, *"When you bring up the picture of the incident, what would you like to believe about yourself now?"*

_____

_____

Validity of Cognition

Say, *"When you bring up the picture of the incident, how true do those words* _____ (repeat the PC) *feel to you now on a scale of 1 to 7, where 1 feels completely false and 7 feels completely true?"*

_____

_____

1	2	3	4	5	6	7
(completely false)				(completely true)		

Emotions

Say, *"When you bring up the picture* (or incident) *and those words* _____ (state the NC), *what emotion do you feel now?"*

_____

_____

Subjective Units of Disturbance

Say, *"On a scale of 0 to 10, where 0 is no disturbance or neutral and 10 is the highest disturbance you can imagine, how disturbing does it feel now?"*

0	1	2	3	4	5	6	7	8	9	10

(no disturbance)   (highest disturbance)

Location of Body Sensations

Say, *"Where do you feel it* (the disturbance) *in your body?"*

_____

_____

MOST DISTURBING HOARDING BEHAVIOR EXPERIENCE

Incident

Say, *"The memory that we will start with today is* _____ (select the incident from the treatment plan)."*

_____

_____

Picture

Say, *"What picture represents the most disturbing part of this incident now?"*

_____

_____

Negative Cognition

Say, *"What words best go with the picture that express your negative belief about yourself now?"*

_____

_____

Positive Cognition

Say, *"When you bring up the picture of the incident, what would you like to believe about yourself now?"*

_____

_____

Validity of Cognition

Say, *"When you bring up the picture of the incident, how true do those words*
_____ (repeat the PC) *feel to you now on a scale of 1 to 7, where 1 feels*
completely false and 7 feels completely true?"

_____

_____

1	2	3	4	5	6	7

(completely false)   (completely true)

Emotions

Say, *"When you bring up the picture* (or incident) *and those words* _____
(state the NC), *what emotion do you feel now?"*

_____

_____

Subjective Units of Disturbance

Say, *"On a scale of 0 to 10, where 0 is no disturbance or neutral and 10 is the*
highest disturbance you can imagine, how disturbing does it feel now?"

0	1	2	3	4	5	6	7	8	9	10

(no disturbance)   (highest disturbance)

Location of Body Sensations

Say, *"Where do you feel it* (the disturbance) *in your body?"*

_____

_____

MOST RECENT HOARDING BEHAVIOR EXPERIENCE

Incident

Say, *"The memory that we will start with today is* _____ (select the incident from the treatment plan)."

_____

_____

Picture

Say, *"What picture represents the most disturbing part of this incident now?"*

_____

_____

Negative Cognition

Say, *"What words best go with the picture that express your negative belief about yourself now?"*

_____

_____

Positive Cognition

Say, *"When you bring up the picture of the incident, what would you like to believe about yourself now?"*

_____

_____

Validity of Cognition

Say, *"When you bring up the picture of the incident, how true do those words* _____ (repeat the PC) *feel to you now on a scale of 1 to 7, where 1 feels completely false and 7 feels completely true?"*

_____

_____

1	2	3	4	5	6	7
(completely false)				(completely true)		

Emotions

Say, *"When you bring up the picture* (or incident) *and those words* _____ (state the NC), *what emotion do you feel now?"*

_____

_____

Subjective Units of Disturbance

Say, *"On a scale of 0 to 10, where 0 is no disturbance or neutral and 10 is the highest disturbance you can imagine, how disturbing does it feel now?"*

0	1	2	3	4	5	6	7	8	9	10
(no disturbance)							(highest disturbance)			

Location of Body Sensations

Say, *"Where do you feel it* (the disturbance) *in your body?"*

_____

_____

Phase 4: Desensitization

The Standard EMDR Protocol is used to process targets in the above order. Remember that during the preparation phase, the installation of the desired state was used to help pave the way for the processing of targets. It can be helpful to access the desired state before starting processing so the client is accessing the positive network related to the desired goal of treatment.

Access the Desired State

Say, *"See* _____ (state the specific, positive goal chosen for the desired goal). *Really see it, imagining how good it would look. Imagine how you would feel about yourself and your home when you accomplish this. Imagine it in Technicolor, seeing it brightly. Imagine* _____ (state the desired goal).*"*

Add BLS in short sets (6 to 8 sets of eye movements).

Say, *"What do you notice now?"*

_____

_____

If positive, add BLS.
If negative, refocus on desired state. Continue, repeating until the client achieves positive enhancement and can picture the target goal with positive emotion free from distress.
The work in phase 4 follows the Standard EMDR Protocol.

Explain the Process

To begin, say the following:

Say, *"Now, remember, it is your own brain that is doing the healing and you are the one in control. I will ask you to mentally focus on the target and to* _____ (state BLS you are using). *Just let whatever happens, happen, and we will talk at the end of the set. Just tell me what comes up and don't discard anything as unimportant. Any new information that comes to mind is connected in some way. If you want to stop, just raise your hand."*

Then say, *"Bring up the picture and the words* _____ (repeat the NC) *and notice where you feel it in your body. Now follow* _____ (state BLS).*"*

_____

_____

This procedure is to be repeated until the SUDs = 0.

Say, *"When you go back to the original image or incident, notice the words* _____ (repeat the NC), *the emotion and body sensation and follow my fingers."*

_____

_____

Then the PC is installed.

Note: Each traumatic event associated with the problem that is not reprocessed during the normal course of the first target must be processed using the above protocol until the SUDs reach an ecological 1 or 0 and the PC is installed.

Continue with sets of BLS until the SUD level reaches 0.

Phase 5: Installation

Check the Initial PC

Say, *"When you bring up that original incident, does your original positive belief* (repeat the PC) _____ *still fit, or is there now a better statement or positive belief about yourself?"*

_____

_____

If the client accepts the original PC, the clinician should check the VoC rating to see if it has improved.

Say, *"As you think about the original incident and those words* _____ (repeat the selected PC), *how do the words feel to you now on a scale where 1 is completely false and 7 is completely true?"*

1   2   3   4   5   6   7

(completely false)   (completely true)

Installation of the PC

Say, *"Think of the event and hold it together with the words* _____ (repeat the PC). *Go with that."*

Add BLS.

_____

_____

Continue this procedure until the VoC reaches 7.

Link the PC and the Target and Install

Say, *"Think about the original incident or event and hold it together with the words* _____ (repeat the PC) *and follow my fingers."*

Add BLS.

_____

_____

Do sets of BLS as long as the client reports new positive associations, sensations, or emotions. Check VoC after each set of BLS, until the PC is fully installed (VoC = 7). Remember to check for a blocking belief if the VoC does not reach a 7.

Check Other Targets

If there is generalization, it is possible that the other targets (ancillary events, first, worst, most recent, and present triggers) delineated during the history-taking phase are no longer distressing, so it is helpful to check the other target events to see if they are still salient. Remember that the targets (ancillary events that were occurring at the time when the Hoarding Disorder began, the first time, the worst time, the most recent time, and present triggers, which were discovered in the history taking and delineated further in the assessment phase) may no longer feel distressing to clients, so it is helpful check the other target events to see if they are still salient.

Say, *"OK, let's check the next target _____ (bring up the next target). On
a scale of 0 to 10, where 0 is no disturbance or neutral and 10 is the highest
disturbance you can imagine, how disturbing does it feel to you now?"*

   0   1   2   3   4   5   6   7   8   9   10

(no disturbance)   (highest disturbance)

If the SUD is greater than 0, proceed with the desensitization phase. Continue processing through targets that are still disturbing, processing the first, worst, most recent, and
current stimuli.

Phase 6: Body Scan

Say, *"Close your eyes and notice what you are feeling in your body. Bring your
attention to the different parts of your body, starting with your head and
working downward. Any place you find any tension, tightness, or unusual
sensation, tell me."*

_____

_____

If any sensation is reported, add BLS.

If it is a positive or comfortable sensation, use BLS to strengthen the positive feelings.

If a sensation of discomfort is reported, reprocess the body sensation until the discomfort subsides.

Present Triggers

Check for any present triggers that are still disturbing. Typical triggers could be anxiety
related to discarding, urges to acquire, or distress at viewing hoarded spaces or family dis-
cord due to the hoarding, for example.

Any Associated Present Stimuli That Are Triggers

Process any situations, events, or stimuli triggers that bring up the hoarding behaviors.

Say, *"What are the situations, events, and/or stimuli triggers that still bring up
the hoarding behaviors?"*

Situations, Events, or Stimuli Trigger List

_____

_____

_____

_____

_____

Incident

Say, *"What situation, event, or stimulus would you like to use as a target today?"*

_____

_____

Picture

Say, *"What picture represents the most disturbing part of this incident now?"*

_____

_____

Negative Cognition

Say, *"What words best go with the picture that express your negative belief about yourself now?"*

_____

_____

Positive Cognition

Say, *"When you bring up the picture of the incident, what would you like to believe about yourself now?"*

_____

_____

Validity of Cognition

Say, *"When you bring up the picture of the incident, how true do those words _____ (repeat the PC) feel to you now on a scale of 1 to 7, where 1 feels completely false and 7 feels completely true?"*

_____

_____

1	2	3	4	5	6	7
(completely false)				(completely true)		

Emotions

Say, *"When you bring up the picture* (or incident) *and those words _____ (state the NC), what emotion do you feel now?"*

_____

_____

Subjective Units of Disturbance

Say, *"On a scale of 0 to 10, where 0 is no disturbance or neutral and 10 is the highest disturbance you can imagine, how disturbing does it feel now?"*

0	1	2	3	4	5	6	7	8	9	10
(no disturbance)								(highest disturbance)		

Location of Body Sensations

Say, *"Where do you feel it* (the disturbance) *in your body?"*

_____

_____

SENSATIONS ASSOCIATED WITH HOARDING BEHAVIORS

Sensation Symptom List

_____

_____

_____

Incident

Say, *"What are the sensations concerning your* _____ (state the hoarding behaviors)? *Let's process them one by one."*

_____

_____

Picture

Say, *"What picture represents the most disturbing part of this incident now?"*

_____

_____

Negative Cognition

Say, *"What words best go with the picture that express your negative belief about yourself now?"*

_____

_____

Positive Cognition

Say, *"When you bring up the picture of the incident, what would you like to believe about yourself now?"*

_____

_____

Validity of Cognition

Say, *"When you bring up the picture of the incident, how true do those words _____ (repeat the PC) feel to you now on a scale of 1 to 7, where 1 feels completely false and 7 feels completely true?"*

_____

_____

1   2   3   4   5   6   7

(completely false)   (completely true)

Emotions

Say, *"When you bring up the picture (or incident) and those words _____ (state the NC), what emotion do you feel now?"*

_____

_____

Subjective Units of Disturbance

Say, *"On a scale of 0 to 10, where 0 is no disturbance or neutral and 10 is the highest disturbance you can imagine, how disturbing does it feel now?"*

0   1   2   3   4   5   6   7   8   9   10

(no disturbance)   (highest disturbance)

Location of Body Sensations

Say, *"Where do you feel it (the disturbance) in your body?"*

_____

_____

Future Template

Installation of the Future Template

Normally, the future template is used when the targets are reprocessed and the body scan is clear. Often, for patients with hoarding behaviors, it may not be possible to fully reprocess all targets in one session. In these circumstances, with incomplete sessions, it is helpful to use the installation of the future template at the end of each session, to help patients maintain the motivation to continue the difficult work of decreasing acquisition behaviors and increasing discarding. Have the client imagine going through the week, with the PC in mind, meeting the challenges of decreasing acquisition behaviors, discarding items, and maintaining appropriate self-caring behaviors.

Say, *"While holding the positive belief about yourself in mind _____ (repeat PC), run a movie imagining that you are going through your week successfully, facing the challenges of not acquiring new items and getting rid of your hoarded items and notice what comes up."*

_____

_____

If the individual reports something negative (e.g., the spouse saying something negative to him about the hoarding while he is reprocessing), reprocess those disturbances until the client can run the whole movie all of the way through successfully accomplishing the goal.

Say, *"Go with that."*

_____

_____

In addition, individuals with Hoarding Disorder can get discouraged about persevering with discarding, as progress can seem slow.

Say, " _____(state patient's name), *you are telling me that you are having a hard time staying on track with our plan for* _____ (state goal, such as discarding the papers on your desk). *What would you like to accomplish this week?"*

_____

_____

It can be helpful during the installation of the future template to have the individual go back to the desired state.

Say, *"See* _____ (state the specific, positive goal chosen for the desired goal). *Really see it, imagining how good it would look. Imagine how you would feel about yourself and your home when you accomplish this. Imagine it in Technicolor, seeing it brightly. Imagine* _____ (state the desired goal)."
Add BLS in short sets (6 to 8 sets of eye movements).

Say, *"What do you notice now?"*

_____

_____

Say, *"Run a movie of yourself doing that successfully. For example,* _____ (state goal, such as imagine seeing yourself sitting at your desk, going through the piles of papers, and successfully discarding items you no longer need or want)."

_____

_____

Have the client imagine specific, future goals and add BLS. The BLS continues as long as the client reports positive insights and increased coping or confidence. The future template is successful when the client is able to picture the distressing situation with positive coping strategies and as little distress as possible.

Say, *"Imagine spending five minutes per day* _____ (state the challenge for your patient, such as sorting through items on the coffee table rapidly, into two piles: a pile to keep and a pile to throw away). *Hold the words in mind* (PC) *'I am worthwhile' while you see yourself* _____ (state activity). *Go quickly, telling yourself, 'Keep or throw away.' Notice any distress that comes up and see yourself coping well. Imagine* _____ (state goal). *Follow my fingers* (or notice any other BLS)."

_____

_____

Or say, *"Imagine going through the week and resisting* _____ (state what needs to be resisted). *Play a movie of the entire week, holding in mind the words 'I am strong'* (PC). *Imagine yourself coping well with any challenges that happen. Notice what you are seeing, thinking, feeling, and experiencing in your body.*

While playing the movie, let me know if there are any blocks. If there are no blocks, tell me when you have viewed the whole movie. Now, follow my fingers (or notice any other BLS)."

_____

_____

In Vivo Practice of Discarding

Have the client bring in some hoarded items. Alternatively, some clinicians work in the individual's home, helping her to practice discarding. Part of the goal of practice discarding is to speed up the process and have the client face the fear that she may discard something incorrectly. It can be helpful to intentionally have the individual discard a useful item. BLS can be added to help the client with the level of distress.

Say, *"Let's go through this stack of items. Work quickly; the only decision you need to make today is 'keep' or 'throw away.' Remember your list of questions:*

- *Do I really need it?*
- *Is keeping it going to help me with my long-term goals* (uncluttered life)?
- *Do I have an immediate plan for its use?* (No projects)
- *Do I have a place to put it?*
- *Do I already have one?*
- *Do I have time to do it?*
- *How many does one need?*
- *Is this available online?*
- *Let's start with this first item. Is this 'keep' or 'throw away?'"*

If the client gets stuck, the clinician can add BLS to decrease distress.

Say, *"Go with that."*

It is important for the clinician to remain positive but firm during this practice exercise. When finished, the clinician can use a future template to install the experience of discarding.

Say, *"Imagine yourself going through a pile of things that you want to discard. Have your positive cognition in mind,* _____(state PC). *See yourself doing it quickly, making two piles: keep and throw away. Then imagine yourself immediately getting rid of the 'throw away pile.' If possible, see yourself putting away things from the 'keep pile.'"*

The client should be encouraged to continue to practice at home. See Phase 7: Closure.

Phase 7: Closure

At the end of every session, consolidate the changes and improvement that have occurred.

Say, *"What is the most positive thing you have learned about yourself during this session with regard to* _____ (state the target or theme)?"

_____

_____

When you discuss specific homework with the client, keep the goal in mind: to work on decreasing acquiring, or discarding items for the week. It is important that the homework be time limited and that the client spend no more than 45 minutes per day (less is preferable) on hoarding homework.

Say, *"Let's think about a specific plan of action for this week. Can you think of a small goal focused on either decreasing acquiring behaviors or increasing discarding behaviors that you would like to work on this week? It is important not to spend too much time on it. I would recommend spending 5 to 15 minutes per day."*

The clinician listens for an answer and helps the client to specify the homework.

Say, *"That sounds great; spending* _____ (state how many minutes) *minutes on* _____ (state the behavior client agrees to do) *is an excellent goal. Let's plan what time of day you are going to do it and where. Remember with junk mail, if you are not going to handle something right away, you can throw it away because they will send you a new one."*

Say, *"Also, I think it is important to plan some pleasant activities this week as part of your homework. What pleasant activities would you like to do?"*

The clinician listens for an answer and then reinforces.

Say, *"OK, that is a great idea to do* _____ (state the pleasant activity) *for your pleasant activities this week. Remember that if you have difficulty with your homework, this is just feedback for us to work on at our next session. Also, remember that you can always call me if you get stuck."*

Say, *"You have done great work today and can be proud of yourself. Sometimes things come up and sometimes nothing is noticed. If they do, this is just feedback. Keep a log and we can make it a target for next time. If you get any new memories, dreams, or situations that disturb you, just take a snapshot of what is disturbing or even interesting. It isn't necessary to give a lot of detail. Just put down enough to remind yourself, so we can target it next time. If negative feelings do come up, you can practice a self-control technique such as the breathing or the Safe Place. Remember to practice a self-control technique each day, even if things are going well. Please remember to practice your homework. You can call me if you would like to."*

Phase 8: Reevaluation

The treatment of Hoarding Disorder is likely to be slow, given that it has probably taken many years for the individual's space to become cluttered; as a result, it may take time to become uncluttered. It is important to remind clients that they may relapse on acquiring behaviors or have increased difficulty with discarding. It is important to remind clients that these setbacks are merely feedback and can be used as targets for subsequent sessions.

Say, *"It has taken a long time for your space to become so cluttered and it will take time to reverse the process. We are changing ingrained patterns and there may be times when it is harder to resist urges to acquire or to discard things. Sometimes, even with the new skills you are learning, you might feel like you are back to square one. This can happen; don't be alarmed, as it is not unusual. When this happens, just note what has happened, what is going on around you, and what you did to handle the situation so that you don't forget what happened and how it felt and then bring it or them to the next session so that we can determine what to target next. Do you have any questions?"*

_____

_____

Say, *"If you go back to the target that we were working on last time, on a scale of 0 to 10, where 0 is no disturbance or neutral and 10 is the highest disturbance you can imagine, how disturbing does it feel to you now?"*

0   1   2   3   4   5   6   7   8   9   10

(no disturbance)   (highest disturbance)

If the disturbance level has increased, the event or issue should be retargeted. The therapist should assess the necessity of teaching the client additional self-control and perhaps relaxation techniques. Individuals with a Hoarding Disorder may need help in decluttering or to employ the assistance of a professional organizer.

Say, *"Are there other resources that might be helpful in dealing with this situation?"*

_____

_____

Reinforce Homework and Practice!

Say, *"You have really been working hard, both in our sessions and at home _____ (praise what the client has done that has been successful, focusing on the small gains he has made)."*

The clinician should continue to help the client to focus on small gains.

Summary

The treatment of Hoarding Disorder with EMDR Therapy is a comprehensive protocol that involves decreasing acquisition behaviors and increasing discarding behaviors. The end goal is for the individual to live a fulfilled and healthy life with work, social activities, relationships, and pleasure in daily activities. Having a clutter-free living environment is part of this goal. Clients implement changing behaviors and cognitions with EMDR Therapy processing. Individuals actually change their relationship with hoarded items in the course of treatment so that they eventually are able to live their lives without either excessive acquiring or hoarding. It is important for the clinician to remember that individuals suffering from Hoarding Disorder have taken many years to clutter their living spaces. While the behavioral and cognitive changes may be put in place rather quickly in EMDR Therapy, the actual decluttering of the client's environment may take more time. However, the changes typically are permanent and the sufferers will eventually achieve an uncluttered living environment.

References

American Psychiatric Association. (2013). *Diagnostic and statistical manual of mental disorders* (5th ed.). Arlington, VA: American Psychiatric Publishing.

Frost, R. O., & Steketee, G. (2013). *The Oxford handbook of hoarding and acquiring.* Oxford, UK: Oxford University Press.

Frost, R. O., Steketee, G., & Tolin, D. (2011, October). Comorbidity in hoarding disorder. *Depression and Anxiety, 28*(10), 876–884. doi:10.1002/da.20861

Gomez, A. (Ed.). (2013). *EMDR therapy and adjunct approaches with children: Complex trauma, attachment and dissociation.* New York, NY: Springer.

Luber, M. (2009). The Safe/Calm Place Protocol. *Eye movement desensitization and reprocessing (EMDR) scripted protocols: Basics and special situations* (pp.67–70). New York, NY: Springer.

Marich, J. (2011). *EMDR made simple: 4 approaches to using EMDR with every client.* Wisconsin: Premier Publishing and Media Eau Claire.

Mataix-Cols, D., Billotti, D., Fernandez de la Cruz, I., & Nordsletten, A. E. (2013). The London field trial for hoarding disorder. *Psychological Medicine, 43*(4), 837–847.

Popky, A. J. (2009). DeTur, an urge reduction protocol for addictions and dysfunctional behaviors. In M. Luber (Ed.), *Eye movement desensitization and reprocessing (EMDR) scripted protocols: Special populations* (pp. 489–516). New York, NY: Springer.

Russell, M., & Figley, C. (2013).*Treating traumatic stress injuries in military personnel: An EMDR practitioner's guide* (Routledge Psychosocial Stress Series). New York, NY: Routledge.

Shapiro, F. (2001). *Eye movement desensitization and reprocessing: Basic principles, protocols, and procedures* (2nd ed.). New York, NY: Guilford Press.

Shapiro, R. (Ed.). (2009). *EMDR solutions II, for depression, eating disorders, performance and more.* New York, NY: W.W. Norton.

Timpano, K. R., Exner, C., Glaesmer, H., Rief, W., Keshaviah, A., Brahler, E., & Wilhelm, S. (2011, June). The epidemiology of the proposed DSM-5 hoarding disorder: Exploration of the acquisition specifier, associated features and distress. *Psychiatry, 72*(6), 780–786.

Treatment Session Summary Notes

For Record-keeping Purposes

Check Appropriate Items

NAME _____ **DATE** ____/____/

PRESENTING ISSUE:

TARGET: ☐ Touchstone Memory   ☐ Past Present Trigger   ☐ First   ☐ Worst   ☐ Most Recent
☐ Future Template

Target Status now: ☐ Completed   ☐ Unfinished

STABILIZATION EXERCISE used at the end of the session?

☐ Safe Place   ☐ Light Stream   ☐ Breathing   ☐ Other _____

CLIENT STABILIZATION STATUS (when leaving session): ☐ Poor   ☐ Fair   ☐ Good
☐ Excellent

HOMEWORK ASSIGNMENT

TREATMENT SUMMARY NOTES:

_____

_____

_____

_____

Issues/associations of importance that arose during reprocessing to be reevaluated at later time:

_____

SUMMARY SHEET:
EMDR Therapy and Hoarding:
The Hoarding Protocol

Priscilla Marquis and Christie Sprowls
SUMMARY SHEET BY MARILYN LUBER

Name: _____ Diagnosis: _____

☑ Check when task is completed, response has changed, or to indicate symptoms or diagnosis.

Note: This material is meant as a checklist for your response. Please keep in mind that it is only a reminder of different tasks that may or may not apply to your client.

Introduction

Determine to What Extent the Client Fulfills Criteria for Hoarding Behavior (APA, 2013)

☐ Ongoing trouble with discarding or parting with possessions, regardless of their value.

☐ The difficulty is due to the person feeling a need to save the items and distress when he or she discards them.

☐ Difficulty with discarding items causes the accumulation of possessions that cause significant clutter and impacts on the intended use of living areas. If the person with hoarding does not have cluttered living areas it is only due to interventions of others (e.g., family members, house cleaners, or authorities).

☐ Hoarding causes significant distress or impairment in social, occupational, or other key areas of functioning (including maintaining safe environment for the person and others).

☐ Hoarding is not due to another medical condition (e.g., brain injury, neurodegenerative disease or Prader--Willi syndrome).

☐ Another psychiatric disorder (e.g., obsessions in OCD, decreased energy in Major Depressive Disorder, delusions in psychotic disorders, cognitive deficits in Major Neurocognitive Disorders, or restricted range of interests in Autism Spectrum Disorder) does not account more accurately for the presenting symptoms of hoarding.

Note if: The individual with hoarding has the following:

☐ Excessive acquisition when items are not needed or when there is no available space.

☐ Good or fair insight: The person recognizes that hoarding-related beliefs and behaviors are a problem.

☐ With poor insight: The individual believes most of the time that hoarding-related beliefs and behaviors are not problematic despite evidence to the contrary.
☐ With lack of insight or delusional beliefs: The person with hoarding is certain that hoarding-related beliefs and behaviors are not an issue despite proof that they are a problem.

Adaptive Information Processing Model

AIP explanation: The individual's past experiences of hoarding and cluttering are like small traumas that remain unprocessed in the individual's information processing system, causing continual upset. Each time the person acquires new items, is unable to discard items, is upset by seeing stacks of items, or feels shame about the condition of the home is like a small trauma for that individual. These persons avoid facing the anxiety of not acquiring an item or of discarding an item, much the way an individual with posttraumatic stress disorder (PTSD) avoids reminders of the trauma. With EMDR Therapy, reprocessing of the targets related to the Hoarding Disorder allows the individual to face the experience of not acquiring or of discarding without activating the negative network associated with Hoarding Disorder. This allows them to make permanent changes in their information processing related to hoarding, which will ultimately result in decreasing clutter and help them to achieve their desired goals.

The EMDR Therapy Hoarding Disorder Protocol Script

Phase 1: Client History

Types of Hoarding and Severity

Items collected, cluttering/hoarding: _____

_____

_____

Need to continue?   ☐ Yes   ☐ No

Difficulty discarding them?   ☐ Yes   ☐ No

Repetitive patterns for acquiring items (daily online shopping/going to certain stores frequently)?

_____

_____

Areas can't be used for intended purpose?   ☐ Yes   ☐ No

Amount of distress associated with discarding items? _____

Certain categories cause more distress than others: ☐ Yes   ☐ No

Amount of items in home or storage excessive and cause difficulty?   ☐ Yes   ☐ No

Identify the Targets

Earlier (ancillary) experience: _____

_____

_____

First time/Touchstone hoarding event: _____

_____

_____

Worst experience of hoarding: _____

_____

_____

Most recent hoarding experience: _____

_____

_____

Other relevant experiences of hoarding: _____

_____

_____

Present Triggers

Associated present stimuli to hoard objects or discard: _____

_____

_____

Physical sensations related to hoarding: _____

_____

_____

Future concerns: _____

_____

_____

Phase 2: Preparation

EMDR Therapy explanation—"*When a trauma occurs, it seems to get locked in the nervous system with the original picture, sounds, thoughts, and feelings. Hoarding can be like having many small traumas occurring repeatedly each day. Each time we see something we want to acquire but shouldn't or see items we want to discard but haven't, these are like small traumas. The eye movements we use in EMDR Therapy seem to unlock the nervous system and allow the brain to process the experience. That may be what is happening in REM or dream sleep; the eye movements may help to process the unconscious material. It is important to remember that it is your own brain that will be doing the healing and that you are the one in control.*"

☐ Desired state—*"See a small part of your home, such as a corner of the coffee table, cleared off and uncluttered. Really see it, imagining how good it would look. Imagine how you would feel about yourself and your home when you accomplish this. Imagine it in Technicolor, seeing it brightly. Imagine using it to set your coffee cup on or putting your feet up on it."*
+ BLS
☐ Safe Place
☐ Rapport
☐ Clarify expectations—*"Rome was not built in a day."* Start with decreasing acquisition behaviors and then discarding hoarded items.

Self-Control Techniques

Abdominal breathing—*"I would like to teach you about abdominal breathing. Sit quietly with room for your abdomen to expand. Do gentle and even breathing, exhaling all of the way. See if you can make your exhale longer than your inhale. As you breathe in think: 'One.' As you breathe out think: 'Nothing.' Just focus on the breathing. If you get distracted, this is normal. Just gently refocus on the breathing, thinking the words: 'One' and 'Nothing.' It is helpful to practice this exercise for five minutes, twice per day, at first. You might try five minutes in the morning and then five minutes in the evening. Gradually you can increase your practice to 20 to 30 minutes per day or more."*

Progressive Muscle Relaxation—*"I would like to introduce you to Progressive Muscle Relaxation. Clench your fists, with your arms extended for 10 seconds, then release. Repeat, simply noticing the tension and release. Extend your arms with fingers up, hands stretched back at the wrists, for 10 seconds, then release and repeat, simply noticing the tension and release. Clench your fists, with your arms doubled up, for 10 seconds, then release. Repeat, simply noticing the tension and release. Now relax your arms and leave them resting comfortably. Lift eyebrows, wrinkling forehead, for 10 seconds and release. Then repeat, simply noticing the tension and release. Close your eyes tightly for 10 seconds, then release. Repeat, simply noticing the tension and release. Smile widely for 10 seconds and release, letting your jaw hang slack. Repeat, simply noticing the tension and release. Press your lips together for 10 seconds and release. Repeat, simply noticing the tension and release. Press your tongue on the roof of your mouth for 10 seconds and release. Repeat, simply noticing the tension and release. Open your jaw wide for 10 seconds and release. Repeat, simply noticing the tension and release. Gently tilt your head to one side for 10 seconds, then tilt head forward for 10 seconds, then to the other side for 10 seconds. Repeat, simply noticing the tension and release. Lift your shoulders up toward your ears for 10 seconds and release. Repeat, simply noticing the tension and release. Lean back slightly, to engage your back muscles (gently), for 10 seconds and release. Repeat, simply noticing the tension and release. Press your stomach muscles back toward your back for 10 seconds and release. Repeat, simply noticing the tension and release. Press your heels into the floor for 10 seconds and release. Repeat, simply noticing the tension and release. Lift your feet up, with your toes toward the ceiling for 10 seconds and then release. Repeat, simply noticing the tension and release. Lift up your heels for 10 seconds and then release. Repeat, simply noticing the tension and release. Lift up your toes for 10 seconds, then release. Repeat, simply noticing the tension and release. Now scan your entire body from the top of your head to the tips of your toes, releasing any residual tension."*

Practice 10 to 15 minutes per day and increase this to up to an hour.

Course of Treatment

☐ Decreasing acquisition behaviors—*"We are going to focus on helping you to decrease acquisition behaviors first. Then we will work on helping you to learn how to discard your hoarded items. The progress may be slow, but will be permanent. Just like crash diets that do not work for people who want to lose weight, trying to discard all your hoarded items at once will not be effective. People who do this 'all or nothing' approach often feel overwhelmed, discouraged, and depressed. Rome wasn't built in a day. We want to focus on decluttering a little every day, then move on, living your life, doing things to take care of yourself and doing pleasant activities. Often a 5 minute tornado is helpful, where you spend 5 minutes going through items, saying, 'Keep. Throw away. Keep. Throw away.' Then discard the items and reward yourself for a job well done!"*

☐ *"Often people with a Hoarding Disorder find it helpful to ask themselves the following questions when trying to determine whether to acquire or discard an item:*

- *Do I really need it?*
- *Is keeping it going to help me with my long-term goals* (i.e., having an uncluttered life, improving my relationship, having time and space to do art, etc.)?
- *Do I have an immediate plan for its use?"*

Note: Typically clients with hoarding will never get to their projects. They have many plans to complete projects, but with their level of clutter, they do not have time or space to complete them.

- *"Do I have a place to put it?*
- *Do I already have one?*
- *Do I have time to do it?*
- *How many does one need?*
- *Is this available online?"*

"You can use this list of questions when going shopping or use this list when trying to decide whether to discard an object."

Phase 3: Assessment

☐ For *acquiring behaviors*, the following cognitions are representative:

Negative Cognition	Positive Cognition
☐ I am powerless	I am in control
☐ I am unlovable (without desired object)	I am loveable
☐ I am in danger	I am safe in the world

☐ For *discarding behaviors*, the following cognitions are representative:

Negative Cognition	Positive Cognition
☐ I am out of control	I am in control
☐ I am worthless (without it)	I am loveable and worthwhile
☐ I am in danger	I am safe now

Past Memories

Targets

☐ **Earlier (Ancillary) Experience**

Target: _____

Picture/Image: _____

NC: _____

Note: If difficulty: *"In your worst moments, when you are remembering some aspect of the event, what thoughts or negative beliefs do you have about yourself?"* _____

PC: _____

VoC: _____ /7

Emotions: _____

SUD: _____ /10

Location of body sensation: _____

☐ **First Time/Touchstone Hoarding Event:**

Target: _____

Picture/Image: _____

NC: _____

Note: If difficulty: *"In your worst moments, when you are remembering some aspect of the event, what thoughts or negative beliefs do you have about yourself?"* _____

PC: _____

VoC: _____ /7

Emotions: _____

SUD: _____ /10

Location of body sensation: _____

☐ **Worst Experience of Hoarding**

Target: _____

Picture/Image: _____

NC: _____

Note: If difficulty: *"In your worst moments, when you are remembering some aspect of the event, what thoughts or negative beliefs do you have about yourself?"* _____

PC: _____

VoC: _____ /7

Emotions: _____

SUD: _____ /10

Location of body sensation: _____

☐ **Most Recent Hoarding Experience**

Target: _____

Picture/Image: _____

NC: _____

Note: If difficulty: *"In your worst moments, when you are remembering some aspect of the event, what thoughts or negative beliefs do you have about yourself?"* _____

PC: _____

VoC: _____ /7

Emotions: _____

SUD: _____ /10

Location of body sensation: _____

☐ **Other Relevant Experiences of Hoarding**

Target: _____

Picture/Image: _____

NC: _____

Note: If difficulty: *"In your worst moments, when you are remembering some aspect of the event, what thoughts or negative beliefs do you have about yourself?"* _____

PC: _____

VoC: _____ /7

Emotions: _____

SUD: _____ /10

Location of body sensation: _____

Phase 4: Desensitization

Introduce according to EMDR Standard Protocol. Helpful to access the desired state:

- ☐ Desired state—*"See a small part of your home, such as a corner of the coffee table, cleared off and uncluttered. Really see it, imagining how good it would look. Imagine how you would feel about yourself and your home when you accomplish this. Imagine it in Technicolor, seeing it brightly. Imagine using it to set your coffee cup on or putting your feet up on it."*
  + BLS
- ☐ Explain the process—*"Now, remember, it is your own brain that is doing the healing and you are the one in control. I will ask you to mentally focus on the target and to _____ (state BLS you are using). Just let whatever happens, happen, and we will talk at the end of the set. Just tell me what comes up and don't discard anything as unimportant. Any new information that comes to mind is connected in some way. If you want to stop, just raise your hand."*

"Bring up the picture and the words _____ (repeat the NC) and notice where you feel it in your body. Now follow _____ (state BLS).

If SUD = 1 or more, continue processing.

If SUD continues to be 0 after 2 sets of BLS, go to the installation phase.

Phase 5: Installation

PC: ☐ Completed

New PC (if new one is better): _____

VoC: _____ /7

Incident + PC + BLS

Continue installation with BLS until material becomes increasingly adaptive. If VoC = 6 or less, check and see if there is a limiting belief: *"Which thoughts or concerns prevent you from feeling those words as completely true?"* _____

Note: If the limiting belief is not resolved quickly, explore to see whether there are any limiting beliefs or unidentified/unprocessed memory(ies)/networks that are causing this difficulty.

The session is then considered incomplete; therefore, return to the incomplete target and continue the installation process in the next session.

Phase Completed   ☐ Yes   ☐ No

    ☐ Check other targets—*"OK, let's check the next target* _____ *(bring up the next target). On a scale of 0 to 10, where 0 is no disturbance or neutral and 10 is the highest disturbance you can imagine, how disturbing does it feel to you now?"* _____ /10

Phase 6: Body Scan   ☐ Completed

"Close your eyes, and keep in mind the original memory and the words _____ *(state the positive belief). Then bring your attention to different parts of your body, starting with your head and working downward. Any place you find any tension, tightness, or unusual feeling, let me know."*

Note: If the client reports any negative feeling, do a set of BLS until it disappears. If the client reports positive feelings, continue with BLS in order to strengthen them.

    Present Triggers

Situations, Events, or Stimuli Triggers

☐ Trigger 1:

Most disturbing part: _____

_____

☐ Trigger 2:

Most disturbing part: _____

_____

☐ Trigger 3:

Most disturbing part: _____

_____

☐ Trigger 4:

Most disturbing part: _____

_____

Target: _____

Picture/Image: _____

NC: _____

Note: If difficulty: *"In your worst moments, when you are remembering some aspect of the event, what thoughts or negative beliefs do you have about yourself?"*

PC: _____

VoC: _____ /7

Emotions: _____

SUD: _____ /10

Location of body sensation: _____

Sensation Symptom List

☐ Trigger 1:

Most disturbing part: _____

_____

☐ Trigger 2:

Most disturbing part: _____

_____

☐ Trigger 3:

Most disturbing part: _____

_____

☐ Trigger 4:

Most disturbing part: _____

_____

Target: _____

Picture/Image: _____

NC: _____

Note: If difficulty: *"In your worst moments, when you are remembering some aspect of the event, what thoughts or negative beliefs do you have about yourself?"*

PC: _____

VoC: _____ /7

Emotions: _____

SUD: _____ /10

Location of body sensation: _____

Future Template

Installation of the Future Template

  ☐ When body scan is clear
  ☐ After incomplete sessions, to maintain motivation to decrease acquisition behaviors and increase discarding
  ☐ Access the desired state: *"See* _____ (state the specific, positive goal chosen for the desired state). *Really see it, imagining how good it would look. Imagine how you would feel about yourself and your home when you accomplish this. Imagine it in Technicolor, seeing it brightly. Imagine* _____ (state the desired goal)." + BLS

☐ Run a moving imagining going through the week + PC + meeting challenges of decreasing acquisition behaviors + discarding items +maintain appropriate self-caring behaviors

☐ *"Imagine spending 5 minutes per day* _____ (state the challenge for your patient, such as sorting through items on a coffee table rapidly, into two piles: a pile to keep and a pile to throw away. *Hold the words in mind* (PC) *'I am worthwhile' while you see yourself* _____ (state activity*). Go quickly, telling yourself, 'Keep or throw away.' Notice any distress that comes up and see yourself coping well. Imagine* _____ (state goal). *Follow my fingers* (or notice any other BLS).

☐ *"Imagine going through the week and resisting* _____ (state what needs to be resisted). *Play a movie of the entire week, holding in mind the words 'I am strong' (PC). Imagine yourself coping well with any challenges that happen. Notice what you are seeing, thinking, feeling, and experiencing in your body. While playing the movie, let me know if there are any blocks. If there are no blocks, tell me when you have viewed the whole movie. Now, follow my fingers* (or notice any other BLS).

In vivo practice of discarding—Client brings in some hoarded items. Practice discarding with speed. It can be helpful to intentionally discard a useful item. Use BLS.

☐ *"Let's go through this stack of items. Work quickly; the only decision you need to make today is 'keep' or 'throw away.' Remember your list of questions:*
  • *Do I really need it?*
  • *Is keeping it going to help me with my long-term goals* (uncluttered life)?
  • *Do I have an immediate plan for its use?* (No projects).
  • *Do I have a place to put it?*
  • *Do I already have one?*
  • *Do I have time to do it?*
  • *How many does one need?*
  • *Is this available online?*
  • *Let's start with this first item. Is this 'keep' or 'throw away'?"*

If the client gets stuck, the clinician can add BLS to decrease distress.

Install the experience of discarding:

☐ *"Imagine yourself going through a pile of things that you want to discard. Have your positive cognition in mind* _____ (state PC). *See yourself doing it quickly, making two piles: keep and throw away. Then imagine yourself immediately getting rid of the 'throw away pile.' If possible, see yourself putting things from the 'keep pile' away."*

Phase 7: Closure

To consolidate changes: *"What is the most positive thing you have learned about yourself during this session with regard to* _____ (state the target or theme)?" _____

_____

_____

Focus on specific plans for the week: *"Let's think about a specific plan of action for this week. Can you think of a small goal focused on either decreasing acquiring behaviors or increasing discarding behaviors that you would like to work on this week? It is important not to spend too much time on it. I would recommend spending 5 to 15 minutes per day."* _____

_____

_____

Support and specificity: *"That sounds great; spending* _____ *(state how many minutes)* minutes _____ *(state the behavior client agrees to do) is an excellent goal. Let's plan what time of day you are going to do it and where. Remember, with junk mail, if you are not going to handle something right away, you can throw it away because they will send you a new one."*

_____

_____

Add pleasant activities: *"Also, I think it is important to plan some pleasant activities this week as part of your homework. What pleasant activities would you like to do?"* _____

_____

_____

Reinforce: *"OK, that is a great idea to do* _____ *(state the pleasant activity) for your pleasant activities this week. Remember that if you have difficulty with your homework, this is just feedback for us to work on at our next session. Also, remember that you can always call me if you get stuck. You have done great work today and can be proud of yourself. Sometimes things come up and sometimes nothing is noticed. If they do, this is just feedback. Keep a log and we can make it a target for next time. If you get any new memories, dreams, or situations that disturb you, just take a snapshot of what is disturbing or even interesting. It isn't necessary to give a lot of detail. Just put down enough to remind yourself, so we can target it next time. If negative feelings do come up, you can practice a self-control technique such as the breathing or the Safe Place. Remember to practice a self-control technique each day, even if things are going well. Please remember to practice your homework. You can call me if you would like to."*

"If nothing comes up, make sure to use the tape every day and give me a call if you need to."

Phase 8: Reevaluation

Remind clients that it takes time for this process: *"It has taken a long time for your space to become so cluttered and it will take time to reverse the process. We are changing ingrained patterns and there may be times when it is harder to resist urges to acquire or to discard things. Sometimes, even with the new skills you are learning, you might feel like you are back to square one. This can happen; don't be alarmed, as it is not unusual. When this happens, just note what has happened, what is going on around you, and what you did to handle the situation so that you don't forget what happened and how it felt and then bring it/them to the next session so that we can determine what to target next. Do you have any questions?"*

SUDS of incident(s) processed: _____ /10

New material: _____

_____

New resources needed?_____

_____

_____

Reprocessed necessary targets: ☐ Completed

Reference

American Psychiatric Association. (2013). *Diagnostic and statistical manual of mental disorders* (5th ed.). Arlington, VA: American Psychiatric Publishing.

Mood disorders are among the presenting problems we see the most as practitioners. Symptoms such as depressed mood, diminished interest or pleasure, weight gain or loss, insomnia or hypersomnia, fatigue, feelings of worthlessness and diminished ability to think or concentrate, and recurring thoughts of death are the types of complaints our patients tell us. Others describe inflated self-esteem, decreased need for sleep, increased goal-directed activity, racing thoughts, distractibility, and so on of a manic episode. Patients present with the mood disorder on its own or it is comorbid with other disorders. It is important to understand accurately the symptomatology of these disorders to respond and develop appropriate treatment plans to work with these challenging patients.

Bipolar Disorder

Bipolar disorder occurs with high frequency; it is a complex disorder characterized by mood changes that range from elevated mood to depressive or mixed moods (see Chapter 7 for an in-depth exposition). There are three subtypes: bipolar disorder I, bipolar disorder II, and cyclothymic disorder. Most often, this illness is treated by medications such as mood stabilizers, atypical antipsychotics, and antidepressants. The goal is to help clients go into clinical remission and to remain stable and euthymic for the long term; however, relapses occur frequently. Patients with bipolar disorder are yet another patient group that is at risk for comorbid adverse life events and trauma and/or trauma-related incidents (Hernandez et al., 2013; McLaughlin et al., 2012; Otto et al., 2004); they found that approximately 20% of bipolar patients also fulfill the criteria for the diagnosis of posttraumatic stress disorder (PTSD). Despite the high number of traumatized bipolar patients, there are very few studies pertaining to these patients. They also are at risk for substance abuse, suicide attempts, rapid cycling, and more affective symptoms (Kessler, Sonnega, Bromet, Hughes, & Nelson, 1995; Quarantini et al., 2009, 2010).

The only research on bipolar disorder, PTSD, and eye movement desensitization and reprocessing (EMDR) is Novo et al.'s (2014) randomized controlled, single-blind pilot study that included 20 bipolar I and II patients, with subsyndromal symptoms and a history of at least three documented traumatic events that were still causing distress, but not necessarily meeting the full criteria for PTSD. The goal was to test the effectiveness of the Standard EMDR Protocol, as an addition to the usual medication, in decreasing traumatic symptoms and improving affective symptomatology. After 3 months of EMDR Therapy (14–18 sessions), patients in the EMDR group showed statistically significant improvement concerning the impact of their trauma and a more stable mood compared to the control group; the effects were maintained at a 6-month follow-up. The authors concluded that EMDR Therapy seemed promising as an effective and safe intervention for patients diagnosed with bipolar I and II and who had also been traumatized.

The Barcelona EMDR Research Group (Benedikt L. Amann, Roser Batalla, Vicky Blanch, Dolors Capellades, Maria José Carvajal, Isabel Fernández, Francisca García, Walter Lupo, Marian Ponte, Maria José Sánchez, Jesús Sanfiz, Antonia Santed, & Marilyn Luber) created "The EMDR Protocol for Bipolar Disorder (EPBD)" based on Novo et al.'s study. The EPBD includes an extensive client history to assist clinicians in assessing patients who will benefit from this protocol, such as those patients in clinical remission with light hypomanic or subdepressive subsyndromal symptoms. When patients have mild depression or are in the hypomanic phase, clinician appraisal is indicated as to the appropriateness of the protocol. EPBD is not recommended for those experiencing moderate to severe mania, mixed or depressive phase.

Preparation is intensive, including explaining how EMDR Therapy works, practicing bilateral stimulation (BLS), signing an informed consent, keeping a mood diary, teaching about bipolar disorder, and installing positive resources such as the Safe Place. For resource building, the Barcelona Group has developed five very helpful subprotocols to address the clinical needs that are often specific to bipolar patients:

- EMDR Mood Stabilizing Protocol for Bipolar Disorder (EMPBD)
- EMDR Illness Awareness Protocol (EIAP)
- EMDR Adherence Enhancer Protocol (EAEP)
- EMDR Prodromal Symptoms Protocol (EPSP)
- EMDR De-Idealization Manic Symptoms Protocol (EDMSP)

It is helpful to include a meeting with a family member, since bipolar disorder affects family members as well as patients. Often, patients may present with problematic symptoms in the present; if so, the Barcelona Group suggests beginning with present triggers for the 3-Pronged Protocol and, if there are no pressing current issues, beginning with past memories. After the treatment plan is made, the authors recommend proceeding with phases 4–8, according to the Standard EMDR Protocol. The Barcelona Group emphasizes the importance of making time for closure.

Major Depression

Treating patients with Major Depression is often a challenge. As Hofmann et al. (see Chapter 8) state, "At first glance, depression looks like a disease that is easy to treat but on closer scrutiny, it appears to be a chronic and severe disease." Ultimately, they conclude, "Depression shows all the signs of a stress regulation disorder with a strong relationship between depression and stressful-traumatic and nontraumatic (regarding criterion A) events and memories." The research shows that there is an increased influence of early adverse events, traumatic events, and medical-related difficulties (Broad & Wheeler, 2006; Felitti & Anda, 2009; Kendler, Hettema, Butera, Gardner, & Prescott, 2003) that can precipitate and/or contribute to these mood-related disorders. This is also in keeping with Francine Shapiro's Adaptive Information Processing model (Shapiro, 2001; Solomon & Shapiro, 2008).

With this data and growing understanding of mood disorders in mind, new treatments and ideas are needed. The early research on EMDR Therapy and mood-related issues has been sparse and focused on comorbid depression rather than unipolar primary depression. In five books, authors documented *case reports* of patients with depression who were successfully treated: Shapiro and Forrest (1997), *EMDR: The Breakthrough Therapy for Overcoming Anxiety, Stress, and Trauma;* Philip Manfield's 1998 cases in *Extending EMDR: A Casebook of Innovative Applications* (1998a, 1998b, 1998c); David Servan-Schreiber's 2004 text, *The Instinct to Heal;* Robin Shapiro's (2009a, 2009b, 2009c, 2009d) tackling of this issue, along with Knipe (2009), in her text, *EMDR Solutions II: For Depression, Eating Disorders, Performance, and More;* or Oppenheim (2009)'s chapter in H. Hornsveld and S. Berendsen's *Casusboek EMDR, 25, voorbeelden uit de praktijk.* Other *case reports* appeared in journals (Bae, Kim, & Park, 2008; Broad & Wheeler, 2006; Gonzalez-Brignardello & Vazquez, 2004; Grey, 2011; Rosas Uribe et al., 2010; Song & Wang, 2007; Srivastava & Mukhopadhyay, 2008; Sun, Wu, & Chiu, 2004), all finding positive results with EMDR Therapy.

In 2013, Wood and Ricketts reviewed the literature concerning EMDR and depression and found 37 suitable references: 18 references reported interventions for depression as a primary diagnosis, while 19 described interventions for PTSD with comorbid depressive symptoms. There were *six randomized controlled trials* (Lee, Gavriel, Drummond, Richards, & Greenwald, 2002; Marcus, Marquis, & Sakai, 1997; Rothbaum, 1997, Rothbaum, Astin, & Marsteller, 2005; Silver, Brooks, & Obenchain, 1995; van der Kolk et al., 2007), *three pilot RCTs* (Arabia, Manca, & Solomon, 2011; Hogberg et al., 2007; Ironson, Freund, Strauss, & Williams, 2002), *one random lagged groups study* (Chemtob, Nakashima, Hamada, & Carlson, 2002), *one case control study* (Narimani, Ahari, & Rajabi, 2010), and *eight case studies* (Korn & Leeds, 2002; Lobenstine & Courtney, 2013; Montefiore, Mallet, Levy, Allilaire, & Pelissolo, 2007; Raboni, Tufik, & Suchecki, 2006; Schneider, Hofmann, Rost, & Shapiro, 2008; Silver et al., 2008; Tarquinio, Schmitt, & Tarquinio, 2012; Tarquinio, Schmitt, Tarquinio, Rydberg, Spitz, 2012).

There were a number of studies discussing the use of EMDR Therapy with PTSD or phantom limb pain with comorbid depression. When PTSD was treated with EMDR Therapy in these studies, comorbid depression scores showed improvement and patients appeared to do better than with imaginal exposure, wait-list controls, standard care, and fluoxetine or placebo pills. Other studies showed that EMDR Therapy was effective—but not significantly different—when compared to cognitive behavioral therapy (CBT) or prolonged exposure. Only one early randomized controlled trial (RCT) did not find improvement for PTSD and comorbid depression in a study where patients were treated with EMDR Therapy, relaxation, or biofeedback. All of the case studies reported success in the treating of depressive symptoms. Wood and Ricketts concluded: "Although each case study on its own is not generalizable because of the nature of the experimental design, the growing number of such reports adds weight to the premise that, in people with PTSD, comorbid depression can be alleviated by treatment with EMDR" (2013, p. 228).

Arne Hofmann and his colleagues (2014) began their retrospective study of EMDR Therapy for Recurrent Depressive Disorder or unipolar primary depression by asking experienced EMDR clinicians to identify patients who met this criterion. The 10 patients in the unpublished study had an average of 6.4 previous depressive episodes and had been treated with CBT or psychodynamic therapy (PD) in 60 treatment sessions, including 7.4 EMDR Therapy memory-processing sessions. At follow-up, approximately 3.7 years later, 7 of the 10 patients were no longer taking medication. Although four to five depression relapses were expected, there was only one. Despite the small number of participants, Hofmann et al. concluded that the study supported their clinical observation that EMDR Therapy might be of significant assistance in preventing relapse in recurrent depression. After several more pilot studies, the results led them to conclude that EMDR Therapy had excellent potential for the treatment of depressive disorders.

In 2009, Hofmann et al. set up a European network of depression researchers from Germany, Italy, Spain, and Turkey; their work is referred to as the European Depression EMDR Network (EDEN) study. They created a "Treatment Manual for the EDEN Study: EMDR for Depressive Patients," published through the EMDR Institute Germany. For the EDEN project, each participant diagnosed with recurrent depression is randomly assigned to one of the following groups: medication alone, EMDR and medication, or CBT and medication. Their RCT will use the Standard EMDR Protocol (see Chapter 8) and will measure improvement using the Beck Depression Inventory (BDI-II; Beck, Brown & Steer, 1996) and social functioning scores. Follow-up will occur at one, two, and hopefully five years to report on the effectiveness of the work for relapse prevention and long-term gains.

In 2014, the *Journal of EMDR Practice and Research* published Hofmann et al.'s "Eye Movement Desensitization and Reprocessing as an Adjunctive Treatment of Unipolar Depression:

A Controlled Study." This was a nonrandomized controlled exploratory study with a mean of 44.5 sessions of CBT and 6.9 sessions of EMDR Therapy versus the control group with 47.1 sessions of CBT alone. They found that patients in the group with CBT + EMDR Therapy had an additional benefit on their BDI-II scores and that number of remissions posttreatment was significantly better. They concluded: "Despite the limitations of this study, this first controlled study that used EMDR with depressive patients can, in our opinion, encourage further studies in this field. It may be that a method such as EMDR that processes stressful memories can add to the therapeutic options in these patients and help more depressive patients to reach full remission from their depressive episodes" (p. 110). Hase et al.'s (2015) study, "Eye Movement Desensitization and Reprocessing (EMDR) Therapy in the Treatment of Depression: A Matched Pairs Study in an Inpatient Setting," enlisted 16 patients with depressive episodes in an inpatient setting. The treatment entailed reprocessing memories of stressful life events in addition to treatment as usual (TAU); they were compared to a matched control group receiving TAU. Results showed that the EMDR group demonstrated a decrease in depressive symptoms as measured by the Symptom Checklist (SCL)-90-R depression subscale. The difference was significant even when adjusted for duration of treatment. On follow-up of more than one year, the EMDR group reported fewer problems related to depression and fewer relapses when compared to the control group. This study concluded that EMDR Therapy shows potential as an effective treatment for depressive disorders and called for more rigorous research.

Wood (2012) reported on her study concerning depression. The Sheffield EMDR and Depression Investigation (SEDI) is an intensive clinical replication series where patients with long-term depression will be treated with EMDR Therapy. Measures will be used to chart the effects of the intervention on the following: depressive symptoms, social functioning, memory narrative, heart rate variability, and skin conductance response. An interview will be conducted with participants about the experience itself.

Wood and Ricketts (2013) report concerning the state of EMDR Therapy and treatment of depressive disorders:

> The research on EMDR is highly variable; there are case studies and RCTs of differing levels of quality from all over the world, in different settings, and with vastly different patient groups of all ethnicities and age groups. From the accumulated case studies and unpublished pilot studies that have taken place, it would appear that it is possible to use EMDR to treat depression successfully, but its specific efficacy is unknown. The practice-based evidence suggests that EMDR has the potential to be an evidence-based treatment for depression. EMDR has been reported to reduce rumination in patients with traumatic grief (Sprang, 2001); however, further research is required to determine if EMDR can add anything to the current psychotherapeutic approaches and to investigate the theoretical process behind EMDR as a treatment for any psychiatric distress. (p. 232)

Wood and Ricketts hope that the SEDI project and the EDEN trial will shed light on these unresolved issues concerning the efficacy of EMDR Therapy for depression; the nature of the patient experience; and the comparative efficacy of EMDR, CBT, and medication, and relapse prevention. They conclude with the following:

> [A]lthough medication and CBT are the recommended treatments for depression, CBT only has a recovery rate of around 50% (Eckers, Richards, & Gilbody, 2008) and the relapse rate among those treated with antidepressants is high (Gloaguen, Cottraux, Cucherat, & Blackburn, 1998). Any additional treatment that can be effective in treating depression will bring significant health and social benefits because it is such a widespread and costly illness (Arnow & Constantino, 2003). EMDR may be such a treatment. (p. 233)

The team of Arne Hofmann, Michael Hase, Peter Liebermann, Maria Lehnung, Luca Ostacoli, Franz Ebner, Christine Rost, Marilyn Luber, and Visal Tumani produced "DeprEnd®—EMDR Therapy Protocol for the Treatment of Depressive Disorders." Their chapter emphasizes the enormous prevalence of depression (affecting 120 million people worldwide); the importance of decreasing relapse, as the illness becomes more severe with each episode; and the risk factor for depression as the number of negative life experiences increases. DeprEnd® is a manual for EMDR Therapy in the treatment of depressive patients;

the conceptualization by this team brings new potency into working with this population. They consider four factors when forming an individual's treatment plan to address episode treatment and relapse prevention: current episode triggers of the current depressive episode, belief systems, depressive states, and suicidal states. By using this structure, clinicians can formulate the best plan to cover the important building blocks of patients' depressive experiences and use EMDR Therapy to resolve them, including the Three-Pronged Protocol. Other targets that may have to be processed are Criterion A experiences related to life-threatening events; Non-Criterion A concerned with losses, separations, shaming and humiliating experiences; and present life stressors/triggers not related to the current depression to reduce stress. They give a clear guide of how to work with these targets.

Specifiers for Depressive Disorders With Peripartum Onset: Postpartum Depression

Postpartum depression (PPD) is coded under "Specifiers for Depressive Disorders With Peripartum" onset and, according to *Diagnostic and Statistical Manual of Mental Disorders*, Fifth Edition (*DSM-5*), "can be applied to the current or, if full criteria are not currently met for a major depressive episode, most recent episode of major depression if onset of mood symptoms occurs during pregnancy or in the 4 weeks following delivery" (American Psychiatric Association, 2013). The prevalence of PPD, according to the RTI-University of North Carolina Evidence-Based Practice Center (Gaynes et al., 2005), is estimated at 7% to 13%. This translates into a huge concern, even more so because often PPD is underreported and/or underdiagnosed. EMDR therapists aware of the magnitude of this problem began using EMDR Therapy for PPD and its prevention early on. Phyllis Klaus's presentations on "The Use of EMDR in Medical and Somatic Problems," including perinatal issues, birth trauma, and the impact of childhood sexual abuse on children (1995, 1996, 2002, 2005a, 2005b, 2007, 2008; Klaus & Casadaban, 1996) began to underline the idea that these types of problems could be successfully resolved with EMDR Therapy. *Case reports* began to appear in journals and in presentations about working with women who have PPD (Amato, 2009; Lucchese, 2008; Parnell, 1998).

As a result of her 26 years of experience as a psychologist at Family Planning Centers in Naples, Italy, De Diviitis (2008) integrated her knowledge of pregnant women and her expertise in EMDR Therapy to help women in the prevention of PPD. She developed an EMDR Therapy-based intervention that she used with pregnant women with good success. Currently, she is conducting research on the effectiveness of her "EMDR Therapy Group Protocol for the Prevention of Birth Trauma and Postpartum Depression" (see Chapter 10). Her preliminary sample consisted of 60 women who had given birth from 10 to 26 weeks earlier and were enrolled in postpartum courses. The experimental group attended a postpartum course that included the EMDR Therapy Group Protocol, while the control group attended a postpartum course that did not include the EMDR Therapy Group Protocol. Each of the two groups was subdivided into women giving birth naturally or by cesarean. Beginning results are promising for the positive effects of the EMDR Therapy Group Protocol (see the chapter for more detail).

In Chapter 9, "EMDR Therapy Protocol for the Prevention of Birth Trauma and Postpartum Depression in the Pregnant Woman," De Diviitis and Luber discuss the goals of this protocol: to treat pregnant women in order to reduce the risks of childbirth trauma by improving their performance in the birthing process, and to strengthen their resiliency in order to reduce the negative effects of stress that occur during childbirth. De Diviitis conceptualizes childbirth as the opportunity for "peak performance" as women are asked to go beyond their perceived safety and comfort zones, and enter the realm of out-of-the-ordinary performances. This protocol asks women to take an active role in the birth of their children by assisting them in developing mastery, self-support, and containment. Lendl and Foster's *EMDR Performance Enhancement Psychology Protocol* (EMDR-PEP; 1997, 2001, 2009; Foster, 2001) was adapted to assist in developing resources for managing childbirth, and the EMDR Protocol for Anticipatory Anxiety for the Future Template (Shapiro, 2001, 2006) was used as a structure to reprocess blocking beliefs.

The World Health Organization has called for the prevention of health care issues such as postpartum problems, since high numbers of women are suffering with PPD. The next chapter, by Diviitis and Luber, "EMDR Therapy Group Protocol for the Prevention of Birth Trauma and Postpartum Depression for Pregnant Women," contributes to the solution of this problem. This EMDR Therapy group protocol has been a successful adjunct to childbirth preparation classes and gives women a chance to share their concerns and fears about childbirth with others who are going through the same types of experience. As in the chapter for individual pregnant women, this protocol also used Lendl and Foster's EMDR-PEP, EMDR Protocol for Anticipatory Anxiety for the Future Template. The authors added the following: *Butterfly Hug* (Artigas & Jarero, 2014) for BLS; *Resource Development and Installation* (RDI; Korn & Leeds, 2002; Leeds & Shapiro, 2000) for increasing resiliency; *Written Workbook for Individual or Group EMDR* (Birnbaum, 2006, 2014) for group structured reprocessing; and the *EMDR Integrative Group Treatment Protocol (IGTP*; Artigas, Jarero, Maurer, Lopez Cano, & Alcalá, 2000a, 2000b; Artigas, Jarero, Alcalà, & Lopez Cano, 2014) for installing specific personal resources for each woman to increase resiliency and for desensitizing and reprocessing information/targets that might interfere with the childbirth process. They also include a Notes Sheet for the women to fill in and take home.

The EMDR Therapy and Mood Disorders section is filled with important information, procedures, and protocols to address the questions that we see in our work on a regular basis. A summary sheet that serves as a checklist showing the important steps needed for your work accompanies each of these chapters, with a CD version format also available to provide mobile access.

References

Amato, M. (2009, June). *EMDR in a screening service in post-partum.* Poster presented at the 10th EMDR Europe Association Conference, Amsterdam, The Netherlands.

American Psychiatric Association. (2013). *Desk reference to the diagnostic criteria from DSM-5.* Arlington, VA: Author.

Arabia, E., Manca, M. L., & Solomon, R. M. (2011). EMDR for survivors of life-threatening cardiac events: Results of a pilot study. *Journal of EMDR Practice and Research, 5,* 2–13.

Arnow, B. A., & Constantino, M. J. (2003). Effectiveness of psychotherapy and combination treatment for chronic depression. *Journal of Clinical Psychology, 59*(8), 893–905.

Artigas, L., & Jarero, I. (2014). The butterfly hug. In M. Luber (Ed.), *Implementing EMDR early mental health interventions for man-made and natural disasters: Models, scripted protocols, and summary sheets* (pp. 127–130). New York, NY: Springer.

Artigas, L., Jarero, I., Alcalà, N., & Lopez Cano, T. (2014). The EMDR Integrative Group Treatment Protocol (IGTP). In M. Luber (Ed), *Eye movement desensitization and reprocessing (EMDR): Basics and special situations.* New York, NY: Springer.

Artigas, L. A., Jarero, I., Maurer, M., Lopez Cano, T., & Alcalà, N. (2000a, September). *EMDR and traumatic stress after natural disasters: Integrative treatment protocol and the butterfly hug.* Poster presented at the 5th EMDR International Association Conference, Toronto, Ontario, Canada.

Artigas, L. A., Jarero, I., Maurer, M., Lopez Cano, T., & Alcalà, N. (2000b). *EMDR and traumatic stress after natural disaster: Integrative treatment protocol and butterfly hug.* Poster presented at the EMDRIA Conference, Toronto, Ontario, Canada.

Bae, H., Kim, D., & Park, Y. C. (2008). Eye movement desensitization and reprocessing for adolescent depression. *Psychiatry Investigations, 5*(1), 60–65.

Beck, A. T., Steer, R. A., & Brown, G. K., (1996). *Beck depression inventory-II (BDI-II).* San Antonio, TX: Harcourt Assessment, Inc.

Birnbaum, A. (2006). *Group EMDR: Theory and practice.* Invited presentation at EMDR Israel Humanitarian Assistance Program Conference, Netanya, Israel.

Birnbaum, A. (2014). A written workbook for individual or group EMDR. In M. Luber (Ed.), *Implementing EMDR early mental health interventions for man-made and natural disasters: Models, scripted protocols, and summary sheets* (pp. 127–130). New York, NY: Springer.

Broad, R. D., & Wheeler, K. (2006, May). An adult with childhood medical trauma treated with psychoanalytic psychotherapy and EMDR: A case study. *Perspectives in Psychiatric Care, 42*(2), 95–105. doi:10.1111/j.1744–6163.2006.00058.x

Chemtob, C. M., Nakashima, J., Hamada, R. S., & Carlson, J. G. (2002). Brief treatment for elementary school children with disaster-related posttraumatic stress disorder: A field study. *Journal of Clinical Psychology, 58,* 99–112.

De Diviitis, A. M. (2008, November). *Applicazione dello sviluppo e installazione delle risorse (RDI) nella psicoprofilassi al parto finalizzata alla prevenzione delle depressione post partum (DPP) [Application of resource development and installation (RDI) in psychoprophylaxis geared to the prevention of postpartum depression(DPP)].* Presentation at Italian EMDR Association, Milan, Italy.

Eckers, D., Richards, D., & Gilbody, S. (2008). A meta-analysis of randomized trials of behavioural treatment of depression. *Psychological Medicine, 38*(5), 611–624.

Felitti, V. J., & Anda, R. F. (2009).The relationship of adverse childhood experiences to adult medical disease and psychiatric disorders, and sexual behavior: Implications for healthcare. In R. Lanius, E. Vermetten, & C. Pain (Eds.), *The hidden epidemic: The impact of early life trauma on health and disease.* Cambridge, England: Cambridge University Press.

Foster. S. (2001). *From trauma to triumph: EMDR and advanced performance enhancement strategies (self-published manual).* San Francisco, CA: Success at Work.

Gaynes, B. N., Gavin, N., Meltzer-Brody, S., Lohr, K. N., Swinson, T., Gartlehner, G.,...Miller, W. C. (2005, February). Perinatal depression: Prevalence, screening accuracy, and screening outcomes. *Evidence Report/Technology Assessment No. 119.* (Prepared by the RTI-University of North Carolina Evidence-Based Practice Center, under Contract No. 290–02-0016; AHRQ Publication No. 05-E006–2). Rockville, MD: Agency for Healthcare Research and Quality.

Gloaguen, V., Cottraux, J., Cucherat, M., & Blackburn, I. M. (1998). A meta-analysis of the effects of cognitive therapy in depressed patients. *Journal of Affective Disorders, 49*(1), 59–72.

Gonzalez-Brignardello, M. P., & Vazquez, A. M. M. (2004). Tratamiento de un caso de trastorno por estrés postraumático con EMDR dentro de un marco cognitivo-conductual [Intervention in a case of post-traumatic stress disorder with EMDR within a cognitive behavioral setting]. *Clínica y Salud, 15*(3), 337–354.

Grey, E. (2011). A pilot study of concentrated EMDR: A brief report. *Journal of EMDR Practice and Research, 5*(1), 14–24. doi: 10.1891/1933-3196.5.1.14.

Hase, M., Balmaceda, U. M., Hase, A., Lehnung, M., Tumani, V., Huchzermeier, C., & Hofmann, A. (2015). Eye movement desensitization and reprocessing (EMDR) therapy in the treatment of depression: A matched pairs study in an inpatient setting. *Brain and Behavior, 5,* 6. doi: 10.1002/brb3.342

Hernandez, J. M., Cordova, M. J., Ruzek, J., Reiser, R., Gwizdowski, I. S., Suppes, T.,...Ostacher, M. J. (2013). Presentation and prevalence of PTSD in a bipolar disorder population: A STEP-BD examination. *Journal of Affective Disorders 5, 150*(2), 450–455. doi: 10.1016/j.jad.2013.04.038. Epub 2013 May 23.

Hofmann, A., Hase, M., Liebermann, P., Ebner, F., Rost, C., & Tumani, V. (2009). *Treatment manual for the EDEN study: EMDR for depressive patients.* Germany: EMDR Institute Germany.

Hofmann, A., Hilgers, A., Lehnung, M., Liebermann, P., Ostacoli, L., Schneider, W., & Hase, M. (2014). Eye movement desensitization and reprocessing as an adjunctive treatment of unipolar depression: A controlled study. *Journal of EMDR Practice and Research, 8*(3), 103–112.

Hogberg, G., Pagani, M., Sundin, Ö., Soares, J., Aberg-Wistedt, A., Tarnell, B., & Hallstrom, T. (2007, February). On treatment with eye movement desensitization and reprocessing of chronic post-traumatic stress disorder in public transportation workers: A randomized controlled trial. *Nordic Journal of Psychiatry, 61*(1), 54–61. doi:10.1080/08039480601129408

Ironson, G., Freund, B., Strauss, J., & Williams, J. (2002, January). Comparison of two treatments for traumatic stress: A community-based study of EMDR and prolonged exposure. *Journal of Clinical Psychology, 58*(1), 113–128. doi:10.1002/jclp.1132

Kendler, K. S., Hettema, J. M., Butera, F., Gardner, C. O., & Prescott, C. A. (2003). Life event dimensions of loss, humiliation, entrapment, and danger in the prediction of onsets of major depression and generalized anxiety. *Archives of General Psychiatry, 60*(8), 789–796.

Kessler, R. C., Sonnega, A., Bromet, E., Hughes, M., & Nelson, C. B. (1995). Posttraumatic stress disorder in the National Comorbidity Survey. *Archives of General Psychiatry, 52,* 1048–1060.

Klaus, P. H. (1995, June). *The use of EMDR in medical and somatic problems.* Presentation at the EMDR Network Conference, Santa Monica, California.

Klaus, P. (1996, June). *Applying EMDR to physical illness, injury, and symptoms in adults and children: The use of EMDR to unlock the potential for healing.* Presentation at the 1st EMDR International Association Conference, Denver, Coorado.

Klaus, P. (2002, May). *Perinatal advances that alter the management of problems of bonding and attachment.* Preconference presentation at the 3rd EMDR Europe Association Conference, Frankfurt, Germany.

Klaus, P. (2005a, June). *Birth trauma—Causes, effects, methods to heal: An EMDR approach.* Presentation at the 6th EMDR Europe Association Conference, Brussels, Belgium.

Klaus, P. (2005b, September). *The impact of childhood sexual abuse on childbearing: EMDR and other therapeutic interventions.* Presentation at the 10th EMDR International Association Conference, Seattle, Washington.

Klaus, P. (2007, June). *The use of EMDR in medical and somatic problems.* Presentation at 8th EMDR Europe Association Conference, Paris, France.

Klaus, P. (2008, June). *The use of EMDR in somatic & medical problems: Special emphasis on early life interventions.* Presentation at the 9th EMDR Europe Association Conference, London, England.

Klaus, P., & Casadaban, A. (1996, June). *Applying EMDR to physical illness, injury, and symptoms in adults and children: The use of EMDR with physically challenged individuals*. Presentation at the 1st EMDR International Association Conference, Denver, Colorado.

Knipe, J. (2009). "Shame is my safe place": Adaptive information processing methods for resolving chronic shame-based depression. In R. Shapiro (Ed.), *EMDR solutions II: For depression, eating disorders, performance, and more* (1st ed., pp. 49–89). New York, NY: W.W. Norton.

Korn, D. L., & Leeds, A. M. (2002). Preliminary evidence of efficacy for EMDR resource development and installation in the stabilization phase of treatment of complex posttraumatic stress disorder. *Journal of Clinical Psychology, 58*(12), 1465–1487.

Lee, C., Gavriel, H., Drummond, P., Richards, J., & Greenwald, R. (2002). Treatment of post-traumatic stress disorder: A comparison of stress inoculation training with prolonged exposure and eye movement desensitization and reprocessing. *Journal of Clinical Psychology, 58*, 1071–1089.

Leeds, A. M., & Shapiro, F. (2000). EMDR and resource installation: Principles and procedures for enhancing current functioning and resolving traumatic experiences. In L. Carlson & L. Sperry (Eds.), *Brief therapy strategies with individuals and couples*. Phoenix, AZ: Zeig/Tucker.

Lendl, J., & Foster, S. (1997). *EMDR performance enhancement for the workplace: A pratictioner's guide*. San Jose, CA: Performance Enhancement Unlimited.

Lendl, J., & Foster, S. (2009). EMDR performance enhancement psychology protocol. In M. Luber (Ed.), *Eyes movement desensitization and reprocessing (EMDR): Basics and special situation* (pp. 377–396). New York, NY: Springer.

Lobenstine, F., & Courtney, D. (2013). A case study: The integration of intensive EMDR and ego state therapy to treat comorbid posttraumatic stress disorder, depression, and anxiety. *Journal of EMDR Practice and Research, 7*(2), 65–80.

Lucchese, D. (2008, November). *Aborto, EMDR e prevenzione della depressione post partum: un caso [Abortion, EMDR and prevention of postpartum depression: A case]*. Presentation at Italian EMDR Association, Milan, Italy.

Manfield, P. (1998a). EMDR terms and procedures: Resolution of uncomplicated depression. In P. Manfield (Ed.), *Extending EMDR: A casebook of innovative applications* (1st ed., pp. 15–36). New York, NY: W. W. Norton.

Manfield, P. (Ed.). (1998b). *Extending EMDR: A casebook of innovative applications* (1st ed.). New York, NY: W.W. Norton.

Manfield, P. (1998c). Filling the void: Resolution of a major depression. In P. Manfield (Ed.), *Extending EMDR: A casebook of innovative applications* (1st ed., pp. 113–137). New York, NY: W.W. Norton.

Marcus, S., Marquis, P., & Sakai, C. (1997). Controlled study of treatment of PTSD using EMDR in an HMO setting. *Psychotherapy, 34*, 307–315.

McLaughlin, K. A., Greif Green, J., Gruber, M. J., Sampson, N. A., Zaslavsky, A. M., & Kessler, R. C. (2012). Childhood adversities and first onset of psychiatric disorders in a national sample of US adolescents. *Archives of General Psychiatry, 69*, 1151–1160.

Montefiore, D., Mallet, L., Levy, R., Allilaire, J. F., & Pelissolo, A. (2007). Pseudo-dementia conversion and post-traumatic stress disorder. *Encephale, 33*(3, Pt. 1), 352–355.

Narimani, M., Ahari, S., & Rajabi, S. (2010). Comparison of efficacy of eye movement desensitization and reprocessing and cognitive behavioural therapy, therapeutic methods for reducing anxiety and depression of Iranian combatants afflicted by post traumatic stress disorder. *Medical Sciences Journal of Islamic Azad University, Tehran Medical Branch, 19*(4), 236–245.

Novo, P., Landin-Romero, R., Radua, J., Vicens, V., Fernandez, I., Garcia, F.,...Amann, B. L. (2014, May). Eye movement desensitization and reprocessing therapy in subsyndromal bipolar patients with a history of traumatic events: A randomized, controlled pilot-study. *Psychiatry Research, 219*, 122–128.

Oppenheim, H. P. (2009). Casus 10—De kwetsbaarheid van kracht: Vrouw met depressies en paniekaanvallen na overlijden van haar vader [Case 10—The vulnerability of strength: A woman with depression and panic attacks after the death of her father]. In H. K. Hornsveld & S. Berendsen (Eds.), *Casusboek EMDR, 25 voorbeelden uit de praktijk* (1st ed., pp. 157–167). Houten, The Netherlands: Bohn Stafleu Van Loghum. doi:10.1007/978–90-313–7358-1_16

Otto, M. W., Perlman, C. A., Wernicke, R., Reese, H. E., Bauer, M. S., & Pollack, M. H. (2004). Posttraumatic stress disorder in patients with bipolar disorder: A review of prevalence, correlates, and treatment strategies. *Bipolar Disorders, 6*, 470–479.

Parnell, L. (1998). Postpartum depression: Helping a new mother to bond. In P. Manfield (Ed.), *Extending EMDR: A casebook of innovative applications* (1st ed., pp. 37–64). New York, NY: W.W. Norton.

Quarantini, L. C., Miranda-Scippa, A., Nery-Fernandes, F., Andrade-Nascimento, M., Galvão-de-Almeida, A., Guimarães, J. L.,...Koenen, K. C. (2010). The impact of comorbid posttraumatic stress disorder on bipolar disorder patients. *Journal of Affective Disorders, 123*, 71–76.

Quarantini, L. C., Netto, L. R., Andrade-Nascimento, M., Galvão-de-Almeida, A., Sampaio, A. S., Miranda-Scippa, A.,...Karestan, C. (2009). Comorbid mood and anxiety disorders in victims of violence with posttraumatic stress disorder. *Review of Brazilian Psychiatry 31*(Suppl. II), 566–576.

Raboni, M. R., Tufik, S., & Suchecki, D. (2006). Treatment of PTSD by eye movement desensitization and reprocessing (EMDR) improves sleep quality, quality of life, and perception of stress. *Annals of the New York Academy of Science, 1071*(1), 508–513.

Rosas-Uribe, M. E., & Ramirez, E. O. L. (2006). The effect of EMDR therapy on the negative information processing of patients who suffer depression. *Revista Electrónica de Motivación y Emoción (REME), 9*, 23–24.

Rosas-Uribe, M. E., Lopez Ramirez, E. O., & Jarero Mena, I. (2010, May). Effect of the EMDR psychotherapeutic approach on emotional cognitive processing in patients with depression. *Spanish Journal of Psychology 13*(1), 396–405.

Rothbaum, B. O. (1997). A controlled study of eye movement desensitization and reprocessing for posttraumatic stress disordered sexual assault victims. *Bulletin of the Menninger Clinic, 61*, 317–334.

Rothbaum, B. O., Astin, M. C., & Marsteller, F. (2005). Prolonged exposure versus eye movement desensitization (EMDR) for PTSD rape victims. *Journal of Traumatic Stress, 18*, 607–616.

Schneider, J., Hofmann, A., Rost, C., & Shapiro, F. (2008, January–February). EMDR in the treatment of chronic phantom limb pain: Theoretical implications, case study, and treatment guidelines. *Pain Medicine, 9*(1), 76–82. doi:10.1111/j.1526-4637.2007.00299.x

Servan-Schreiber, D. (2004). *The instinct to heal.* New Delhi, India: Diamond Pocket Books.

Shapiro, F. (2001). *Eye movement desensitization and reprocessing: Basic principles, protocols, and procedures* (2nd ed.). New York, NY: Guilford Press.

Shapiro, F. (2006). *EMDR: New notes on adaptive information processing with case formulation principles, forms, scripts and worksheets.* Watsonville, CA: EMDR Institute.

Shapiro, F., & Forrest, M. S. (1997). *EMDR: The breakthrough therapy for overcoming anxiety, stress, and trauma* (1st ed.). New York, NY: Basic Books.

Shapiro, R. (2009a). Attachment-based depression: Healing the "hunkered-down." In R. Shapiro (Ed.), *EMDR solutions II: For depression, eating disorders, performance, and more* (1st ed., pp. 90–105). New York, NY: W.W. Norton.

Shapiro, R. (2009b). Endogenous depression and mood disorders. In R. Shapiro (Ed.), *EMDR solutions II: For depression, eating disorders, performance, and more* (1st ed., pp. 24–48). New York, NY: W.W. Norton.

Shapiro, R. (2009c). Introduction to assessment and treatment of depression with EMDR. In R. Shapiro (Ed.), *EMDR solutions II: For depression, eating disorders, performance, and more* (1st ed., p. 9). New York, NY: W.W. Norton.

Shapiro, R. (2009d). Trauma-based depression. In R. Shapiro (Ed.), EMDR solutions II: For depression, eating disorders, performance, and more (1st ed., p. 21). New York, NY: W. W. Norton.

Silver, S. M., Brooks, A., & Obenchain, J. (1995). Eye movement desensitization and reprocessing treatment of Vietnam war veterans with PTSD: Comparative effects with biofeedback and relaxation training. *Journal of Traumatic Stress, 8*, 337–342.

Silver, S. M., Rogers, S., & Russell, M. C. (2008, August). Eye movement desensitization and reprocessing (EMDR) in the treatment of war veterans. *Journal of Clinical Psychology, 64*(8), 947–957. doi: 10.1002/jclp.20510

Solomon, R., & Shapiro, F. (2008). EMDR and the adaptive information processing model: Potential mechanisms of change. *Journal of EMDR Practice and Research, 2*(4), 315–325.

Song, L., & Wang, Z.-Y. (2007, November). Sertraline treatment of depression combined EMDR research: A control study of sertraline combined with EMDR in the treatment of depression. *Journal of Clinical Psychosomatic Disease, 13*(4) 307–308. doi:10.3969/j.issn.1672-187X.2007.04.008

Sprang, G. (2001, May). The use of eye movement desensitization and reprocessing (EMDR) in the treatment of traumatic stress and complicated mourning: Psychological and behavioral outcomes. *Research on Social Work Practice, 11*(3), 300–320. doi:10.1177/104973150101100302

Srivastava, U., & Mukhopadhyay, A. (2008, September). Application of EMDR in the treatment of major depressive disorder: A case study. *Indian Journal of Clinical Psychology, 35*(2), 163–172.

Sun, T. F., Wu, C. K., & Chiu, N. M. (2004, June). Mindfulness meditation training combined with eye movement desensitization and reprocessing in psychotherapy of an elderly patient. *Chang Gung Medical Journal, 27*(6), 464–469.

Tarquinio, C., Schmitt, A., & Tarquinio, P. (2012, January–March). Violences conjugales et psychothérapie eye movement desensitization reprocessing (EMDR): études de cas [Conjugal violence and eye movement desensitization and reprocessing (EMDR): Case studies]. *L'évolution Psychiatrique, 77*(1), 97–108. doi:10.1016/j.evopsy.2011.11.002

Tarquinio, C., Schmitt, A., Tarquinio, P., Rydberg, J.-A., & Spitz, E. (2012, April–June). Intérêt de la psychothérapie « eye movement desensitization reprocessing » dans le cadre de la prise en charge de femmes victimes de viols conjugaux [Benefits of "eye movement desensitization and reprocessing" psychotherapy in the treatment of female victims of intimate partner rape]. *Sexologies, 21*(2), 92–99. doi:10.1016/j.sexol.2011.05.001

van der Kolk, B. A., Spinazzola, J., Blaustein, M. E., Hopper, J. W., Hopper, E. K., Korn, D. L.,...Simpson, W. C. (2007). A randomized clinical trial of eye movement desensitization and reprocessing (EMDR), fluoxetine, and pill placebo in the treatment of posttraumatic stress disorder: Treatment effects and long-term maintenance. *Journal of Clinical Psychiatry, 68*(1), 37–46.

Wood, E. F. (2012, September). *Sheffield EMDR and depression investigation (SEDI)*. Poster presented at the 18th International Network for Psychiatric Nursing Research Conference, Oxford, England.

Wood, E. F., & Ricketts, T. (2013). Is EMDR an evidence-based treatment for depression? A review of the literature. *Journal of EMDR Practice and Research, 7*(4), 225–235. doi:10.1891/1933–3196.7.4.225

The EMDR Therapy Protocol for Bipolar Disorder

Benedikt L. Amann, Roser Batalla, Vicky Blanch,
Dolors Capellades, Maria José Carvajal, Isabel Fernández,
Francisca García, Walter Lupo,
Marian Ponte, Maria José Sánchez, Jesús Sanfiz,
Antonia Santed, and Marilyn Luber

Introduction

Bipolar disorder is a disease that occurs with high frequency and affects the brain circuits regulating affective states. This complex mental disorder is characterized by dynamic mood changes from elevated mood to depressive or mixed episodes:

- *Mania*: Patients in a manic episode are normally admitted to a psychiatric hospital due to the severity of frequently presented symptoms, such as an elevated and expansive mood, hyperactivity, hypersexuality, need to spend money, talkativeness, and reduced need for sleep.
- *Hypomania*: Hypomania is defined as a less severe euphoric state than mania—with similar symptoms—that does not require admission to a psychiatric hospital.
- *Depression*: Depressed patients often suffer from symptoms such as anhedonia; lack of motivation, energy, and concentration; suicidal ideas; and also somatic symptoms, such as changes in sleeping patterns and decreased or increased appetite.
- *Mixed phase*: Patients in a mixed phase are normally admitted to a psychiatric hospital and fulfill criteria for both a depressive and a manic episode. Frequently presented symptoms are hyperactivity, talkativeness, rapid thoughts, irritability, anxiousness, sad mood, and suicidal ideas or plans.
- *Euthymia*: Bipolar patients in a euthymic phase present with a normal or neutral mood, in the absence of a hypomanic, manic, mixed, or depressed episode.
- *Rapid cycling*: This is a temporary complication of the disease and refers to four or more affective episodes a year.
- *Prodromal symptoms*: Prodromal symptoms are described as cognitive, affective, and behavioral symptoms of bipolar disorder before a depressive, (hypo)manic, or mixed episode.
- *Subsyndromal symptoms*: Bipolar patients do not enter clinical remission but continue with mild depressive or hypomanic symptoms. Subsyndromal symptoms are a risk factor for more affective relapses and poor functioning in daily life.

Note: Patients in a manic, mixed, or severe depressed phase can also present with psychotic symptoms, such as hallucinations, delusions, catatonia, or thought disorders.

Bipolar disorder is classified into the following main subtypes:

- *Bipolar disorder I*: Characterized by at least one severe manic or mixed episode, alternating also with depressed episodes.
- *Bipolar disorder II*: Characterized by several protracted depressive episodes and at least one hypomanic episode, but no manic or mixed episode.
- *Cyclothymic disorder*: Constant changes from several hypomanic to depressive symptoms, but symptoms do not meet criteria for hypomania or depression.

Bipolar disorder is a neurobiological disease and the basis of the treatment is pharmacological, using mood stabilizers, atypical antipsychotics, and antidepressants (e.g., Geddes & Miklowitz, 2013). Typical mood stabilizers for bipolar patients include:

- Lithium
- Anticonvulsants, such as valproate, lamotrigine, oxcarbamazepine, or carbamazepine
- Atypical antipyschotics, such as olanzapine, risperidone, quetiapine, aripiprazol, asenapine, or ziprasidone

The therapeutic aim is that bipolar patients go into clinical remission, are euthymic, and remain stable for the long term; but, as a matter of fact, they relapse frequently with full-blown affective episodes (Simhandl, König, & Amann, 2014) or continue with subsyndromal symptoms (de Dios et al., 2012) that are of clinical importance because they are considered a risk factor for more affective relapses and worse functioning in daily life when compared to euthymic bipolar patients (Altshuler et al., 2006).

Among further risk factors for bipolar patients are the following:

- Poor insight into the disease
- Poor compliance with prescribed medication
- Idealization of euphoric symptoms
- Cognitive deficits
- Unhealthy lifestyle habits
- Substance abuse
- Personality disorders
- Anxiety disorders
- Posttraumatic stress disorder (PTSD)/trauma/life events

Bipolar patients, therefore, need a more complex treatment approach, including psychosocial interventions, such as cognitive behavior therapy, psychoeducation, and interpersonal and/or family therapies (Colom et al., 2003; Geddes & Miklowitz, 2013). A new functional remediation therapy, which consists of 21 group therapy sessions, also targets often-observed cognitive and functional impairments in bipolar patients (Torrent et al., 2013). The aim of a more holistic treatment approach is to ameliorate those problems and finally improve the course of the illness with fewer affective relapses and hospitalizations.

An underestimated risk factor for bipolar patients is that of comorbid adverse life events, trauma, and/or PTSD. This is of concern because various studies have found that early childhood adverse events can trigger severe mental disorders—such as bipolar disorder—later in life, with a negative impact on the course of the illness (e.g., McLaughlin et al., 2012). Also, it is well established that adverse life events that occur later in life can affect the course of the disease in a negative manner and can be important contributors to a poorer outcome (e.g., Ellicott, Hammen, Gitlin, Brown, & Jamison, 1990). A recent study found an increase of depressive episodes in bipolar disorder when patients were suffering from life events six months prior to the affective episode (Simhandl, König, & Amann, 2015). Finally, around 20% of bipolar patients also fulfill the criteria for the diagnosis of PTSD (Hernandez et al., 2013; Otto et al., 2004).

Research with bipolar patients and PTSD show that they suffer from more substance abuse, suicide attempts, rapid cycling, and affective symptoms (e.g., Kessler, Sonnega, Bromet, Hughes, & Nelson, 1995; Quarantini et al., 2010). Furthermore, it is important to note that patients primarily diagnosed with PTSD develop unipolar depressive episodes or dysthymia frequently, but seem especially vulnerable to present with (hypo)manic symptoms (men more than women); this means they are more prone to the diagnosis of bipolar disorder than unipolar depression (Kessler et al., 1995).

Note: The Barcelona Group recommends that trauma therapists take into account this elevated risk for PTSD patients to develop bipolar disorder and include a psychiatrist in the treatment strategy if mood symptoms are prominent and are complicating the psychotherapeutic approach in primarily traumatized patients.

Bipolar Disorder, PTSD, and EMDR Therapy

Despite the documented high frequency of traumatic events and PTSD in bipolar disorder patients' histories (Hernandez et al., 2013; Kessler et al., 1995; Otto et al., 2004; Quarantini et al., 2010), there are strikingly few studies concerning traumatized bipolar patients.

This Eye Movement Desensitization and Reprocessing (EMDR) Therapy Protocol for Bipolar Disorder (EPBD)—with its five subprotocols—is based on the results of a controlled randomized, single-blind pilot study of 20 bipolar I and II patients with subsyndromal symptoms and a history of various traumatic events (Novo et al., 2014). Patients who were included in this study had to have experienced at least three documented traumatic events over their lifetime that were still causing distress (subjective units of disturbance or SUD ≥ 5), without necessarily fulfilling a current diagnosis of PTSD. Patients were excluded if they had a neurological disease, suicidal thoughts, substance abuse, or dissociative symptoms evaluated by the Dissociation Experience Scale or DES > 20 (Bernstein & Putnam, 1986).

The objective was to evaluate the efficacy of the EMDR Standard Protocol, as an adjunctive treatment to their habitual mood stabilizers, in reducing the impact of trauma and in improving affective symptoms. After 3 months of 14 to 18 sessions of EMDR Therapy, patients in this group showed a statistically significant improvement in the reduction of the impact of their trauma and a more stable mood when compared with the control group. This effect was maintained after 6 months follow-up. After the EMDR Therapy intervention, none of the patients in the EMDR group relapsed with an affective episode. In conclusion, following the data of this pilot study, EMDR Therapy preliminarily seems an effective and safe intervention for traumatized patients diagnosed with bipolar I and II disorders.

Note: The EPBD was not used for the study but designed after having finished the trial; therefore, the EPBD is based on findings and observations that resulted from patients with bipolar disorder who participated in the trial.

EMDR Therapy Protocol for Bipolar Disorder

Phase 1: Clinical History

General Aspects: Diagnosis and Comorbidity

ASSESS THE CURRENT STATE OF THE CLIENT WITH BIPOLAR DISORDER IN ORDER TO APPLY EMDR

The Barcelona Group normally will assess patients who are possible candidates for EMDR Therapy but who have been diagnosed with bipolar disorder and are currently treated by a psychiatrist. Always assess the current affective state of the patient and check whether or not it is possible to work with EMDR Therapy processing.

- EMDR Therapy recommended for clients in clinical remission and with light hypomanic or subdepressive symptoms (subsyndromal symptoms; Novo et al., 2014).

- EMDR Therapy applicability criteria are to be assessed by the clinician in case of a mild depression or hypomanic phase. If psychotic symptoms are present, please consult protocol for the treatment of psychotic symptoms with EMDR (see van den Berg et al., 2015; and Chapter 5).
- EMDR Therapy not recommended when clients are experiencing a moderate to severe manic, mixed, or depressive episode, as it is impossible to work with a patient psychotherapeutically due to those clinical symptoms. Furthermore, it would also be harder to access traumatic experiences because such patients have no awareness of the difficulties and no connection with previous events in their traumatic history. In addition, when patients present with affective dysregulation, resulting from attachment trauma and/or lack of resources and management of subsequent emotions, the authors observed that the patients had difficulties when reprocessing traumatic events.

Note: The Barcelona Group *does not recommend* EMDR Therapy if the patient is currently in a moderate to severe manic, mixed, or depressive episode. In this case, refer the patient to the treating psychiatrist and consider restarting EMDR Therapy, in addition to the pharmacological therapy, once the patient is affectively more stable. If you are not clear about the current affective state of your patients, consider using the following scales to evaluate affective symptoms:

- Young Mania Rating Scale (Young, Biggs, Ziegler, & Meyer, 1978)
- Montgomery–Asberg Depression Rating Scale (Montgomery & Asberg, 1979)
- Bipolar Depression Rating Scale (Berk et al., 2007; in Spanish: Sarró et al., 2015).

Note: Often clients present with dissociative symptoms, so the authors recommend completing the usual dissociation rating scales, such as the DES (Bernstein & Putnam, 1986) or others. It is also important to consider comorbidity with other Axis II disorders (following *Diagnostic and Statistical Manual of Mental Disorders*, Fifth Edition, *DSM-5*, criteria). For example, in the case of complex trauma and/or an additional personality disorder diagnosis, this protocol can be used, but a different case conceptualization and treatment would also be needed.

For an accurate assessment of bipolar patients, it is essential to collect an extensive client history, including early relationships and attachment type, traumas, and life stressors. These data provide a comprehensive understanding of the impact of traumatic experiences on psychobiological, social, emotional, and mental levels. The authors pay special attention to those triggers that precede affective episodes, with a focus on those that have taken place before the first episode.

Note: The Barcelona Group recommends for bipolar patients a close treatment alliance between psychiatrist and EMDR therapist, combining pharmacological treatment with EMDR Therapy.

Phase 2: Preparation

During the preparation phase, it is important to do the following:

- Create a good therapeutic relationship with your client.
- Explain how EMDR Therapy works.
- Practice bilateral stimulation (BLS).
- Create consciousness of changes during therapy by advising the client to pay close attention to any mental, cognitive, or physical changes during the therapy.
- Go over the informed consent form and ask the client to sign it.
- Check whether your client is aware of his or her disease and whether your client received a psychoeducational program about bipolar disorder.
- Install positive resources as needed; they might include Safe Place (Shapiro, 2001) and the five specifically designed protocols for bipolar patients, addressing mood stabilization, adherence, insight, de-idealization of manic symptoms, and prodromal

symptoms mentioned earlier and scripted in this chapter. After this is accomplished, continue with the treatment plan.

Subprotocols

The EPBD includes five specific, brief subprotocols that address important clinical needs of bipolar patients and can be applied in phase 2 as positive resources, depending on clients' needs.

1. THE EMDR THERAPY MOOD-STABILIZING PROTOCOL FOR BIPOLAR DISORDER

The *aim* of the EMDR Therapy Mood-Stabilizing Protocol for Bipolar Disorder (EMPBD) is to reinforce the positive experiences of affective stability and self-control in bipolar patients. The *major goal* in the treatment process of bipolar patients is long-term normalization in mood. We propose that bipolar patients can benefit from EMDR Therapy as a mood stabilizer, as it provides an elegant way to access the neuronal networks in order to control and stabilize mood states. Initially, the method is to use positive cognitions to strengthen the adaptive system of beliefs. When this installation is reinforced many times, patients experience an improvement in their self-esteem and affective stability, which, in turn, is connected with positive body sensations. Hypothetically, this will produce a homeostasis of neurotransmitters and/or a normalization of activations and deactivations in relevant brain regions (Landin et al., 2013), resulting in a more stable mood with easier access to positive memories. Therefore, we recommend applying the EMPDB protocol during every visit and over the long term as a preventive intervention.

2. THE EMDR THERAPY ILLNESS AWARENESS PROTOCOL

Insight has several dimensions, such as insight into symptoms or disease and insight into need for treatment. Insight decreases with more psychopathology but does not always improve when psychopathological symptoms do. It is mainly associated with medication compliance, prognosis, voluntary versus involuntary admission, and the cultural concepts of disease (Ghaemi & Pope, 1994). Interventions to improve insight into bipolar disorder are scarce; therefore, this group created the EMDR Therapy Illness Awareness Protocol (EIAP). The *aim* is to help clients become more aware of the disease. Good awareness is associated with less affective symptoms and risk behavior, better adherence to treatment, and a healthier lifestyle. Being aware of bipolar disorder can help the client do the following: take medication more reliably, act more consistently concerning eating and sleeping habits, reduce risky behaviors, and ask for professional help when necessary.

3. THE EMDR THERAPY ADHERENCE ENHANCER PROTOCOL

An important risk factor for affective relapses is that of poor adherence. Poor adherence in bipolar patients is mainly caused by the feeling of being controlled by drugs, (hypo)manic episodes, lack of insight, a negative view on pharmacological treatment, substance abuse, lack of treatment response, and side effects, such as weight gain and sedation (Leclerc, Mansur, & Brietzke, 2013). The EMDR Therapy Adherence Enhancer Protocol (EAEP) aims to identify and improve these issues and strengthen adherence to avoid further affective relapses.

4. THE EMDR THERAPY PRODROMAL SYMPTOMS PROTOCOL

The recognition of prodromal symptoms is crucial to relapse prevention. The most often reported prodromal symptoms in bipolar disorder patients include sleep disturbances, mood changes or lability, psychotic symptoms, agitation, restlessness, increased anxiety, changes in appetite, or suicidal ideas (Jackson, Cavanagh, & Scott, 2003). The aim of the EMDR Therapy Prodromal Symptoms Protocol (EPSP) is to help bipolar patients identify early prodromal symptoms so that they can request rapid therapeutic intervention to avoid an affective relapse.

5. THE EMDR DE-IDEALIZATION MANIC SYMPTOMS PROTOCOL

Often, bipolar patients in diagnostic interviews are more focused on their depressive episodes and tend to idealize (hypo)manic episodes. Pleasant aspects of euphoria frequently cause a negation of devastating high-risk behavior during manic episodes. The latter include severe conflictive behavior, engaging in unrestrained buying sprees, impulsive sex and sexual indiscretions, or foolish business investments.

The aim of the EMDR De-Idealization Manic Symptoms Protocol (EDMSP) is to assist patients who are aware of manic episodes but still idealize specific pleasant euphoric symptoms to avoid poor adherence and further affective relapses. The EDMSP is designed for patients who idealize pleasant manic symptoms but ignore the devastating results of these symptoms during a manic episode. Often, clients with bipolar disorder are barely aware of their manic and impulsive symptoms or underestimate them, as they are under the influence of the expansiveness and extroversion of the manic episode, and the mood sensations are pleasant. When asked to do an introspective exercise on their general symptomatology, they usually place more importance on their depressive symptoms than on those of euphoria.

While in Phase 2: Stabilization and Preparation, do not focus on the emotional and somatic aspects, as this could lead to more complex reprocessing. Instead, aim for the cognitive understanding of "realization" and "becoming aware" that manic symptoms are symptoms of illness and not something desirable in the long run.

The EMDR Therapy 3-Pronged Protocol

The EMDR Therapy 3-Pronged Protocol (past, present, future) is used to reprocess past traumatic experiences, work with present triggers, and address future concerns to bring the client to the highest level of adaptive response. The standard 3-Pronged Protocol developed by Shapiro (1995, 2001) recommends starting to reprocess sequentially all traumatic incidents from the earliest to the present ones. As a result of the Barcelona Group's pilot study, the authors implemented some modifications to the EMDR Standard Protocol to best address the issues of this special population. Clients with the diagnosis of bipolar disorder usually present with a rich constellation of traumatic events over their lifetimes, but especially with a variety of disturbing negative life events in the present. Therefore, it is often necessary to begin the treatment from the perspective of symptom-focused therapy (Korn, Rozelle, & Weir, 2004; Leeds, 2009) or the Inverted EMDR Standard Protocol for Unstable Complex Post-Traumatic Stress Disorder developed by Hofmann (2009). According to these authors, beginning to process symptoms in the present that cause the greater(est) discomfort allows clients to access the specific past traumatic memories that are associated with these symptoms and take into account clients' explicit present needs. This will prevent processing many of the individual's life events which may not be connected to the client's current symptomatology.

The Barcelona Group suggests that patients start with present targets when their most disturbing concerns or traumatic events are in the present. If this is not the case, start with past traumatic events, according to the Standard EMDR Protocol and procedures.

Past

There are a number of different ways to organize the processing of past targets:

- If your client does not present with a dominant current dysfunction, reprocess past memories in chronological order.
- In the case of multiple targets, choose—as stated earlier—those related to the symptoms that are contributing to the current dysfunction and start with the processing of the present. Identify these memories through direct questions as well as the Float-Back and affect bridge techniques (Shapiro, 1995). The criteria for target selection include the first, the worst, and the most recent ones that are related to the symptom chosen to work on.
- It is also relevant to address the most important impacts of the disease, choosing as targets the first crisis, the diagnosis, and the first hospitalization.

According to the Three-Pronged Protocol, and in case you followed the standard protocol and started with the past, the next step is to reprocess the corresponding present triggers.

Present

We will emphasize the following present triggers that represent the symptoms and consequences of the disease:

- Affect instability, such as rapid changes in mood, light depressive, or hypomanic symptoms
- Cognitive problems such as problems in memory, attention, or planning
- Disturbing physical sensations and emotions
- Family, social, and work problems
- Flashbacks and intrusive memories experienced by the client in daily life
- Difficulties in the organization of daily life, boredom, or feelings of lack of control and life project

Following the established treatment plan, reprocess the present triggers linked to the chosen symptoms.

Future

Future patterns are incorporated for each trigger and each anticipated future situation. Consider installing a new image of the self, using the resource development and installation protocol to consolidate the benefits obtained in treatment (Leeds, 2009).

EMDR Therapy Protocol for Bipolar Disorder Script

Phase 1: Clinical History

Identify the First Episode, Age, and Type (Mania, Hypomania, Mixed Phase, Depression)

Identify the client's first episode, age at that time, and the type of affective state he or she was in (hypomanic, manic, mixed phase, depressed).

Say, *"Tell me about when you experienced your first episode of _____ (state hypomania, mania, mixed phase, depression)."*

_____

Say, *"How old were you?"*

_____

Say, *"What was happening in your life in the months prior to the crisis?"*

_____

_____

Say, *"Were you affected by or exposed to any stressful or difficult situations?"*

_____

_____

Say, *"Were you using any substances such as alcohol, cannabis, cocaine, heroin, ecstasy, amphetamines, benzodiazepines, or anything else?"*

_____

If so, say, *"If so, how much were you using and what effect did it or they have on you?"*

_____

_____

Use the same set of questions for the first episode of each type of mood change(s) that is or are applicable.

Identify the Worst Episode, Age, and Type

Identify the client's worst episode, age at that time, and the type of affective state he or she was in (hypomanic, manic, mixed phase, depressed).

Say, *"Tell me about the worst episode that you have had. Please include your age at the time and what type it was. For instance, were you in a hypomanic, manic, mixed phase, or depressed mood?"*

_____

_____

Say, *"What was happening in your life in the months prior to the crisis?"*

_____

_____

Say, *"Were you affected by or exposed to any stressful or difficult situations?"*

_____

_____

Say, *"Were you using any substances such as alcohol, cannabis, cocaine, heroin, ecstasy, amphetamines, benzodiazepines, or anything else?"*

_____

_____

If so, say, *"If so, how much were you using and what effect did it or they have on you?"*

_____

_____

Identify the Most Recent Episode, Age, and Type

Identify the client's most recent episode, age at that time, and the type of affective state he or she was in (hypomanic, manic, mixed phase, depressed).

Say, *"Tell me about the most recent episode that you have had. Please include your age at the time and what type it was. For instance, were you in a hypomanic, manic, mixed phase, or depressed mood?"*

_____

_____

Say, *"What was happening in your life in the months prior to the crisis?"*

_____

_____

Say, *"Were you affected by or exposed to any stressful or difficult situations?"*

_____

_____

Say, *"Were you using any substances such as alcohol, cannabis, cocaine, heroin, ecstasy, amphetamines, benzodiazepines, or anything else?"*

_____

If so, say, *"If so, how much were you using and what effect did it or they have on you?"*

_____

_____

Identify Later Episodes, Age, and Type

Identify the client's later episodes, age at that time, and the type of affective state he or she was in (hypomanic, manic, mixed phase, depressed).

Say, *"Tell me about further episodes that you have had. Please include your age at the time and what type it was. For instance, were you in a hypomanic, manic, mixed phase, or depressed mood?"*

_____

_____

_____

_____

_____

_____

_____

Say, *"What was happening in your life in the months prior to each crisis?"*

_____

_____

Say, *"Were you affected by or exposed to any stressful or difficult situations?"*

_____

_____

Say, *"Were you using any substances such as alcohol, cannabis, cocaine, heroin, ecstasy, amphetamines, benzodiazepines, or anything else?"*

_____

If so, say, *"If so, how much were you using and what effect did it or they have on you?"*

_____

_____

Identify Last Episode, Age, and Type

Identify the client's last episode, age at that time, and the type of affective state he or she was in (hypomanic, manic, mixed phase, depressed).

Say, *"Tell me about the last episode that you have had. Please include your age at the time and what type it was. For instance, were you in a hypomanic, manic, mixed phase, or depressed mood?"*

_____

_____

_____

Say, *"What was happening in your life in the months prior to that crisis?"*

_____

_____

Say, *"Were you affected by or exposed to any stressful or difficult situations?"*

_____

_____

Say, *"Were you using any substances such as alcohol, cannabis, cocaine, heroin, ecstasy, amphetamines, benzodiazepines, or anything else?"*

_____

If so, say, *"If so, how much were you using and what effect did it or they have on you?"*

_____

_____

Hospitalizations

Collect information about hospitalizations and experiences in hospital environments (in the event that there have been any).

Say, *"Were you ever hospitalized?"*

_____

If so, say, *"How many times were you hospitalized?"*

_____

Say, *"Were these voluntary hospitalizations or had you been admitted involuntarily as well?"*

_____

_____

Say, *"How were you treated upon arrival?"*

_____

_____

Say, *"How was your stay during the hospitalization?"*

_____

_____

Say, *"Did you experience isolation or mechanical restraint?"*

_____

_____

Say, *"How were your experiences with doctors and caregivers during the hospitalization?"*

_____

_____

Say, *"How did the episode evolve? Did you recover from your episode?"*

_____

_____

Say, *"Did you receive visits from family or friends?"*

_____

_____

Say, *"Did you feel supported by your family?"*

_____

_____

Say, *"How were the relationships you established with other patients?"*

_____

_____

Impact of Bipolar Diagnosis

Assess the impact of the diagnosis on the patient, family members, and other social relationships.

Say, *"How did you respond when you found out that you were diagnosed with a bipolar disorder?"*

_____

_____

Say, *"How did your diagnosis affect your self-esteem, and did it change your perception of yourself?"*

_____

_____

Say, *"Has it affected your vision of the future?"*

_____

_____

Say, *"How was your diagnosis communicated to your family and what was the impact on them?"*

_____

_____

Say, *"Have you had family and professional support?"*

_____

_____

Say, *"Currently, does having a bipolar disorder have any repercussions for you and your family?"*

_____

_____

Say, *"Did any of your social relationships change after the diagnosis?"*

_____

_____

Say, *"Do you have trouble accepting medication?"*

_____

_____

If yes, consider applying the EAEP (see later).

Say, *"Is anyone else familiar with your medication regimen besides yourself?"*

_____

_____

Say, *"Do some of your family members attend your medical visits?"*

_____

_____

Say, *"Have you changed professionals during the course of the disease?"*

_____

_____

If yes, say, *"How has this affected you?"*

_____

_____

Say, *"Has the illness affected your work in general?"*

_____

Cognitive Consequences of the Disease

Ask about the cognitive consequences of bipolar disorder.

Say, *"Do you have the impression that your concentration, attention, and memory are affected?"*

_____

_____

If so, say, *"Has this affected your performance at work, or your tasks at home or anywhere else?"*

_____

Issues of Attachment

Ask about issues of attachment.

Say, *"Please tell me what you know about your birth. Was it a normal birth or were you told about any complications?"*

_____

_____

_____

Say, *"During the time of your birth, did your mother experience any stress about being a mother, or did she suffer other disorders such as depression, mania, hypomania, mixed phase, psychosis, or PTSD?"*

_____

_____

Say, *"Do you know if there was any physical and/or emotional separation from your mother at birth?"*

_____

_____

Say, *"Did your mother have any miscarriages prior to her pregnancy with you and/or did she lose any other children?"*

_____

_____

Say, *"How was your relationship with your father and mother?"*

_____

_____

Say, *"How was the relationship between your parents?"*

_____

_____

Say, *"Please tell me about a typical scene in your family from an everyday situation such as lunchtime, games, or bedtime."*

_____

_____

_____

Assess illness in the patient and other relatives that could cause separation, neglect or overprotection, and role reversal.

Say, *"Did you move or change residences a great deal growing up?"*

_____

_____

Say, *"Did you have many different caregivers growing up?"*

_____

_____

Say, *"Did any of your family members have problems with substance abuse?"*

_____

_____

Say, *"How did your caregivers respond to challenges and needs? Please tell me about any examples that come to mind."*

_____

_____

Say, *"When you had challenges or needs, were you able to talk about it with someone?"*

_____

_____

Say, *"If you spoke, did the person(s) respond to you in a helpful way, or were there reprimands and/or punishments?"*

_____

_____

Say, *"How was your care with regard to food, health, rest, and leisure activities?"*

_____

_____

Say, *"Who played with you? Who consoled you? Who told you stories?"*

_____

_____

Say, *"Please tell me about your family's financial and work situation."*

_____

_____

Trauma

Ask about the patient's history of traumatic experiences.

Say, *"I am going to ask you about any traumatic experiences that you might have had. Please tell me about anyone to whom you were close who died."*

_____

_____

_____

Say, *"How did you manage your feelings of sadness and grief?"*

_____

_____

_____

Say, *"Was there anyone to whom you were close who died through suicide?"*

_____

_____

_____

Say, *"How did you manage all your feelings related to _____ (state the person's name) suicide?"*

_____

_____

Say, *"Were there people around who were able to support your feelings and grief?"*

_____

Say, *"Do you feel that you were neglected growing up?"*

_____

_____

Say, *"Did anyone make you feel bad emotionally and/or psychologically while you were growing up? If so, how did they act toward you?"*

_____

_____

_____

Say, *"Did anyone touch you inappropriately or without your consent? If so, what happened?"*

_____

_____

Say, *"Did you have any break-ups that went badly for you? If so, what happened?"*

_____

_____

_____

Say, *"Were there hurtful consequences due to manic episodes?"*

_____

_____

If so, consider applying the EDMSP (see later).

Say, *"Are there any particular work, social, financial, and/or family stressors that have been going on for you lately?"*

_____

_____

_____

Say, *"When you think back on your time in school, were there any traumatic and/or adverse experiences that you had there with teachers, peers, and/or anyone else?"*

_____

_____

_____

Say, *"Were you in any type of accident where there was a threat of death or serious injury to yourself or someone else? If so, what happened?"*

_____

_____

_____

Say, *"Were you in any type of critical incident due to a natural or man-made disaster such as a flood, hurricane, tsunami, war, terrorist act, kidnapping, robbery, etc.?"*

_____

_____

_____

Say, *"How did you manage your feelings of sadness and grief?"*

_____

_____

Say, *"Have you had a serious physical illness where you felt that you would not survive or felt that you were not treated well during the course of your illness?"*

_____

_____

_____

Say, *"Did you have any surgeries that were upsetting to you?"*

_____

_____

_____

Say, *"Are there any other important life experiences that we have not covered so far that have affected you in a negative way?"*

_____

_____

_____

Significant Life Experiences

Say, *"Thinking about all of the things we just talked about and including anything that you might remember that was not included earlier, let's make a list of memories of significant life experiences beginning with the earliest ones. Include positive and negative experiences. For each positive and negative experience, consider thinking about at least one person, situation, or experience that helped you to cope with it or was part of the situation"* (Leeds, 2009).

Positive Experiences   Sharing Person

_____

_____

_____

_____

_____

_____

Negative Experiences   Helpful Person

_____

_____

_____

_____

_____

Psychiatric History of Family Members and Effects

Assess the psychiatric background of family members and the effects of any difficulties on the attachment system of the patient.

Say, *"Is or are there any family member(s) who has or have been diagnosed with a psychiatric illness?"*

_____

_____

Say, *"Do you have any knowledge of any person in the family who shows strange behavior?"*

_____

_____

If so, say, *"How has _____ (state the name of the family member(s)) illness affected you?"*

_____

_____

Preparation for the Treatment Plan

As you will have accumulated a great deal of information, revise the history of the patient so far by structuring it in a hierarchical way from worst to least worst. You can write down the traumatic event and then add the year and SUD.

Say, *"We have a great deal of information about what has happened to you during the course of your life; let's create a list together of the adverse life experiences and/or traumatic events that affected you. Let's start with the one that affected you the most, what year it happened, and please rate it on a scale of 0 to 10 where 0 is no disturbance or neutral and 10 is the highest disturbance you can imagine."*

Negative events   Year   SUD

1. _____

2. _____

3. _____

4. _____

5. _____

6. _____

7. _____

8. _____

9. _____

10. _____

Treatment Plan

The case conceptualization for the treatment plan includes the 3-Pronged Protocol, and possibly starts with symptoms in the present related to the traumatic events in the past. The Barcelona Group suggests that patients start with present targets when their most disturbing concerns or traumatic events are in the present. If this is not the case, start with past traumatic events, according to the Standard EMDR Protocol and procedures.

PRESENT LEADS TO PAST

Ask for the incidents or symptoms in the present causing discomfort.

Say, *"What causes you the most discomfort currently?"*

_____

_____

_____

Say, *"What image represents the most traumatic part of* _____ (state the issue)?"

_____

_____

_____

Say, *"What words best go with the image that express your negative belief about yourself now?"*

_____

Say, *"When you bring up that image or* _____ (state the issue), *what would you like to believe about yourself now?"*

_____

_____

Say, *"In which other moment in the past did you experience similar negative thoughts?"*

_____

_____

Say, *"When did you have those negative thoughts earliest?"*

_____

Say, *"What was the most debilitating symptom?"*

_____

Say, *"Think of the image, the NC _____ (repeat the NC) and the emotions and let your mind float back to the past. Identify when you experienced this for the first time."*

The procedure is the same for every symptom and traumatic experience.

Future

Check for the future template for all behaviors, events, or stimuli that continue to be associated with maladaptive responses. The client uses the most adaptive information learned from experiences in the past and present. The objective is to find new coping strategies for situations in the future similar to those that caused symptoms before.

Imagine with the client a future anticipated situation with a person or situation.

Say, *"Bring up the picture of the future situation of _____ (describe the specific situation) _____, and the words _____ (repeat the PC), and notice what emotions you feel _____ (repeat them) and where you feel it in your body."*

Phase 2: Client Preparation

Create a good therapeutic relationship with your client.

Say, *"As you agreed to work on your traumatic events and your bipolar disorder, it is important for us to meet on a regular basis. All issues we will work with are confidential, which means that we will not discuss what happens here unless you give us your permission. If you feel uncomfortable in a certain situation or if you are concerned about something, please do not hesitate to inform me about it so that we can address it."*

Coordinate with the family and professional team.

Say, *"As bipolar disorder not only affects patients like you but also family members, I want to propose to you that we also talk to someone in your family about this treatment approach. Who do you think would be a good person for us to contact?"*

Name of relative: _____

Degree of kinship: _____

Say, *"Would it be OK with you if we call that person and ask her or him to attend one session? What is the best way to contact _____ (state the name of the family member)?"*

Name of relative: _____ Tel: _____

Say, *"Also, I will need permission to contact your psychiatrist to inform her or him about the therapy so that we can all make sure that you get the best possible treatment."*

Name of psychiatrist: _____ Tel: _____

Use a diary or record to monitor treatment response and adjust treatment plans.

Say, *"I also would recommend using a diary to monitor your mood. You might use just a simple book and note your mood three times a week (from −5 extremely depressed, to 0 very stable, to +5 very manic or mixed). In your journal, it is also helpful to note how many hours you slept and the time when you took or did not take your medication. It is also helpful to note any positive or negative life events."*

Say, *"Alternatively, you might download an app from your mobile phone to monitor your mood (e.g., App: Moody Me-Mood Diary and Tracker [MedHelp])."*

Method chosen to monitor mood: _____

Check Whether Client Received Psychoeducation

Say, *"Did you attend a psychoeducation program on bipolar disorder? If so, what did you learn from it?"*

_____

_____

Say, *"What do you know about bipolar disorder?"*

_____

_____

Say, *"Please tell me about medication and how it is or is not working for you."*

_____

_____

Say, *"Are you aware of any symptoms that signal to you that your illness is about to happen?"*

Jot down relevant protocols.

_____

Explain the EMDR Therapy approach to the client, telling him or her that it is intended to solve traumatic experiences that underlie the symptoms. It is important that the client understand the impact of trauma on his or her condition, the phases of the treatment plan (past, present, and future), and what he or she can expect from the reprocessing.

Say, *"Traumatic experiences are frequent in patients with bipolar disorder and worsen the course of the disease. Our aim is to help you stabilize yours by reprocessing your traumatic events. If a traumatic event happens, often it gets saved in a dysfunctional way. Images, emotions, sensations, and thoughts of the experience might be isolated from the rest of the functional memory. This might provoke intense symptoms as if the traumatic event were happening right now. EMDR seems to stimulate the brain, allowing the processing of this experience and integrating it into memory networks. EMDR is a very effective method to reprocess traumatic events and works via a bilateral cerebral stimulation, including accessing your physical state, your thoughts about yourself, feelings, and images. We will start with an experience in the present that bothers you most and then go back to the past."*

Use the train metaphor to explain EMDR Therapy to clients (Leeds & Shapiro, 2000), as this allows them to observe or be consciously aware of their position or experience without pressuring or judging themselves.

Say, *"To understand how EMDR Therapy works, I will use the train metaphor: You can get into a train at the main station with a big suitcase full of memories from the past. In the train, you can observe the landscape through the window.*

Sometimes it changes quickly, or sometimes it changes very slowly, if at all. Sometimes you do not see anything, as if you were in a tunnel. Using this approach of letting whatever happens to happen during BLS is important to allowing your mind to move in the direction it needs to go rather than holding on to where you have been before. Just think about nothing specifically. When the train stops in a station, breathe deeply and tell me what you notice while the train is at rest. Just describe what you noticed when the train was moving. When the train starts again, be aware of changes in the landscape without judging what should occur until the train stops again at the next station."

Help clients understand how affect regulation will enable them to better manage their disorder and provide the ability to prevent relapses.

Say, *"You will see when we have processed your traumatic events that your mood will get better as well. This is because your own adaptive information processing system eliminated various disturbing feelings related to the traumatic events. These traumatic events influenced your mood in the past in a negative way and might have triggered your depressive or manic episodes."*

Foster an attitude of conscious observation that helps with effective reprocessing.

Say, *"I would also like to ask you to observe carefully any physical, emotional, and cognitive changes you might experience during the therapy."*

Introduce BLS to clients. It is helpful for therapists to study the client's tolerance to different speeds and types of stimulation before accessing any positive or negative memories.

Say, *"Let's sit in the position of two ships passing in the night. Also, let's experiment with the kinds of bilateral stimulation such as eye movements, tones, or tapping we will use. If you find them uncomfortable, just hold your hand up like this* (demonstrate) *or turn your head away to let me know. Remember, I just need accurate feedback about what you are experiencing."*

Make sure to have the client's consent for treatment. Depending on the country, this might or might not be an important legal issue. If it is an issue, prepare an informed consent in your language about EMDR Therapy with bipolar traumatized patients that then should be signed by the client and yourself.

Say, *"Now that you know how EMDR Therapy works and what the principal ideas of the therapy are, I would like you to sign the following informed consent that you agree it is OK to go forward with the EMDR Therapy I have been proposing to you and that I have informed you in an extensive manner about the therapy."*

Patient has signed an informed consent   ☐ Yes   ☐ No

Positive Resources

Use the Safe Place protocol and the five specific subprotocols for bipolar patients that can be applied in a flexible way in phase 2 to further enhance mental stability.

Five Protocols to Enhance Mental Stability

1. EMDR MOOD-STABILIZING PROTOCOL FOR PATIENTS WITH BIPOLAR DISORDER

Positive Mood

Say, *"As you know, in bipolar patients the mood can change often from depression to an exaggerated, elevated mood. Furthermore, daily stress and tensions make us susceptible to whatever is happening around us. With this exercise we will determine memories and moments where you felt well and your mood was stable. Concentrating on this will stabilize your mood and increase the sensation of control in your life."*

Say, *"Please describe a moment in your life in which you had the experience and sensation of a stable mood, and where you were in control of your life. You can go as early in your life as you wish. It is important that you feel the sensation of a stable mood and control."*

_____

_____

_____

Say, *"Which image represents this best situation?"*

_____

_____

Say, *"Which positive thought accompanies this situation?"*

_____

_____

Say, *"Which emotion accompanies this image and the positive thought?"*

_____

_____

Say, *"In which part of the body do you feel this?"*

_____

_____

Say, *"Now concentrate on this image of your stable mood, control and* _____ (state the positive words), *and the body sensations, and* _____ (state whatever type of BLS you chose)."

_____

_____

Do 6 to 12 sets of BLS.

Say, *"What do you get now?"*

_____

_____

If the experience continues to be positive or even increases, reinforce with another 6 to 12 sets of BLS.

Say, *"Concentrate on this and follow my fingers."*

_____

_____

If the experience continues to be positive or even increases, choose from the various possibilities. Reinforce as often as you think might be helpful.

Say, *"Go with that."*

Concentrate on the PC and the body sensation.

> Say, *"Focus on the positive words* _____ (state PC) *and the body sensation and go with that."*

_____

Do the same but intensify the body sensations.

> Say, *"Focus on the positive words* _____ (state PC) *and really experience the body sensations and go with that."*

_____

Anchor or reinforce with a keyword.

> Say, *"When you think of that positive experience, what is the word or phrase that represents your positive experience?"*

_____

_____

If a negative sensation or memory comes up, leave that and go on to another positive experience.

Note: It is recommended to repeat the procedure in a stable and constant form during the therapeutic process to support clients in stabilizing their mood.

2. EMDR ILLNESS AWARENESS PROTOCOL

As a first step, it is recommended that the therapist review with the client the presence of affective symptoms suggestive of bipolar disorder that the client experienced in the past.

Check symptoms of hypomania and mania.

> Say, *"Do or did you ever suffer from interrupted sleep?"*

_____

> Say, *"Have you ever experienced a decreased need for sleep, feeling refreshed with only 3 or 4 hours a night?"*

_____

> Say, *"Do you know the sensation that you feel when you have made too many plans, projects, and activities?"*

_____

> Say, *"Do you remember episodes of an uncontrollable need to spend money, have sex, shop, or eat?"*

_____

> Say, *"Did you have moments in your life when you felt tense or more conflictive?"*

_____

> Say, *"Did you live episodes with an increased vitality, energy, or strength?"*

_____

Say, *"Did you ever notice that you have so many thoughts in your head and that you cannot pay adequate attention to each one of them?"*

_____

Say, *"Have you ever been more talkative than usual?"*

_____

Say, *"Did you ever feel the need to move around aimlessly and restlessly?"*

_____

Say, *"Did you ever have difficulties in concentrating or maintaining attention when you read, worked, or you were talking to someone?"*

_____

Say, *"Do you have a feeling of being watched or observed by others?"*

_____

Say, *"Do you have a feeling that someone may be following you?"*

_____

Say, *"Did you ever hear voices in your head?"*

_____

If so, *"How many voices do or did you hear?"*

_____

Say, *"Do they communicate amongst themselves?"*

_____

Check Symptoms of Depression

Say, *"Does or did your mood ever feel low, melancholic, or very sad?"*

_____

Say, *"Do or did you ever feel an excessive need to sleep?"*

_____

Say, *"Do you ever have the experience that your thinking is slowed down?"*

_____

Say, *"Have you ever thought about suicide?"*

_____

If so, *"Do or did you have a plan?"*

_____

Say, *"Do or did you ever lose your appetite or feel that you can't stop eating?"*

_____

Say, *"Do or did you ever suffer from anxiety?"*

_____

Say, *"Do or did you ever experience a complete loss of sexual desire?"*

_____

Check Symptoms of a Mixed Episode

Say, *"Do or did you ever feel excessive irritability and are or were you prone to argue excessively?"*

_____

Say, *"Do or did you ever feel restless and agitated?"*

_____

Say, *"Do or did you ever feel excitement and sadness at the same time?"*

_____

Say, *"Do or did you go from being lively and cheerful to being sad for no apparent reason?"*

_____

Say, *"Do or did you suffer from other symptoms we have not mentioned and you may think are part of bipolar disorder?"*

_____

_____

_____

_____

Say, *"We have collected a number of symptoms that might be typical of bipolar disorder. Next, I wonder if we can find any positive beliefs that are useful to better manage the disease."*

List of Positive Beliefs

The therapist can propose positive beliefs that can help clients manage the symptoms that were worked on previously.

Say, *"I wonder if any of the following beliefs could be useful to you to better manage your disease?"* (Please make a cross where client responds positively)

Say, *"Accepting my illness allows me to better regulate my leisure time."*   ☐ Yes   ☐ No

Say, *"Accepting my illness allows me to choose a better job and/or a better job schedule."*   ☐ Yes   ☐ No

Say, *"Accepting my illness allows me to have a better relationship."*   ☐ Yes   ☐ No

Say, *"Accepting my illness allows me to be in better control of my life."* ☐ Yes ☐ No

Say, *"I feel like I take care of myself if I accept my disease and take my medication."* ☐ Yes ☐ No

Say, *"I am able to call my therapist and ask for help if I feel unstable."*

☐ Yes ☐ No

Say, *"Being aware of the illness I have makes me less sick."* ☐ Yes ☐ No

Say, *"When I notice the first symptoms of my illness, I know that I have to contact _____ (name a person of trust) because he or she gives me a trustworthy and realistic point of view about my condition."* ☐ Yes ☐ No

Say, *"Please tell me if there are any other beliefs about yourself that we have not mentioned."*

_____

_____

_____

The next step is to reinforce illness awareness by using PCs so that the client is able to better cope with it.

Say, *"Now let's talk about how the awareness of your symptoms allows you to take care of yourself and ask for help. During which life experiences have you been aware of your illness, and how has that been for you?"*

_____

_____

_____

Say, *"What bodily sensations do you experience when remembering this experience?"*

_____

Say, *"What image best represents this experience?"*

_____

Say, *"What positive thought* (of the previously presented PCs) *goes along with this experience?"*

_____

Say, *"What emotion goes along with that image and positive thought?"*

_____

Say, *"Where do you feel it in your body?"*

_____

Say, *"Now, focus on that image of _____ (state the time when client was in control and aware of his or her illness), those positive words, and the body sensation, and follow my fingers."* (Use 6 to 12 sets of BLS).

Say, *"What do you get now?"*

_____

If the experience continues to be positive or becomes stronger, reinforce with a second set of 6 to 12 BLS.

Say, *"Focus on that and follow my fingers."*

Say, *"What do you get now?"*

_____

If it continues to be positive, reinforce with a new set of BLS.

Say, *"Is there a word or phrase that can help you remember this as a resource?"*

_____

Say, *"Connect it with the pleasant bodily sensations, and follow my fingers."* (Do 6 to 12 sets of BLS.)

Say, *"What do you notice now?"*

_____

If there are any negative sensations or any negative memories that come up, leave this resource and move on to another positive experience.

You can repeat the EIAP in the same session or in different ones throughout the therapeutic process.

3. EMDR ADHERENCE ENHANCER PROTOCOL

Clients with bipolar disorder have a chronic illness that includes lifelong drug treatment. Among the problems reported to clinicians by their clients that arise in meeting treatment requirements are the following (Leclerc et al., 2013):

- Loss of a sense of control over their lives due to taking medication
- Missing (hypo)manic phases
- Lack of awareness of the disease
- Adverse attitude toward treatment
- Substance abuse
- Lack of treatment response
- Side effects experienced caused by drugs

The goal of this protocol is to strengthen adherence to drug treatment in clients with bipolar disorder, and to help them appreciate the positive aspects of taking their medication.

Negative feelings about taking medication for bipolar disorder
First, we have to find out what bothers the client most about receiving drug treatment.

Say, *"What bothers you most about taking medication for your disease, bipolar disorder?"*

_____

Positive feelings about taking medication for bipolar disorder
The therapist acknowledges the client's issue about taking medication but suggests some possible positive outcomes from taking medication and asks the following question:

Say, *"I understand that _____ (state the issue) bothers you. However, what would you say is good about taking medication?"*

_____

Say, *"Have you ever thought that taking medication has been beneficial for you with regard to your family and social environment?"*

_____

Say, *"Have you ever thought that taking medication has been beneficial for you with regard to developing your professional and intellectual activity?"*

_____

Say, *"Have you ever thought that taking medication has been beneficial for you with regard to being better organized in daily life, in your daily tasks?"*

_____

Say, *"What further issues do you remember in your life in which taking medication has been beneficial for you?"*

_____

_____

_____

Say, *"After everything we've talked about, when you take the medication, what can you say that is positive about yourself now?"*

_____

Check for possible positive beliefs (make a cross if positive):

Say, *"Do you feel that one of the following positive beliefs is correct for you now?"*

I control my life.	☐ Yes	☐ No
I control my disease.	☐ Yes	☐ No
I control my medication.	☐ Yes	☐ No
I can take care of myself.	☐ Yes	☐ No
I am worth it.	☐ Yes	☐ No
I am able to ask for help.	☐ Yes	☐ No
I am strong.	☐ Yes	☐ No
I have options, I can choose.	☐ Yes	☐ No
I am responsible for my actions.	☐ Yes	☐ No

Say, *"Do any further positive beliefs come into your mind when you think about taking medication and/or when you took medication?"*

_____

_____

_____

The next step is to identify each specific positive experience related to taking medication regularly, and to work on them one by one to strengthen treatment adherence with the following procedure.

Say, *"What experiences or positive memories of your life come into your mind associated with taking medication regularly?"*

Narrative of the Positive Experiences

_____

_____

_____

Choose an experience that is vivid for the client.

Say, *"What sensations do you have when you think of that particular experi-ence?"*

_____

_____

_____

The therapist can help develop the sensory aspects related to that experience.

Say, *"What image represents this experience best?"*

_____

Say, *"What positive thought goes along with this experience?"*

_____

Say, *"What emotion goes along with the image and the positive thought?"*

_____

Say, *"Where do you feel it in your body?"*

_____

Say, *"Now, focus on that image of control, those positive words, and the sensa-tion in your body and follow my fingers."* (Do 6 to 12 sets of BLS.)

Say, *"What do you notice now?"*

_____

If the experience continues to be positive or becomes stronger, reinforce it with a second set of 6 to 12 BLS.

Say, *"Focus on that and follow my fingers."*

Say, *"What do you notice now?"*

_____

Say, *"Now, while you focus on the pleasant bodily sensation, bring to mind the words _____ (repeat PC related to the memory), and follow my fin-gers."* (Do 6 to 12 sets of BLS.)

Say, *"What happens now?"*

_____

If it continues to be positive, reinforce with a new set of BLS.

Say, *"Is there a word or phrase that could help you remember this as a resource?"*

_____

Say, *"Connect it with the pleasant bodily sensations, and follow my fingers."* (Do 6 to 12 sets of BLS).

If any negative feeling or negative memories come up, leave this resource and move on to another positive experience.

You can repeat the EAEP procedure in the same session or different ones throughout the therapeutic process.

4. EMDR PRODROMAL SYMPTOMS PROTOCOL

Check for Prodromal Symptoms

First, the therapist will ask the client which prodromal symptoms usually occur before an affective episode.

Say, *"What are the first symptoms you usually notice before a depressive episode starts?"*

_____

Say, *"What are the first symptoms you usually notice before a hypomanic or manic episode starts?"*

_____

Say, *"What are the first symptoms you usually notice before a mixed episode starts?"*

_____

In case you want to evaluate more affective symptoms as possible prodromal symptoms, please check with questions from the EIAP (see earlier).

Once the client can recognize his or her prodromal symptoms, the therapist can propose some positive beliefs that can help the client manage the symptoms previously identified and worked on.

List of Positive Beliefs

Say, *"Could any of the following positive beliefs or suggestions be useful to you to avoid a possible full depressive, manic, or mixed episode?"*

Mark useful positive beliefs with a check.

Say, *"When I notice* _____ (state prodromal symptom), *I know I have to ask for help."*   ☐ Yes   ☐ No

Say, *"When I notice* _____ (state prodromal symptom), *I recognize it is a symptom of my illness."*   ☐ Yes   ☐ No

Say, *"When I notice* _____ (state prodromal symptom), *I have to take and/or maintain my medication as prescribed."*   ☐ Yes   ☐ No

Say, *"When I notice* _____ (state prodromal symptom), *I am about to suffer from a new episode."*   ☐ Yes   ☐ No

Say, *"When I notice* _____ (state prodromal symptom), *I have to plan the following steps cautiously and calm down."*   ☐ Yes   ☐ No

Say, *"When I notice* _____ (state prodromal symptom), *I have to be aware of not getting into an argument."*   ☐ Yes   ☐ No

Say, *"When I notice* _____ (state prodromal symptom), *I have to avoid conflictual relationships."*   ☐ Yes   ☐ No

Say, *"When I notice* _____ (state prodromal symptom), *I have to com-municate with a person I trust."*   ☐ Yes   ☐ No

Say, *"When I notice* _____ (state prodromal symptom), *I have to avoid the use of alcohol, coffee, Coca-Cola, Red Bull, amphetamines, and drugs."*   ☐ Yes   ☐ No

Say, *"When I notice* _____ (state prodromal symptom), *I should smoke less."*   ☐ Yes   ☐ No

Repeat the list of positive beliefs if necessary with every prodromal symptom.

Say, *"Can you tell me if you have any other beliefs we have not mentioned related to the good part about recognizing the symptoms that precede an episode?"*

_____

Reinforce Prodromal Symptoms Awareness With PCs

The next step is to reinforce prodromal symptoms awareness with PCs, allowing the client to better cope with the crisis.

Say, *"Now let's talk about how awareness of the symptoms that precede your episodes allows you to take care of yourself and ask for help. In what life experiences have you been aware of symptoms that precede your episodes and this has been good for you?"*

List all experiences and start with the most vivid one:

1. _____
2. _____
3. _____
4. _____

Say, *"What image represents this experience best?"*

_____

Say, *"What positive thought* _____ (of the previously presented positive beliefs) *goes along with this experience?"*

_____

Say, *"What emotion goes along with this image and the positive thought?"*

_____

Say, *"Where do you feel this in your body?"*

_____

Say, *"Now, focus on that image of* _____ (state experience), *those positive words* _____ (state words), *and the body sensation, and follow my fingers."* (Do 6 to 12 sets of BLS.)

Say, *"What do you get now?"*

_____

If the experience continues to be positive or becomes stronger, reinforce with a second set of 6 to 12 BLS movements.

Say, *"Focus on that and follow my fingers."*

Say, *"What do you get now?"*

If it continues to be positive, reinforce with a new set of BLS.

Say, *"Is there a word or phrase that can help you remember this as a resource?"*

Say, *"Connect it with the pleasant body sensations, and follow my fingers."* (Do 6 to 12 sets of BLS.)

If there are any negative sensations or any negative memories that come up, leave this resource and move on to another positive experience.

You can repeat the EPSP procedure in the same session or in different ones throughout the therapeutic process.

5. EMDR DE-IDEALIZATION MANIC SYMPTOMS PROTOCOL

The steps for the EDMSP are the following:

- *Step 1*: Create a list with clients of the types of life experiences they have had while in a manic state that ended in disastrous consequences.
- *Step 2*: Activate the neural networks for each manic experience that contain those memories of manic symptoms and impulses, along with the associated consequences, feelings, and beliefs or thoughts.
- *Step 3*: Work with each one of the experiences to strengthen the client's awareness that it is positive—in a preventive way—to connect the impulsivity and disastrous experiences with the manic state.

Manic Symptoms or Impulses That Lead to Negative Consequences

Step 1: Together with the client, create a list of manic-state life experiences that ended in disastrous consequences.

Say, *"Do or did you suffer from negative experiences as a consequence of manic symptoms and/or impulsivity? Can you give some examples of the impulses you have had and the types of experiences you had as a result of them?"*

	Manic symptoms or impulses	Negative consequences
Experience 1:	_____	_____
Experience 2:	_____	_____
Experience 3:	_____	_____
Experience 4:	_____	_____
Experience 5:	_____	_____
Experience 6:	_____	_____

Step 2: Connect each experience that occurs during a mixed or manic state with the corresponding impulse, action, sensation, belief, and thought.

Say, *"When you felt such a strong impulse, how would you describe the impulse?"*

Say, *"What action followed the impulse?"*

_____

Say, *"Do you remember the sensations you felt in that moment?"*

_____

Say, *"What beliefs did you have in that moment?"*

_____

Say, *"What was the result of the impulse and action? What consequences did it have?"*

_____

Step 3: Strengthen the client's awareness that it is preventive to connect the mania and impulsivity with disastrous consequences.

Say, *"When you think about the negative consequences of your experience* _____ (state the experience), *how important is it for you to know that they are a symptom of your illness, on a scale from 0 to 10, where 0 = not positive at all and 10 = being totally positive?"*

_____

Strengthen the positive awareness response with 6 to 12 sets of BLS.

Say, *"What do you get now?"*

_____

Follow with BLS until 9/10 or 10/10 is reached.

Say, *"How positive is this awareness for you now on a scale from 0 to 10, where 0 = being not positive at all and 10 = being totally positive?"*

_____

Strengthen the positive awareness response with 6 to 12 sets of BLS.

Say, *"What do you get now?"*

_____

Follow with BLS until 9/10 or 10/10 is reached.

Continue and link all the client's experiences of impulses and manic symptoms with negative consequences.

Phase 3: Assessment

Use the trauma targets established in the treatment plan with the EMDR Standard Protocol.

	Description	Year	SUD
Trauma 1:			
Trauma 2:			
Trauma 3:			
Trauma 4:			
Trauma 5:			

Trauma 7: _____

Trauma 8: _____

Trauma 9: _____

Trauma 10: _____

Incident

_____

Say, *"The memory that we will start with today is* _____ (select the next
    incident to be targeted)*."*

_____

_____

_____

Say, *"What happens when you think of the* _____ (state the issue)*?"*

_____

_____

_____

Or say, *"When you think of* _____ (state the issue), *what do you get?"*

_____

_____

Picture

Say, *"What picture represents the entire* _____ (state the issue)*?"*

_____

_____

_____

If there are many choices or if the client becomes confused, the clinician assists by asking
the following:

Say, *"What picture represents the most traumatic part of* _____ (state the
    issue)*?"*

_____

_____

_____

Sometimes bipolar patients have difficulty accessing NCs; however, it is helpful to try
the standard method first.

Negative Cognition

Say, *"What words best go with the picture that express your negative belief about yourself now?"*

_____

_____

Regarding negative beliefs, if clients do not access their disturbing emotions and cannot connect with a negative assessment, ask them the following (following Leeds, 2009):

Say, *"In your worst moments, when you are remembering some aspect of the event, what thoughts or negative beliefs do you have about yourself?"*

_____

_____

Positive Cognition

Say, *"When you bring up that picture or* _____ (state the issue), *what would you like to believe about yourself now?"*

_____

_____

Validity of Cognition

Say, *"When you think of the incident* (or picture), *how true do those words* _____ (repeat the PC) *feel to you now on a scale of 1 to 7, where 1 feels completely false and 7 feels completely true?"*

1	2	3	4	5	6	7

(completely false)   (completely true)

Emotions

Say, *"When you bring up the picture or* _____ (state the issue) *and those words* _____ (state the NC), *what emotion do you feel now?"*

Subjective Units of Disturbance

Say, *"On a scale of 0 to 10, where 0 is no disturbance or neutral and 10 is the highest disturbance you can imagine, how disturbing does it feel now?"*

0	1	2	3	4	5	6	7	8	9	10

(no disturbance)   (highest disturbance)

Location of Body Sensation

Say, *"Where do you feel it* (the disturbance) *in your body?"*

_____

_____

Phase 4: Desensitization

Introduction to Reprocessing

Say, *"Now we will begin to reprocess. As we apply sets of eye movements (taps or tones) sometimes there will be changes and sometimes not. You may notice other images, thoughts, emotions, or memories. Also, new memories may emerge; other times you will only be aware of the eye movements (taps or tones). Remember the train metaphor. There are no right and wrong answers, just notice what happens. If you need to stop, use the stop sign."*

Say, *"Now, remember, it is your own brain that is doing the healing and you are the one in control. I will ask you to mentally focus on the target and to follow my fingers (or any other BLS you are using). Just let whatever happens, happen, and we will talk at the end of the set. Just tell me what comes up, and don't discard anything as unimportant. Any new information that comes to mind is connected in some way. If you want to stop, just raise your hand."*

Then say, *"Bring up the picture and the words _____ (repeat the NC) and notice where you feel it in your body. Now follow my fingers with your eyes (or other BLS)."*

After a set of BLS, say the following.

Say, *"Let your mind go and take a deep breath. What do you get now?"*

_____

_____

Processing and Checking New Channels

Continue processing with several sets of BLS until no new material arises.

Say, *"When you go back to the original experience, what do you get now? Focus on that."*

_____

_____

Check SUDs.

Say, *"On a scale of 0 to 10, where 0 is no disturbance or neutral and 10 is the highest disturbance you can imagine, how disturbing does the incident feel to you now?"*

0	1	2	3	4	5	6	7	8	9	10

No disturbance   Worst disturbance

If SUD = 1 or more, go on with processing.
If SUD continues to be 0 after two sets of BLS, go to the installation phase.

Phase 5: Installation

The objective of the installation phase is to strengthen the reprocessing and integrate a new and more adaptive perspective on the problem that clients are working on.
Steps to perform during installation:

Link the desired PC to the original incident or memory.

Say, *"How does _____ (repeat the PC) sound?"*

_____

_____

Say, *"Do the words _____ (repeat the PC) still fit, or is there another posi-*
tive statement that feels better?"

_____

_____

If the client accepts the original PC, the clinician should ask for a VoC rating to see if it has improved:

Say, *"As you think of the incident, and those wolds _____ (state PC), how*
do the words feel, from 1 (completely false) to 7 (completely true)?"

1   2   3   4   5   6   7

(completely false)   (completely true)

Say, *"Think of the event and hold it together with the words _____ (repeat*
the PC)."

Do a long set of BLS to see if there is more processing to be done.

Say, *"Do the words _____ (repeat PC) still fit, or is there another positive*
statement that seems more appropriate?"

_____

_____

Say, *"As you think of the incident, and those wolds _____ (state PC), how*
do the words feel, from 1 (completely false) to 7 (completely true)?"

1   2   3   4   5   6   7

(completely false)   (completely true)

Say, *"Hold them together."* Do BLS.

Say, *"As you think of the incident, and those wolds _____ (state PC), how*
do the words feel, from 1 (completely false) to 7 (completely true)?"

1   2   3   4   5   6   7

(completely false)   (completely true)

Continue installation with sets of BLS until the material becomes increasingly adaptive. When the client reaches a 6 or 7, offer a set of BLS to strengthen the installation, and continue as needed. If the client reports a VoC of 6 or less, check its adequacy and locate the limiting belief (if necessary) with additional reprocessing.

Say, *"Which thoughts or concerns prevent you from feeling those words as com-*
pletely true?"

_____

_____

This limiting belief should be resolved with a set of BLS. If not, explore whether there are any further limiting beliefs or unidentified or unprocessed memory(ies) network(s) that is or are causing this difficulty.

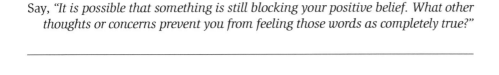

Say, *"It is possible that something is still blocking your positive belief. What other thoughts or concerns prevent you from feeling those words as completely true?"*

_____

_____

If the client continues reporting a VoC of 6 or less, suggest continuing this work in the next session.

Say, *"As this is a process and takes time, I suggest that we continue in the next session."*

If this session is considered incomplete, return to the incomplete target and continue the installation process in the next session. Check the incident again at that time just to make sure that nothing else came up during the week.

Phase 6: Body Scan

It is important to reinforce the positive feelings and the well-being achieved and detect if there is any aspect that has not been reprocessed and is affecting the client at a somatic level.

Say, *"Close your eyes, and keep in mind the original memory and the words _____ (state the positive belief). Then bring your attention to different parts of your body, starting with your head and working downward. Any place you find any tension, tightness, or any unusual feeling, let me know."*

If the client reports any negative feeling, do a set of BLS until it disappears.

If the client reports positive feelings, continue with BLS in order to strengthen them.

Phase 7: Closure

For clients with bipolar disorder, it is important to allow time for closure. It increases integration of the reprocessed material, ensures client stability, and provides a guide for the client to observe, record, and continue integrating the changes that come up after the session. Thank the client for the work done and discuss what he or she has observed during this session.

If the session is complete (VoC = 7/7 and SUDs = 0/10), you can make the following summary:

Say, *"Things may come up or they may not. If they do, great. Write it down and it can be a target for next time. You can use a log to write down triggers, images, thoughts or cognitions, emotions, and sensations; you can rate them on our 0 to 10 scale where 0 is no disturbance or neutral and 10 is the worst disturbance. Please write down the positive experiences, too.*

"If you get any new memories, dreams, or situations that disturb you, just take a good snapshot. It isn't necessary to give a lot of detail. Just put down enough to remind you so we can target it next time. The same thing goes for any positive dreams or situations. If negative feelings do come up, try not to make them significant. Remember, it's still just the old stuff. Just write it down for next time. Then use the tape or the Safe Place exercise to let go of as much of the disturbance as possible. Even if nothing comes up, make sure to use the tape every day and give me a call if you need to."

The session is incomplete when there is still unresolved material:

- If there is still discomfort or the SUD score is greater than 1
- The VOC score is less than 6
- Negative feelings persist in the body scan
- If the SUDs is greater than 1, skip phases 5 and 6

Congratulate the client for the work done and assess the need for stabilization techniques and relaxation, containment, and/or sensory orientation exercises.

> Say, *"We're almost out of time and need to stop soon. You've done a good job and I really appreciate the effort you made. How do you feel?"*

_____

_____

> Say, *"We will not go on with installation of positive cognition nor body scan because there is still material to be processed. However, we will do a containment exercise."*

> Say, *"I would like for us to do a relaxation exercise before stopping. Would you like to do the _____ (suggest a form of relaxation, such as Safe Place or EMPBD)?"*

Once stabilized, say the following:

> Say, *"Things may come up or they may not. If they do, great. Write it down and it can be a target for next time. You can use a log to write down triggers, images, thoughts or cognitions, emotions, and sensations; you can rate them on our 0 to 10 scale where 0 is no disturbance or neutral and 10 is the worst disturbance. Please write down the positive experiences, too.*

> *"If you get any new memories, dreams, or situations that disturb you, just take a good snapshot. It isn't necessary to give a lot of detail. Just put down enough to remind you so we can target it next time. The same thing goes for any positive dreams or situations. If negative feelings do come up, try not to make them significant. Remember, it's still just the old stuff. Just write it down for next time. Then use the Safe Place exercise to let go of as much of the disturbance as possible. Even if nothing comes up, make sure to use the Safe Place every day and give me a call if you need to. Next time, we will practice the Mood-Stabilizing EMDR Bipolar Protocol again, which we will use in every session from now on."*

Phase 8: Reevaluation

In the following session, the client is reevaluated by accessing the network treated in the previous session. Note that if an SUD has increased compared to the previous session, it is likely that the memory is associated with other memory channels. It has been observed that this is common in clients with bipolar disorder, as a result of the large amount of past memories that are linked to other events over time. Often, what seemed like a very clear target in the session can be broken into several others in the next session.

Reprocessing an Incomplete Target

If the target was incomplete in the previous session, return to the incomplete target and continue reprocessing.

> Say, *"Bring back to mind the incident _____ (state the incident) we worked on in the previous session. What comes up? What thoughts arise? What emotions? What physical sensations?"*

Accessing the Baseline

> Say, *"On a scale of 0 to 10, where 0 is no disturbance or neutral and 10 is the highest disturbance you can imagine, how disturbing does it feel now?"*

0	1	2	3	4	5	6	7	8	9	10

(no disturbance)   (highest disturbance)

Continue reprocessing.

Say, *"Stay with that."*

Continue until phases 4, 5, and 6 are complete. This is when the client has reached SUDs = 0 and VOC = 7 and the body scan presents no disturbances.

If target is complete, we recommend continuing with the treatment plan and reprocessing further targets.

Summary

Traumatic events play a fundamental role in the course of bipolar patients' disease. On the basis of a first positive pilot randomized controlled trial of EMDR Therapy in traumatized bipolar patients, the Barcelona Group developed a complex EMDR Bipolar Disorder Protocol to address this clinical need. We recommend using this protocol for bipolar patients in remission, with subsyndromal symptoms or—at most—in a hypomanic, mild mixed, or mild depressive episode. Furthermore, we suggest taking a detailed history of your client, emphasizing among other aspects traumatic prior events. If patients present with disturbing symptoms in the present, start processing targets in the present and later work with traumatic events in the past. In this protocol, five flexible subprotocols address the specific needs of clients with this disorder: a mood stabilization, illness awareness, aldherence enhancer (of medication), recognition of prodromal symptoms, and de-idealization of manic symptoms.

Acknowledgment

This work was made possible through the continuing support of the Spanish and European EMDR Associations. Additional generous support came from the Centro de Investigación Biomédica en Red de Salud Mental (CIBERSAM) and from the Instituto de Salud Carlos III, Spain, with a Stabilization Contract grant (CES 12/024) to B. L. Amann.

References

Altshuler, L. L., Post, R. M., Black, D. O., Keck, P. E., Jr. Nolen, W. A., Frye, M. A.,...Mintz, J. (2006). Subsyndromal depressive symptoms are associated with functional impairment in patients with bipolar disorder: Results of a large, multisite study. *Journal of Clinical Psychiatry, 67*, 1551–1560.

Bernstein, E. M., & Putnam, F. W. (1986). Development, reliability, and validity of a dissociation scale. *Journal of Nervous Mental Disorder, 174*, 727–735.

Colom, F., Vieta, E., Martinez-Aran, A., Reinares, M., Goikolea, J. M., Benabarre, A.,...Corominas, J. (2003). A randomized trial on the efficacy of group psychoeducation in the prophylaxis of recurrences in bipolar patients whose disease is in remission. *Archives of General Psychiatry, 60*, 402–407.

de Dios, C., Ezquiaga, E., Agud, J. L., Vieta, E., Soler, B., & García-López, A. (2012). Subthreshold symptoms and time to relapse: Recurrence in a community cohort of bipolar disorder outpatients. *Journal of Affective Disorders, 20*, 143, 1605.

Ellicott, A., Hammen, C., Gitlin, M., Brown, G., & Jamison, K. (1990). Life events and the course of bipolar disorder. *American Journal of Psychiatry, 147*, 1194–1198.

Geddes, J. R., & Miklowitz, D. J. (2013). Treatment of bipolar disorder. *Lancet, 381*(9878), 1672–1682.

Ghaemi, S. N., & Pope, H. G., Jr. (1994). Lack of insight in psychotic and affective disorders: A review of empirical studies. *Harvard Review of Psychiatry, 2*(1), 22–33.

Hernandez, J. M., Cordova, M. J., Ruzek, J., Reiser, R., Gwizdowski, I. S., Suppes, T., & Ostacher, M. J. (2013). Presentation and prevalence of PTSD in a bipolar disorder population: A STEP-BD examination. *Journal of Affective Disorders, 150*, 2, 450–455. doi: 10.1016/j.jad.2013.04.038. PMID: 23706842.

Hofmann, A. (2009). The inverted EMDR standard protocol for unstable complex post-traumatic stress disorder. In M. Luber (Ed.), *Eye movement desensitization and reprocessing: EMDR scripted protocols: Special populations* (pp. 313–328). New York, NY: Springer.

Jackson, A., Cavanagh, J., & Scott, J. (2003). A systematic review of manic and depressive prodromes. *Journal of Affective Disorders, 74*(3), 209–217.

Kessler, R. C., Sonnega, A., Bromet, E., Hughes, M., & Nelson, C. B. (1995). Posttraumatic stress disorder in the National Comorbidity Survey. *Archives of General Psychiatry, 52*, 1048–1060.

Korn, D., Rozelle, D., & Weir, J. (2004). *Looking beyond the data. Clinical lessons learned from an EMDR treatment outcome study.* Paper presented at the EMDR International Association Annual Conference, Montreal, Canada.

Landin, R., Novo, P., Santed, A., Vicens, V., Pomarol-Clotet, E., McKenna, P.,...Amann, B. L. (2013). Clinical and brain functional improvement in a bipolar patient with subsyndromal mood symptoms following EMDR therapy. *Neuropsychobiology, 67*, 181–184.

Leclerc, E., Mansur, R. B., & Brietzke, E. (2013). Determinants of adherence to treatment in bipolar disorder: A comprehensive review. *Journal of Affective Disorders, 149*, 247–252.

Leeds, A. (2009). *A guide to the standard EMDR protocols for clinicians, supervisors and consultants.* New York, NY: Springer.

Leeds, A. M., & Shapiro, F. (2000). EMDR and resource installation: Principles and procedures for enhancing current functioning and resolving traumatic experiences. In J. Carlson & L. Sperry (Eds.), *Brief Therapy Strategies With Individuals and Couples.* Phoenix, Az: Zeig/Tucker.

McLaughlin, K. A., Greif Green, J., Gruber, M. J., Sampson, N. A., Zaslavsky, A. M., & Kessler, R. C. (2012). Childhood adversities and first onset of psychiatric disorders in a national sample of US adolescents. *Archives of General Psychiatry, 69*, 1151–1160.

Novo, P., Landin, R., Vicens, V., McKenna, P., Pomarol-Clotet, E., Fernandez, I.,...Amann B. L. (2014). EMDR as add-on to pharmacological treatment in subsyndromal, traumatized bipolar patients: A randomized, single-blind, controlled pilot-study. *Psychiatry Research, 219*, 122–128.

Otto, M. W., Perlman, C. A., Wernicke, R., Reese, H. E., Bauer, M. S., & Pollack, M. H. (2004). Posttraumatic stress disorder in patients with bipolar disorder: A review of prevalence, correlates, and treatment strategies. *Bipolar Disorders, 6*, 470–479.

Quarantini, L. C., Miranda-Scippa, A., Nery-Fernandes, F., Andrade-Nascimento, M., Galvão-de-Almeida, A., Guimarães, J. L.,...Koenen, K. C. (2010). The impact of comorbid posttraumatic stress disorder on bipolar disorder patients. *Journal of Affective Disorders, 123*, 71–76.

Shapiro, F. (1995). *Eye movement desensitization and reprocessing. Basic principles, protocols and procedures.* New York, NY: Guilford Press.

Shapiro F. (2001). *Eye movement desensitization and reprocessing: Basic principles, protocols and procedures* (2nd ed.). New York, NY: Guilford Press.

Simhandl, C., König, B., & Amann, B. L. (2014). A prospective 4 year naturalistic follow-up of treatment and outcome of 300 bipolar I and II patients. *Journal of Clinical Psychiatry, 3*, 254–262.

Simhandl, C., König, B., & Amann, B. L. (2015). The prevalence and effect of life events on 222 bipolar I and II patients: A 4 year prospective follow-up study. *Journal of Affective Disorders, 170*, 166–171.

Torrent, C., Del Mar Bonnin, C., Martínez-Arán, A., Valle, J., Amann, B. L., González-Pinto, A.,...Vieta, E. (2013). Efficacy of functional remediation in bipolar disorder: A multicentre, randomized-controlled study. *American Journal of Psychiatry, 170*, 852–859.

van den Berg, D. P., de Bont, P. A., van der Vleugel, B. M., de Roos, C., de Jongh, A., van Minnen, A., & van der Gaag, M. (2015, January). Prolonged exposure vs. eye movement desensitization and reprocessing vs. waiting list for posttraumatic stress disorder in patients with a psychotic disorder: A randomized clinical trial. *JAMA Psychiatry, 72*, 3, 259–267. doi: 10.1001/jamapsychiatry.2014.2637.

Scales

Berk, M., Malhi, G. S., Cahill, C., Carman, A. C., Hadzi-Pavlovic, D., Hawkins, M. T.,...Mitchell, P. B. (2007). The Bipolar Depression Rating Scale (BDRS): Its development, validation and utility. *Bipolar Disorders, 9*, 571–579.

Montgomery, S. A., & Asberg, M. (1979). A new depression scale designed to be sensitive to change. *British Journal of Psychiatry, 134*, 382–389.

Sarró, S., Madre, M., Fernandez, P., Valentí, M., Goikolea, J., Berk, M., & Amann, B. L. (2015). Transcultural adaption and validation of the Spanish version of the Bipolar Depression Rating Scale (BDRS-S). *Journal of Affective Disorders.* doi:10.1016/j.jad.2014.10.009

Young, R. C., Biggs, J. T., Ziegler, V. E., & Meyer, D. A. (1978). A rating scale for mania: Reliability, validity and sensitivity. *British Journal of Psychiatry, 133*, 429–435.

SUMMARY SHEET:
The EMDR Therapy Protocol for Bipolar Disorder

Benedikt L. Amann, Roser Batalla, Vicky Blanch,
Dolors Capellades, Maria José Carvajal, Isabel Fernández,
Francisca García, Walter Lupo, Marian Ponte,
Maria José Sánchez, Jesús Sanfiz,
Antonia Santed, and Marilyn Luber
SUMMARY SHEET BY MARILYN LUBER

Name: _____ Diagnosis: _____

☑ Check when task is completed, response has changed, or to indicate symptoms or diagnosis.

Note: This material is meant as a checklist for your response. Please keep in mind that it is only a reminder of different tasks that may or may not apply to your client.

Introduction

Basic terms of bipolar disorder are:

- ☐ *Mania/hypomania*: It is a less severe euphoric state that does not require admission to a psychiatric hospital. Patients in a manic episode frequently present with the following:
  - ☐ Elevated, expansive mood
  - ☐ Hyperactivity
  - ☐ Hypersexuality
  - ☐ Talkativeness
  - ☐ Reduced need for sleep
- ☐ *Depression*: Depressed patients often suffer from symptoms such as
  - ☐ Anhedonia
  - ☐ Lack of motivation
  - ☐ Reduced energy and concentration
  - ☐ Suicidal ideas
  - ☐ Somatic symptoms, that is, changes in sleeping patterns and decreased or increased appetite
- ☐ *Mixed phase*: Patients in a mixed phase often show
  - ☐ Hyperactivity
  - ☐ Talkativeness
  - ☐ Rapid thoughts

☐ Irritable, anxious, and sad in their mood
☐ Suicidal ideas or plans
☐ *Euthymia*: Bipolar patients in a euthymic phase present with the following:
☐ Normal or neutral mood, in absence of a hypomanic, manic, mixed, or depressed episode
☐ *Rapid cycling* is defined as four or more affective episodes a year, which might be temporary
☐ *Prodromal symptoms*: Prodromal symptoms are described as the first cognitive, affective, and/or behavioral symptoms of bipolar disorder before a depressive, (hypo)manic, or mixed episode.
☐ *Subsyndromal symptoms*: When bipolar patients do not enter clinical remission but continue with mild depressive or hypomanic symptoms. They are a risk factor for more affective relapses and poor functioning in daily life.

Note: Patients in manic, mixed, or severe depressed phase can also present with psychotic symptoms, such as hallucinations, delusions, catatonia, or thought disorders.

Bipolar disorder is classified into the following subtypes:

☐ *Bipolar disorder I*: Characterized by at least one severe manic or mixed episode, alternating also with depressed episodes.
☐ *Bipolar disorder II*: Characterized by several protracted depressive episodes and at least one hypomanic episode, but no manic or mixed episode.
☐ *Cyclothymic disorder*: Several periods of hypomanic and depressive symptoms but symptoms do not meet criteria for hypomania or depression.

Typical mood stabilizers for bipolar patients include:

☐ Lithium
☐ Anticonvulsants, such as valproate, lamotrigine, or carbamazepine
☐ Atypical antipsychotics, such as olanzapine, risperidone, quetiapine, aripiprazol, asenapine, or ziprasidone

Therapeutic aim: Bipolar patients go into clinical remission, are euthymic, and remain stable for the long term.

Risk factors for bipolar patients are:

☐ Poor insight into the disease
☐ Poor compliance with prescribed medication
☐ Idealization of euphoric symptoms
☐ Cognitive deficits
☐ Unhealthy lifestyle habits
☐ Substance abuse
☐ Personality disorders
☐ Anxiety disorders
☐ Posttraumatic stress disorder (PTSD)/trauma/life events

Bipolar patients, therefore, need a more complex treatment approach, including psychosocial interventions:

☐ Cognitive behavioral therapy
☐ Psychoeducation
☐ Interpersonal and/or family therapies
☐ Cognitive rehabilitation
☐ Eye movement desensitization and reprocessing (EMDR)

Bipolar Disorder, PTSD, and EMDR Therapy

EMDR preliminarily seems an effective and safe intervention for traumatized patients diagnosed with bipolar I and II disorders.

EMDR Therapy Protocol for Bipolar Disorder Script Notes

Phase 1: Clinical History

General Aspects: Diagnosis and Comorbidity

Collect the following:

- ☐ Extensive client history
  - ☐ Early relationships
  - ☐ Attachment type
  - ☐ Traumas
  - ☐ Life stressors
  - ☐ Triggers preceding affective episodes
  - ☐ Assess current state of client for EMDR Therapy
- ☐ EMDR Therapy recommended

In clinical remission and light hypomanic or subdepressive symptoms (subsyndromal symptoms)

> For mild depression and hypomanic phase, clinician assessment is indicated
> Psychotic symptoms: consult protocol for psychotic symptoms (Chapter 5)
> EMDR Therapy NOT recommended: Experiencing a moderate to severe manic, mixed, or depressive phase

When the patient is experiencing a manic, mixed phase, or severe depression, it is essential to contact the psychiatrist of the patient.

If you are not sure about the current affective state of your client you might use the following scales:

- ☐ Young Mania Rating Scale
- ☐ Montgomery–Asberg Depression Rating Scale
- ☐ Bipolar Depression Rating Scale

Assess for:

- ☐ Dissociative disorders
- ☐ Other Axis II disorders

Phase 2: Preparation

During the preparation phase, it is important to do the following:

- ☐ Explain how EMDR Therapy works
- ☐ Practice bilateral stimulation
- ☐ Go over the informed consent form and ask the client to sign it
- ☐ Install positive resources as needed; they might include Safe Place (Shapiro, 2001), and or/the five specifically designed protocols for bipolar patients, addressing mood stabilization, adherence, insight, de-idealization of manic symptoms, and prodromal symptoms.
- ☐ After this is accomplished, continue with the treatment plan

Sub Protocols to Address Important Clinical Needs of Bipolar Patients

EMDR MOOD-STABILIZING PROTOCOL FOR BIPOLAR DISORDER

Aim: Reinforce positive experiences of affective stability and self-control over the long term. Procedure: Use PCs to strengthen the adaptive systems of beliefs; reinforce the installation on a regular basis.

EMDR ILLNESS AWARENESS PROTOCOL

Aim: Help clients become more aware of the disease, as this promotes fewer affective symptoms and risk behavior, better adherence to treatment, and a healthier lifestyle.

EMDR ADHERENCE ENHANCER PROTOCOL

Aim: To identify issues that cause poor adherence and improve those issues in order to strengthen adherence, to avoid further relapses.

EMDR PRODROMAL SYMPTOMS PROTOCOL

Aim: To help identify early prodromal symptoms so client can ask for help to avoid relapse.

EMDR DE-IDEALIZATION MANIC SYMPTOMS PROTOCOL

Aim: To use for patients who are aware of manic episodes and still idealize specific pleasant euphoric symptoms, so they can learn to avoid poor adherence and further affective relapses.

The Three-Pronged Protocol—Modifications for Bipolar Disorder Patients

Note: If your client presents with symptoms in the present that cause the greatest discomfort, start processing them first. If not, follow the standard protocol and start processing traumatic events in the past.

Present

Choose symptoms related to current dysfunction (use Float-Back and affect bridge)

 ☐ Choose first, worst, and most recent targets related to the symptom chosen to work on

Present triggers might include:

 ☐ Disturbing physical sensations and emotions
 ☐ Family, social, and work problems
 ☐ Flashbacks and intrusive memories experienced by the client in daily life
 ☐ Difficulties in the organization of daily life, boredom, or feelings of lack of control and life project.

Following the established treatment plan, reprocess the present triggers linked to the chosen symptoms.

Past

 ☐ Reprocess in chronological order
 ☐ Address impact of the disease targets, such as first crisis, diagnosis, and first hospitalization

Future

 ☐ Future patterns for each trigger
 ☐ Future patterns for each anticipated future situation

EMDR Therapy Protocol for Bipolar Disorder Script

Phase 1: Clinical History

Assess the Current State of the Client With Bipolar Disorder in Order to Apply EMDR Therapy

First episode: Identify the first episode, age, and type (mania, hypomania, mixed phase, depression). Then, identify first episodes of each type of mood change.

    1. First episode of either hypomania, mania, mixed phase, depression (circle one).

Age: _____

Events prior to crisis: _____

_____

Affected by/exposed to stressful/difficult situations: _____

_____

Substance use: ☐ Yes   ☐ No

Type: _____

How much? _____ Effect: _____

    2. First episode of either hypomania, mania, mixed phase, depression (circle one).

Age: _____

Events prior to crisis: _____

_____

Affected by/exposed to stressful/difficult situations: _____

_____

Substance use: ☐ Yes   ☐ No

Type: _____

How much? _____ Effect: _____

    3. First episode of either hypomania, mania, mixed phase, depression (circle one).

Age: _____

Events prior to crisis: _____

_____

Affected by/exposed to stressful/difficult situations: _____

_____

Substance use: ☐ Yes   ☐ No

Type: _____

How much? _____ Effect: _____

Worst episode: Identify the worst episode, age, and type

    1. Worst episode of either hypomania, mania, mixed phase, depression (circle one).

Age: _____

Events prior to crisis: _____

_____

Affected by/exposed to stressful/difficult situations: _____

_____

Substance use: ☐ Yes   ☐ No

Type: _____

How much? _____   Effect: _____

Most recent episode: Identify the most recent episode, age, and type

    1. Most recent episode of either hypomania, mania, mixed phase, depression (circle one).

Age: _____

Events prior to crisis: _____

_____

Affected by/exposed to stressful/difficult situations: _____

_____

Substance use: ☐ Yes   ☐ No

Type: _____

How much? _____   Effect: _____

Identify Later/Other Episodes, Age, and Type

    1. Other episode of either hypomania, mania, mixed phase, depression (circle one).

Age: _____

Events prior to crisis: _____

_____

Affected by/exposed to stressful/difficult situations: _____

_____

Substance use: ☐ Yes   ☐ No

Type: _____

How much? _____   Effect:_____

2. Other episode of either hypomania, mania, mixed phase, depression (circle one).

Age: _____

Events prior to crisis: _____

_____

Affected by/exposed to stressful/difficult situations: _____

_____

Substance use: ☐ Yes   ☐ No

Type: _____

How much? _____   Effect: _____

Hospitalizations

Hospitalized: ☐ Yes   ☐ No

How many times?

    1. First hospitalization

☐ Voluntary   ☐ Involuntary

Treatment upon arrival: _____

_____

Treatment during your stay: _____

_____

Experienced: ☐ Isolation   ☐ Mechanical Restraint

Experiences with doctors and caregivers: _____

_____

_____

Evolution of episode: _____

_____

Did you recover from your episode?   ☐ Yes   ☐ No

Visits from family?   ☐ Yes   ☐ No

Visits from friends?   ☐ Yes   ☐ No

Felt supported by family?   ☐ Yes   ☐ No

Did you establish relationships with other patients?   ☐ Yes   ☐ No

    2. Second hospitalization

☐ Voluntary   ☐ Involuntary

Treatment upon arrival: _____

_____

Treatment during your stay: _____

_____

Experienced: ☐ Isolation   ☐ Mechanical Restraint

Experiences with doctors and caregivers: _____

_____

_____

Evolution of episode: _____

_____

Did you recover from your episode?	☐ Yes	☐ No
Visits from family?	☐ Yes	☐ No
Visits from friends?	☐ Yes	☐ No
Felt supported by family?	☐ Yes	☐ No
Did you establish relationships with other patients?	☐ Yes	☐ No

Impact of Bipolar Diagnosis

Response to bipolar disorder diagnosis: _____

_____

Effect of diagnosis on self-esteem: _____

_____

Effect on your vision of the future: _____

_____

How diagnosis communicated to family: _____

_____

Impact on family: _____

_____

Family support?	☐ Yes	☐ No
Professional support?	☐ Yes	☐ No

Does having BD have repercussions for you and your family? _____

_____

Social relationships changed after diagnosis?   ☐ Yes   ☐ No

Do you have trouble accepting medication?   ☐ Yes   ☐ No (If yes, apply EAEP)

Others familiar with your medication regimen: _____

Family members attend your medical visits?   ☐ Yes ☐ No

Changed professionals during course of disease?   ☐ Yes ☐ No

If yes, how did it affect you? _____

Has the illness affected your work in general?   ☐ Yes ☐ No

Cognitive Consequences of the Disease

Are your concentration, attention, and memory affected?   ☐ Yes ☐ No

If yes, has this affected your performance at work, home, or elsewhere? ☐ Yes ☐ No

Issues of Attachment

Birth: ☐ Normal   ☐ Complications

If complicated, what happened? _____

_____

During your birth, did your mother experience any of the following?

☐ stress about being a mother   ☐ depression   ☐ mania

☐ hypomania   ☐ mixed phase   ☐ psychosis   ☐ PTSD

Physical separation from mother: ☐ Yes ☐ No

Emotional separation: ☐ Yes ☐ No

Prior to your birth, did mother have miscarriages?   ☐ Yes ☐ No

Prior to your birth, did mother lose a child/children?   ☐ Yes ☐ No

Describe relationship with your mother and father: _____

_____

Describe relationship between your parents: _____

_____

Describe a typical everyday scene in your family: _____

_____

Moves/changes of residences: ☐ Yes ☐ No

Many different caregivers growing up?   ☐ Yes ☐ No

Family members with substance abuse problems?   ☐ Yes ☐ No

Typical caregiver response to challenge and needs: _____

_____

Could you talk to someone about challenges or needs growing up?   ☐ Yes ☐ No

If so, person was   ☐ Helpful   ☐ Gave reprimands and/or punishments

Care concerning food, health, rest, and leisure activities   ☐ Good   ☐ Poor

Who played with you? _____

Who consoled you? _____

Who told you stories? _____

Describe family's financial and work situation: _____

_____

Trauma History

LOSS

Tell about anyone close to you who died: _____

_____

_____

How did you manage your feelings of sadness and grief? _____

_____

Anyone to whom you were close who committed suicide? _____

_____

Did you feel neglected growing up?   ☐ Yes   ☐ No

Did anyone make you feel bad emotionally/psychologically while
growing up?   ☐ Yes   ☐ No

How did they act toward you? _____

_____

Did anyone touch you inappropriately/without your consent?   ☐ Yes   ☐ No

If so, what happened? _____

_____

Did you have any bad breakups?   ☐ Yes   ☐ No

If so, what happened? _____

_____

Were there hurtful consequences due to manic episodes?   ☐ Yes   ☐ No

Note: If so, consider EDMSP.

STRESSORS/TRAUMA

Current work, social, financial, and/or family stressors?   ☐ Yes   ☐ No

In school, any traumatic and/or adverse experiences with teachers, peers,
and/or anyone else?   ☐ Yes   ☐ No

Any accidents with a threat of serious injury to yourself or someone else?   ☐ Yes   ☐ No

If so, what happened? _____

_____

Any critical incidents due to man-made/natural disasters?   ☐ Yes   ☐ No

If so, what happened? _____

_____

How did you manage feelings of sadness and grief? _____

_____

Serious physical illnesses that you thought you would not survive?   ☐ Yes   ☐ No

Serious physical illnesses where you were not treated well?   ☐ Yes   ☐ No

Upsetting surgeries?   ☐ Yes   ☐ No

Any other important negative life experiences we have not covered yet?   ☐ Yes   ☐ No

If so, what happened? _____

_____

Significant Life Experiences—List Memories of Significant Life Experiences Beginning With the Earliest Ones

Positive Experiences   Helpful Person

_____

_____

_____

_____

_____

Negative Experiences   Helpful Person

_____

_____

_____

_____

_____

Psychiatric History of Family Members and Effects

Family member(s) diagnosed with psychiatric illness: ☐ Yes   ☐ No

If so, who? _____

Person in the family showing strange behavior?   ☐ Yes   ☐ No

If so, who? _____

Effect on you concerning family member's illness: _____

_____

Preparation for the Treatment Plan—Structure History From Worst to Least Worst

Negative events	Year	SUD (0–10/10)

1. _____

2. _____

3. _____

4. _____

5. _____

6. _____

7. _____

8. _____

9. _____

10. _____

Treatment Plan

PRESENT LEADS TO PAST

Cause of most discomfort currently: _____

Target/Memory/Image: _____

NC: _____

PC: _____

Times experienced similar negative thoughts in the past: _____

_____

Earliest time experienced similar negative thoughts in the past: _____

_____

Most debilitating symptom? _____

_____

Image + NC + Emotions + Float-Back to the past, then identify when you experienced this for the first time: _____

_____

Cause of most discomfort currently:

Target/Memory/Image: _____

NC: _____

PC: _____

Times experienced similar negative thoughts in the past: _____

_____

Earliest time experienced similar negative thoughts in the past: _____

_____

Most debilitating symptom? _____

_____

Image + NC + Emotions + Float-Back to the past, then identify when you experienced this for the first time: _____

_____

Cause of most discomfort currently:

Target/Memory/Image: _____

NC: _____

PC: _____

Times experienced similar negative thoughts in the past: _____

_____

Earliest time experienced similar negative thoughts in the past: _____

_____

Most debilitating symptom? _____

_____

Image + NC + Emotions + Float-Back to the past, then identify when you experienced this for the first time: _____

_____

Note: This procedure is the same for every symptom and traumatic experience. Future—To find new coping strategies for similar situations in the future.

> *"Bring up the picture of the future situation of* _____ (describe the specific situation) *and the words* _____ (repeat the PC)*, and notice what emotions you feel* _____ (repeat them) *and where you feel it in your body."*

Phase 2: Client Preparation

General Aspects

☐ Create a good therapeutic relationship with your client
☐ Explain confidentiality

☐ Ask to speak to someone in the family.
  Permission granted: ☐ Yes   ☐ No
  Name of relative: _____
  Degree of kinship: _____
  Telephone #: _____
  Permission to speak to psychiatrist granted: ☐ Yes   ☐ No
  Name of psychiatrist: _____
  Telephone #: _____
☐ Use a diary/download an app (e.g., Moody Me—Mood Diary and Tracker from MedHelp) to monitor the following:
  ☐ Mood every day (-5 = extremely depressed, 0 = very stable, $+5$ = very manic or mixed)
  ☐ How many hours you slept
  ☐ When you took/did not take your medication
  ☐ Note positive or negative life events

Check Whether Your Client Received Psychoeducation

Received psychoeducation concerning bipolar disorder   ☐ Yes   ☐ No

If yes, what learned?_____

_____

Describe what you know about bipolar disorder: _____

_____

Describe how medication is/is not working for you: _____

_____

What are the symptoms that signal to you that your illness is about to happen? _____

_____

If no awareness, consider using the following protocols:

  ☐ The EMDR Illness Awareness Protocol
  ☐ EMDR Adherence Enhancer Protocol
  ☐ EMDR Prodromal Symptoms Protocol

Explain EMDR Therapy

  ☐ Explain how EMDR Therapy works
  ☐ Create consciousness of changes during therapy
    ☐ Use metaphors (such as the train metaphor)
    ☐ Explain affect regulation
    ☐ Explain Adaptive Information Processing
    ☐ Explain conscious observation for effective reprocessing
  ☐ Introduce two ships passing in the night
  ☐ Practice BLS: _____ EMs _____ Tones _____ Taps (check appropriate one(s))
  ☐ Go over the informed consent form and ask the client to sign it

Positive Resources

☐ Install positive resources as needed, such as the Safe Place

Five Protocols to Enhance Mental Stability

1. EMDR MOOD-STABILIZING PROTOCOL FOR PATIENTS WITH BIPOLAR DISORDER

> *"As you know, in bipolar patients the mood can change often from depression to an exaggerated, elevated mood. Furthermore, daily stress and tensions make us susceptible to whatever is happening around us. With this exercise we will determine memories and moments where you felt well and your mood was stable. Concentrating on this will stabilize your mood and increase the sensation of control in your life."*

Describe a moment in your life where you had the experience and sensation of a stable mood and feel it: _____

_____

Image of best situation: _____

PC: _____

Emotion: _____

Where in body? _____

Image of stable mood, control + PC + Body Sensations + 6 to 12 sets BLS

Feelings in body? _____
If positive, reinforce with 6 to 12 sets BLS

Feelings in body? _____

If positive, reinforce with 6 to 12 sets BLS

Options to continue:

- ☐ Reinforce as often as helpful
- ☐ PC + Body Sensations + BLS
- ☐ PC + Really Experience the Body Sensations + BLS
- ☐ Positive Experience + Word That Represents Your Positive Experience

Concentrate on Your Pleasant Body Sensations + PC Related to the Situation + BLS

Notice? _____

If positive, reinforce with BLS

Word/Phrase to remember this resource: _____

Word + Pleasant Body Sensations + BLS

Note: If negative sensation/memory, leave it and try another positive experience.

Usage: Repeat often during the therapeutic process to support stabilization of client's mood.

2. EMDR ILLNESS AWARENESS PROTOCOL

Check Symptoms of Hypomania/Mania

Interrupted sleep?	☐ Yes	☐ No
Decreased need for sleep, feeling refreshed with only 3 to 4 hours/night?	☐ Yes	☐ No
Knows sensation when making too many plans, projects, and activities:	☐ Yes	☐ No
Episodes of uncontrollable need to spend money, have sex, shop/eat:	☐ Yes	☐ No

Moments felt tense or more conflictive:	☐ Yes	☐ No
Episodes of increased vitality/strength:	☐ Yes	☐ No
Lots of thoughts in head and can't pay attention to each:	☐ Yes	☐ No
Times when more talkative than usual:	☐ Yes	☐ No
Need to move around aimlessly and restlessly:	☐ Yes	☐ No
Difficulties in concentrating/maintaining attention when read, worked, or talked to someone:	☐ Yes	☐ No
Feeling of being watched/observed by others:	☐ Yes	☐ No
Feeling someone may be following you:	☐ Yes	☐ No
Hear voices:	☐ Yes	☐ No
If so, how many? _____		
Do they communicate among themselves?	☐ Yes	☐ No

Check Symptoms of Depression

Mood ever low, melancholic, or sad:	☐ Yes	☐ No
Feel excessive need to sleep:	☐ Yes	☐ No
Experience thinking as slowed down:	☐ Yes	☐ No
Thoughts of suicide:	☐ Yes	☐ No
Plan for suicide:	☐ Yes	☐ No

Experience of loss of appetite or can't stop eating:	☐ Yes	☐ No
Suffer from anxiety:	☐ Yes	☐ No
Experience a complete loss of sexual desire:	☐ Yes	☐ No

Check Symptoms of a Mixed Episode

Excessive irritability and feeling conflictive:	☐ Yes	☐ No
Feel restless and agitated:	☐ Yes	☐ No
Feel excitement and sadness at the same time:	☐ Yes	☐ No
Went from being lively and cheerful to sad for no reason:	☐ Yes	☐ No
Other symptoms not mentioned:	☐ Yes	☐ No

List of Positive Beliefs

Could any of the following beliefs be useful to better manage your disease?

"Accepting my illness allows me to better regulate my leisure time."	☐ Yes	☐ No
"Accepting my illness allows me to choose a better job and/or a better job schedule."	☐ Yes	☐ No
"Accepting my illness allows me to have a better relationship."	☐ Yes	☐ No

"Accepting my illness allows me to be in better control of my life." ☐ Yes ☐ No

"I feel like I take care of myself if I accept my disease and take my medication." ☐ Yes ☐ No

"I am able to call my therapist and ask for help if I feel unstable." ☐ Yes ☐ No

"Being aware of the illness I have makes me less sick." ☐ Yes ☐ No

"When I notice the first symptoms of my illness, I know that I have to contact _____ (name a person of trust) *because he/she gives me a trustworthy and realistic point of view about my condition."* ☐ Yes ☐ No

"Please tell me if there are any other beliefs about yourself that we have not mentioned."

_____

Reinforce illness awareness by using PCs so the client can cope with it better.

Describe life experiences where you have been aware of your illness and it has been good for you:

_____

_____

_____

Body sensations of experience: _____

Image: _____

PC: _____

Emotion: _____

Location of sensations in body: _____

Image + Time Client In Control and Aware of Illness + PC + Body Sensation + BLS

Feelings in body: _____

If positive, reinforce with BLS.

Notice: _____

If positive, reinforce with BLS.

Word/phrase to remember resource: _____

Word/Phrase + Pleasant Body Sensations + BLS

Notice: _____

Note: If negative sensation/memory, leave it and try another positive experience.
Usage: Repeat often during the therapeutic process.

3. EMDR ADHERENCE ENHANCER PROTOCOL

Negative Feelings About Taking Medication for Bipolar Disorder

"What is the worst thing about taking medication for bipolar disorder?" _____

_____

Positive Feelings About Taking Medication for Bipolar Disorder

"What are some of the positive outcomes from taking medication?" _____

_____

"Medication benefits regarding your family and social environment": _____

_____

"Medication benefits regarding developing your professional and intellectual activity": _____

_____

"Medication benefits regarding being better organized in daily life and tasks": _____

_____

"Medication benefits regarding other issues in your life": _____

_____

"After everything we've talked about, when you take the medication, what would you say that is positive for you now?"

List of positive beliefs (check if positive):

I control my life.	☐ Yes	☐ No
I control my disease.	☐ Yes	☐ No
I control my medication.	☐ Yes	☐ No
I can take care of myself.	☐ Yes	☐ No
I am worth it.	☐ Yes	☐ No
I am able to ask for help.	☐ Yes	☐ No
I am strong.	☐ Yes	☐ No
I have options, I can choose.	☐ Yes	☐ No
I am responsible for my actions.	☐ Yes	☐ No
Other positive beliefs when you think of taking medication?	☐ Yes	☐ No

Positive experiences/memories of your life associated with taking medication regularly:

_____

Narrative of the positive experiences:

_____

_____

_____

_____

Vivid client positive experience: _____

_____

_____

Body sensations of experience: _____

Image: _____

PC: _____

Emotion: _____

Location of sensations in body: _____

Image + Time Client In Control and Aware of Illness + PC + Body Sensation + BLS

Feelings in body: _____

If positive, reinforce with BLS.

Notice: _____

If positive, reinforce with BLS.

Word/phrase to remember resource: _____

Word/Phrase + Pleasant Body Sensations + BLS

Notice: _____

If continues positive, reinforce with BLS.

Word/phrase to remember resource: _____

Word/Phrase + Pleasant Body Sensations + BLS

Notice: _____

Note: If negative sensation/memory arises, leave it and try another positive experience.

Usage: Repeat often during the therapeutic process.

4. EMDR PRODROMAL SYMPTOMS PROTOCOL

Check for Prodromal Symptoms

First symptoms you notice before a depressive episode: _____

_____

First symptoms you notice before a hypomanic/manic episode: _____

_____

First symptoms you notice before a mixed episode: _____

_____

List of Positive Beliefs to Help Manage the Identified Symptoms

> *"Could any of the following positive beliefs/suggestions be useful to you to avoid a possible full depressive, manic, or mixed episode?"*

Mark useful positive beliefs with a check.

"When I notice _____ (state prodromal symptom), *I know I have to ask for help.*" □ Yes □ No

"When I notice _____ (state prodromal symptom), *I recognize it is a symptom of my illness.*" □ Yes □ No

"When I notice _____ (state prodromal symptom), *I have to take and/or maintain my medication as prescribed.*" □ Yes □ No

"When I notice _____ (state prodromal symptom), *I am about to suffer from a new episode.*" □ Yes □ No

"When I notice _____ (state prodromal symptom), *I have to plan the following steps cautiously and calm down.*" □ Yes □ No

"When I notice _____ (state prodromal symptom), *I have to be aware of not getting into an argument.*" □ Yes □ No

"When I notice _____ (state prodromal symptom), *I have to avoid conflictual relationships.*" □ Yes □ No

"When I notice _____ (state prodromal symptom), *I have to concentrate/communicate with a person I trust.*" □ Yes □ No

"When I notice _____ (state prodromal symptom), *I have to avoid the use of alcohol, coffee, Coca-Cola, Red Bull, amphetamines, and drugs.*" □ Yes □ No

"When I notice _____ (state prodromal symptom), *I should smoke less.*" □ Yes □ No

Repeat the list of positive beliefs, if necessary, with every prodromal symptom.

Other beliefs not mentioned related to the good part about recognizing the symptoms that precede an episode: _____

Reinforce Prodromal Symptoms Awareness With PCs

Talk about how awareness of the symptoms that precede your episodes allows you to take care of yourself and ask for help.

Start with the most vivid life experiences where you have been aware of symptoms that precede your episodes and this has been good for you:

1. _____

2. _____

3. _____

4. _____

Body sensations of experience: _____

Image: _____

PC: _____

Emotion: _____

Location of sensations in body: _____

Image of Experience + PC + Body Sensation + BLS

Feelings in body: _____

If positive, reinforce with BLS.

Notice: _____

If positive, reinforce with BLS.

Word/phrase to remember resource: _____

Word/Phrase + Pleasant Body Sensations + BLS

Notice: _____

If continues positive, reinforce with BLS.

Word/phrase to remember resource: _____

Word/Phrase + Pleasant Body Sensations + BLS

Notice: _____

Note: If negative sensation/memory arises, leave it and try another positive experience.
Usage: Repeat often during the therapeutic process.

5. EMDR DE-IDEALIZATION MANIC SYMPTOMS PROTOCOL

Manic Symptoms/Impulses That Lead to Negative Consequences

Step 1: Create a list of manic-state life experiences that ended in disastrous consequences

Manic symptoms/impulses	Negative consequences
Experience 1: _____	_____
Experience 2: _____	_____
Experience 3: _____	_____
Experience 4: _____	_____
Experience 5: _____	_____
Experience 6: _____	_____

Step 2: Assess each experience that occurs during a mixed or manic state with the corresponding impulse, action, sensation, belief, and thought.

Describe the impulse: _____

Action that followed the impulse: _____

_____

Sensations: _____

Beliefs: _____

Result of the impulse and action: _____

_____

Consequences: _____

Step 3: Strengthen the client's awareness that it is preventive to connect the mania and impulsivity with disastrous consequences.

> *"When you think about the negative consequences of your experience*
> _____ (state the experience), *how important is it for you to know that*
> *they are a symptom of your illness, on a scale from 0 to 10, 0 being not posi-*
> *tive at all and 10 being totally positive?*

Positive Awareness + BLS (6 to 12 sets)

Notice: _____

Use BLS until 9/10 to 10/10 is reached.
Link each of the experiences of impulses and manic symptoms with negative consequences.

Phase 3: Assessment

Use the trauma targets from the treatment plan with the EMDR Standard Protocol.

Target: _____

Picture/Image: _____

NC: _____

Note: If difficulty, ask: *"In your worst moments, when you are remembering some aspect of the event, what thoughts or negative beliefs do you have about yourself?"*

PC: _____

VoC: _____ /7

Emotions: _____

SUD: _____ /10

Location of body sensation: _____

Phase 4: Desensitization

Introduce according to EMDR Standard Protocol.
If SUD = 1 or more, continue processing.
If SUD continues to be 0 after 2 sets of BLS, go to the installation phase.

Phase 5: Installation

PC: □ Completed

New PC (if new one is better): _____

VoC: _____ /7

Incident + PC + BLS

Continue installation with BLS until material becomes increasingly adaptive. If VoC = 6 or less, check and see if there is a limiting belief:

"Which thoughts or concerns prevent you from feeling those words as completely true?"

_____

Note: If the limiting belief is not resolved quickly, explore to see whether there are any limiting beliefs or unidentified/unprocessed memory(ies)/network(s) that are causing this difficulty.
The session is then considered incomplete; therefore, return to the incomplete target and continue the installation process in the next session.

Phase completed   □ Yes   □ No

Phase 6: Body Scan

"Close your eyes, and keep in mind the original memory and the words _____ (state the positive belief). Then bring your attention to different parts of your body, starting with

your head and working downward. Any place you find any tension, tightness, or any unusual feeling, let me know."

Note: If the client reports any negative feeling, do a set of BLS until it disappears. If the client reports positive feelings, continue with BLS in order to strengthen them.

Phase 7: Closure

For clients with bipolar disorder, it is important to allow time for closure. It increases integration of the reprocessed material, ensures client stability, and provides a guide for the client to observe, record, and continue integrating the changes that come up after the session. Thank the client for the work done and discuss what he or she has observed during this session.

The session is incomplete when there is still unresolved material:

- If there is still discomfort or the SUD score is greater than 1
- The VOC score is less than 6
- Negative feelings persist in the body scan
- If the SUD is greater than 1, skip phases 5 and 6

Congratulate the client for the work done and assess the need for stabilization techniques and relaxation, containment, and/or sensory orientation exercises.
Once stabilized, say the following:

"Things may come up or they may not. If they do, great. Write it down and it can be a target for next time. You can use a log to write down triggers, images, thoughts or cognitions, emotions, and sensations; you can rate them on our 0 to 10 scale where 0 is no disturbance or neutral and 10 is the worst disturbance. Please write down the positive experiences, too."

"If you get any new memories, dreams, or situations that disturb you, just take a good snapshot. It isn't necessary to give a lot of detail. Just put down enough to remind you so we can target it next time. The same thing goes for any positive dreams or situations. If negative feelings do come up, try not to make them significant. Remember, it's still just the old stuff. Just write it down for next time. Then use the tape or the Safe Place exercise to let go of as much of the disturbance as possible. Even if nothing comes up, make sure to use the tape every day and give me a call if you need to."

Phase 8: Reevaluation

SUDS of incident(s) processed: _____ /10

New material: _____

_____

Reprocessed necessary targets: ☐ Completed

Reference

Shapiro, F. (2001). *Eye movement desensitization and reprocessing: Basic principles, protocols and procedures* (2nd ed.). New York, NY: Guilford Press.

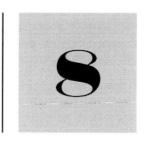

DeprEnd©—EMDR Therapy Protocol for the Treatment of Depressive Disorders

Arne Hofmann, Michael Hase, Peter Liebermann,
Luca Ostacoli, Maria Lehnung, Franz Ebner,
Christine Rost, Marilyn Luber, and Visal Tumani

Introduction

Depression is the most common mental disorder, affecting 120 million people worldwide. It is the third most common cause for primary health consultation and the leading cause of disability from ages 15 to 44. In Europe, every 9 minutes a person commits suicide. Most depressions respond to psychotherapeutic treatment. Unfortunately, studies show that there is a high risk for relapse in major depression (MD):

- After 6 months—24%
- After 1 year—37%
- After 5 years—75%
- After 15 years—85%

Each depressive episode increases the risk of relapse by 15% and the episodes get more severe with each relapse (Angst, 1992; Maj, Veltro, Pirozzi, Lobrace, & Magliano, 1992). Risk factors for relapse are the number of depressive episodes and incomplete remission after the last episode. Ongoing medication reduces the risk of relapses by about 50% and ongoing psychotherapy reduces relapses about the same. These protective effects are reduced with the number of relapses (Reid & Barbui, 2010). The result is that more than 70% of all depressions are chronic diseases. *So, reducing relapse is an important therapy goal.*

In a meta-analysis of 28 studies (*N* = 1880), the results showed the following:

- Cognitive behavioral therapy (CBT) reduces relapses better than medication (after 1 year 29% and after 2 years—54% relapses).
- Other specific psychotherapies work in a similar fashion and reduce relapses further (Vittengl, Clark, Dunn, & Jarrett, 2007).

At first glance, depression looks like a disease that is easy to treat, but on closer scrutiny, it appears to be a *chronic and severe disease*. Even extreme interventions like electroconvulsive therapy (ECT) do not prevent relapses.

The literature on depression reveals many factors playing a role in depression: genetics, hormones, light, cognitive factors, and losses. The literature is overwhelming; however, most guidelines for the treatment of depression focus on medication. Although most studies focus on treating depression with medication, half of the study results are not published.

Adding this missing data in to the equation shows that medication for moderate depression fares no better than the placebo effect.

An important message about depression comes from recent genetic research. In a National Institute of Mental Health (NIMH) meta-analysis of 25 studies on serotonin transporter gene variants, negative life events and risk for depression were studied. Although there is a clear relationship between genes and depression, the relationship is so weak that it was not significant in this big meta-analysis, nor was the relationship between life events, genes, and depression. However, there was one highly significant relationship: the risk of depression and the number of *negative life events alone* (Risch et al., 2009)! Many of these stressful life events produce posttraumatic stress disorder (PTSD)-like symptoms such as intrusions.

In a study by Gold, Marx, Soler-Baillo, and Sloan (2005), they found that 800 college students responded differently to Criterion A (life threat) events and non-Criterion A (life stress) events. Interestingly, the group that had suffered non-Criterion A events suffered significantly ($p < .05$) more from PTSD symptoms like intrusions ($N = 216$) than those who had experienced Criterion A events ($N = 214$). Most of the non-Criterion A experiences in this study were expected deaths of a loved one, while the other events producing PTSD-like symptoms were family and romantic problems.

It is important to note that traumatic events (fulfilling Criterion A) are not the only ones leading to depressive episodes. Often those stressful non-Criterion A events precipitate depressive phases. In Kendler, Hettema, Butera, Gardner, and Prescott's (2003) study on twins in Virginia ($N = 7322$), major depressive episodes and generalized anxieties (GAD) were registered, and noted stressful life events like *losses* (death, separations, material) and *humiliations* (other initiated separation, being put down, threat to core role, rape); *danger* (to life) was registered as well. The study found that there was a significant link between loss and humiliation and the beginning of a major depressive episode during the next month ($p < .001$). The link to MD was especially strong when it included defeat and submission. Danger events had a link to GAD only and not to depressive episodes. Also, it took longer than a month for the disorder to begin.

In summary, *depression shows all the signs of a stress regulation disorder with a strong relationship between depression and stressful—traumatic and nontraumatic (regarding Criterion A)—events and memories.* However, few therapeutic approaches for depressive disorders include this perspective concerning pathogenic memories and the need to work with them. It is probable that Eye Movement Desensitization and Reprocessing (EMDR) Therapy's ability to process pathogenic memories is significant when clinicians are ready to treat the stressful—traumatic and nontraumatic—events and memories of depression.

Research: EMDR Therapy and Depression

There have been a number of reports concerning EMDR Therapy and the treatment of individuals with depression (Manfield, 1998; Shapiro & Silk-Forrest, 1997; Shapiro, 2009); also, a case series has been reported (Bae, Kim, & Park, 2008). As yet, there are no controlled or randomized trials.

In van der Kolk et al.'s (2007) randomized controlled study, 88 participants with PTSD were divided into two groups: one had eight sessions of EMDR Therapy and the other 8 weeks of fluoxetine versus placebo. At follow-up, the EMDR group had a significantly better Beck Depression Inventory (BDI; Beck, Brown, & Steer, 1996) response ($< .001$) than the fluoxetine group. This fits with the observation of a meta-analysis showing that EMDR has a significantly stronger effect on comorbid depression in PTSD than other treatments like CBT (Ho & Lee, 2012).

Bae, Kim, and Park (2008) reported on the treatment of a 16-year-old girl whose father had died 1 year prior to treatment. She had decompensated in boarding school and was diagnosed with her first episode of a major depressive disorder (MDD) but no PTSD. After three sessions of EMDR Therapy, where the focus was on the death of the father and the future, her BDI score decreased as well as the Hamilton Depression Rating Scale (HDRS) score. In the other case in this study, a 14-year-old girl's father got involved in a new business, had an affair, and divorced his wife. The adolescent left school, lost 10 kg (22 pounds) within 3 months, and had suicidal thoughts; she was diagnosed with MDD. After six sessions of EMDR Therapy, where the focus was on her lost friends, father's affair, anxieties, and the future, she too had a significant decrease in her BDI and HDRS scores.

In a retrospective study of EMDR Therapy in recurrent depressive disorder (N = 10 patients), the authors asked a handful of experienced EMDR clinicians if they had treated patients with recurrent depression some time ago. Clinicians identified ten patients (nine women and one man, who were on average 52 years of age). There were five with MD, two with double depressions, and three with chronic depressions (> 2 years). The average number of previous depressive episodes was 6.4 (with a range of 1–13). The three patients with more than ten relapses all reported a history of sexual abuse and had the highest number of hospital stays. Outpatient treatment had included CBT or psychodynamic therapy (PD) in 60 treatment sessions including 7.4 EMDR memory-processing sessions.

The authors asked the clinicians to contact their patients again, interview them, and ask them how they were doing. The follow-up was done 3.7 years after the initial therapy had been terminated. At follow-up, nine reported a complete remission of their depression (seven had already had a full remission at end of treatment). Seven of the ten patients were no longer taking medication at the point of follow-up.

Four to five depression relapses were expected in this group, but only one patient reported relapse. The episode trigger for the patient who reported relapse was her partner's diagnosis of cancer. Three others had significant stressors (e.g., death of partner, myocardial infarction) but reported no relapse. In summary, most of the ten chronic-relapsing, depressed patients had lost their diagnosis of depression after seven to eight sessions of EMDR Therapy were included in their treatments (Hofmann et al., 2012). This study may not have been large or methodically elaborated, but it supported the authors' clinical observation that EMDR Therapy may be a major help in relapse prevention of recurrent depression.

Two additional pilot studies convinced the authors that EMDR Therapy has a significant potential regarding the treatment of depressive disorders. As a result, in 2009, the authors helped build a European network of depression researchers, who later, in 2012, started a multicenter randomized study in Germany (Cologne and Ulm), Italy, Spain, and Turkey.

A draft of the authors' treatment protocol can be read in the following pages. It is based on the manual for the European Depression EMDR Network (EDEN) Study (EMDR Depression Manual; Hofmann et al., 2009). As many details are still flexible in this research protocol, the protocol that follows shows only the essential aspects of the treatment. This draft is, of course, subject to change as the studies continue.

DeprEnd©—Manual for EMDR Therapy in the Treatment of Depressive Patients

Depression is in many cases a complex disorder with many contributing causes. However, at its core, it seems to be a stress regulation disorder. Stressful events are not necessarily traumatic, although many depressed patients report traumatic events in their lives, such as abuse, loss, neglect, and childhood sexual abuse. These may create a depressive episode themselves, but also a vulnerability to later depressive episodes. Research shows that distinct psychosocial stressors precede most of the depressive episodes by 1 or 2 months (*episode triggers*). Most of these episode triggers are *not* life-threatening events that trigger the defense system in the brain (fight or flight) but rather events that include losses, separations, shaming, and humiliating events that are more connected to the attachment system of the brain, leading to pathogenic memories there (Kendler, Hettema, Butera, Gardner, & Prescott, 2003). These episode triggers seem to be the central events that set the pathology in motion in most depressive patients. Consequently, the memories identified as episode triggers are usually prime targets for EMDR processing in a current depressive episode (Bae et al., 2008, Hofmann et al., 2014). In our experience, episode triggers may also be targets for relapse prevention in a remitted episode.

Note: The strength of EMDR Therapy, however, seems to be not with the single-episode depression (where many other psychotherapy methods work well, too), but rather with the more complicated, and often chronic cases, where the classic approaches often fail and patients stay chronic or continue relapsing. In these cases, the individual life history plays a major role and broad generalizations are difficult. This is also the reason why the following manual describes different EMDR Therapy interventions that we have found useful in our studies and that have to be adapted to the individual case. (One also has to keep in mind that there are more factors involved in severe depressions.)

All in all, four factors seem to play a major role in the emergence, maintenance, and recurrence of depressive episodes. Depending on the specific case, it is helpful to consider these four factors when constructing an individual's treatment plan:

1. *Current episode triggers of the current depressive episode*: The present episode seems to be triggered—for the most part—by a stressful, often non-Criterion A event, the episode trigger. Many episode triggers are events that include losses and other interpersonal stressors such as relationship losses, separation, death, humiliation, rape, and bullying.
   Note: The term *trigger* refers here to the triggering of the depressive episode itself, *not* the triggering of a past event. A stressful event—as a result of vulnerabilities, and not always as old or past stressful memories—can result in a depressive episode. A memory that is an episode trigger is defined by the time relationship with a depressive episode (the depression usually follows the triggering event by 1 to 2 months), the persisting high subjective units of disturbance (SUDs) of the memory, and possibly the intrusions it creates.
   Treatment: The episode-trigger event of the current depressive episode is the primary focus to relieve the symptoms of the current episode. (If there is no clear episode trigger, a Float-Back can be done.)
2. *Belief systems*: Series of repeated experiences (mostly non-Criterion A events like humiliations) may crystallize in the form of *belief systems*. They increase the vulnerability for depressive episodes and also help to maintain them. Work with the memories that created the belief systems is helpful for both episode treatment and relapse prevention. The most important characteristics of belief systems are the intrusive negative cognition(s) that have generalized.
   Treatment: Address the belief systems by working with the proof memories and the touchstone memories of the memory network(s) that underlie the belief(s).
3. *Depressive states*: In some patients, earlier, longer, more intense or repeated depressive episodes can be remembered in a state-specific way. One classic example is the "Christmas depression." In this example, the patient suffered repeatedly in her family of origin when her addicted parent was home all the time and her other codependent parent decompensated repeatedly at Christmas. The patient may react to the outer signs of Christmas, such as candles, Christmas tree, and so on, by having the experience of that childhood atmosphere without being aware of the detail of her memories; in other words, she is in that *childhood state of chaos without realizing she has gone back in time*. Such states may also appear after long severe diseases (including severe depressive episodes) as well as loneliness memories of childhood that can be remarkably empty of traumatic material other than the fact that they can have very high SUDs (8 to 10).
   Treatment: The first step is that patients need to understand the difference between a current feeling that reacts to a current situation and a memory (state). To most patients, the state feels "older" than a feeling caused by current events. It is important not to be confused by the high SUDs and the initially "little" other content of the memory. These memory states have to targeted and processed anyway. It is preferable, of course, to focus on a distinct memory first, but if only a state is present, target it. Through observation, it is clear that some of these states can even be transmitted transgenerationally.

4. *Suicidal states*: In most depressive patients, suicidality goes away when the depression is remitting. However, in some patients, this is not the case. In these cases, the *memory of suicidality itself* (or of suicidal attempts) may have become a memory structure of its own. As this is the most experimental part of this protocol, it is important to be most careful with processing these networks. Two rules of thumb are:
   • Don't focus on acute suicidality
   • Check for other forms of dissociation before processing the suicidality directly
   Treatment: Typically, suicidality of this type feels somewhat ego dystonic to the patient, but creates great suffering nevertheless. If the patient's other significant material has been processed (episode triggers, other traumatic material and belief systems) and the suicidality persists, focusing on the possible persisting suicidal state may be an option. In a number of such treatment-resistant cases of chronic suicidality, the state could be processed in one or two EMDR Therapy sessions.

Depending on the individual life history of the depressive patient, any or all of these forms of pathogenic memory networks can be a focus in EMDR Therapy. Also, the EMDR targets can be prioritized depending on the present clinical state of the patient. In cases where complex PTSD and chronic depression are combined, resources must be developed and/or an inverted strategy of targeting may be applied that focuses present stressors before past memories (Korn & Leeds, 2002; see the Inverted EMDR Standard Protocol for Unstable Complex Post-Traumatic Stress Disorder, Hofmann, 2009b; Hofmann, 2014).

Note: In most cases, the pathogenic memories that cause the current depression—the episode triggers—should be processed first.

DeprEnd©—EMDR Therapy in the Treatment of Depressive Patients Notes

Phase 1: History Taking

Trauma Map

During phase 1, it is important to make sure to screen for complex PTSD (especially when there are earlier depressive episodes) and dissociation, because in these cases, the depression is linked to much more memory material than in other cases. The goal is to develop a Trauma Map that allows treatment planning (Hofmann & Luber, 2009). This map can be created while taking the patient history. From the map, events can be prioritized that should be worked on first. It is important to note that not every episode trigger or traumatic event that the patient experienced is linked to the current depressive state or episode. Usually, the events that are prioritized are the events that *are* linked with the *present* depressive state. Drawing a line in the Trauma Map that symbolizes the state of well-being (up) and depression (down) can help identify events that influenced the beginning and course of the depression (Symptom Line). The same scale that is used for events can be used for that line (0 = well-being, no depression; 10 = the worst depression I can think of).

Note: While looking for the events on the Trauma Map, after checking for the trigger event of the current episode, start with the memories of the best events and then ask for the other negative events (during a session). This is especially important when working with clients who may have problems with affect regulation when hearing about or recounting stressful memories.

Continue to gather this information and fill out the form so that it can be placed in the client's chart and the important memories and resources can be seen easily. Also, when processing is complete, there is a place to put that (new) SUD score.

Use the questions that follow to gather the rest of the information. When all of the influential memories are collected, it is helpful to plot them onto a Positive and Negative Memories Map (Beere, 1997; Shapiro, 2006). This map allows a visual presentation along the timeline of the client's life and offers a window into what the important landmarks of the client's life were for the clinician and client to see together. Often, just seeing the events in a visual chronological pattern helps both the therapist and the client see the gestalt of the client's life experience: the themes, the clusters, the gaps in memory, and the positives—or lack of positives—along the way.

Note: In some cases it is very difficult to gather older memories if the present depressive symptoms are too strong or the patient has problems in handling stressful memories; this may compromise the patient's ability to complete the Trauma Map. In most of these cases, working with the present episode is the priority and the trigger event of the current episode or intrusive memories should be processed before the timeline or Trauma Map can be completed. The timeline can be done when the patient is better.

Present Triggers and Future Concerns

It is also important to understand the future concerns and anticipated triggers that the patient connects to the presenting problem(s) or any other issues of concern that the client has revealed during the history-taking process. These future concerns or anticipated triggers can be added to the form throughout the course of treatment.

In depressed patients, in addition to traumatic events, look for the following:

- Past depressive episodes
- Events that were episode triggers, that is, events that triggered the current depressive episode
- Grade of remissions of earlier episodes

Note: The grade of remission is the most important predictor for future episodes. A full remission means being symptom free; for example, a HDRS score of < 7 or a BDI-II score < 12).

There are many different factors contributing to depression. There are also many different forms of depression. According to the *International Classification of Diseases-10* (ICD-10) system, the three main forms of depression are:

- Single-episode depression (only one—the present—depressive episode)
- Relapsing depression (with earlier depressive episodes)
- Chronic depression (duration of more than 2 years) and is ongoing with no relapses

Each of these three forms of depression can contain some or all of the types of memory networks (current depressive episode triggers; belief systems; depressive states and suicidal states) that we target in EMDR Therapy. As a result, EMDR Therapy for the depressive patient must be individualized based on the memory networks involved in the depression.

In single-episode depression, usually one event (or group of events) can be identified as the episode trigger. This event usually is the first that must be processed.

The two last forms are chronic forms of depression that call for a more complex approach, as more, and often more complex, memories are involved.

As a general rule in the treatment of depression, *improving the patient's present depression is a priority*, and relapse prevention is the second priority (even if the patient is in full remission).

Working with chronically depressive patients necessitates its own particular sensitivity concerning the targets chosen to work on:

- *Major depressive episodes*: check for all of the major depressive episodes and ask if the patient had a full remission
- *Episode triggers*: look for episode triggers that triggered episodes from which the patient did not recover fully
- *Chronic dysthymia*: look for episodes that left a chronic dysthymia or initiated a major episode in a patient with chronic dysthymia (double depression = dysthymia plus major episode)

Note: Especially in chronic and relapsing patients, many of the events in the Trauma Map may be linked with increased risk for relapse.

If the present episode has improved, the prognosis is better and the full treatment, including relapse prevention, is easier.

Treatment Planning and Case Conceptualization

Treatment planning and case conceptualization work in the following way.

TARGETING

The targeting sequence plan has to be individualized, but usually includes the types of memory networks just mentioned (or some of them):

- *Episode triggers*: events that triggered the current depressive episode
- *Irrational belief system(s)*: memory networks that resulted in (an) irrational belief system(s)
- *Altered states*: depressive states and persisting suicidal states

More often than not, the sequence of targets processed follows this sequence. The targeting sequence depends, of course, on the strategy selected (e.g., comorbidity), as well as the symptom level of the patient. Other targets that require processing can also include:

- *Criterion A experiences*: Experiences such as near-death, rape, torture, catastrophic motor vehicle accidents, and so on, related to life-threatening events that trigger the defense system in the brain (fight or flight)
- *Non-Criterion A or traumatic experiences*: Experiences related to losses, separations, shaming and humiliating experiences connected to the attachment system of the brain
- Present life stressors or triggers not related to the current depression (to reduce general stress)

TARGETING SEQUENCE FOR FOUR CATEGORIES OF MEMORY NETWORKS IN DEPRESSION

These are the four categories of memory networks that can be at the base of a depression:

1. *Episode triggers*: The primary focus, in the DeprEnd© EMDR Therapy treatment strategy, is the episode trigger(s).
   a. *Target events preceding depressive symptoms*: Target the events that precede the depressive symptoms and set it in motion (usually one to two months before the depression starts).
   b. *Check Criterion A and non-Criterion A events*: Look for Criterion A events, as well as non-Criterion A events such as losses, separations, shaming, and humiliations, as they are often trigger(s) of the current depressive episode.
   Note: In most cases, target the memories that are linked with the present episode first (1a).
      i. Stressful or traumatic events are more important for the depression if *connected in time* with an episode of depression and/or presently intrusive.
   c. *Episode triggers*: If the patient reached a full remission after earlier depressive episodes, the later episode triggers are the primary target for EMDR (rule of free interval). The earlier episodes may be targeted in a later stage of therapy (relapse prevention).
2. *Irrational beliefs*: If an irrational belief system (e.g., "I am unable") blocks the therapy, it gets priority as a target. Behind an irrational belief system usually stands a network of often small, stressful (social) experiences that create cognitive intrusions as symptoms. Many of these beliefs have their roots in childhood, although some do not. Target the network of traumatic memories behind the irrational belief

first, before focusing on the present belief. Target irrational belief systems that maintain and/or trigger depressive episodes. If the present depression is successfully treated, but an irrational belief system persists, it should be targeted as relapse prevention. A good strategy to find and target the network behind the irrational belief is the following:

a. *Look for proof memories*: These are memories that the patients mention as proof for their irrational beliefs (de Jongh, 2010).

b. *Do affect bridge*: Do an affect bridge from a present trigger of the belief to find a touchstone memory (Shapiro, 2001)

c. *First target has highest charge*: Process the past memories, using the touchstone or the proof memory with the highest charge as the first target.

d. *Process present triggers*: Process present triggers of the irrational belief(s) (sometimes they trigger short feelings of depression even if the depressive episode is over).

e. *Process future triggers*: Process possible future triggers of the irrational belief(s).

3. *Depressive and suicidal ideation states*:

a. *Depressive states*: Many depressive patients report depressive thoughts and feelings. These usually subside with the depression getting better. In some patients, however, there is a type of depressive feeling that often feels "old" to the patient. The patient may not remember the origin, but she often attributes the feeling (or "not-feeling") to the present depressive episode. On request, she may remember that she had the same feeling during earlier times (episodes).

   i. Process the depressive feeling state itself. If all other memories possibly linked to the depressive episode have been processed, this feeling may well be a kind of state that feels like a flashback to an earlier depressive episode. If focused on with EMDR Therapy, it usually processes well.

b. *Suicidal ideation states*: In case of a suicidal ideation that persists after the depression is significantly reduced, a suicidal state can be the reason. This type of state often feels ego dystonic (as if it does not belong to oneself).

   Note: This type of work is still experimental, and the patient has to be informed about this (get informed consent). Also, this type of EMDR Therapy work is only possible if, in the practitioner's clinical judgment, the patient is able to do the work and the patient contracts to do the work with the therapist.

   i. Target suicidal thoughts and feelings state. Practically, in this work, these types of suicidal thoughts and feelings can be targeted directly with EMDR Therapy.

   Note: Do this only in a situation where the suicidal ideas have become ego dystonic and stay active while the clinical situation of the patient improves.

   Do NOT attempt this if the suicidal ideation is ego syntonic and the patient is still highly depressive and possibly highly suicidal.

   Note: This is one of the most experimental strategies in our manual, and patient safety has to be maintained here at all times.

4. *Present and future life stressors or triggers (in the case of complex PTSD plus depressive episode)*:

a. *Target present life stressors/triggers*: Target present life stressors or triggers (such as predictable stressors with the boss, family of origin, children, and partner) to reduce the general stress of the patient. This is an important strategy to reduce the patient's susceptibility to being triggered into future depressions. In many cases, this can be done after the Trauma Map has been worked through.

   Note: In a few cases, this has to be done first, especially in chronic cases where the stressors from the present time seem more important than the events that initiated the pathology (see the inverted EMDR protocol).

b. *Use EMDR Therapy future template*: Target possible future stressors using the EMDR future template ("What would need to happen for you to have another depressive episode?")

Phase 2: Preparation

During phase 2, the preparation phase, if the patient suffers from everyday life stressors and/or her affect tolerance is compromised, it can be very helpful to develop resources before working with memories related to the depression. The same is true if phase 1 cannot be completed because of a high symptom level (or strong intrusive symptoms) that requires processing of the memory networks that keep this symptom level high, before the patient is able to explore other memories. Keep the updating of the Trauma Map in mind as well during phase 2.

Phase 3: Assessment and Phase 4: Desensitization

Phase 3: Assessment and Phase 4: Desensitization are undertaken according to the Standard EMDR Protocol.

Phase 5: Installation

In Phase 5: Installation, for many patients with depression, in the authors' experience, the cognitive processing of the installation phase seems to be as important as the processing of the memories in phase 4. If you have the (new) Positive Cognition (PC) and Validity of Cognition (VoC) for the installation, and after stimulation a cognitive association process follows, do not interrupt it by going back to the memory to take the VoC, but follow it until it ends and then go back. Also, the therapist may divide the installation of one PC into the checking and installation of two different PCs that the patient connects with the event that was worked with. These processes seem to be very helpful for some depressive patients.

Phase 6: Body Scan, Phase 7: Closure, and Phase 8: Reevaluation

Phase 6: Body Scan, Phase 7: Closure, and Phase 8: Reevaluation are done according to the Standard EMDR Protocol.

EMDR Therapy in the Treatment of Depressive Patients Script

Phase 1: Client History Taking

These are questions that are pertinent to history taking with depressive patients.

Current Depression

Say, *"Please describe the current depressive episode that you are experiencing."*

_____

_____

_____

_____

Current Depression Episode Triggers (Including More Current
Criterion A and Non-Criterion A Events)

Say, *"What happened before the depression began? What could be the trigger for this episode? Often, triggers occurred 1 to 2 months before your depression began."*

_____

_____

_____

_____

Say, *"Have you had any losses, separations, or deaths of significant people or people who have affected you recently? If so, please tell me what happened."*

_____

_____

_____

_____

Say, *"Have you had any recent experiences where you have been embarrassed and/or humiliated? If so, please tell me what happened."*

_____

_____

_____

_____

Say, *"Are there other memories that you link with this current episode of depression? If so, please tell me what happened."*

_____

_____

_____

_____

Say, *"Have you had any recent experiences where you were assaulted physically and/or emotionally, such as being bullied?"*

_____

_____

_____

_____

Say, *"Has there been an event or experience where you were threatened in a central position or role you have?"*

_____

_____

_____

_____

Say, *"Are there any traumatic events linked with this current episode of depression? If so, please tell me what happened."*

_____

_____

_____

_____

History of Depressive Episodes

Say, *"Please think back, including childhood and adolescence: Were there any times that you felt depressed or wanted to end your life? If so, please tell me what happened."*

_____

_____

_____

_____

History of Adverse Childhood Experiences

Say, *"When you think about your past—including your early childhood—were there negative events or experiences that affected you deeply?"*

_____

_____

_____

_____

History of Traumatic Experiences

Say, *"Do you have any memories of early physical, mental, and/or sexual abuse?"*

_____

If so, say, *"Please tell me about the first or earliest time any abuse happened."*

_____

_____

_____

_____

If so, say, *"Please tell me about the worst time any abuse happened."*

_____

_____

_____

_____

If so, say, *"Please tell me about the most recent time any abuse happened."*

_____

_____

_____

_____

Say, *"Also, were there other times that you experienced traumatic events and/or witnessed an event/s?"*

_____

_____

_____

_____

Say, *"After these adverse experiences in your childhood, did you have a time when you felt good and well? If so, how long were these good times and when did they end?"*

_____

_____

_____

_____

Negative Belief Systems

Say, *"When you think about yourself, please tell me all of the negative thoughts about yourself that occupy your thinking."*

_____

_____

_____

_____

_____

_____

_____

_____

Ask the following for each negative irrational belief:

Say, *"When you think about _____ (state NC), what are the memories that you have that are the 'proof' to yourself that this belief is true?"*

Or, *"What are the experiences that you have had that led you to believe this about yourself?"*

_____

_____

Say, *"When you think about _____ (state NC), what is the earliest time that you remember having that thought about yourself?"*

_____

_____

Say, *"When you think about* _____*(state NC), what triggers it in the present?"*

_____

_____

Say, *"When you think about* _____ *(state NC), what are the triggers in the future that concern you?"*

_____

_____

Depressive States

Say, *"If you are in contact with that depressive feeling you have, do you think it is a new feeling, or is it something you know from earlier times?"*

_____

_____

Say, *"If you are in contact with that depressive feeling, how old does it feel?"*

_____

_____

Say, *"Where do you feel it in your body?"*

Use an affect bridge here to search for earlier presence of that depressive state.

Say, *"When you think about that depressive feeling, let your mind scan back to the earliest time you remember feeling that way."*

_____

_____

Create a Positive and Negative Memories Map with the client.

Say, *"Now that we have talked about the memories that are the most important to you in your life, let's create a map. We can put the positive or best ones on top of the Age line and we can put the negative or worst ones under the Age line. I have found it very helpful to see the important events in a person's life along the timeline. Where would you like to start?"*

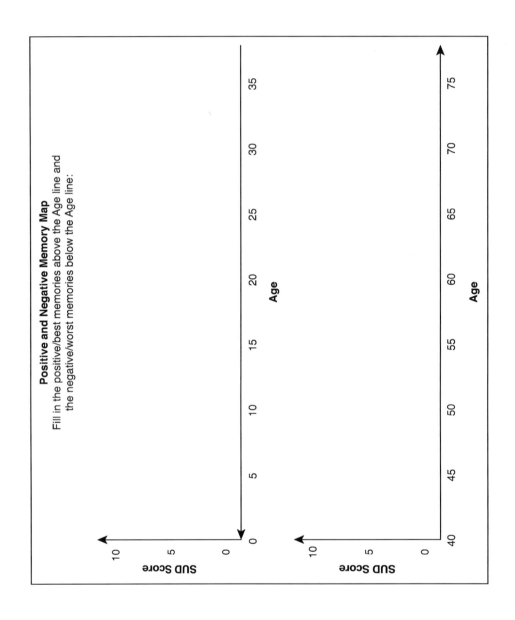

Positive and Negative Memory Map

Fill in the positive/best memories above the Age line and the negative/worst memories below the Age line:

302

Treatment Planning and Case Conceptualization

Use the targets established in phase 1 with the Standard EMDR Protocol.

> *Description*   *Year*   *SUD*

Episode Triggers

Events that precede the depressive symptoms and set it in motion—usually 1 to 2 months before the depression starts. Check for Criterion A and non-Criterion A events around that time frame.

> Episode Trigger 1: _____
>
> Episode Trigger 2: _____
>
> Episode Trigger 3: _____

Irrational Belief Systems

Target the network of traumatic memories behind the irrational belief first, before focusing on the present belief, by asking for the patient's proof memories for the belief. Do an affect bridge to find the touchstone memory; follow with present, then future triggers.

> Irrational Belief 1: _____
>
> > Proof Memory 1a: _____
> >
> > Proof Memory 1b: _____
> >
> > Touchstone Memory 1c: _____
>
> Irrational Belief 2: _____
>
> > Proof Memory 2a: _____
> >
> > Proof Memory 2b: _____
> >
> > Touchstone Memory 2c: _____
>
> Irrational Belief 3: _____
>
> > Proof Memory 3a: _____
> >
> > Proof Memory 3b: _____
> >
> > Touchstone Memory 3c: _____

Depressive State (if appropriate)

Target the type of depressive feeling that often feels "old" to the patient. The patient may not remember the origin, but often attributes the feeling (or "not-feeling") to the present depressive episode. Process the depressive feeling state itself.

> Depressive State 1: _____

Suicidal Feeling State

When suicidal ideation persists after the depression is significantly reduced, a suicidal state can be the reason. This type of state often feels ego dystonic (as if it does not belong to oneself).

Note: This type of work is still experimental, and the patient has to be informed about this (get informed consent). Also, this type of EMDR Therapy work is only possible if, in the practitioner's clinical judgment, the patient is able to do this work and the patient contracts to do the work with the therapist. Target the suicidal thoughts and feeling state itself.

Suicidal Feeling State 1: _____

Criterion A Events

Target any remaining Criterion A events from the past, after the episode triggers and irrational beliefs have been targeted.

Criterion A Event 1: _____

Criterion A Event 2: _____

Criterion A Event 3: _____

Non-Criterion A Events

Target any remaining non-Criterion A events from the past, after the episode triggers and irrational beliefs have been targeted.

Non-Criterion A Event 1: _____

Non-Criterion A Event 2: _____

Non-Criterion A Event 3: _____

Present Life Stressors/Triggers

Target any remaining present life triggers that remain, after the episode triggers, irrational beliefs, Criterion A, and non-Criterion A events have been targeted.

Present Life Stressor or Trigger 1: _____

Present Life Stressor or Trigger 2: _____

Present Life Stressor or Trigger 3: _____

Future Life Stressors/Triggers

Target any remaining future life triggers that remain, after the episode triggers, irrational beliefs, Criterion A, non-Criterion A events, and present life stressors or triggers have been targeted.

Future Life Stressor or Trigger 1: _____

Future Life Stressor or Trigger 2: _____

Future Life Stressor or Trigger 3: _____

Phase 2: Preparation

Resources are crucial to supporting the well-being of patients with depressive episodes. The Absorption Technique is one that is used regularly for the EDEN Study.

The Absorption Technique Script (Hofmann, 2009a; Hofmann, 2014)

SKILL OR STRENGTH

Do at least one session of the Absorption Technique to establish a resource state and check the reaction to bilateral stimulation (BLS).

Take an everyday stressor as target (even standing up in the morning or walking outside). Take the SUDs of that target (e.g., "my child is crying").

Say, *"What is the issue in the future* (present or past) *that you want to focus on?"* _____

_____

_____

Only ask for the SUD scale for the worst memories.

Say, *"If you think of that situation now, how stressful is that to you on a scale of 0 to 10, where 0 is no disturbance or neutral and 10 is the highest disturbance you can imagine? How disturbing does it feel now?"*

0   1   2   3   4   5   6   7   8   9   10

(no disturbance)   (highest disturbance)

The following is a list of three positive abilities or needed resources.

Say, *"What skills would you need to deal with that issue of* _____ (state the future concern) *better?"*

It is helpful to just get a theoretical answer from the head or cortex of the patient.

1. _____
2. _____
3. _____

FIRST ABILITY

Say, *"Think of the FIRST ability. In the last few years or so, was there ever a situation or time in your life where you remember having or feeling this ability?"*

_____

_____

Say, *"Can you think of an image that represents that situation?"*

_____

_____

Say, *"When you focus on the image, at that specific moment of time* (make sure your voice reflects or stresses this point), *where do you feel that you had some of that skill in your body of* _____ (name the resource chosen)*?"*

_____

_____

ENHANCE

Say, *"Think of that* _____ (name the resource), *the image, and the feeling in your body and go with that."*

_____

_____

Do up to 6 sets of slower BLS.

Say, *"What are you noticing?"*

_____

_____

If the feeling is positive, do another set. If it has not changed, do another set.

Say, *"Go with that."*

If it changes to a negative feeling, look for another resource and start from the beginning again.
Do this with the second and third ability.

Then link all three abilities (via the body feeling) and do 4 to 6 sets of slow BLS. Then tell the patient to link with this body state and look again at the initial stressor (take another SUD score).

Phase 3: Assessment

From the treatment plan, use the targeting sequence plan to target each of the pertinent memories with the assessment.

Incident

Say, *"The memory that we will start with today is* _____ (select the next incident to be targeted).*"*

_____

_____

_____

Say, *"What happens when you think of the* _____ (state the issue)?*"*

_____

_____

_____

Or say, *"When you think of* _____ (state the issue), *what do you get?"*

_____

_____

Picture

Say, *"What picture represents the entire* _____ (state the issue)?*"*

_____

_____

_____

If there are many choices or if the client becomes confused, the clinician assists by asking the following:

Say, *"What picture represents the most traumatic part of* _____ *(state the issue)?"*

_____

_____

_____

Negative Cognition

Say, *"What words best go with the picture that express your negative belief about yourself now?"*

_____

_____

Positive Cognition

Say, *"When you bring up that picture or* _____ *(state the issue), what would you like to believe about yourself now?"*

_____

_____

Validity of Cognition

Say, *"When you think of the incident* (or picture), *how true do those words* _____ *(repeat the PC) feel to you now on a scale of 1 to 7, where 1 feels completely false and 7 feels completely true?"*

1	2	3	4	5	6	7

(completely false)　　　　　　　(completely true)

Emotions

Say, *"When you bring up the picture or* _____ *(state the issue) and those words* _____ *(state the NC), what emotion do you feel now?"*

_____

_____

Subjective Units of Disturbance

Say, *"On a scale of 0 to 10, where 0 is no disturbance or neutral and 10 is the highest disturbance you can imagine, how disturbing does it feel now?"*

0	1	2	3	4	5	6	7	8	9	10

(no disturbance)　　　　　　　　　　(highest disturbance)

Location of Body Sensation

Say, *"Where do you feel it* (the disturbance) *in your body?"*

_____

_____

Phase 4: Desensitization

The work in phase 4 follows the Standard EMDR Protocol.
To begin, say the following:

Say, *"Now, remember, it is your own brain that is doing the healing and you are the one in control. I will ask you to mentally focus on the target and to _____ (state BLS you are using). Just let whatever happens, happen, and we will talk at the end of the set. Just tell me what comes up, and don't discard anything as unimportant. Any new information that comes to mind is connected in some way. If you want to stop, just raise your hand."*

Then say, *"Bring up the picture and the words _____ (repeat the NC) and notice where you feel it in your body. Now follow _____ (state BLS)."*

_____

_____

This procedure is to be repeated until the SUDs = 0. Then the PC is installed. Each traumatic event associated with the problem that is not reprocessed during the normal course of the first target must be processed using the preceding protocol until the SUDs reach an ecological 1 or 0 and the PC is installed.

Phase 5: Installation

For many patients with depression, this phase is as important as the processing done in phase 4.

Say, *"How does _____ (repeat the PC) sound?"*

_____

_____

Say, *"Do the words _____ (repeat the PC) still fit, or is there another positive statement that feels better?"*

_____

_____

If the client accepts the original PC, the clinician should ask for a VoC rating to see if it has improved.

Say, *"As you think of the incident, how do the words feel to you now on a scale of 1 to 7, where 1 feels completely false and 7 feels completely true?"*

    1   2   3   4   5   6   7

(completely false)   (completely true)

If you have the (new) PC and VoC for the installation, and after stimulation a cognitive association process follows, do not interrupt it by going back to the memory to take the VoC, but follow it until it ends; then go back.

Say, *"Think of the event and hold it together with the words _____ (repeat the PC)."*

_____

_____

Do a long set of BLS to see if there is more processing to be done.

You may divide the installation of one PC into the checking and installation of two different PCs that the patient connects with the event you worked with. These processes seem to be very helpful for some depressive patients.

Say, *"As you think of the incident, how do the words of the second positive cognition feel to you now on a scale of 1 to 7, where 1 feels completely false and 7 feels completely true?"*

1   2   3   4   5   6   7

(completely false)   (completely true)

Say, *"Think of the event and hold it together with the words _____ (repeat the second PC)."*

_____

_____

Do a long set of BLS to see if there is more processing to be done.

Phase 6: Body Scan

Say, *"Close your eyes and keep in mind the original memory and the positive cognition. Then bring your attention to the different parts of your body, starting with your head and working downward. Any place you find any tension, tightness, or unusual sensation, tell me."*

_____

_____

Phase 7: Closure

Say, *"Things may come up or they may not. If they do, great; write it down and it can be a target for next time. If you get any new memories, dreams, or situations that disturb you, just take a good snapshot. It isn't necessary to give a lot of detail. Just put down enough to remind you so we can target it next time. The same thing goes for any positive dreams or situations. If negative feelings do come up, try not to make them significant. Remember, it's still just the old stuff. Just write it down for next time. Then use the tape or the Safe Place exercise to let go of as much of the disturbance as possible. Even if nothing comes up, make sure to use the tape everyday and give me a call if you need to."*

_____

_____

Phase 8: Reevaluation

Say, *"Please tell me about any new material from last time and/or the results that you recorded in your log."*

_____

_____

Subjective Units of Disturbance

Say, *"On a scale of 0 to 10, where 0 is no disturbance or neutral and 10 is the highest disturbance you can imagine, how disturbing does it feel now?"*

0	1	2	3	4	5	6	7	8	9	10

(no disturbance)   (highest disturbance)

Check the treatment plan to make sure all memories, triggers, and future issues are resolved.

Summary

Depression is a multicausal and complex disorder from which a growing number of patients suffer. Following the Adaptive Information Processing (AIP) model, DeprEnd© is an EMDR Therapy protocol that addresses an important cause of depression that may also contribute to the maintenance of the symptoms of the disorder: pathogenic memory networks.

In the DeprEnd© protocol, four main types of memories are addressed and worked with: classic traumatic memories (Criterion A), often non-Criterion A-based episode triggers, belief systems, and depressive and suicidal states. In two controlled studies, the DeprEnd© protocol increased the rate of complete remissions from 38% to more than 80% and also reduced the number of relapses significantly in a one-year follow-up. Two randomized controlled trial (RCT) studies are under way to study the protocol further.

References

Angst, J. (1992). How recurrent and predictable is depressive illness. In S. Montgomery & F. Roullon (Eds.), *Long-term treatment of depression: Perspectives in psychiatry* (vol. 3, pp. 1–13). Chichester, England: John Wiley.

Bae, H., Kim, D., & Park, Y. C. (2008). Eye movement desensitization and reprocessing for adolescent depression. *Psychiatry Investigation, 5*(1), 60–65.

Beck, A. T., Brown, G. K., & Steer, R. A. (1996). *Beck Depression Inventory-II (BDI-II)*. San Antonio, TX: The Psychological Corporation.

Beere, D. B. (1997). The memory line: A measure of amnesia and continuity of memory. In L. VandeCreek (Ed.), *Innovations in clinical practice: A source book* (Vol. 15, pp. 83–95). Sarasota, FL: Professional Resource Exchange Inc.

de Jongh, A., & ten Broeke, E. (2010). Two method approach: A case conceptualization model in the context of EMDR. *Journal of EMDR Practice and Research, 4*(1), 12–21. doi: 10.1891/1933-3196.4.1.12

Gold, S. D., Marx, B. P., Soler-Baillo, J. M., & Sloan, D. M. (2005). Is life stress more traumatic than traumatic stress? *Journal of Anxiety Disorders, 19*, 687–698.

Ho, M. S. K., & Lee, C. W. (2012). Cognitive behaviour therapy versus eye movement desensitization and reprocessing for post-traumatic disorder: Is it all in the homework then? *Revue européenne de psychologie appliquée, 62*, 253–260.

Hofmann, A. (2009a). The absorption technique. In M. Luber (Ed.), *Eye movement desensitization and reprocessing (EMDR) scripted protocols: Special populations* (pp. 275–280). New York, NY: Springer.

Hofmann, A. (2009b). The inverted standard protocol for unstable complex post-traumatic stress disorder. In M. Luber (Ed.), *Eye movement desensitization and reprocessing (EMDR) scripted protocols: Special populations* (pp. 313–328). New York, NY: Springer.

Hofmann, A. (2014). *EMDR-Praxishandbuch. 5th Edition*. Editor A. Hofmann. Thieme Publishers Stuttgart

Hofmann, A., Hase, M., Liebermann, P., Ebner, F., Rost, C., & Tumani, V. (2009). *Treatment manual for the EDEN study: EMDR for depressive patients*. Cologne, Germany: EMDR Institute Germany.

Hofmann, A., Hilgers, A., Lehnung, M., Liebermann, P., Ostacoli, L., Schneider, W., & Hase, M. (2014). Eye movement desensitization and reprocessing as an adjunctive treatment of unipolar depression: A controlled study. *Journal of EMDR Practice and Research, 8*(3), 103–112. doi:10.1891/1933-3196.8.3.103

Hofmann, A., Lehnung, M., Hilgers, A., Baurhenn, U., & Hase, M. (2012, June). *EMDR in the treatment of depressive disorders*. Presentation at the 13th EMDR Europe Association Conference, Madrid, Spain.

Hofmann, A., & Luber, M. (2009). History taking: The time line. In M. Luber (Ed.), *Eye movement desensitization and reprocessing (EMDR) scripted protocols: Special populations* (pp. 5–10). New York, NY: Springer.

Kendler, K. S., Hettema, J. M., Butera, F., Gardner, C. O., & Prescott, C. A. (2003). Life event dimensions of loss, humiliation, entrapment, and danger in the prediction of onsets of major depression and generalized anxiety. *Archives of General Psychiatry, 60*(8), 789–796.

Korn, D. L., & Leeds, A. M. (2002). Preliminary evidence of efficacy for EMDR resource development and installation in the stabilization phase of treatment of complex posttraumatic stress disorder. *Journal of Clinical Psychology, 58*(12), 1465–1487.

Maj, M., Veltro, F., Pirozzi, R., Lobrace, S., & Magliano, L. (1992). Pattern of recurrence of illness after recovery from an episode of major depression: A prospective study. *American Journal of Psychiatry, 149*(6), 795–800.

Manfield, P. (Ed.). (1998). *Extending EMDR: A casebook of innovative applications*. New York, NY: W.W. Norton.

Reid, S., & Barbui, C. (2010). Long-term treatment of depression with selective serotonin reuptake inhibitors and newer antidepressants. *British Medical Journal, 340*, c1468.

Risch, N., Herrell, R., Lehner, T., Liang, K.-Y., Eaves, L., Hoh, J., . . . Merikangas, K. R. (2009). Interaction between the serotonin transporter gene (5-HTTLPR), stressful life events, and risk of depression: A meta-analysis. *Journal of the American Medical Association, 301*(23), 2462–2471.

Shapiro, F., & Silk-Forrest, M. (1997). *EMDR, the breakthrough therapy*. New York, NY: Basic Books.

Shapiro, F. (2001). *Eye movement desensitization and reprocessing: Basic principles, protocols and procedures* (2nd ed.). New York, NY: Guilford Press.

Shapiro, F. (2006). *EMDR: New notes on adaptive information processing with case formulation principles, forms, scripts and worksheets*. Watsonville, CA: EMDR Institute.

Shapiro, R. (Ed.). (2009). *EMDR solutions II*. New York, NY: W.W. Norton.

van der Kolk, B. A., Spinazzola, J., Blaustein, M. E., Hopper, J. W., Hopper, E. K., Korn, D. L., & Simpson, W. B. (2007). A randomized clinical trial of eye movement desensitization and reprocessing (EMDR), fluoxetine, and pill placebo in the treatment of posttraumatic stress disorder: Treatment effects and long-term maintenance. *Journal of Clinical Psychiatry, 68*(1), 37–46.

Vittengl, J. R., Clark, L. A., Dunn, T. W., & Jarrett, R. B. (2007). Reducing relapse and recurrence in unipolar depression: A comparative meta-analysis of cognitive-behavioral therapy's effects. *Journal of Consulting and Clinical Psychology, 75*(3), 475–488.

DeprEnd©—EMDR Therapy Protocol for the Treatment of Depressive Disorders

Arne Hofmann, Michael Hase, Peter Liebermann,
Luca Ostacoli, Maria Lehnung, Franz Ebner,
Christine Rost, Marilyn Luber, and Visal Tumani
SUMMARY SHEET BY MARILYN LUBER

Name: _____ Diagnosis: _____

Medications: _____

Test Results: _____

☑ Check when task is completed, response has changed, or to indicate symptoms.

Note: This material is meant as a checklist for your response. Please keep in mind that it is only a reminder of different tasks that may or may not apply to your incident.

Manual for DeprEnd©-EMDR Therapy Protocol for the Treatment of Depressive Disorders Script Notes

General Targeting Plan for a Depressive Patient Outline

The targeting sequence plan has to be individualized, but usually includes these types of memory networks (or some of them):

- ☐ *Episode triggers*: events that triggered the current depressive episode
- ☐ *Irrational belief system(s)*: memory networks that resulted in (an) irrational belief system(s)
- ☐ *Altered states*: depressive states and persisting suicidal states

More often than not, the sequence of targets processed follows this sequence. The targeting sequence depends on the strategy selected (e.g., comorbidity) as well as the patient's symptom level. Other targets that require processing can also include:

- ☐ *Criterion A experiences* such as near-death, rape, torture, catastrophic motor vehicle accidents, and so on related to life-threatening events that trigger the defense system in the brain (fight/flight)
- ☐ *Non-Criterion A/traumatic experiences* related to losses, separations, shaming and humiliating experiences connected to the attachment system of the brain
- ☐ *Present life stressors/triggers* not related to the current depression (to reduce general stress)

TARGETING SEQUENCE FOR FOUR CATEGORIES OF MEMORY NETWORKS IN DEPRESSION

These are the four categories of memory networks that can be at the base of a depression.

1. *Episode triggers*: The primary focus, in the DeprEnd© EMDR Therapy treatment strategy, is the episode trigger(s).
   a. *Target events preceding depressive symptoms*: Target the events that precede the depressive symptoms and set it in motion (usually 1–2 months before the depression starts).
   b. *Check Criterion A and Non-Criterion A events*: Look for Criterion A events, as well as non-Criterion A events such as losses, separations, shaming, and humiliations, as they are often trigger(s) of the current depressive episode.
      Note: In most cases, target first the memories that are linked with the present episode (1a).
      i. Stressful or traumatic events are more important for the depression if connected in time with an episode of depression and/or presently intrusive.
   c. *Episode triggers*: If the patient reached a full remission after earlier depressive episodes, the later episode triggers are the primary target for eye movement desensitization and reprocessing (EMDR; rule of free interval). The earlier episodes may be targeted in a later stage of therapy (relapse prevention).
2. *Irrational beliefs*: If an irrational belief system blocks the therapy, it gets priority as a target. Behind an irrational belief system usually stands a network of often small, stressful (social) experiences that create cognitive intrusions as symptoms. Many of these beliefs have their roots in childhood, although some do not. Target the network of traumatic memories behind the irrational belief first, before focusing on the present belief. Target irrational belief systems that maintain and/or trigger depressive episodes. If the present depression is successfully treated, but an irrational belief system persists, it should be targeted as relapse prevention. A good strategy to find and target the network behind the irrational belief is the following:
   a. *Look for proof memories*: These are memories that the patients mention as proof for their irrational beliefs (de Jongh & ten Broeke, 2010).
   b. *Do affect bridge*: Do an affect bridge from a present trigger of the belief to find a touchstone memory (Shapiro, 2001).
   c. *First target has highest charge*: Process the past memories, using the touchstone or the proof memory with the highest charge as the first target.
   d. *Process present triggers*: Process present triggers of the irrational belief(s) (sometimes they trigger short feelings of depression even if the depressive episode is over).
   e. *Process future triggers*: Process possible future triggers of the irrational belief(s).
3. *Depressive and suicidal ideation states*:
   a. *Depressive states*: Many depressive patients report depressive thoughts and feelings. These usually subside with the depression getting better. In some patients, however, there is a type of depressive feeling that often feels "old" to the patient. The patient may not remember the origin, but she often attributes the feeling (or "not-feeling") to the present depressive episode. On request, she may remember that she had the same feeling during earlier times (episodes).
      i. Process depressive feeling state itself. If all other memories possibly linked to the depressive episode have been processed, this feeling may well be a kind of state that feels like a flashback to an earlier depressive episode. If focused on in EMDR Therapy, it usually processes well.
   b. *Suicidal ideation states*: If a suicidal ideation persists after the depression is significantly reduced, a suicidal state can be the reason. This type of state often feels ego dystonic (as if it does not belong to oneself).
      Note: This type of work is still experimental, and the patient has to be informed about this (get informed consent). Also, this type of EMDR Therapy work is

only possible if, in the practitioner's clinical judgment, the patient is able to do this work and the patient contracts to do the work with the therapist.

  i. Target suicidal thoughts and feelings state. Practically, in this work, these types of suicidal thoughts and feelings can be targeted directly with EMDR Therapy.

  Note*:* Do this only in a situation where the suicidal ideas have become ego dystonic and stay active while the patient's clinical situation improves.

  Do NOT do this if the suicidal ideation is ego syntonic and the patient is still highly depressive and possibly highly suicidal.

  Note: This is one of the most experimental strategies in our manual and patient safety here has to be maintained at all times.

4. *Present and future life stressors/triggers (in the case of a complex PTSD plus a depressive episode)*:

  a. *Target present life stressors/triggers:* Target present life stressors/triggers (such as predictable stressors with the boss, family of origin, children, and partner) to reduce the patient's general stress. This is an important strategy to reduce the patient's susceptibility to being triggered into future depressions. In many cases, this can be done after the Trauma Map has been worked through.

  Note: In a few cases, this has to be done first, especially in chronic cases where the stressors from the present time seem more important than the events that initiated the pathology (see the inverted EMDR protocol).

  b. *Use EMDR future template:* Target possible future stressors using the EMDR future template ("What would need to happen for you to have another depressive episode?").

EMDR Therapy in the Treatment of Depressive Disorders Script

Phase 1: History Taking

Current depression: _____

_____

_____

Treatment Planning and Case Conceptualization

Description   Year   SUD

Episode Triggers

Events that precede the depressive symptoms and set it in motion—usually 1 to 2 months before the depression starts. Check for Criterion A and non-Criterion A events around that time frame.

Episode Trigger 1: _____

Episode Trigger 2: _____

Episode Trigger 3: _____

Irrational Belief Systems

Target the network of traumatic memories behind the irrational belief first, before focusing on the present belief, by asking for the patient's proof memories for the belief. Do an affect bridge to find the touchstone memory; follow with present, then future triggers.

Irrational Belief 1: _____

Proof Memories 1a: _____

Proof Memories 1b: _____

Touchstone Memory 1c: _____

Irrational Belief 2: _____

Proof Memories 2a: _____

Proof Memories 2b: _____

Touchstone Memory 2c: _____

Irrational Belief 3: _____

Proof Memories 3a: _____

Proof Memories 3b: _____

Touchstone Memory 3c: _____

Depressive State (If Appropriate)

Target the type of depressive feeling that may feel "old" to the patient. The patient may not remember the origin, but often attributes the feeling (or "not-feeling") to the present depressive episode. Process the depressive feeling state itself.

Depressive State 1: _____

Suicidal Feeling State

When suicidal ideation persists after the depression is significantly reduced, a suicidal state can be the reason. This type of state often feels ego dystonic (as if it does not belong to oneself).

Note: This type of work is still experimental, and the patient has to be informed about this (get informed consent). Also, this type of EMDR Therapy work is only possible if, in the practitioner's clinical judgment, the patient is able to do this work and the patient contracts to do the work with the therapist. Target the suicidal thoughts and feeling state itself.

Suicidal Feeling State 1: _____

Criterion A Events

Target any remaining Criterion A events from the past, after the episode triggers and irrational beliefs have been targeted.

Criterion A Event 1: _____

Criterion A Event 2: _____

Criterion A Event 3: _____

Non-Criterion A Events

Target any remaining non-Criterion A events from the past, after the episode triggers and irrational beliefs have been targeted.

Non-Criterion A Event 1: _____

Non-Criterion A Event 2: _____

Non-Criterion A Event 3: _____

Present Life Stressors/Triggers

Target any present life triggers that remain after the episode triggers, irrational beliefs, Criterion A and non-Criterion A events have been targeted.

Present Life Stressors/Triggers 1: _____

Present Life Stressors/Triggers 2: _____

Present Life Stressors/Triggers 3: _____

Future Life Stressors/Triggers

Target any future life triggers that remain after the episode triggers, irrational beliefs, Criterion A and non-Criterion A events, and present life stressors/triggers have been targeted.

Future Life Stressors/Triggers 1: _____

Future Life Stressors/Triggers 2: _____

Future Life Stressors/Triggers 3: _____

Create a Positive and Negative Memories Map with the client.

Phase 2: Preparation

The Absorption Technique installed: ☐ Yes   ☐ No

Skill or Strength

Issue in the future to focus on: _____

_____

SUD: _____ /10

Abilities/Skills/Strengths/Resources to deal with the issue:

Ability 1: _____

Ability 2: _____

Ability 3: _____

First Ability

Time in past had the ability: _____

_____

Image that represents that situation: _____

Image at that moment in time + Where do you feel you had some of that skill in your body of _____ (name resource)?

Location of sensation: _____
Enhance (Resource + Image + Feeling in Body + BLS [short set])

Notice: _____

If positive/negative, do another set.

If continues negative, look for another resource: ☐ Yes   ☐ No

Second Ability

Time in past had the second ability: _____

_____

Image that represents that situation: _____

Image at that moment in time + Where do you feel you had some of that skill in your body of _____ (name resource)?

Location of sensation: _____

Enhance (Resource + Image + Feeling in Body + BLS [short set])

Notice: _____

If positive/negative, do another set.

If continues negative, look for another resource: ☐ Yes   ☐ No

Third Ability

Time in past had the third ability: _____

_____

Image that represents that situation: _____

Image at that moment in time + Where do you feel you had some of that skill in your body of _____ (name resource)?

Location of sensation: _____

Enhance (Resource + Image + Feeling in Body + BLS [short set])

Notice: _____

If positive/negative, do another set.

If continues negative, look for another resource: ☐ Yes   ☐ No

Getting the Resources Together

Abilities Together + Location of Them in Body + Nod When in Contact with All Three Body Feelings
If nods, add BLS.

Check for the Issue

Feel Resources + Look Back at Issue That Troubles You = SUD: _____ /10

Phase 3: Assessment

For each charged trigger, use the Standard EMDR Protocol.
1. *Episode triggers*—Events that precede the depressive symptoms and set it in motion, usually one to two months before the depression starts. Check for Criterion A and non-Criterion A events around that time frame.

   List of episode triggers

   1. _____

2. _____

3. _____

4. _____

Target/Memory/Image: _____

_____

NC: _____

PC: _____

VoC: _____ /7

Emotions: _____

SUD: _____ /10

Sensation: _____

2. _Irrational beliefs and proof memories_—Target the network of traumatic memories behind the irrational belief first, before focusing on the present belief, by asking for the patient's proof memories for the belief. Do an affect bridge to find the touchstone memory; follow with present, then future triggers.

List of irrational beliefs

1. _____

2. _____

3. _____

4. _____

List of proof memories

1. _____

2. _____

3. _____

4. _____

Touchstone memory: _____

_____

Target/Memory/Image: _____

_____

NC: _____

PC: _____

VoC: _____ /7

Emotions: _____

SUD: _____ /10

Sensation: _____

3. *Depressive state*—Target the type of depressive feeling may feel "old" to the patient. The patient may not remember the origin, but often attributes the feeling (or "not-feeling") to the present depressive episode. Process the depressive feeling state itself.

_____

Target/Memory/Image: _____

_____

NC: _____

PC: _____

VoC: _____ /7

Emotions: _____

SUD: _____ /10

Sensation: _____

4. *Suicidal feeling state*—When suicidal ideation persists after the depression is significantly reduced, a suicidal state can be the reason. This type of state often feels ego dystonic (as if it does not belong to oneself).

Note: This type of work is still experimental, and the patient has to be informed about this (get informed consent). Also, this type of EMDR work is only possible if, in the practitioner's clinical judgment, the patient is able to do this work and the patient contracts to do the work with the therapist. Target the suicidal thoughts and feeling state itself.

_____

Target/Memory/Image: _____

_____

NC: _____

PC: _____

VoC: _____ /7

Emotions: _____

SUD: _____ /10

Sensation: _____

5. *Criterion A PTSD event(s) or losses*—Target any remaining Criterion A events from the past, after the episode triggers and irrational beliefs have been targeted.

   List of Criterion A PTSD events:

   1. _____

   2. _____

3. _____

4. _____

Target/Memory/Image: _____

_____

NC: _____

PC: _____

VoC: _____ /7

Emotions: _____

SUD: _____ /10

Sensation: _____

6. *Non-Criterion A event(s) or losses*—Target any remaining non-Criterion A events from the past, after the episode triggers and irrational beliefs have been targeted.

List of Non-Criterion A events:

1. _____

2. _____

3. _____

4. _____

Target/Memory/Image: _____

_____

NC: _____

PC: _____

VoC: _____ /7

Emotions: _____

SUD: _____ /10

Sensation: _____

7. *Present life stressors/triggers not related to depression to reduce general stress*—Target any present life triggers that remain, after the episode triggers, irrational beliefs, Criterion A and non-Criterion A events have been targeted.

List of present life stressors/triggers not related to depression to reduce general stress:

1. _____

2. _____

3. _____

4. _____

5. _____

Target/Memory/Image: _____

_____

NC: _____

PC: _____

VoC: _____ /7

Emotions: _____

SUD: _____ /10

Sensation: _____

8. *Future life stressors/triggers not related to depression to reduce general stress*—Target any future life triggers that remain, after the episode triggers, irrational beliefs, Criterion A and non-Criterion A events, and present life stressors/triggers have been targeted.

List of present life stressors/triggers not related to depression to reduce general stress:

1. _____

2. _____

3. _____

4. _____

5. _____

Target/Memory/Image: _____

_____

NC: _____

PC: _____

VoC: _____ /7

Emotions: _____

SUD: _____ /10

Sensation: _____

Phase 4: Desensitization

Apply the Standard EMDR Protocol for all targets.

Phase 5: Installation

Install the PC

Original PC: _____

Use Original PC _____

Use new PC (if new one is better): _____

VoC: _____ /7

Incident + PC + BLS

Note: If you have the (new) PC and VoC for the installation, and after stimulation a cognitive association process follows, do not interrupt it by going back to the memory to take the VoC. Instead, follow it until it ends, then go back.

Incident + PC + BLS

You may divide the installation of one PC into the checking and installation of two different PCs that the patient connects with the event you worked with. These processes seem to be very helpful for some depressive patients.

Second PC: _____ /7

Incident + Second PC + BLS

Phase 6: Body Scan

Unresolved Tension/Tightness/Unusual Sensation: _____

_____

Unresolved tension/tightness/unusual sensation + BLS

Strengthen positive sensation using BLS.

If there is more discomfort, reprocess until discomfort subsides + BLS. Then repeat body scan.
VoC: _____ /7

Phase 7: Closure

> Say, *"Things may come up or they may not. If they do, great; write it down and it can be a target for next time. If you get any new memories, dreams, or situations that disturb you, just take a good snapshot. It isn't necessary to give a lot of detail. Just put down enough to remind you so we can target it next time. The same thing goes for any positive dreams or situations. If negative feelings do come up, try not to make them significant. Remember, it's still just the old stuff. Just write it down for next time. Then use the tape or the Safe Place exercise to let go of as much of the disturbance as possible. Even if nothing comes up, make sure to use the tape everyday and give me a call if you need to."*

Phase 8: Reevaluation

New material since last session: _____

_____

Log results: _____

_____

SUDs of incident from last session: _____ /10

Target resolved: ☐ Yes   ☐ No

Check treatment plan to make sure that memories of relapse, intense craving triggers, and current problems are targeted and reprocessed.

References

de Jongh, A., & ten Broeke, E. (2010). Two method approach: A case conceptualization model in the context of EMDR. *Journal of EMDR Practice and Research, 4*(1), 12–21. doi: 10.1891/1933-3196.4.1.12

Shapiro, F. (2001). *Eye movement desensitization and reprocessing: Basic principles, protocols and procedures* (2nd ed.). New York, NY: Guilford Press.

EMDR Therapy Protocol for the Prevention of Birth Trauma and Postpartum Depression in the Pregnant Woman

Anna Maria De Divitiis and Marilyn Luber

Introduction

The need for an intervention aimed at preventing postpartum depression (PPD) became evident while working with women before and after childbirth, and observing and hearing their many accounts of their pregnancy and delivery experiences.

Postpartum Depression (PPD) Diagnosis

The *Diagnostic and Statistical Manual of Mental Disorders, Fourth Edition* (*DSM-IV*); American Psychiatric Association, 2000) included in its nosology the "postpartum depression" diagnosis under the heading "Mood Disorders with a Postpartum Onset Specifier." Most researchers and clinicians today agree on the existence and independent condition of postpartum mood disorder.

In the *Diagnostic and Statistical Manual of Mental Disorders, Fifth Edition* (*DSM-5*; American Psychiatric Association, 2013), PPD is still classified as "Mood Disorder" and continues to use the specifier "onset," although the indicator has been modified from "postpartum" to "peripartum." This modification of the indicator is based on the observation that between 3% and 6% of women experience the onset of bad peripartum depression during pregnancy; unfortunately, this does not take into account that the real suffering often presents itself during the course of the first year after childbirth. It is hoped that, in the future, peripartum depression will be recognized as an autonomous diagnostic entity.

There are a number of ways that women respond to their postpartum experience, and it is important to understand how they differ rather than simply lumping any negative responses in to the category of postpartum depression, as often occurs. Actually, their etiopathogenesis (the cause and development of a disease or abnormal condition), their onset period, and their course differ widely.

The term *peripartum* refers to the period before and after delivery. In this chapter, the authors use the term *postpartum* to refer only to the period after delivery.

There are four postpartum types of responses to understand:

- *Baby blues:* Baby blues is a light, benign, and transient form of a drop in mood tone; it affects on average 70% of patients in their third or fourth day after delivery, and subsides spontaneously within a couple of weeks, with its incidence varying from 30% to 85%. Women feel sad, exhausted, and cry easily. Baby blues is the woman's physiological response to the drop in estrogen and progesterone (Harris et al., 1994), and to the psychophysical stress of the delivery. Only 20% of patients with baby blues develop PPD symptoms.

- *Puerperal psychosis*: Puerperal psychosis is a serious psychiatric disorder affecting 1 to 2 women per 1,000. Its onset may range from the immediate postpartum period to 6 months after delivery, with symptoms such as hallucinations, mania, obsessions, reality distortions, mystical crises, and so on. Five percent of these women are at risk of suicide and 4% of infanticide. Obviously, this type of disorder mandates *immediate* intervention with medication and hospitalization.

- *PPD*: PPD is a mood disorder and includes all major and minor depressive episodes experienced by patients, from delivery to when the child is 1 year old. The symptoms may last between a few weeks to 1 year. PPD affects 15% of women who give birth, and the estimated relapse rate for successive deliveries ranges between 50% and 75%. It should be noted, though, that PPD is often underdiagnosed: in fact, minor depressive episodes are often undiagnosed, because the functionality of the woman is apparently good. These are the major symptoms of PPD that can be part of the clinical picture:
  - Symptoms of depressive disorder
  - Feeling inadequate to care for the baby
  - Fear of being alone with the baby
  - Guilt for not experiencing the joy of the child's birth
  - Guilt for not experiencing affection toward the baby
  - Fear of losing control and hurting the baby
  - Difficulty caring for self and the child
  - Overwhelmed by chores

- *Post traumatic Delivery Disorder:* The inception of posttraumatic delivery disorder, is one to six months after delivery, and there is a high risk of developing a serious depression. The symptoms are the same as those that characterize posttraumatic stress disorder (PTSD). The latest Childbirth Connection surveys (Declercq, Sakala, Corry, & Applebaum, 2008a, 2008b) show that at least 9% of women who give birth meet childbirth-related PTSD criteria. Beck (2008) showed that up to 34% of women reported suffering from some kind of trauma during childbirth. According to several recent surveys and research, childbirth-related PTSD is underdiagnosed; this is because symptoms developed after childbirth are often not recognized and are erroneously ascribed to PPD (Ballard, Stanley, & Brockington, 1995). This diagnostic mistake could be caused by mental health professionals' unfamiliarity with (childbirth-related) PTSD, as well as by the overlap of many symptoms of these two diagnostic categories. The most frequently reported delivery-related traumatic experiences are:
  - Excessively painful or long labor
  - Unexpected cesarean cut
  - Experiencing a strong feeling of powerlessness
  - Incapability, or loss of control
  - Unexpected circumstances during delivery
  - Lack of respect and/or consideration by hospital staff
  - Intense fear of dying or of serious physical damage to the self or the child
  - Retraumatization during a natural childbirth following a rape

Motherhood

Changing Roles and Identity

Motherhood is a heavily evocative experience with deep emotional implications:

- *Parental role structuring process*: Actually, the parental role structuring process consists of the construction of a mental space where the child can be accommodated in order for the mother to care for him or her. This implies a total transformation and reorganization of her identity, her self-representation, her role and interpersonal relations.

- *Female identity development*: Motherhood is a turning point in female identity development, because it marks the transition from the role of daughter to that of mother.

This transition implies a double identification process for the mother: with her own child and with her own parent. In her interaction with the child, a mother must identify with him or her, reactivating the image of her "child self," internalized in the attachment process with her own parents. This brings the emotional states and self-cognitions developed in childhood to the surface. At the same time, the mother, in her relationship with her child, refers to her "internalized parental image," rekindling associated emotional states and cognitive models. Therefore, if these internalized images evoke positive emotional states and self-cognitions, her maternal role structuring process and the childbirth management will be facilitated; otherwise, the mother will face substantial difficulties in managing both the moment of delivery and her role as a parent. These problems may become a significant risk factor in the development of PPD and childbirth-related PTSD.

PPD and Childbirth-Related PTSD Risk Factors

Recent studies on PPD and on childbirth-related PTSD have identified the following risk factors.

Anxiety and Depression Related

- Anxiety and/or depression during pregnancy
- Personal and/or family history with reported anxiety and/or depressive disorders
- Insecure attachment
- History of premenstrual dysphoric disorder
- Previous experience of PPD or childbirth-related PTSD

Trauma Related

- Traumatic experience caused by difficult and/or particularly painful and/or premature deliveries
- Traumatic experience caused by prolonged hospitalization
- Traumatic experience caused by difficult pregnancies and/or gravidic pathologies
- Spontaneous abortion experience (particularly if repeated) or stillbirth
- Previous voluntary pregnancy termination
- Traumatic experience caused by sexual abuse or violence
- Caesarean birth (particularly if not planned)
- Complicated grief

Family and/or Relationship Related

- Parental conflicts and/or problems caused by attachment to parental figures
- Unwanted or unplanned pregnancy
- Little support from partner
- Partner conflicts
- Little support from and/or conflictual relationship(s) with family of origin and/or that of partner
- Adolescent pregnancy
- Single mother
- Large family

Financial and/or Work Related

- Financial difficulties
- Professional and/or work problems caused by pregnancy

Hospital and/or Medical Related

- Little support and/or psychological abuse (disrespectful and/or unsympathetic attitude) during delivery on the part of medical and/or nursing staff
- Hospitalization of newborn baby because of health problems

PPD Prevention

Intervention in PPD prevention represents, in itself, important work in the prevention of mental illness in general. Numerous studies have demonstrated that a mother's mental illness has a negative impact on the process of mother–child attachment and creates a serious vulnerability for development of the child's secure sense of self. In contrast, a psychologically healthy mother creates significant protection with respect to the mental health of the child (Lima et al., 2014).

To be comprehensive, a preventive intervention program must address all three levels of prevention: primary, secondary, and tertiary. For this reason, three PPD prevention protocols were created to address the specific concerns and needs at each level.

Primary prevention has two major goals:

- Reduce or avoid exposure to risk factors
- Enhance the defenses to prevent or minimize the effects of exposure to risk factors

The Eye Movement Desensitization and Reprocessing (EMDR) Therapy Protocol for the Prevention of Birth Trauma and PPD in the Pregnant Woman was designed with two major purposes:

- Improve the woman's *performance* in the implementation of the complex process of childbirth, in order to reduce the risks of childbirth trauma

Note: Statistics show there is a strong correlation between childbirth trauma and the beginning of PPD.

- Strengthening the woman's *resiliency* while reducing the negative effects of stress suffered in childbirth. This enables the woman to feel more competent and secure, yet less anxious, by being more active and constructive

As difficult as the experience of childbirth can be, the more it is an ego syntonic experience, the more probable it is that the woman will increase her self-esteem and avoid the risk of reactivating old, adverse, cognitive patterns related to herself.

It is often the case that negative core beliefs are reactivated during the challenges of childbirth. In these scenarios, women often assume passive attitudes and feel powerless going into their birthing experiences. By strengthening women's resilience, connections catalyzing positive information are activated and support women adopting positive cognitive and proactive schemas. This ego-syntonic experience of childbirth occurs when women are active participants in the birth of their children, resulting in their feeling capable and in control; at the same time, turning off those negative cognitive schemas, emotions, and behaviors that result in PPD.

Primary PPD prevention can take place in a group setting or in an individual setting.

Assessment

Prenatal Assessment

In order to collect as much useful data as possible, both for assessment and research, and to optimize time, it is helpful to have expectant mothers fill out the anamnesis that is composed of the Anamnestic Questionnaire for Pregnancy (De Divitiis, 2010), the assessment measures, and the clinical interview specific to the pregnancy and birth process. Apart from information on personal and socioeconomic data, the questionnaire collects information on risk factors and on women's expectations regarding childbirth. In addition to the clinical interview, make sure the patients complete the anamnesis and fill out assessment measures to evaluate the extent of related disorders such as depression, anxiety, trauma, and so on, and to ascertain the style of attachment.

Assessment Measures

Apart from the Anamnestic Questionnaire for Pregnancy, include psychodiagnostic instruments to evaluate important concerns, such as depression, anxiety, and the style of attachment. Appropriate instruments include the following:

- *Beck Depression Inventory (BDI)*: The BDI is a questionnaire for evaluation of the symptoms and attitudes that characterize depression. The BDI is composed of 21 items regarding symptoms and attitudes that are typical of depressed subjects. The questionnaire is self-administered. For each item there are four alternative answers that correspond to the gravity of the symptom, from 0 = absent to 3 = serious (Beck, Steer, & Brown, 1996).
- *State-G Trait Anxiety Inventory (STAI—Y1 and Y2)*: The STAI form Y is a self-administered questionnaire that asks subjects to evaluate, on a scale of 1 to 4 (1 = not at all and 4 = a lot), to what extent certain statements apply to their behavior. The STAI is composed of 40 questions, 20 regarding state anxiety (Y1) and 20 regarding trait anxiety (Y2) (Spielberger, Gorsuch, Lushene, Vagg, & Jacobs, 1983).
- *Separation Anxiety Test (SAT)*: The SAT is a semi-structured test prepared by John Bowlby (Klagsbrun & Bowlby, 1976) and subsequently modified and validated in Italy by Attili (2001).

Childbirth and Resilience

Childbirth can be a very destabilizing experience because of the psychophysical stress involved and the dysfunctional self-schemas likely to be reactivated with motherhood. The level of women's resilience significantly affects their ability to cope with the childbirth experience, and influences the risk of developing childbirth-related PTSD or PPD.

Since the literature does not report any effective intervention to prevent PPD and childbirth-related PTSD, this author adapted the Resource Development and Installation (RDI; Korn & Leeds, 2002).

Childbirth is an extremely demanding psychophysical performance, requiring strength, self-control, resistance, and courage. Throughout labor, mothers must concentrate on their bodies and maintain a state of relaxation allowing them to control the pain and contain emotional responses during the process of childbirth. During the expulsive stage, they must coordinate their breathing and pushing, while keeping the pelvic floor relaxed. In order to do so, they must refrain from taking postures that would be less painful, as those postures would close the birth canal, so they must undertake painful postures and "go toward" the pain. This makes childbirth a real peak performance in its own right, as it goes beyond a person's perceived safety and comfort zone and into the area of out-of-the-ordinary performances.

Childbirth leads women to confront their limits and can precipitate a rush of negative cognitions (NCs) about the self developed in the past, as well as allowing them to access many and/or all of the resources they have acquired over the years. This is why childbirth is a testing ground for women's courage, determination, and true grit. When women are overwhelmed by the critical moments in childbirth, they can experience this passage as something they have to bear as passive victims, defeated and demeaned. When women succeed in playing active roles in the birth of their children, they emerge stronger from the experience. By helping expectant women develop mastery, self-support, and containment, the practitioner helps foster their active cooperation during childbirth, in contrast to the dysfunctional passive attitude.

EMDR Therapy Protocol for the Prevention of Birth Trauma and PPD in the Pregnant Woman Script Notes

When there is a positive or an ego-syntonic experience of childbirth, this process becomes a self-confirmation and reinforces the self-confidence needed to cope with the delicate period that follows childbirth. In order to promote childbirth as a positive and reinforcing experience, this author adapted Lendl and Foster's (1997) Peak Performance Protocol, with the goal of developing resources likely to improve women's ability to manage childbirth. This protocol is included at the end of a prenatal class, when women are already informed of all childbirth phases and of the appropriate breathing and relaxation techniques, pushing positions and modes, and so on.

The EMDR Therapy Protocol for the Prevention of Birth Trauma and PPD for the Pregnant Woman recognizes that the concerns of pregnant women regarding their performance during childbirth deal with a future event. Lendl and Foster's (1997) EMDR Protocol for Peak Performance was determined to be an appropriate structure to help women create a positive future schema for the process of childbirth that includes adaptive responses in the face of an important event. Three aspects of this protocol are essential:

- Future based
- RDI oriented toward the peak performance strategies used in sport psychology in order to promote a client's sense of possibility rather than safety (as in the standard protocol) before initiating desensitization
- "Skills of peak performance enhanced to increase the probability of reaching and sustaining high-stake goals and promoting the conditions for enjoying a fully satisfying life" (Foster & Lendl, 2000, p. 2)

Finally, the EMDR Protocol for Anticipatory Anxiety for the Future Template (Shapiro, 2001, 2006) offers a perfect procedural model to use for reprocessing of the blocking beliefs that may hinder installation of the desired performances.

EMDR Therapy Protocol for the Prevention of Birth Trauma and PPD in the Pregnant Woman Script

Phase 1: History Taking

The presence of issues in one of the following areas could represent a risk factor both in carrying out the psychophysical performance during childbirth (causing a possible childbirth-related PTSD) and as a contributing factor to PPD.

Pregnancy

Say, *"Tell me about the history of this pregnancy."*

_____

_____

Say, *"How are you dealing with it?"*

_____

_____

Say, *"Were you trying to get pregnant, or is it an unplanned pregnancy?"*

_____

_____

Say, *"Was it difficult to get pregnant, or did it happen easily?"*

_____

_____

Say, *"Has this pregnancy presented any problems or any disorders, or has everything always gone well?* (risks of miscarriage, confined to bed for a period of time, bad nausea, sialorrhoea [excessive salivation or drooling], etc.*)."*

_____

_____

Say, *"Has this pregnancy had any negative consequences such as loss of job, interruption of studies, tensions with or separation from partner, tensions and/ or arguments with some members of your family or your partner's family?"*

_____

_____

For pluriparae (women who have already had one or more childbirths), say the following:

Say, *"How was the experience of your previous pregnancy?"*

_____

_____

Say, *"How do you feel about it?"*

_____

_____

Delivery

Say, *"Have there been any close relatives or friends who had any difficulties in their pregnancy, delivery, or postpartum?"*

_____

_____

If so, say, *"Could you tell me what happened?"*

_____

_____

Say, *"What are your thoughts about having to give birth?"*

_____

_____

Say, *"Has anybody ever told you about any childbirth experience that upset and/ or worried you?"*

_____

_____

Say, *"Have you ever had any experience with obstetric–gynecological surgery?"*

_____

_____

If so, say, *"What was the experience like?"*

_____

_____

For pluriparae, say the following:

Say, *"What was or were your experience(s) of your previous delivery or deliveries like?"*

_____

_____

Say, *"What do you remember about it or them?"*

Say, *"Have you ever assisted at a delivery live or through audiovisual means (e.g., television, the Internet, etc.)?"*

_____

_____

If so, say, *"What are your impressions of childbirth?"*

_____

_____

Say, *"Have you or your baby had any health problems that could complicate the delivery?"*

_____

_____

Say, *"What do you think about childbirth?"*

_____

_____

Say, *"What do you think about the fact that you are going to give birth?"*

_____

_____

Say, *"Are there any negative thoughts that you are having about yourself when you think of giving birth?"*

_____

_____

Maternity

Say, *"What do you think about the fact that your role will change from that of a daughter to that of a mother?"*

_____

_____

Say, *"What do you think about your partner being the father of your child?"*

_____

_____

Say, *"Do you have any worries about you and/or your partner being parents?"*

_____

_____

Say, *"What about when the baby arrives—how are you feeling about caring for your child?"*

_____

_____

Say, *"Are you concerned about being alone with your child?"*

_____

_____

Say, *"Are there any negative thoughts that you are having about yourself when you think about after the birth?"*

_____

_____

Say, *"Do you know the gender of your baby?"*

_____

_____

If so, say, *"Are you happy about the gender of your baby?"*

_____

_____

Say, *"Describe how you imagine your baby will be."*

_____

_____

Say, *"What are you looking forward to the most when your child arrives?"*

_____

_____

Say, *"What are your hopes, dreams, and expectations for your child?"*

_____

_____

Sexuality

Say, *"Have you ever been subject to sexual abuse or aggression?"*

_____

_____

If so, say, *"Could you tell me what happened?"*

_____

_____

Physical Safety

Say, *"Have you ever had an accident, of any kind, where your life was at risk?"*

_____

_____

If so, say, *"Could you tell me what happened?"*

_____

_____

Say, *"Have you been hospitalized at any time during your life?"*

_____

_____

Say, *"Have you ever been subject to physical violence (assault)?"*

_____

_____

If so, say, *"Could you tell me what happened?"*

_____

_____

Say, *"What are your hopes, dreams, and expectations for your child?"*

_____

_____

Phase 2: Preparation

Explain the work that you and your client will do to increase her awareness and encourage her to participate in the process.

> Say, *"Now we'll proceed with work that is aimed at reinforcing your resources, so that you can feel stronger in the critical moments that you could have during delivery, as well as acquiring efficient tools to confront such moments or situations. In order to increase your strength and resistance to stressors, we will develop your personal resources. The goal is to develop specific characteristics or qualities that you consider to be crucial to your success in giving birth. At first, we will identify those characteristics that you would need and then anchor them in your body so that you can use them when necessary. We'll use bilateral stimulation, which is rhythmic and alternate stimulation of the two hemispheres in your brain, to install these resources."*

Have the expectant mother try the different kinds of BLS so that she can choose the kind of stimulation that is the most comfortable for her.

> Say, *"Numerous scientific research studies have shown that bilateral stimulation accelerates the innate adaptive information processing system. By stimulating neural connectors with adequate information, the adaptive information that was unable to link into memory networks holding the dysfunctionally stored information is now able to link in to these dysfunctional neural networks and facilitate normal memory processing."*

In keeping with RDI work (Korn & Leeds, 2002; Leeds & Shapiro, 2000), use 1 or 2 short sets of bilateral stimulation (BLS; 6 to 12 saccades for eye movement) to install each resource.

Develop Resources

This series of positive resources is suggested for EMDR Peak Performance work (Foster, 2001) and RDI (Korn & Leeds, 2002) using material generated by the client. One or two short sets of 6 to 12 BLS is used (Leeds & Korn, 2012; Leeds & Shapiro, 2000), to install each resource separately.

Work with the client to develop the necessary abilities to perform what was learned during the delivery preparation course, as well as the following work of resource installation: concentration, relaxation ability, and self-contentment.

> Say, *"At the moment of delivery, no one can 'make you deliver.' On the contrary, you will have to give birth with your own body, actively participating*

throughout the entire process and essentially counting on yourself. You'll be the leading figure in the birth of your child. For this reason, it's of fundamental importance to remain concentrated on yourself, in particular listening carefully to your body sensations to 'actively' help the progress of childbirth in its different phases."

CONCENTRATION AND BODY FOCUS

This technique is to help expectant mothers develop the skills to remain concentrated on themselves and in touch with their body sensations. The sensations used in delivery preparation are the ones reinforced here: weight, heat, contact, and "full space."

Note: *Full space* refers to the summation of all the sensations mentioned previously (weight, heat, contact) that were learned in the delivery preparation course; or use the appropriate term from the course that you have used.

The first ability that is acquired is *concentration*. By being able to concentrate, the mother-to-be can remain centered in herself, staying sufficiently relaxed so that she can use the breathing and relaxation techniques she has learned during her psychoprophylaxis course on delivery.

Say, *"Now, remain concentrated on your body, listening to everything that happens. Notice what occurs in your body when you breathe. What moves? Feel the air enter and exit ... feel the weight of the body, its heat...perceive all that touches your skin ... and finally ... remain concentrated on the 'full space' sensation of your body ... remain concentrated on all the sensations that are occurring in your body as they happen. Go with that."*

Use 2 sets of 6 to 12 BLS.

Say, *"Well, now imagine how to be better focused and concentrated on your body during the labor phase, while applying the respiratory techniques to contain the pain of contractions and while you actively look for the most favorable position to move the child forward into the birth canal.*

Pay attention to how your body expands and relaxes when you breathe in.

Feel how your birth canal dilates when you breathe in.

Now, imagine how you succeed in concentrating during the expulsion phase, while you apply the respiratory techniques to strengthen your push that you learned in your course.

Remember to use the respiratory techniques you have been practicing and how to modify them, depending on what is happening. Go with that."

Do two slow sets of BLS. Then, ask for feedback and be sure that the client can imagine being able to do the techniques acquired in the course, during the delivery phase.

Say, *"How did it go?"*

_____

_____

Say, *"Were you able to imagine doing the techniques during delivery?"*

_____

_____

Say, *"What does your body feel when you visualize these images?"*

_____

_____

In general, pregnant clients are always able to imagine these scenes without any problems, because they have already been trained in relaxation. However, in case someone imagines some difficulty, or a critical situation connected to the upcoming delivery, you can respond as follows:

Say, *"Well, let's note this difficulty because we can work on this in a while, using it as a target, but now, notice only the pleasant and beneficial effects of relaxing and concentrating on your body. Go with that."*

Do 2 sets of 6 to 10 slow BLS.

ESTABLISH A SAFE PLACE SCRIPT (SHAPIRO, 1995, 2006)

Besides the ability to concentrate, it is necessary that the woman be able to stay self-contained and relax. For this purpose, it is useful to install the "Safe/Calm Place" as a resource.

The Safe/Calm Place can be used with other desired qualities, depending on the client's preference; for example, the Peaceful Place, the Control Place, the Quiet Place, and so on. The Safe/Calm Place installation is useful not only as preparation for the EMDR Protocol, but also because it can be used as a resource to cope with the critical moments during the stage of labor and between contractions, to recover energies and to keep relaxed.

Creating a Safe and Quiet Place

IMAGE

Say, *"Imagine a place, real or virtual, in which you feel a sense of refuge, well-being, freedom, and peace of mind."*

Say, *"Where would you be?"*

_____

_____

Say, *"Focus on your safe (or calm) place. Note the details: its sights, sounds, smells, colors, temperature. Tell me about what you are noticing."*

_____

_____

EMOTIONS AND SENSATIONS

Say, *"Notice the emotions and physical sensations that you feel when imagining being in the place."*

Say, *"Where do you notice these feeling and these sensations in your body?"*

_____

_____

CHECK RESOURCE VALIDITY

Say, *"Notice the emotions, the physical sensations and where you feel them in your body, when imagining being in the place."*

Say, *"What do you notice?"*

_____

_____

If the emotions and body sensations are positive, proceed with the installation (two slow sets of BLS). Otherwise, help the woman find another suitable Safe Place.

ENHANCEMENT

Say, *"Focus on your safe (or calm) place, its sights, sounds, smells, and body sensations. Tell me more about what you are noticing."*

_____

_____

When the expectant mother holds or reaches a valid safe or secure place, you can then proceed with BLS.

Say, *"Go with that."*

Do 2 sets of slow (6 to 12) BLS.

Say, *"Bring up the image of that place. Concentrate on where you feel the pleasant sensations in your body and allow yourself to enjoy them."*

Do 2 slow sets of 6 to 12 BLS.

Say, *"How do you feel now?"*

_____

_____

Repeat several times if the process has enhanced the woman's positive feelings and sensations.

If positive, say, *"Focus on that."*

Repeat BLS.

Say, *"What do you notice now?"*

_____

_____

IDENTIFICATION OF THE CUE WORD FOR THE SAFE PLACE

Cue words are verbal stimuli associated with the resource, capable of activating the relevant psychophysical state.

Say, *"What word goes best with that place?"*

_____

_____

Or say, *"Is there a word or phrase that represents your calm or safe place?"*

_____

_____

Say, *"Think of_____* (cue word or phrase) *and your calm place and notice the positive feeling you have when you think of that word or phrase. Now concentrate on those sensations and the cue word."*

_____

_____

Use 2 sets of slow BLS (6 to 12 for each set).

INSTALLING THE CUE WORD

Say, *"Link the memory, the physical sensations, and your cue words together. Go with that."*

Use 2 sets of slow BLS (6 to 10 each).
Between the sets, always ask how your client is doing by saying the following:

Say, *"How do you feel now?"*

_____

_____

Say, *"How are you now?"*

_____

_____

CUING WITH DISTURBANCE

Say, *"Now imagine a minor annoyance and how it feels."* (Pause)

_____

_____

Say, *"Do you feel disturbance? Notice what you are feeling in your body, and where you feel it."*

_____

_____

Say, *"Now bring up your safe (or calm) place and notice any shifts in your body."*

_____

_____

Do slow sets of BLS.
Guide the client through the process until she is able to experience the positive emotions and sensations.

SELF-CUING WITH DISTURBANCE

This technique can also be used as an emotional self-containment resource, to cope with the critical moments that may occur through childbirth (Shapiro, 2006).

> Say, *"Now imagine yourself during those moments of respite among the contractions."*
> Pause.
>
> Say, *"Do you feel disturbance? Notice what you are feeling in your body, and where you feel it."*
> Pause.
>
> Say, *"Now bring up your safe (or calm) place and notice any shifts in your body as you relive that sense of well-being. Go with that."*

Do 2 sets of 6 to 12 BLS.
At the end of the set, it is recommended to ask for feedback.

> Say, *"What do you notice now?"*

_____

_____

MASTERY RESOURCE SCRIPT (KORN & LEEDS, 2002)

Identify the Challenging or Critical (Target) Situation

> Say, *"Consider the whole process of childbirth, from the beginning of labor to the end of the delivery stage and identify the most demanding, critical, or challenging moment that you expect."*

Note the response and in which domain the cognition falls, such as safety, responsibility, or choice/control.

_____

_____

_____

_____

Identifying the Personality Traits or Features

Identify the resource(s) that are needed, such as courage, strength, resistance, self-control, tenacity, self-confidence, strong will, serenity, optimism, patience, and so on.

Domain	Critical Issues/Difficult Moments	Quality or Features
Responsibility	"I've always been weak, I'm afraid I won't be able to push in the expulsion stage"	Strength (in body or mind)
Responsibility	"I can't do it on my own; if I imagine myself during delivery, I don't think I can succeed"	Faith in oneself Personal strength
Control	"I cannot bear seeing blood, I am sure I will faint" (I cannot bear it)	Self-control Self-containment
Safety	I can't stand the idea of entrusting my body to others, even if they are professionals	Capacity of trusting (in body and mind)

Say, *"At that critical or challenging moment or situation, what would you like to be able to do?"*

_____

_____

Say, *"What would you like to believe about yourself?"*

_____

_____

Say, *"What would you like to feel?"*

_____

_____

Say, *"So, what quality or feature do you think would be useful to better cope with that critical or challenging moment or situation of your childbirth?"*

_____

_____

Or say, *"What quality or feature do you think you need to develop to better cope with critical or challenging moments or situations of your childbirth?"*

_____

_____

Or say, *"What quality or feature do you believe that you need to develop in order to deal effectively with this critical or challenging moment or situation of your childbirth?"*

_____

_____

Identifying Resource (Mastery Episode or Mastery Resource Script)

Say, *"Scan your memory for a positive episode or experience where you felt particularly _____ (repeat the feature or quality identified by the client)."*

_____

_____

Check the Validity of the Resource

Say, *"Now concentrate on the episode identified and notice the accompanying emotions and body sensations."*

_____

_____

Note: If negative emotions or body sensations arise, their causes should not be investigated. Help the client to identify another mastery memory capable of eliciting positive emotions and body sensations. When she has a valid resource available, then proceed to the installation phase.

Installation Resource of Mastery Episode/Script

Say, *"Now concentrate on the episode (resource) you've identified and on your bodily sensations."*

Ask the mother-to-be to self-administer the BLS (6 to 12) via the Butterfly Hug.

Say, *"Please use the Butterfly Hug about 6 to 12 times."*

Demonstrate how to do the Butterfly Hug.

Say, *"What do you feel in your body?"*

_____

_____

Say, *"Where do you feel it?"*

_____

_____

Use a set of 6 to 12 BLS.

Say, *"How do you feel?"*

_____

_____

Use a set of 6 to 12 BLS.

Say, *"What do you believe about yourself when you remember that episode?"*

_____

_____

Use a set of 6 to 12 BLS.

Say, *"Concentrate again on the episode and on your emotions and bodily sensations."*

Use 2 sets of 6 to 12 BLS.

Say, *"What do you notice now?"*

_____

_____

Identifying the Cue Words Associated with the Mastery Episode

Say, *"What word is associated with that memory?"*

_____

_____

Or say, *"When you think of that positive experience, what are the most positive words you can say to yourself now?"*

_____

_____

Expectant women in general find words or phrases aimed at self-soothing, self-containment, and self-support helpful, such as the following:

- "Go on"
- "I can make it"
- "Keep up!"
- "I am able to remain calm, relax!"
- "I'm strong enough, I can resist"
- "I am trained, I can do it"
- "I can trust the hospital staff, they are here to help me!"
- "I can hold on, it's just a moment, it will go away"

Installation of the Cue Word Associated with the Mastery Episode

Say, *"Link the memory, the physical sensations, the emotion, and your words together. Go with that."*

Use 2 or 3 sets of 6 to 12 BLS.

INNER ADVISOR/COACH SCRIPT (LENDL & FOSTER, 2009, PP. 390–391)

Identify the Inner Advisor or Coach

Say, *"Imagine a person or virtual being who could be an inner resource for you, like an Inner Coach supporting and soothing you during the critical states of childbirth. This may be some part of yourself, like your Higher or Wiser Self. Imagine this person's or being's voice, calming you when you are upset or frustrated and reminding you of your strengths, talents, and positive qualities. Go ahead and do that now and let me know what you find."*

_____

_____

Say, *"Great. Go with that!"*

Use a set of slow BLS.

Say, *"Now imagine calling* _____ *(him/her), the way* _____ *(he/she) appears to you, where* _____ *(he/she) is located in your field of vision, how* _____ *(he/she) greets you,* _____ *(his/her) voice tone,* _____ *(his/her) facial expression, and where* _____ *(he/she) goes to place space between you, that is, in front, beside, or slightly behind you."*

Say, *"How do you feel when* _____ *(he/she) is with you?"*

_____

_____

Say, *"Do you feel stronger or more positive?"*

_____

_____

Say, *"Do you need to add or delete anything to make it more positive?"*

_____

_____

If yes, say the following:

Say, *"Go ahead and do that now. Go with that."*

Do a set of slow BLS.

Check the Validity of the Inner Coach

Say, *"Now concentrate on the inner Coach. What do you notice?"*

_____

_____

Say, *"What do you feel in your body and where?"*

_____

_____

If negative emotions or body sensations arise, do not investigate them. Identify another Inner Coach. When your client has a valid Inner Coach, proceed with the installation.

Installation of Inner Coach

Say, *"Imagine this person's voice soothing or encouraging you in difficult times and reminding you of your strong points and positive features and link what you feel in your body."*

Do a set of 6 to 12 slow BLS.

Cue Word or Sentence Identification

Say, *"Imagine _____'s (state Inner Coach) voice soothing or encouraging you in difficult times and reminding you of your strong points and positive features. What words would you want your Inner Coach to say?"*

_____

_____

Install the Cue Word or Sentence Identification

Say, *"Now see and hear _____(him/her) coming toward you, smiling at you, saying hello, staying close to you and telling you the words of encouragement you would like to hear, reminding you of your strong points and positive features and offering advice when you need it."*

_____

_____

Use 2 sets of slow BLS (6 to 12).

Phase 3: Assessment

Selecting the Target

Say, *"Before, when considering all the childbirth process, you identified a critical/challenging situation/moment/idea that represents an issue for you. What happens when you think of _____ (state the issue)?"*

Image

Say, *"What image represents the entire* _____ (state the issue)?*"*

Negative Cognition

Most frequent negative cognitions (NCs) are: *"I'm not in control"; "I'm weak"; "I can't do it"; "I'm powerless"; "I'm vulnerable"; "I'm not capable."*

Say, *"What words best go with the picture of* _____ *(state critical or challenging moment/situation/idea) that express your negative belief (worry/concern/self-doubt) about yourself now?"*

Positive Cognition

Most frequent PCs include: *"I'm smart"; "I'm strong enough"; "I can do it"; "I'm in control"; "I'm capable."*

Say, *"When you bring up that picture or* _____ *(state the issue), what would you like to believe about yourself now?"*

Validity of Cognition

Say, *"When you think of* _____ *(state the issue, or picture/scene), how true do those words* _____ *(repeat the PC) feel to you now on a scale of 1 to 7, where 1 feels completely false and 7 feels completely true?"*

1	2	3	4	5	6	7

(completely false)   (completely true)

Emotions

Say, *"When you bring up the picture or* _____ *(state the issue) and those words* _____ *(state the NC), what emotion(s) do you feel now?"*

_____

_____

Subjective Units of Disturbance

Say, *"On a scale of 0 to 10, where 0 is no disturbance or neutral, and 10 is the highest disturbance you can imagine, how disturbing does it feel to you now?"*

0	1	2	3	4	5	6	7	8	9	10

(no disturbance)   (highest disturbance)

Localization of Body Sensation

Say, *"Where do you feel it (the disturbance) in your body?"*

_____

_____

Phase 4: Desensitization

Say, *"Bring up the picture of the* _____ *(repeats the critical/challenging/demanding situation/moment/idea) and the words* _____ *(repeat the NC) and notice where you feel it in your body. Now follow my fingers with your eyes."*

Do sets of BLS until the SUD drops to a value of 0.

The goal is to help the client integrate past experiences underlying the present performance problem in order to minimize future upsets. Most past memories will surface during the reprocessing. However, if looping occurs or past memories are compartmentalized and do not surface, use a Float-Back, affect scan, and/or cognitive interweave.

> Say, *"When you see yourself stuck in* _____ (state the critical moment, issue of delivery), *when have you had that* _____ (state the NC, or the negative body feeling) _____ *in the past?"*

> Say, *"Good, go with that and just notice."*

Do a set of BLS.

> Say, *"Well, now let's take a deep breath* (pause) *and then just notice what you get now."*

Do sets of BLS until the SUD drops to a value of 0.

Phase 5: Installation

When the SUD = 0 and the VoC = 7, proceed with the installation phase.

Check the PC

> Say, *"When remembering the moment/situation critical to delivery that you identified at the beginning, and the words* _____ (repeat the PC), *are the words still valid, or is there another positive cognition that is more suitable?"*

Check the VoC

If the client accepts the original PC, the clinician should ask for a VoC rating to see if it has increased; otherwise, help her find another more suitable cognition.

When the client has identified her PC, say the following:

> Say, *"When you think of the critical/demanding/challenging situation/moment of delivery, how true do those words* _____ (repeat the PC) *feel to you now on a scale of 1 to 7, where 1 feels completely false and 7 feels completely true?"*

> 1   2   3   4   5   6   7

> (completely false)   (completely true)

When the client evaluates the PC to be true at a level of 5, then it is possible to proceed to tie the PC to the critical moment.

Installation

Tie the PC to the problematic/critical situation/moment.

> Say, *"Now join the identified problematic situation and the words* _____ (state the PC). *Go with that."*

Do a long set of BLS to see if there is more processing to be done. Continue repeating the sets as long as the material is becoming more adaptive. When the client reports the VoC = 7, do BLS again to strengthen and continue until it no longer strengthens.

Phase 6: Body Scan

> Say, *"Close your eyes and keep in mind the original target and the positive cognition. Then bring your attention to the different parts of your body, starting*

with your head and working downward. Any place you find any tension, tightness, or unusual sensation, tell me."

The Final Installation: The Expanded Future Template

By using the expanded future template, the expectant mother projects into the future her real ability to use the techniques learned during the delivery preparation course and the resources previously installed during the preparation phase. This allows for the installation of the desired results and the reprocessing, using BLS, of any other possible disturbing element.

Say, *"Imagine an internal space such as a comfortable room, or a beautiful space outdoors, in which you can comfortably sit and see a large projection screen in front of you. On this screen, you can project scenes of yourself effectively dealing with all the difficulties and critical/challenging moments/situations that you think you will come across during childbirth, from the beginning of the labor to the end of the delivery phase. Visualize how you would actually use the resources to cope with these difficulties and how that feels in your body. Pay attention to your body as you competently go through the birthing process. Let me know whenever any discomfort arises and we will stop the visualization and reprocess any discomforts until you can imagine the task with a positive full-body experience."*

After processing any block that arises and focusing on the successes, say the following:

Say, *"Imagine being in that space in which you can picture and mentally rehearse your childbirth experience. See a projection screen in front of you and imagine that you can see images of yourself projected onto that screen _____ (state whatever task needs to be done)."*

When the reprocessing of the issue is complete (VoC = 7; SUD = 0; body scan clear), the expanded future template can be useful to check if all the material concerning the issue, upon which the client has worked, has been resolved, or if there is more material that has escaped detection so far.

Phase 7: Closure

In this protocol, the client is encouraged to practice her performance skills.

Say, *"The work we have done today could continue. You may or may not notice new bodily sensations, thoughts, memories, or dreams. Should this happen, note it, describing it as a picture, and the next time we'll take it into consideration. Please write down the positive experiences, too. Remember to practice your relaxation techniques and Safe Place every day to increase your expertise in supporting yourself during the birth process."*

Phase 8: Reevaluation

It is important to pay attention to the following questions when the client returns after doing EMDR Therapy work.

Say, *"When you think of whatever is left of the problem that we worked on last time, how disturbing does it feel now on a scale of 0 to 10, where 0 is no disturbance or neutral and 10 is the highest disturbance you can imagine?"*

0   1   2   3   4   5   6   7   8   9   10

(no disturbance)   (highest disturbance)

Say, *"Have you noticed any other material associated with the original memory since the last session?"*

_____

_____

Say, *"Have all the necessary targets been reprocessed so that you can feel at peace with the past, empowered in the present, and able to make choices for the future?"*

_____

_____

Say, *"Has the work that we have done with EMDR helped you be more adaptive in your day-to-day life?"*

_____

_____

Summary

The present protocol allows clinicians who work in maternal health care service to make use of the extensive potential of EMDR Therapy in the field of prevention. By means of BLS, expectant mothers can both reprocess any maladaptive encoding information that would interfere with future childbirth performances, and anchor positive information associated with images and scenes, which represent personal resources to be used in coping with the critical moments of childbirth.

The authors hope that this protocol will stimulate the development of a series of future interventions structured on EMDR Therapy in numerous healthcare areas regarding prevention.

References

American Psychiatric Association. (2000). *Diagnostic and statistical manual of mental disorders* (4th ed.). Washington, DC: Author.

American Psychiatric Association. (2013). *Diagnostic and statistical manual of mental disorders* (5th ed.). Arlington, VA: American Psychiatric Publishing.

Attili, G. (2001). *Ansia da separazione e misura dell'attaccamento normale e patologico: Versione modificata e adattamento italiano del Separation Anxiety Test (SAT) di Klagsbrun e Bowlby*. Milano, Italy: Edizioni Unicopli.

Ballard, C. G., Stanley, A. K., & Brockington, I. F. (1995). Post traumatic stress disorder (PTSD) after childbirth. *British Journal of Psychiatry, 166*, 525–528.

Beck, A. T., Steer, R. A., & Brown, G. K. (1996). *Manual for the Beck Depression Inventory-II*. San Antonio, TX: Psychological Corporation.

Beck, C. T. (2008). Impact of birth trauma on breastfeeding. *Nursing Research, 57*(4), 228–236.

Declercq, E. R., Sakala, C., Corry, M. P., & Applebaum, S. (2008a). *Childbirth connection. New mothers speak out*. New York, NY: Childbirth Connection.

Declercq, E. R., Sakala, C., Corry, M. P., & Applebaum, S. (2008b, August). *New mothers speak out: National survey results highlight women's postpartum experiences*. New York, NY: Childbirth Connection. Retrieved from http://www.childbirthconnection.org/pdfs/new-mothers-speak-out.pdf

De Divitiis, A. M. (2010, June). *Application of resource development and installation (RDI) in delivery preparation in order to prevent postpartum depression*. In *Female issues*. Symposium conducted at the 11th EMDR Europe Association Conference, Hamburg, Germany.

Foster, S., & Lendl, J. (2003). *EMDR performance enhancement for the workplace: A practitioners' manual* (2nd European ed.).

Foster, S. (2001a). A case of EMDR-integrated performance enhancement coaching. In J. E. Auerbach, *Personal and executive coaching*. Ventura, CA: Executive College Press.

Foster, S. (2001b). *From trauma to triumph: EMDR and advanced performance enhancement strategies* (self-published training manual). San Francisco, CA: Success at Work.

Foster, S., & Lendl, J. (2000, August). *Peak performance EMDR: Adapting trauma treatment to positive psychology outcomes and self-actualization.* Poster presented at the 108th Annual Convention of the American Psychological Association, Washington, DC.

Harris, B., Lovett, L., Newcombe, R. G., Read, G. F., Walker, R., & Riad-Fahmy, D. (1994). Maternity blues and major endocrine changes: Cardiff Puerperal Mood and Hormone Study II. *BMJ, 308*(9), 949–952.

Klagsbrun, M., & Bowlby, J. (1976). Responses to separation from parents: A clinical test for young children. *Projective Psychology, 21*(2), 7–27.

Korn, D. L., & Leeds, A. M. (2002). Preliminary evidence of efficacy for EMDR resource development and installation in the stabilization phase of treatment of complex posttraumatic stress disorder. *Journal of Clinical Psychology, 58*(12), 1465–1487.

Leeds, A. M., & Korn, D. L. (2012). A commentary on Hornsveld et al. (2011). A valid test of resource development and installation? Absolutely not. *Journal of EMDR Practice and Research, 6*(4), 170–173. doi: 10.1891/1933-3196.6.4.170

Leeds, A. M., & Shapiro, F. (2000). EMDR and resource installation: Principles and procedures for enhancing current functioning and resolving traumatic experiences. In L. Carlson & L. Sperry (Eds.), *Brief therapy strategies with individuals and couples* (pp. 469–534). Phoenix, AZ: Zeig/Tucker.

Lendl, J., & Foster, S. (1997). *EMDR performance enhancement for the workplace: A practitioner's guide.* San José, CA: Performance Enhancement Unlimited.

Lendl, J., & Foster, S. (2009). EMDR performance and enhancement psychology protocol. In M. Luber (Ed.), *Eye movement desensitization and reprocessing (EMDR) scripted protocols: Basics and special situations* (pp. 377–396). New York, NY: Springer.

Lima, A. R., Mello, M. F., Andreoli, S. B., Fossaluza, V., de Araújo, C. M., Jackowski, A. P., . . . Mari, J. J. (2014). The impact of healthy parenting as a protective factor for posttraumatic stress disorder in adulthood: A case-control study. *PLoS ONE, 9*(1), e87117.

Shapiro, F. (1995). *Eye movement desensitization and reprocessing. Basic principles, protocols, and procedures.* New York, NY: Guilford Press.

Shapiro, F. (2001). *Eye movement desensitization and reprocessing: Basic principles, protocols, and procedures* (2nd ed.). New York, NY: Guilford Press.

Shapiro, F. (2006). *EMDR new notes on adaptive information processing with case formulation principles, forms, scripts and worksheet.* Watsonville, CA: EMDR Institute.

Spielberger, C. D., Gorsuch, R. L., Lushene, R., Vagg, P. R., & Jacobs, G. A. (1983). *Manual for the State-Trait Anxiety Inventory (Form Y self-evaluation questionnaire).* Palo Alto, CA: Consulting Psychologists Press.

Additional Reading

Balaskas, J. (1983a). *Active birth.* London, UK: Unwin Paperbacks.

Balaskas, J. (1983b). *Manuale del parto attivo: Gli esercizi per arrivare al parto con la sicurezza e le energie necessarie.* Novara, Itala: Red Edizioni.

Campbell, S. B., & Cohon, J. F. (1991). Prevalence and correlates of postpartum depression in first time mothers. *Journal of Abnormal Psychology, 100*(4), 594–599.

Cox, J., & Holden, J. (2003). *Perinatal mental health: A guide to Edinburgh Postnatal Depression Scale.* London, UK: The Royal College of Psychiatrists.

DeMier, R. L., Hynan, M. T., Harris, H. B., & Manniello, R. L. (1996). Perinatal stressors as predictors of symptoms of posttraumatic stress in mother and infants at high risk. *Journal of Perinatology, 16*(4), 276–280.

Dennis, C. L. (2004). Can we identify mothers at risk for postpartum depression in the immediate post-partum period using the Edinburgh Postnatal Depression Scale? *Journal of Affective Disorders, 78*(2), 163–169.

Dennis, C. L. (2005). Psychosocial and psychological interventions for prevention of postnatal depression: Systematic review. *British Medical Journal, 331*(7507), 15.

Edwards, D. R. L., Porter, S. A. M., & Stein, G. S. (1994). A pilot study of postnatal depression following caesarean section using two retrospective self-rating instruments. *Journal of Psychosomatic Research, 38*, 111–117.

Figueira, P. (2009). *Edinburgh Postnatal Depression Scale for screening in the public health system. Revista Saúde Pública, 43*(Suppl. 1) 79–84.

Foster, S. (2001a). *A case of EMDR-integrated performance enhancement coaching.* In J. E. Auerbach (Ed.), *Personal and executive coaching.* Ventura, CA: Executive College Press.

Foster, S. (2001b). *From trauma to triumph: EMDR and advanced performance enhancement strategies* (Self-published training materials). San Francisco, CA: Success at Work.

Foster, S., & Lendl, J. (1995). Eye movement desensitization and reprocessing: Initial applications for enhancing performance in athletes. *Journal of Applied Sport Psychology, 7*(Suppl.), 63.

Gotlib, I. H., Whiffen, V. E., Wallace, P. M., & Mount, J. H. (1991). Prospective investigation of postpartum depression: Factors involved in onset and recovery. *Journal of Abnormal Psychology, 100*(2), 122–132.

Grossman, F. K., Eichler, L. S., & Winickoff, S. A. (1980). *Pregnancy, birth, and parenthood.* San Francisco, CA: Jossey-Bass.

Harris, B. (1993). A hormonal component of postnatal depression. *British Journal of Psychiatry, 163,* 403–405.

Hayworth, J., Little, B. C., Bonham Carter, S., Raptopoulos, P., Priest, R. G., & Sandler, M. (1980). A predictive study of postpartum depression: Some predisposing characteristics. *British Journal of Medical Psychology, 53,* 161–167.

Lendl, J., & Foster, S. (2003). *EMDR per il miglioramento della performance sul posto di lavoro: manuale per terapeuti, Seconda Edizione Europea . (EMDR performance enhancement for the workplace: A practitioners' manual.* San Jose, CA: Performance Enhancement Unlimited, 1997).

Lendl, J., & Foster, S. (2004). *EMDR performance enhancement for the workplace: A practitioner's manual (2nd European ed.) Milano, Italia: Ed. Associazione per l'EMDR Italia. (EMDR performance enhancement for the workplace: A practitioners' manual.* San Jose, CA: Performance Enhancement Unlimited, 1997)

Luber, M. (Ed.). (2009a). *Eye movement desensitization and reprocessing (EMDR) scripted protocols: Basics and special situations.* New York, NY: Springer.

Luber, M. (2009b). Future template worksheet. In M. Luber (Ed.), *Eye movement desensitization and reprocessing (EMDR): Basics and special situations* (pp. 422–429). New York, NY: Springer.

Manage, J. (1993). Posttraumatic stress disorders in women who have undergone obstetric and or gynaecological procedures: A consecutive series of 30 cases of PTSD. *Journal of Reproductive and Infant Psychology, 11,* 221–228.

Meares, R. A., Grimwade, J., & Wood, C. (1976). A possible relationship between anxiety in pregnancy and pueperal depression. *Journal of Psychosomatic Research, 20,* 605–610.

Moehler, E., Brunner, R., Wiebel, A., Reck, C., & Resch, F. (2006, September). Maternal depressive symptoms in the postnatal period are associated with long-term impairment of mother-child bonding. *Archives of Women's Mental Health, 9*(5), 273–278.

Murray, L., & Cooper, P. J. (1996). The impact of postpartum depression on child development. *International Review of Psychiatry, 8*(1), 55–63.

Nilsson, A., Kaij, L., & Jacobson, L. (1967). Postpartum mental disorder in an unselected sample: The importance of the unplanned pregnancy. *Journal of Psychosomatic Research, 10,* 341–347.

O'Hara, M. W. (1987). Post-partum "blues," depression, and psychosis: A review. *Journal of Psychosomatic Obstetric and Gynaecology, 7,* 205–227.

Pearlstein, T. (2008). Perinatal depression: Treatment options and dilemmas. *Journal of Psychiatry & Neuroscience, 33*(4), 302–318.

Piacentini, D., Levenia, D., Primerano, G., Cattaneo, M., Volpia, L., Biffia, G., & Mirabella, F. (2009). Prevalence and risk factors of postnatal depression among women attending antenatal course. *Epidemiologia e Psichiatria Sociale, 18*(3), 214–220.

Piscicelli, U. (1977). *Training autogeno respiratorio e psicoprofilassi ostetrica.* Padova, Italy: Piccin Editions.

Porges, S. (2007). The polyvagal perspective. *Biological Psychology, 74,* 116–143.

Prezza, M., Di Mauro, D., Giudici, M. G., Violani, C., Vaccari, S., & Faustini, F. (1984). Studio longitudinale sulla disforia post parto. In U. Montemagno & L. Zichella (Eds.), *Psicosomatica ginecologica ed ostetrica.* Bologna, Italy: Monduzzi.

Read, D. G. (1944). *Childbirth without fear.* New York, NY: Harper.

Reynolds, J. L. (1997). Post-traumatic stress disorders after childbirth: The phenomenon of traumatic birth. *Canadian Medical Association Journal, 156,* 831–835.

Rizzolatti, G., & Sinigaglia, C. (2006). *So quel che fai, il cervello che agisce e i neuroni specchio.* Milano, Italia: Raffaello Cortina Editore.

Robinson, J. (2002). Post-traumatic stress disorder—a consumer view. In A. B. MacLean & J. Neilson (Eds.), *Maternal Morbidity and Mortality* (pp. 313–322). London: RCOG.

Stein, G. (1982). *The maternity blues.* In I. F. Brockington & R. Kumar (Eds.), *Motherhood and mental illness.* New York, NY: Grune & Stratton.

Watson, J. P., Elliott, S. A., Rugg, A. J., & Brough, D. I. (1984). Psychiatric disorder in pregnancy and the first postnatal year. *British Journal of Psychiatry, 144,* 453–462.

Weiss, D. S. (2007). The Impact of Event Scale: Revised. In J. P. Wilson & C. S. Tang (Eds.), *Cross-cultural assessment of psychological trauma and PTSD* (pp. 219–238). New York, NY: Springer.

Addendum: Anamnestic Questionnaire for Pregnancy

Anna Maria De Divitiis

(The present questionnaire is only for clinical and preventative reasons. Results may also be utilized for research, if absolute rights of privacy are respected.)
Note: Answers to this questionnaire are strictly confidential.

Date _____

Name _____ Surname _____ Age _____

Home Telephone _____ Cellular _____

Email _____

Week of Pregnancy _____ Presumed Date of Birth _____

1. Have you ever suffered any of the following?

Anxiety	YES	NO
Depression	YES	NO
Panic Attacks	YES	NO
Alimentary Disorders	YES	NO
Sleep Disorders	YES	NO
Psychosomatic Disorders	YES	NO
Obsessive-Compulsive Disorders (compulsive ruminations (brooding) on thoughts; excessive controls, forced rituals, hygienic and/or cleanliness manias)	YES	NO
Phobias resulting in a limitation in your life	YES	NO
Other psychological or psychiatric disorders	YES	NO

If the answer is YES to this last question, specify what and at what age

2. Have you ever had an abortion or miscarriage?

YES	NO

3. Have you ever had one or more traumas in your life (experiences of a death, departure of or an abandonment by someone affectionately close or significant, any various types of accidents, surgical interventions, abortions, lengthy or stressful hospitalizations, personal serious sicknesses or sickness of someone dear to you, physical aggression, beating, sexual rape

or molestations, earthquake, flooding, or any other natural or man-made catastrophe, robbery, etc.)?

| YES | NO |

If you answer YES, please briefly describe the event or events, stating the relative age at occurrence.

4. Have you ever been to a psychologist or psychiatrist, neurologist or neuropsychiatric doctor before?

| YES | NO |

If the answer is YES, please briefly describe the motives for the consultation and your age at the time.

5. Have you ever had a loss that still hurts you deeply?

| YES | NO |

If the answer is YES, please briefly report who was concerned and when it happened.

6. Do you have other children?

| YES | NO |

If so, specify how many.

7. Have you ever had any negative experiences relative to any previous childbirth?

| YES | NO |

8. Are there any conflicts at the moment with the father of the expected child?

| YES | NO |

9. Do you have any valid support from friends and/or family?

| YES | NO |

10. Are there any conflicts with your family of origin and/or that of your partner?

| YES | NO |

11. Are you presently single?

| YES | NO |

12. With respect to your professional/working life, how much could this pregnancy be a problem, on a scale of 1 to 4 (1 = none, 2 = some, 3 = enough, 4 = a lot/quite a lot)?

| 1 | 2 | 3 | 4 |

13. Taking into consideration your present economic resources, how big of a problem do you think the birth of this child could be for your budget, on a scale of 1 to 4 (1 = none, 2 = some, 3 = enough, 4 = a lot/quite a lot).

| 1 | 2 | 3 | 4 |

Are there any particular things that are concerning you now about your pregnancy?

_____

_____

_____

How is your current emotional state?

_____

_____

_____

Have there been any close relatives or friends who have had any difficulties
in their pregnancy, delivery, or postpartum?

YES	NO

If so, please briefly describe what happened?"

_____

_____

_____

How satisfying do you consider the following aspects of your relationship
with your mother when you were a child, on a scale of 1 to 4 (1 = none,
2 = some, 3 = enough, 4 = a lot/quite a lot)?

Physical and alimentary treatments	1	2	3	4	Trust/appreciation	1	2	3	4
Expressions of emotional warmth/affection	1	2	3	4	Consideration of needs	1	2	3	4
Empathy/understanding	1	2	3	4	Acceptance	1	2	3	4
Communicative quality	1	2	3	4	Support	1	2	3	4

When you were a child, which of the following characteristics did your mother have,
on a scale of 1 to 4 (1 = none, 2 = some, 3 = enough, 4 = a lot/quite a lot)?

Anxious	1	2	3	4	Agitated/nervous	1	2	3	4
Depressed	1	2	3	4	Intrusive	1	2	3	4
Accommodating	1	2	3	4	Caring	1	2	3	4
Aggressive	1	2	3	4	Abusive	1	2	3	4
Soothing–consoling/reassuring	1	2	3	4	Whining/victimizing	1	2	3	4
Emotionally detached	1	2	3	4	Fondling/pampering	1	2	3	4
Understanding	1	2	3	4	Manipulative	1	2	3	4
Punishing	1	2	3	4	Self-assured	1	2	3	4
Mentally absent	1	2	3	4	Cheerful/good-humored	1	2	3	4
Physically present	1	2	3	4	Hypercritical	1	2	3	4
Strong	1	2	3	4	Available	1	2	3	4
Discomforting	1	2	3	4	Apprehensive	1	2	3	4
Authoritative	1	2	3	4	Enterprising/propositional	1	2	3	4
Positive/optimistic	1	2	3	4	Irrational/emotional	1	2	3	4
Tolerant	1	2	3	4	Distracted/mentally absent	1	2	3	4
Narcissist/egocentric	1	2	3	4	Supportive/encouraging	1	2	3	4
Responsible/reliable	1	2	3	4	Tense/preoccupied	1	2	3	4

Oppressive	1	2	3	4
Coherent	1	2	3	4
Formal	1	2	3	4
Busy/committed	1	2	3	4
Thoughtful	1	2	3	4
Talkative	1	2	3	4
Courageous	1	2	3	4

Autonomous	1	2	3	4
Impulsive	1	2	3	4
Affectionate	1	2	3	4
False/liar	1	2	3	4
Satisfied/realized	1	2	3	4
Extrovert	1	2	3	4
Passive	1	2	3	4

How would you define your present relationship with the father of the child you are expecting (place a mark next to all the characteristics you consider to be true)?

	Mentally absent		of Reciprocal empathy		of Reciprocal support
	Cooperative		Physically present		Not very affectionate
	Conflictual		Rivalrous		of Reciprocal understanding
	Passionate		Sharing		of Reciprocal respect

How sensitive to pain do you consider yourself to be, on a 1 to 10 scale, with 1 being nothing to 10 being very sensitive?

1	2	3	4	5	6	7	8	9	10

How much do you imagine you will suffer during childbirth (or immediately after delivery in case of a caesarean) on a 1 to 10 scale, with 1 being nothing to 10 being very painful?

1	2	3	4	5	6	7	8	9	10

Are there any negative thoughts that you are having about yourself when you think of your pregnancy and giving birth?

_____

_____

_____

Have you given any thought to the birth process? What are your thoughts about it?

_____

_____

_____

_____

Do you feel like you are ready to give birth?

_____

_____

_____

For Expectant Mothers at the Completion of Application of the EMDR Therapy Protocol for the Prevention of Birth Trauma and Postpartum Depression

How much do you feel that the exercises of the psychoprophylaxis delivery course can help you in handling pain during delivery, on a scale of 1 to 4 (1 = none, 2 = little, 3 = enough, 4 = a lot)?

1	2	3	4

How much do you feel that the information obtained during the course and the exercises, can help you, in general, in preparing for delivery as well as for your future maternity, on a scale of 1 to 4 (1 = none, 2 = little, 3 = enough, 4 = a lot)?

1	2	3	4

How much do you feel that the resource (practice proficiency with the key word/ phrase; interior trainer/Inner Coach) can help you in handling the difficult moments of delivery, on a scale of 1 to 4 (1 = none, 2 = little, 3 = enough, 4 = a lot)?

1	2	3	4

Suggestions for the psychoprophylaxis delivery course?

_____

_____

_____

Anna Maria De Divitiis and Marilyn Luber
SUMMARY SHEET BY MARILYN LUBER

Name: _____ Diagnosis: _____

☑ Check when task is completed, response has changed, or to indicate symptoms or diagnosis.

Note: This material is meant as a checklist for your response. Please keep in mind that it is only a reminder of different tasks that may or may not apply to your client.

Psychoprophylaxis is a method of preparing women for natural childbirth by means of special breathing and relaxation.
Logistics: 8 to 10 pregnant women; 90 to 120 minutes; protocol usually the last class.

DSM-5: In the *DSM-5* (American Psychiatric Association, 2013), postpartum depression is still classified as "Mood Disorder" and continues to use the specifier "onset," although the "indicator" has been modified from "postpartum" to "peripartum." This modification of the indicator is based on the observation that between 3% and 6% of women experience the onset of bad peripartum depression during pregnancy, but unfortunately this does not take into account that the real suffering often presents itself during the course of the first year after childbirth.

Diagnosing Postpartum Depression

☐ Baby blues: a light, benign, and transient form of a drop in mood tone; it affects on average 70% of patients in their third or fourth day after delivery, and subsides spontaneously within a couple of weeks, with its incidence varying from 30% to 85%. Women feel sad, exhausted, and cry easily. Baby blues is the woman's physiological response to the drop in estrogen and progesterone (Harris et al., 1994), and to the psychophysical stress of the delivery. Only 20% of patients with Baby blues develop postpartum depression symptoms.

☐ Puerperal psychosis: a serious psychiatric disorder affecting 1 to 2 women per 1,000. Its onset may range from immediately postpartum to 6 months after delivery, with symptoms such as hallucinations, mania, obsessions, reality distortions, mystical crises, and so on. Five percent of these women are at risk of suicide and 4% of infanticide. Obviously, this type of disorder mandates *immediate* intervention with medication and hospitalization.

☐ Postpartum depression (PPD): PPD is a mood disorder and includes all major and minor depressive episodes experienced by patients, from delivery to when the child is 1 year old. The symptoms may last between a few weeks to 1 year. PPD affects 15% of women who give birth, and the estimated relapse rate for successive deliveries ranges between 50% and 75%. It should be noted, though, that postpartum depression is often under-diagnosed: in fact, minor depressive episodes are often undiagnosed, because the functionality of the woman is apparently good. These are the major symptoms of postpartum depression that can be part of the clinical picture:

☐ Symptoms of depressive disorder
☐ Feeling inadequate to care for the baby
☐ Fear of being alone with the baby
☐ Guilt for not experiencing the joy of the child's birth
☐ Guilt for not experiencing affection toward the baby
☐ Fear of losing control and hurting the baby
☐ Difficulty caring for self and the child
☐ Overwhelmed by chores
☐ Posttraumatic delivery disorder: Inception is 1 to 6 months after delivery, and there is a high risk of developing a serious depression. The symptoms are the same as those that characterize posttraumatic stress disorder (PTSD). Childbirth Connection surveys (DeClercq, Sakala, Corry, & Applebaum, 2008a, 2008b) show that at least 9% of women who give birth meet childbirth-related PTSD criteria. Beck (2008) showed that up to 34% of women reported suffering from some kind of trauma during childbirth. According to several recent surveys and research, childbirth-related PTSD is underdiagnosed; this is because symptoms developed after childbirth are often not recognized and are erroneously ascribed to PPD (Ballard, Stanley, & Brockington, 1995).

Delivery-related traumatic experiences:

☐ Excessively painful or long labor
☐ Unexpected cesarean cut
☐ Experiencing a strong feeling of powerlessness
☐ Incapability, or loss of control
☐ Unexpected circumstances during delivery
☐ Lack of respect and/or consideration by hospital staff
☐ Intense fear of dying or of serious physical damage to the self or the child
☐ Retraumatization during a natural childbirth following a rape

Postpartum Depression and Childbirth-Related PTSD Risk Factors

☐ Anxiety and depression related
   ☐ Anxiety and/or depression during pregnancy
   ☐ Personal and/or family history with reported anxiety and/or depressive disorders
   ☐ Insecure attachment
   ☐ History of premenstrual dysphoric disorder
   ☐ Previous experience of postpartum depression or childbirth-related PTSD
☐ Trauma related
   ☐ Traumatic experience caused by difficult and/or particularly painful and/or premature deliveries
   ☐ Traumatic experience caused by prolonged hospitalization
   ☐ Traumatic experience caused by difficult pregnancies and/or gravidic pathologies
   ☐ Spontaneous abortion experience (particularly if repeated) or stillbirth
   ☐ Previous voluntary pregnancy termination
   ☐ Traumatic experience caused by sexual abuse or violence
   ☐ Caesarean birth (particularly if not planned)
   ☐ Complicated grief
☐ Family and/or relationship related
   ☐ Parental conflicts and/or problems caused by attachment to parental figures
   ☐ Unwanted or unplanned pregnancy
   ☐ Little support from partner
   ☐ Partner conflicts

□ Little support from and/or conflictual relationship(s) with family of origin and/or that of partner
□ Adolescent pregnancy
□ Single mother
□ Large family
□ Financial and/or work related
   □ Financial difficulties
   □ Professional and/or work problems caused by pregnancy
□ Hospital and/or medical related issues
   □ Little support and/or psychological abuse (disrespectful and/or unsympathetic attitude) during delivery on the part of medical and/or nursing staff
   □ Hospitalization of newborn baby because of health problems

EMDR Therapy Group Protocol for the Prevention of Birth Trauma and Postpartum Depression in the Pregnant Woman Script

Phase 1: Client History

Pregnancy

History of pregnancy: _____

_____

_____

□ Trying to get pregnant   □ Unplanned pregnancy   □ Difficult to get pregnant

□ Easy to get pregnant   □ Problems in pregnancy   □ No problems in pregnancy

Describe: _____

Negative consequences of pregnancy: _____

_____

_____

Experience of other pregnancies: _____

_____

_____

_____

Delivery

Family/friends with pregnancy, delivery/postpartum issues: □ Yes □ No

Describe: _____

Thoughts about giving birth: _____

_____

_____

_____

Worries based on what others said about giving birth: _____

_____

_____

Obstetric/gynecological surgery: ☐ Yes   ☐ No

Describe: _____

Experience with past deliveries: _____

_____

Assisted at live delivery/audiovisual: ☐ Yes   ☐ No

Describe: _____

Health problems for you/baby that could complicate delivery: ☐ Yes   ☐ No

Describe: _____

Thoughts about giving birth: _____

Negative thoughts about giving birth: ☐ Yes   ☐ No

Describe: _____

Maternity

Thoughts about role change from daughter to mother: _____

_____

_____

Thoughts about partner being father of child: _____

_____

Worries about partner being parent: ☐ Yes   ☐ No

Describe: _____

Worries about both of you being parents: ☐ Yes   ☐ No

Describe: _____

Worries about caring for your child: ☐ Yes   ☐ No

Describe: _____

Worries about being alone with child: ☐ Yes   ☐ No

Describe: _____

Negative thoughts about self when you think about after the birth: ☐ Yes   ☐ No

Describe: _____

Know the gender of baby?   ☐ Yes   ☐ No

Happy about gender of baby?   ☐ Yes   ☐ No

What looking forward to when child arrives:

_____

_____

Sexuality

Subject to sexual abuse or aggression: □ Yes   □ No

Describe: _____

Physical Safety

Accident where life at risk: □ Yes   □ No

Describe: _____

Hospitalized during life: □ Yes   □ No

Describe: _____

Subject to physical violence/assault: □ Yes   □ No

Describe: _____

Hopes, dreams, and expectations for child: _____

_____

_____

□ Completed above interview/history
□ Assessment measures
    □ Beck Depression Inventory (BDI)
    □ State-G Trait Anxiety Inventory (STAI—Y1 and Y2):
    □ Separation Anxiety Test (SAT)
□ Divitiis Anamnestic Questionnaire for Pregnancy

Phase 2: Preparation

"Now we'll proceed with work that is aimed at reinforcing your resources, so that you can feel stronger in the critical moments that you could have during delivery, as well as acquiring efficient tools to confront such moments/situations. In order to increase your strength and resistance to stressors, we will develop your personal resources. The goal is to develop specific characteristics/qualities that you consider to be crucial to your success in giving birth. At first, we will identify those characteristics that you would need and then anchor them in your body so that you can use them when necessary. We'll use bilateral stimulation (BLS), which is rhythmic and alternate stimulation of the two hemispheres in your brain to install these resources."

"Teach bilateral stimulation: *"Numerous scientific research studies have shown that bilateral stimulation (BLS) accelerates the innate adaptive information processing system. By stimulating neural connectors with adequate information, the adaptive information that was unable to link into memory networks holding the dysfunctionally stored information is now able to link in to these dysfunctional neural networks and facilitate normal memory processing."*

"Teach the following resources: (see EMDR Group Protocol for the Prevention of Birth Trauma and Postpartum Depression for Pregnant Women Notes Sheet.)

□ Concentration and Body Focus

"Now, remain concentrated on your body, listening to everything that happens. Notice what occurs in your body when you breathe. What moves? Feel the air enter and exit … feel the weight of the body, its heat… perceive all that touches your skin… and finally… remain concentrated on the 'full space' sensation of your body… remain concentrated on all the sensations that are occurring in your body as they happen."

"Now imagine how to be better focused and concentrated on your body during the labor phase, while applying the respiratory techniques to contain the pain of contractions and while you actively look for the most favorable position to move the child forward into the birth canal. Pay attention to how your body expands and relaxes when you breathe in. Feel how your birth canal dilates when you breathe in. Now, imagine how you succeed in concentrating during the expulsion phase, while you apply the respiratory techniques to strengthen your push that you learned in your course. Remember to use the respiratory techniques you have been practicing and how to modify them, depending on what is happening. Go with that."

"How did it go?" _____

_____

_____

"Were you able to imagine doing the techniques during delivery?"   □ Yes   □ No

Describe: _____

"What does your body feel when you visualize these images?" _____

_____

_____

□ *Establish A Safe Place Script*

Image: _____

Emotions and sensations: _____

Safe Place clue word/phrase: _____

Self-cuing: _____

□ *Mastery Resource Script*

Critical/Challenging moment/aspect/situation: _____

_____

_____

Personal quality or feature: _____

Mastery episode or mastery resource/script: _____

_____

_____

Mastery episode cue word/sentence: _____

□ *Inner Advisor/Coach Script*

Inner Coach resource: _____

_____

_____

Inner Coach cue word/sentence: _____

Phase 3: Assessment

Target Selection

"Before, considering all the childbirth processes, you identified a critical/challenging situation/moment/idea that represents an issue for you. What happens when you think of _____ (state the issue)?"

Incident:

Picture:

NC exs: "I'm weak"; "I can't do it"; "I'm powerless"; "I'm vulnerable"; "I'm not capable."

_____

PC exs.: "I'm smart"; "I'm strong enough"; "I can do it"; "I'm in control"; "I'm capable."

VoC: _____/7

Emotions: _____

SUD: _____/10

Location of body sensation: _____

Phase 4: Desensitization

Introduce according to EMDR Standard Protocol.

If looping occurs or past memories are compartmentalized and do not surface, use a Float-Back, affect scan, and/or cognitive interweave:

> *"When you see yourself stuck in _____ (state the critical moment, issue of delivery), when have you had that _____ (state the NC, or the negative body feeling) _____ in the past?"*

If SUD = 1 or more, continue processing.

If SUD continues to be 0 after two sets of BLS, go to the installation phase.

Phase 5: Installation

PC: ☐ Completed

New PC (if new one is better): _____

VoC: _____/7

Incident + PC + BLS

Continue installation with BLS until material becomes increasingly adaptive.

If VoC = 6 or less, check and see if there is a limiting belief:

> *"Which thoughts or concerns prevent you from feeling those words as completely true?"* _____

Note: If the limiting belief is not resolved quickly, explore to see whether there are any limiting beliefs or unidentified/unprocessed memory(ies)/networks that are causing this difficulty.

The session is then considered incomplete; therefore, return to the incomplete target and continue the installation process in the next session.

Phase completed   ☐ Yes   ☐ No

Phase 6: Body Scan

> *"Close your eyes, and keep in mind the original memory and the words _____ (state the positive belief). Then bring your attention to different parts of your body, starting with your head and working downward. Any place you find any tension, tightness, or any unusual feeling, let me know."*

Note: If the client reports any negative feeling, do a set of bilateral stimulation until it disappears. If the client reports positive feelings, continue with bilateral stimulation in order to strengthen them.

The Final Installation: The Expanded Future Template

> *"Imagine an internal space such as a comfortable room, or a beautiful space outdoors, in which you can comfortably sit and see a large projection screen in front of you. On this screen, you can project scenes of yourself effectively dealing with all the difficulties and critical/challenging moments/situations that you think you will come across during childbirth, from the beginning of the labor to the end of the delivery phase. Visualize how you would actually use the resources to cope with these difficulties and how that feels in your body. Pay attention to your body as you competently go through the birthing process. Let me know whenever any discomfort arises and we will stop the visualization and reprocess any discomforts until you can imagine the task with a positive full-body experience."*

After processing any blocks that arise, focus on the successes:

> *"Imagine being in that space in which you can picture and mentally rehearse your childbirth experience. See a projection screen in front of you and imagine that you can see images of yourself projected onto that screen _____ (state whatever task needs to be done)."*

Phase completed   ☐ Yes   ☐ No

Phase 7: Closure

> *"The work we have done today could continue. You may or may not notice new bodily sensations, thoughts, memories, or dreams. Should this happen, note it, describing it as a picture and the next time we'll take it into consideration. Please write down the positive experiences, too."*

> *"Remember to practice your relaxation techniques and Safe Place every day to increase your expertise in supporting yourself during the birth process."*

Phase completed   ☐ Yes   ☐ No

Phase 8: Reevaluation

Phase completed   ☐ Yes   ☐ No

References

American Psychiatric Association. (2013). *Diagnostic and statistical manual of mental disorders* (5th ed.). Arlington, VA: American Psychiatric Publishing.

Ballard, C. G., Stanley, A. K., & Brockington, I. F. (1995). Post traumatic stress disorder (PTSD) after childbirth. *British Journal of Psychiatry, 166*, 525–528.

Beck, C. T. (2008). Impact of birth trauma on breastfeeding. *Nursing Research, 57*(4), 228–236.

Declercq, E. R., Sakala, C., Corry, M. P., & Applebaum, S. (2008a). *Childbirth connection. New mothers speak out*. New York, NY: Childbirth Connection.

Declercq, E. R., Sakala, C., Corry, M. P., & Applebaum, S. (2008b, August). *New mothers speak out: National survey results highlight women's postpartum experiences*. New York, NY: Childbirth Connection. Retrieved from http://www.childbirthconnection.org/pdfs/new-mothers-speak-out.pdf

Harris, B., Lovett, L., Newcombe, R. G., Read, G. F., Walker, R., & Riad-Fahmy, D. (1994). Maternity blues and major endocrine changes: Cardiff Puerperal Mood and Hormone Study II. *BMJ, 308*(9), 949–952.

EMDR Therapy Group Protocol for the Prevention of Birth Trauma and Postpartum Depression for Pregnant Women

Anna Maria De Divitiis and Marilyn Luber

Introduction

The growing attention of the World Health Organization concerning prevention has led to many health care programs and procedures aimed at the three types of prevention: primary, secondary, and tertiary. In Italy, this call for prevention in the Family Services field was to think about what would be most beneficial for issues of parenting and family health and well-being; the answer was to institute a prepartum course for delivery preparation and a postpartum course for parenting support. This has been a resounding success. The possibility of enhancing the effectiveness of these health procedures for prevention in pre- and postpartum care motivated this author to develop integrated protocols for individuals and groups of women to support the prevention of birth trauma and postpartum depression.

The Obstetric Psychoprophylaxis in Childbirth
Course/Childbirth Preparation Class

Private and public health care facilities routinely offer courses on preparing for childbirth. They usually consist of a course referred to as *psychoprophylaxis*; this is a method of preparing women for natural childbirth by means of special breathing and relaxation. For primary prevention, the goal is giving mothers (and fathers/partners) the resources needed to handle the demands that occur in the process of childbirth. These types of courses prepare women for childbirth by teaching them about the process that they have begun and teaching them the types of skills that they will need to make the experience a successful one for all involved. The group format supports the participants in sharing the experience of pregnancy and imminent birth experience with other pregnant women. In this way, women have the opportunity to open up—within the parameters set in the group—about their uncertainties, fears, weaknesses, and difficulties. By realizing that others have fears too, and often are thinking the same kinds of thoughts, these pregnant women can begin to realize that they are not so different from the other members and do not have to face their concerns alone. In this way, they receive comfort and support.

This course usually consists of 8 to 10 group meetings lasting approximately 90 to 120 minutes. Attendance is kept at a maximum of 10 women. The women who attend these courses are usually prepared to learn new information regarding childbirth and future motherhood, and share with the other pregnant women their experience of pregnancy and the impending birth.

The EMDR Therapy Protocol for the Prevention of Birth Trauma and Postpartum Depression for Pregnant Women can be inserted into these types of courses. This protocol is included at the end of a prenatal class, when women are already informed about all of the phases of childbirth and have been trained to use the appropriate breathing and relaxation techniques, pushing positions, modes, and so on.

Obstetric Psychoprophylaxis in Childbirth Course/Childbirth Preparation Class and EMDR Therapy

This author has introduced EMDR Therapy into the Obstetric Psychoprophylaxis in Childbirth Course/Childbirth Preparation Class that includes Piscicelli's Respiratory Autogenic Training (RAT) method (1977, 1987). Piscicelli's RAT is a delivery preparation method that has been recognized by the Italian Ministry of Health and is used in all the Italian public and private health centers (family planning centers and obstetric departments in hospitals and clinics). The aim of this method, as well as any other preparation method for childbirth, is to support pregnant women in gaining a series of competences, including strengthening abilities of relaxation and concentration, the understanding of the body, and increased proprioception (ability to sense stimuli arising within the body regarding position, motion, and equilibrium), by using exercises consisting of breathing, sensory integration, and visualization.

The EMDR Therapy Group Protocol for the Prevention of Birth Trauma and Postpartum Depression for Pregnant Women can be used easily with any other delivery preparation method, such as *Childbirth Without Fear* (Read, 1944), *Active Birth* (Balaskas, 1983), *Metodo Leboyer* (Leboyer, 1975), and so on.

Research

At present, research is being conducted to ascertain the effectiveness of the EMDR Therapy Group Protocol for the Prevention of Birth Trauma and Postpartum Depression. The first preliminary sample consisted of 60 women, ages 21 to 46, who had given birth from 10 to 26 weeks earlier, and were enrolled in the postpartum courses. The experimental group consisted of half of the sample and was made up of new mothers who had previously attended the delivery preparation course and had the EMDR Therapy Group Protocol for the Prevention of Birth Trauma and Postpartum Depression. The members of the control group made up the other half and were new mothers who attended the delivery preparation course at other centers (or had not attended any course) and had not followed the present protocol. Women suffering from psychotic problems, dissociative disorders, and active substance abuse disorders were excluded. Both groups were further subdivided into women who had given birth naturally and women who had given birth by cesarean. Women were given several assessment measures: the Edinburgh Postnatal Depression Scale (EDPS; Cox & Holden, 2003; Cox, Holden, & Sagovsky, 1987), the Impact of Event Scale–Revised (IES-R; Weiss, 2007), and the Anamnestic Questionnaire for Postpartum (De Divitiis, 2010).

The test results indicate that the experimental group presented a smaller number of postpartum depression cases or birth trauma disorders than did the control group, in particular in the subgroup of women who gave birth by cesarean. Regarding the EPDS results, no new mother in the experimental group reached the criteria for postnatal depression, whereas three women in the control group reached the criteria for postnatal depression (two of them had given birth by cesarean). The average EPDS scores of the entire experimental group were also lower than those of the control group. As for the IES-R, only three women in the experimental group partially met the criteria for a posttraumatic stress disorder (PTSD) diagnosis, whereas four new mothers in the control group exceeded the cutoff for the diagnosis of PTSD (three of them had given birth by cesarean). The average IES-R scores of the experimental group were significantly lower than those of the control group. Further details of this research will be published in the future.

EMDR Therapy Group Protocol for the Prevention of Birth Trauma and Postpartum Depression for Pregnant Women Script Notes

The main objective of this group protocol is to reduce the incidence of childbirth PTSD and postpartum depression so that women can prepare for the critical moments in the process of childbirth in the same way an athlete would prepare for a peak performance. This is done by strengthening their resilience and reducing—as much as possible—the negative effects of the risk factors described in Chapter 9. This protocol integrates the use of the following EMDR-related protocols:

- Butterfly Hug (BH; Artigas & Jarero, 2009, 2010; Artigas, Jarero, Maurer, Alcalà, & Lopez Cano, 2000) for bilateral stimulation (BLS)
- Resource Development and Installation (RDI; Korn & Leeds, 2002; Leeds & Shapiro, 2000) for increasing resiliency
- EMDR Performance Enhancement Psychology Protocol (EMDR-PEP; Lendl & Foster, 2009)
- Written Workbook for Individual or Group EMDR (Birnbaum, 2006, 2009, 2013) for group structured reprocessing
- EMDR Integrative Group Treatment Protocol (IGTP; Artigas, Jarero, Alcalà, & Lopez Cano, 2009, 2014 & Jarero, Artigas, 2010) for installing specific personal resources for each woman to increase resiliency and for desensitizing and reprocessing information/ targets that might interfere with the childbirth process
- Future template: Anticipatory anxiety (Shapiro, 2001, 2006) for the processing of issues related to the childbirth process as an event that happens in the future.

Consequently, the present protocol includes the following advantages:

- *Resiliency*: Teaches women to feel strong, powerful, and in control during childbirth
- *Positive childbirth experience*: Facilitates positive childbirth experiences
- *Positive post-childbirth training*: Supports self-esteem and self-efficacy concerning taking care of newborn and handling new requirements connected to the altered family context
- *Reprocessing nonpathological issues*: Reprocesses nonpathological issues such as fear of failure, not being sufficiently strong or capable, negative prejudices regarding childbirth, setbacks, and so on
- *Increased access*: Extends primary prevention to the greatest number of women possible
- *Building competence versus resolving personal problems*: Allows women to develop competency in managing childbirth even if they are not interested in facing personal problems
- *EMDR Therapy*: Uses EMDR Therapy with a group of pregnant women who are already a cohesive group
- *Mother–child dyad*: Increases favorable conditions for the establishment of a fulfilling mother–child dyad that supports effective communication and secure attachment
- *Couple support*: Supports the mother in being more present within the couple and her other social relationships so that she does not create an exclusive relationship with her child

Group Selection

Only the pregnant women who have attended the Obstetric Psychoprophylaxis in Childbirth Course/Childbirth Preparation Course can participate in the EMDR Therapy Group Protocol for Primary Depression. The ideal number of participants ranges from 5 to 8, with a maximum of 10. Women suffering from psychotic problems, dissociative disorders, and active substance abuse disorders are excluded from these groups and referred to specific, specialized centers, or, when possible, are treated by the clinician herself. The participants are selected taking into consideration the following information:

- Information collected from the interview for entry into the Obstetric Psychoprophylaxis in Childbirth Course/Childbirth Preparation Course
- Measurements administered (EPDS, IES-R, and Anamnestic Questionnaire for Postpartum)
- De Divitiis Anamnestic Questionnaire for Pregnancy (see Addendum in Chapter 9)

Individual Issues

Before applying the EMDR Therapy Group Protocol for the Prevention of Birth Trauma and Postpartum Depression for Pregnant Women, the authors suggest that clinicians treat women who present issues related to complicated grief; traumatic experiences related to assault, rape, abortion (spontaneous and induced), difficult/dangerous delivery (oneself or loved ones); and critical incidents with the Standard EMDR Protocol, as these adverse life experiences and/or traumas are easily reactivated by the childbirth process. The authors advise against using EMDR Therapy, at this time, with women presenting with complex posttraumatic stress disorders (CPTSD) and/or dissociative disorders or serious trauma attachment issues, for the following reasons:

- Lack of sufficient time to resolve such matters
- Greater emotional reactivity and less mood stability, due to the hormonal variations caused by pregnancy
- High risk of destabilizing the expectant mother by reactivating highly disturbing memories

However, if during the application of the following protocol, traumatic experiences of this kind emerge, make a note of them and address them after childbirth.

Timing

The EMDR Therapy Group Protocol for the Prevention of Birth Trauma and Postpartum Depression for Pregnant Women is administered in a single session, and as the last session, at the end of the delivery preparation course. It is set up this way so that the pregnant women are aware in detail of everything that happens physiologically during the various phases of childbirth, and in what order, and the obstetric techniques needed. Thus, women are well prepared for the types of challenges they will face and how they will need to pace themselves as they go through this process. Based on prior experience, application of the protocol takes, on average, from 120 to 150 minutes, depending on the number of participants.

Clinicians

It is preferable that the clinician who conducts the childbirth preparation course also be the person who leads the EMDR Therapy Group Protocol for the Prevention of Birth Trauma and Postpartum Depression for Pregnant Women. If this is not possible, it is essential for the clinician to have a complete and precise knowledge of the techniques that are taught and the information that is supplied to the expectant mothers, so that the clinician can refer to it during the application of the protocol. The practitioner for the group should have completed the EMDR Therapy Basic Training.

The staff consists of the Lead Clinician (LC) and the Assistant Clinician (AC) who have been trained in the administration of this protocol. The role of the AC is to supply emotional support to the expectant mothers who might need assistance during the course of the class. The AC also walks around among the participants, offering help and clarification about how to fill out the Notes Sheet (see the end of this chapter).

Note: The Notes Sheet information is helpful not only in this primary prevention protocol, but can also be used for secondary prevention work during the postpartum course.

EMDR Therapy Group Protocol for the Prevention of Birth Trauma and Postpartum Depression for Pregnant Women Script

Phase 1: History

During enrollment for the delivery preparation course, the clinician conducts an individual interview with all the women who are to take the course, including the following questions.

Pregnancy

Say, *"Tell me about the history of this pregnancy."*

_____

_____

Say, *"How are you dealing with it?"*

_____

_____

Say, *"Were you trying to get pregnant, or is it an unplanned pregnancy?"*

_____

_____

Say, *"Was it difficult to get pregnant, or did it happen easily?"*

_____

_____

Say, *"Has this pregnancy presented any problems or any disorders, or has everything always gone well?* (risks of miscarriage, confined to bed for a period of time, bad nausea, sialorrhoea [i.e., excessive salivation or drooling], etc.)."

_____

_____

Say, *"Has this pregnancy had any negative consequences such as loss of job, interruption of studies, tensions with or separation from partner, tensions and/ or arguments with some members of your or your partner's family?"*

_____

_____

For multiparous women, say the following:

Say, *"How was the experience of your previous pregnancy?"*

_____

_____

Say, *"How do you feel about it?"*

_____

_____

Delivery

Say, *"Have there been any close relatives or friends who had any difficulties in their pregnancy, delivery, or postpartum?"*

_____

_____

If so, say, *"Could you tell me what happened?"*

_____

_____

Say, *"What are your thoughts about having to give birth?"*

_____

_____

Say, *"Has anybody ever told you about any childbirth experience which upset and/or worried you?"*

_____

_____

Say, *"Have you ever had any experience with obstetric–gynecological surgery?"*

_____

_____

If so, say, *"What was the experience like?"*

_____

_____

For pluriparae, say the following:

Say, *"What was/were your experience(s) of your previous delivery/deliveries like?"*

_____

_____

Say, *"What do you remember about it/them?"*

_____

_____

Say, *"Have you ever assisted at a delivery live or even through audiovisual means (e.g., television, the Internet, etc.)?"*

_____

_____

If so, say, *"What are your impressions of childbirth?"*

_____

_____

Say, *"Have you or your baby had any health problems that could complicate the delivery?"*

_____

_____

Say, *"What do you think about childbirth?"*

_____

_____

Say, *"What do you think about the fact that you are going to give birth?"*

_____

_____

Say, *"Are there any negative thoughts that you are having about yourself when you think of giving birth?"*

_____

_____

Maternity

Say, *"What do you think about the fact that your role will change from that of a daughter to that of a mother?"*

_____

_____

Say, *"What do you think about your partner being the father of your child?"*

_____

_____

Say, *"Do you have any worries about you and/or your partner being parents?"*

_____

_____

Say, *"What about when the baby arrives? How are you feeling about caring for your child?"*

_____

_____

Say, *"Are you concerned about being alone with your child?"*

_____

_____

Say, *"Are there any negative thoughts that you are having about yourself when you think about after the birth?"*

_____

_____

Say, *"Do you know the gender of your baby?"*

_____

_____

If so, say, *"Are you happy about the gender of your baby?"*

_____

_____

Say, *"Describe how you imagine your baby will be."*

_____

_____

Say, *"What are you looking forward to the most when your child arrives?"*

_____

_____

Sexuality

Say, *"Have you ever been subject to sexual abuse or aggression?"*

_____

_____

If so, say, *"Could you tell me what happened?"*

_____

_____

Physical Safety

Say, *"Have you ever had an accident of any kind where your life was at risk?"*

_____

_____

If so, say, *"Could you tell me what happened?"*

_____

_____

Say, *"Have you been hospitalized at any time during your life?"*

_____

_____

Say, *"Have you ever been subject to physical violence (assault)?"*

_____

_____

If so, say, *"Could you tell me what happened?"*

_____

_____

_____

Say, *"What are your hopes, dreams, and expectations for your child?"*

_____

_____

This information, together with the results obtained from the specific tests and the De Divitiis Anamnestic Questionnaire for Pregnancy (see Addendum to Chapter 9), allows the clinician to conceptualize the case of every woman in the group.

Phase 2: Preparation

Note: No formal introduction is needed, as this is the eighth session of the course.

Explanations of the Modality, Objectives, and Fundamentals of the Work

It is important to explain to the women the purpose of the group, as well as its structure and how it will unfold.

> Say, *"Today, we are going to work on reinforcing the resources that you have, or adding to them, to increase your strength and support your dealing with the stress that you will encounter during those difficult times that might occur during the delivery process.*
>
> *Since you are each unique, with your own strengths and weaknesses, I will encourage you to find the resources that will be most suitable to you and assist you in preparing for this process."*

Self-Administered BLS: BH

> Say, *"I will be introducing you to something called the Butterfly Hug (BH) that uses bilateral stimulation (BLS). BLS consists of the rhythmic and alternate stimulation of the two hemispheres of our brain that allows for the installation of the resources we will be learning.*
>
> *Please watch me and do what I am doing. Cross your arms over your chest, so that the tip of the middle finger from each hand is placed below the clavicle or*

the collarbone and the other fingers and hands cover the area that is located under the connection between the collarbone and the shoulder and the collarbone and sternum or breastbone. Hands and fingers must be as vertical as possible so that the fingers point toward the neck and not toward the arms.

Now interlock your thumbs to form the butterfly's body and the extension of your other fingers outward will form the butterfly's wings.

Your eyes can be closed, or partially closed, looking toward the tip of your nose. Next, you alternate the movement of your hands, like the flapping wings of a butterfly. Let your hands move freely. You can breathe slowly and deeply (abdominal breathing) while you observe what is going through your mind and body, such as thoughts, images, sounds, odors, feelings, and physical sensations, without changing, pushing your thoughts away, or judging. You can pretend as though what you are observing is like clouds passing by."

Develop Resources and Instructions for the Group

Emphasize the importance of learning these new resources to assist in the delivery:

Say, *"During this course, you are all moving toward the birthing of your baby. It is important for you to know that no one can make you deliver your baby; it is a process that occurs and works best when your body and mind work together. With this in mind, I will be teaching you ways to support your learning how to stay concentrated on yourself by listening to the signals that your body will be sending so that you can respond during each moment of the birthing process."*

Reinforce the instructions for the group:

Say, *"Later we'll be reprocessing disturbing information, which will help us to overcome every possible physical or mental block, every doubt or fear, which could interfere with the carrying-out of what we learned during the delivery preparation course. We'll use the Butterfly Hug as BLS and the Notes Sheet you were given to note down briefly all your thoughts, feelings, sensations, pictures, and scenes that emerge during the process.*

Please take out your Note Sheet so that I can step you through how we will be using it.

I suggest you reply very concisely, using only one word or one sentence, because our time is limited. You can see the step-by step instructions on your Notes Sheet and can proceed at your own pace. You can keep it with you to help you remember what you have done here. I will also keep a copy to use for the follow-up that will take place after your babies are born."

These positive resources are taken from the work on EMDR-PEP and RDI, using material elicited from the client. Use 1 or 2 short sets of 6 to 12 BHs, to install each resource separately, as indicated later.

1. CONCENTRATION AND BODY FOCUS

This technique is to help expectant mothers develop the skills to remain concentrated on themselves and in touch with their body sensations. The sensations used in delivery preparation are the ones reinforced here: weight, heat, contact, and "full space."

Note: *Full space* refers to the summation of all the sensations mentioned previously (weight, heat, contact) that were learned in the delivery preparation course; or use the appropriate term from the course that you have used.

Concentration is a skill that allows the women to remain centered on themselves—while staying sufficiently relaxed—so that they can implement the delivery techniques they have learned in their birthing classes.

Say, *"Now, remain concentrated on your body, listening to everything that happens. Notice what occurs in your body when you breathe. What moves? Feel the air enter and exit ... feel the weight of the body, its heat...perceive all that touches your skin ... and finally ... remain concentrated on the 'full space' sensation of your body... remain concentrated on all the sensations that are occurring in your body as they happen."*

Invite the women to do 2 slow, short sets of 6 to 12 BLS.

Say, *"Go with that."*

Say, *"Take a deep breath and describe what you are noticing."*

_____

_____

Say, *"Well, now imagine how to be better focused and concentrated on your body during the labor phase, while applying the respiratory techniques to contain the pain of contractions and while you actively look for the most favorable position to move the child forward into the birth canal.*

Pay attention to how your body expands and relaxes when you breathe in.

Feel how your birth canal dilates when you breathe in.

Now, imagine how you succeed in concentrating during the expulsion phase, while you apply the respiratory techniques to strengthen your push that you learned in your course.

Remember to use the respiratory techniques you have been practicing and how to modify them, depending on what is happening. Go with that."

Do two slow sets of BLS.

Ask for feedback and be sure that all the women can imagine being able to do the techniques acquired in the course during the delivery phase.

Say, *"Take a deep breath and describe what you are noticing."*

Say, *"How did it go?"*

_____

_____

Say, *"Were you able to imagine doing the techniques during delivery?"*

_____

_____

Say, *"What does your body feel when you visualize these images? Describe what you are noticing."*

_____

_____

After installation, to be sure that they have acquired the skills to stay concentrated and body-focused, it is helpful to have the women do the exercise even in the presence of a distracting element such as loud acoustic disturbances. While the women practice the preceding exercise, at two-minute intervals the clinician produces loud noises such as banging on a triangle, clapping hands, and/or beating on objects to help women learn to get away from the distracting element and continue to remain relaxed and centered on themselves. A single acoustic disturbance lasts from 50 to 60 seconds, which is the length of one contraction and occurs every 2 minutes, so as to give the women a facsimile of what they will have to deal with during the birth process. This exercise is helpful because it allows the women to learn how to stay focused and relaxed—without panicking—even with a distracting element such as the intense pain of contractions.

> Say, *"Let's repeat the exercise, but this time I am going to 'bother you' with loud noises. The challenge for you will be to remain relaxed and centered on yourselves even when there is a great deal of noise going on, because this will help you during the childbirthing process. Any questions?"*

_____

_____

> Say, *"OK. Let's start. Well, now imagine how to be better focused and concentrated on your body during the labor phase, while applying the respiratory techniques to contain the pain of contractions and while you actively look for the most favorable position to move the child forward into the birth canal."*

Go up to each woman individually and introduce a loud sound.

> *"Pay attention to how your body expands and relaxes when you breathe in.*
>
> *Feel how your birth canal dilates when you breathe in.*
>
> *Now, imagine how you succeed in concentrating during the expulsion phase, while you apply the respiratory techniques to strengthen your push that you learned in your course.*
>
> *Remember to use the respiratory techniques you have been practicing and how to modify them, depending on what is happening. Go with that."*

Do two slow sets of BLS.

Ask for feedback and be sure that all the women can imagine being able to do the techniques acquired in the course during the delivery phase.

> Say, *"Take a deep breath and describe what you are noticing."*
>
> Say, *"How did it go?"*

_____

_____

When all the women can relax and concentrate on their own bodies, perceiving pleasant bodily sensations, it is helpful to assist the women to acquire self-containment and relaxation. Install the Calm/Safe Place, a resource that is used between contractions to help replenish energy and stay relaxed.

2. ESTABLISH A SAFE PLACE SCRIPT (SHAPIRO, 1995, 2006)

Image

> Say, *"Imagine a place, real or virtual, in which you feel a sense of refuge, well-being, freedom, and peace of mind. Perhaps being on the beach or sitting by a mountain stream."* (Pause)
>
> Say, *"Where would you be?"*

Say, *"Focus on your safe (or calm) place. Note the details: its sights, sounds, smells, colors, temperature. Describe it briefly in the space provided on your Notes Sheet."*

_____

_____

Emotions and Sensations

Say, *"Notice the emotions and physical sensations that you feel when imagining being in the place."* (Pause)

Say, *"What do you feel in your body?"*

_____

_____

If all the mothers-to-be report pleasant physical sensations, you can proceed to the next step; otherwise, it is necessary to help those who have not perceived any positive sensations to find an adequate Safe Place.

Enhancement

When the whole group holds/reaches a valid safe/secure place, you can then proceed with the BH.

Say, *"Bring up the image of that place. Concentrate on where you feel the pleasant sensations in your body and allow yourself to enjoy them."*

Two sets of slow BHs are advised.

Say, *"How do you feel now?"*

The expectant mothers can use a conventional signal to communicate their sensations; for instance, they can raise the index finger of the right hand when the sensations are positive and the index finger of the left hand when the sensations are unpleasant.

Say, *"To signal us how you are feeling, raise the index finger of your right hand when the sensations are positive* (demonstrate raising the index finger of the right hand) *and raise the index finger of your left hand when the sensations are negative* (demonstrate raising the index finger of the left hand)."

If positive, say, *"Focus on that."*
Repeat BLS.

Say, *"What do you notice now?"*

Repeat several times if the process has enhanced the women's positive feelings and sensations.

Identification of the Cue Word for the Safe Place

Cue words are verbal stimuli associated with the resource, capable of activating the relevant psychophysiological state when recalled to mind.

Say, *"What word goes best with that place?"*

Or say, *"Is there a word or phrase that represents your safe (or calm) place?"*

Say, *"Note it down on your Notes Sheet."*

_____

_____

Then say, ""*Think of* _____ (cue word or phrase) *and your safe (or calm) place and notice the positive feeling you have when you think of that word/phrase. Now concentrate on those sensations and the cue word and do two slow sets of Butterfly Hugs.*"

Say, *"How do you feel now?"*

Enhance positive feelings with BLS two or three times.

Installing the Cue Word

Say, *"Link the memory, the physical sensations, and your cue words together. Use three sets of Butterfly Hugs."*

Use 3 sets of 6 to 12 BLS with BH.
Between the sets, always ask how your client is doing by saying the following:

Say, *"How do you feel now?"*

Say, *"How are you now?"*

Cuing With Disturbance

Say, *"Now imagine a minor annoyance and how it feels."* (Pause)

Say, *"Do you feel disturbance? Notice what you are feeling in your body, and where you feel it."*

Say, *"Now bring up your safe (or calm) place and notice any shifts in your body and do some slow sets of Butterfly Hugs."*

Use slow sets of BHs.

Self-Cuing With Disturbance

This technique can also be used as an emotional self-containment resource, to cope with the critical moments that may occur throughout childbirth (Shapiro, 2006).

Say, *"Now imagine yourself during those moments of respite among the contractions or while you are pushing."*

Pause.

Say, *"Do you feel disturbance? Notice what you are feeling in your body, and where you feel it."*

Pause.

Say, *"Now bring up your safe (or calm) place and notice any shifts in your body as you relive that sense of well-being. Do 2 or 3 sets of 6 to 10 Butterfly Hugs."*

Say, *"Raise the index finger of your right hand when the sensations are positive and the finger of your left hand when the sensations are negative."*

Guide the women through the process until they are able to experience the positive emotions and sensations. Repeat as often as necessary.

Say, *"If you like, write something about it on your Notes Sheet."*

_____

_____

Practice

Say, *"I'd like you to practice using your safe place daily, thinking of those moments of respite among the contractions or during the pushing, between now and your childbirth, so as to keep this resource vivid in your mind and continue to benefit from its relaxing effect. Do you have any questions?"*

3. MASTERY RESOURCE SCRIPT (KORN & LEEDS, 2002)

Identify the Challenging or Critical (Target) Situation

Say, *"Consider the whole process of childbirth, from the beginning of labor to the end of the delivery stage, and identify the most demanding, critical, or challenging moment that you expect."*

Say, *"Please note them briefly on the Notes Sheet."*

_____

_____

Identifying the Resource(s) From Client's Past: Personality Features or Qualities

Ask participants to identify the personality features or qualities they think should be strengthened to better cope with the previously identified critical moment or fear, such as, for instance, courage, strength, self-control, self-confidence, serenity, optimism, tenacity, patience, and so on.

Note: Major themes include safety, responsibility, and choice/control.

Domain	Critical Issues/Difficult Moments	Quality or Features
Responsibility	"I've always been weak, I'm afraid I won't be able to push in the expulsion stage"	Strength (in body or mind)
Responsibility	"I can't do it on my own; if I imagine myself during delivery, I don't think I can succeed"	Faith in oneself; personal strength
Choice/Control	"I cannot bear seeing blood, I am sure I will faint"	Self-control; self-containment
Safety	"I can't stand the idea of entrusting my body to others, even if they are professionals"	Capacity of trusting (in body and mind)

Say, *"At that critical/challenging moment/situation, what would you like to be able to do?"*

Say, *"What would you like to believe about yourself?"*

Say, *"What would you like to feel?"*

Say, *"So, what personality quality or feature do you think would be useful to better cope with the critical/challenging moments of your childbirth?"*

Or say, *"What quality or feature do you believe that you need to develop in order to deal effectively with this critical/challenging moment/situation?"*

Say, *"Describe it briefly in the space provided on your Notes Sheet."*

_____

_____

Identifying Resource (Mastery Episode or Mastery Resource Script)

Say, *"Scan your memory for a positive episode or experience where you felt that particular quality you identified before."*

Say, *"Describe it briefly in the space provided on your Notes Sheet."*

_____

_____

Check the Validity of the Resource

Say, *"Now concentrate on the episode identified and notice the accompanying emotions and body sensations."*

Note: If negative emotions or body sensations arise, the causes should not be investigated.

The client is helped by the AC to identify another mastery memory capable of eliciting positive emotions and body sensations. When all the women have a valid resource available, then proceed to the installation phase.

Installation Resource of Mastery Episode/Script

Say, *"Concentrate on the episode identified and use the Butterfly Hug about 6 to 12 times."*

Say, *"What do you feel in your body?"* Pause.

Say, *"Where do you feel it?"* Pause.

Say, *"Concentrate again on the episode identified and the body sensations and use 2 sets of 6 to 12 Butterfly Hugs."*

Say, *"What do you notice?"*

Say, *"Do a set of 6 to 12 Butterfly Hugs each."*

Identifying the Cue Words Associated With the Mastery Episode

Say, *"What word goes together with that memory?"*

Or, say, *"When you go back to that experience, what are the most positive words you can say to yourself now?"*

Say, *"Write down the words/statement on your Notes Sheet."*

_____

_____

Expectant women in general find words or phrases aimed at self-soothing, self-containment, and self-support helpful.

Say, *"Some expectant women find these words helpful when trying to self-soothe, contain their emotions, or give words of encouragement."*

"Go on!"

"I can make it!"

"Keep up!"

"I am able to remain calm. Relax!"

"I'm strong enough, I can resist!"

"I am trained, I can do it!"

"I can trust the hospital staff, they are here to help me!"

"I can hold on, it's just a moment, it will go away!"

Installation of the Cue Word Associated With the Mastery Episode

Say, *"Link the memory, the physical sensations, and your words together and let's do two to three sets of Butterfly Hugs."*

4. INNER ADVISOR/COACH SCRIPT (LENDL & FOSTER, 2009, PP. 390–391)

Identify the Inner Advisor or Coach

Say, *"Imagine an actual person or virtual being who can be an inner resource for you, like an Inner Coach supporting and soothing you during the critical states of childbirth. This may be some part of yourself, like your Higher or Wiser Self. Imagine this person's or being's voice calming you when you are upset or frustrated and reminding you of your strengths, talents, and positive qualities. Go ahead and do that now and let me know what you hear."*

Say, *"Write down who you have chosen."*

_____

_____

Say, *"Great. Go with that and do a slow set of 6 to 12 Butterfly Hugs."*

Say, *"Now imagine calling _____ (him/her), the way _____ (he/she) appears to you, where _____ (he/she) is located in your field of vision, how _____ (he/she) greets you, _____ (his/her) voice tone, _____ (his/her) facial expression, and where _____ (he/she) goes to place space between you; that is, in front, beside, or slightly behind you."*

Say, *"How do you feel when _____ (he/she) is with you?"*

Say, *"Do you feel stronger or more positive?"*

Say, *"Do you need to add or delete anything to make it more positive?"*

Say, *"Do a slow set of 6 to 12 Butterfly Hugs."*

Check the Validity of the Inner Coach

Say, *"Now concentrate on the Inner Coach. What do you notice?"* Pause.

Say, *"What do you feel in your body and where?"* Pause.

If negative emotions or body sensations arise, do not investigate them. Identify another Inner Coach. When all the pregnant women have a valid Inner Coach, proceed with the installation.

Installation of Inner Coach

Say, *"Imagine this person's voice soothing or encouraging you in difficult times and reminding you of your strong points and positive features and link what you feel in your body. Do a set of 6 to 12 slow Butterfly Hugs."*

Cue Word or Sentence Identification

Say, *"Imagine _____ (state Inner Coach) voice soothing or encouraging you in difficult moments/situations of your childbirth and reminding you of your strong points and positive features. What words would you want your Inner Coach to say?"*

Say, *"Note the word or sentences on your Notes Sheet."*

_____

_____

Install the Cue Word or Sentence Identification

Say, *"Now see and hear_____ (the Inner Coach) coming toward you, smiling at you, saying hello, staying close to you and telling you the words of encouragement you would like to hear, reminding you of your strong points and positive features and offering advice when you need it. Do 2 sets of 6 to 12 Butterfly Hugs."*

Ask for feedback and suggest that participants write down what they noticed. Conclude this part by saying the following:

Say, *"I suggest you practice the resources we have just installed at home in order to strengthen their effectiveness to further enhance your preparations for childbirth. You can then use them as you feel the need, and in the way you prefer, during the childbirth process."*

Phase 3: Assessment

Instructions for the Assessment and Desensitization Phases

Say, *"After this work, we focus in on our target and answer a few questions about thoughts and feelings surrounding it. We will begin processing using the Butterfly Hug. After each set of Butterfly Hugs, we will briefly write something about our response, and then continue with Butterfly Hugs and processing. Some things will come up or change, and sometimes they won't. There are no 'supposed to's' in this process. Just go with the flow and let whatever happens, happen, without judging it. If you have a problem or feel you have to stop, raise your hand."*

Target

Say, *"Consider the whole childbirth, from the beginning of labor to the end of the delivery stage, and identify the most demanding, critical, or challenging moment that you expect. Or, which aspect worries or frightens you the most?"*

Pause.

Say, *"Please take 30 seconds to write down your target on the Notes Sheet."*

_____

_____

Image

Say, *"What picture represents the entire issue?"*

Pause.

Say, *"Describe it briefly in the space provided on your Notes Sheet."*

_____

_____

If some women report several choices, the clinician assists by asking the following:

Say, *"What picture represents the worst part of your issue?"*

Say, *"Describe it briefly in the space provided on your Notes Sheet."*

_____

_____

Negative Cognition

Say, *"What words go best with the picture that express your negative belief about yourself now? For instance, others say things like, 'I'm weak'; 'I can't do it'; 'I'm powerless'; 'I'm vulnerable'; 'I'm not capable.'"*

Pause.

Say, *"Please write down your sentence on your Notes Sheet."*

_____

_____

Positive Cognition

Say, *"When you bring up that picture, or issue, what would you like to believe about yourself now? For instance, 'I'm smart'; 'I'm strong enough'; 'I can do it'; 'I'm in control'; 'I'm capable.'"*

Pause.

Say, *"Write down your sentence on your Notes Sheet."*

_____

_____

Validity of Cognition

Say, *"When you think of your picture, or your issue, how true do those positive words feel to you now, on a scale of 1 to 7, where 1 feels completely false and 7 feels completely true?"*

1   2   3   4   5   6   7

(completely false)   (completely true)

Emotions

Say, *"When you bring up the picture or your issue and negative words that go with it, what emotion do you feel now? For instance: afraid, discouraged, ashamed, or something else?"*

Pause

Say, *"Write down this emotion on your Notes Sheet."*

_____

_____

Subjective Units of Disturbance

Say, *"On a scale of 0 to 10, where 0 is no disturbance or neutral and 10 is the highest disturbance you can imagine, how disturbing does it feel now?"*

0   1   2   3   4   5   6   7   8   9   10

(no disturbance)   (highest disturbance)

Localization of Body Sensation

Say, *"Where do you feel it* (the disturbance) *in your body?"*

Say, *"Describe on your Notes Sheet your sensation and where you feel it in your body."*

_____

_____

Pause.

Phase 4: Desensitization

Say, *"Let's move on to processing. For each set, we'll do the Butterfly Hug for about 30 seconds. Then we'll pause, take a deep breath together, and briefly jot down a few words about what we noticed in the space provided on the Notes Sheet. Then, we'll repeat: Butterfly Hugs..., deep breath..., writing and so on. We'll do this for about five to six minutes. I'll let you know a couple of minutes before it's time to move on together to the next stage. So we'll begin with the target, and let ourselves go with whatever comes up. Any questions?"*

Say, *"Well, now go ahead and bring up the picture of the critical moment or issue that you are concerned about during your childbirth, those negative words you were saying about yourself. Notice where you are feeling it in your body, and begin with your Butterfly Hugs."*

The Lead Clinician starts doing BH to model how to do it for the group and inserts supportive comments to facilitate processing; for instance:

Say, *"Good"; "Go with that"; "Just notice."*

After about 30 seconds of processing with BH, say the following:

Say, *"Well, now let's take a deep breath... and then just notice what you get now... please take 30 seconds to write down a few words."*

_____

_____

A pause of 30 seconds.

Say, *"OK, let's continue with Butterfly Hugs and processing. Again, go with the flow, let whatever happens happen. After about 30 seconds, or when you feel a change, take a deep breath, and write something about what you noticed."*

Note: The LC continues to do BHs and to provide positive comments during the entire session. The LC will decide on the number of sets to be used, and intervenes with cognitive interweave(s) if any woman gets stuck with a dysfunctional cognition. The AC walks around among the women, offering help and clarification about how to fill in the Notes Sheet. The AC can also intervene if any woman needs emotional support.

Say, *"In two minutes we'll move on to the next stage together. So, now we can do two more sets of Butterfly Hugs. Come on, let's go!"*

BHs for 30 seconds.

Say, *"OK, deep breath, notice what you get now, and take a few moments to write your thoughts in the space provided on your Notes Sheet."*

After repeating another set of BH and writing on the Notes Sheet, say the following:

Say, *"When you bring up the original target (critical moment or worst part of your childbirth), on a scale of 0 to 10, where 0 is no disturbance or neutral and 10 is the highest disturbance you can imagine, how disturbing does it feel to you now?"*

0   1   2   3   4   5   6   7   8   9   10

(no disturbance)   (highest disturbance)

It is possible to go to the next phase when the SUD = 0 for all the women, or when it has at least dropped to an ecological level for all concerned.

Phase 5: Installation

Check the PC

Say, *"Before we started processing, you chose a positive statement you wanted to believe about yourself. Do these positive words still fit, or is there another positive statement you feel would be more suitable? When you think of the original target (critical moment or worst part of your childbirth), what would you like to believe about yourself now?"*

Pause

Say, *"Please write down your PC on your Notes Sheet."*

Say, *"As you think of the original target, how true do those words feel, from 1 (completely false) to 7 (completely true)?"*

1   2   3   4   5   6   7

(completely false)   (completely true)

When all the pregnant women evaluate the PC to be true at a level of 5, then it is possible to proceed to tie the PC to the critical moment.

Installation of the PC

Say, *"Think of the event, and hold it together with the positive words you chose. Let's do one set of 10 Butterfly Hugs."*

Say, *"How true does it feel to you now?"*

1   2   3   4   5   6   7

(completely false)   (completely true)

Say, *"Do sets of Butterfly Hugs to enhance the feeling of the PC."*

Phase 6: Body Scan

Say, *"Now close your eyes and keep in mind the original target and your positive thought. (Pause) Now bring your attention to the different parts of your body, starting with your head and working downward. Any place you find tension, tightness, or unusual sensation, just notice it and then start to do Butterfly Hugs. Keep doing Butterfly Hugs until you sense a change, and continue tapping as long as it seems to be helping you feel better. Good. We'll do this for the next couple of minutes."*

Pause. After about 90 seconds, say the following:

Say, *"Let's do another half minute of Butterfly Hugs and let go of any residual disturbance in our bodies that we don't need to hold onto right now."*

Say, *"Very good. Now take a deep breath, and jot down what you noticed and how you feel now."*

_____

_____

The Expanded Future Template (Lendl & Foster, 2009, pp. 395–396)

Using the expanded future template, the expectant mothers can project into the future their real ability to use the techniques learned during the delivery preparation course and the resources previously installed during the preparation phase. This is done to assist them in coping with the critical moments of childbirth by envisioning themselves collaborating actively and responding adaptively to the physiological changes occurring to their bodies during delivery. This allows the installation of the desired results and the reprocessing, using BHs, of any other possible disturbing element.

The Final Installation: The Expanded Future Template

Say, *"Imagine an internal space such as a comfortable room, or a beautiful space outdoors, in which you can comfortably sit and see a large projection screen in front of you. On this screen, you can project scenes of yourself effectively dealing with all the difficulties and critical/challenging moments/situations that you think you will come across during childbirth, from the beginning of the labor to the end of the delivery phase. Visualize how you would actually use the resources to cope with these difficulties and how that feels in your body. Pay attention to your body as you competently go through the birthing process. Let me know whenever any discomfort arises and we will stop the visualization and reprocess any discomforts until you can imagine the task with a positive full-body experience.*

After you do that, please describe briefly what you create on the Notes Sheet."

_____

_____

Say, *"Go with that and do 2 slow sets of 6 to 12 Butterfly Hugs as more positive sensations emerge, in order to install all of your desired skills."*

If negative sensations emerge, the LC makes sure that the participant has the time to reprocess any doubts, physical or mental blocks, or discomfort that may arise until the expectant mother(s) can imagine the entire process of childbirth with a positive full-body experience. If any of them cannot complete this during the allotted time, the clinician either makes an individual or group appointment (depending on the number of women) in which to conclude the reprocessing.

At the end say, *"OK, play the movie one more time from beginning to end. Go with that and use a slow set of Butterfly Hugs."*

Phase 7: Group Closure

Say, *"We will be stopping soon. You have done very good work, as individuals and as a group. Please write a few words about how you are feeling."*

Say, *"Once again, I would like to urge you to practice the resources we have installed previously. The processing we have done today may continue after the session. You may or may not notice new insights, thoughts, memories, or dreams. If so, just notice what you are experiencing—take a snapshot of it— what you are seeing, feeling, thinking, and the trigger, and keep a log. Go to your Calm/Safe Place if you need to process through any disturbances. In case this isn't sufficient, you can contact me to make an appointment, and we can use the new material as targets to be reprocessed."*

Phase 8: Reevaluation

As this protocol is applied in a single session, and is the last intervention of the delivery preparation course, the follow-up takes place during the first session of the postpartum course, 2 to 6 months after childbirth, in order to find out how the women have used it and how effective it was. The data gathered from this follow-up will constitute the basis of the work to be done during the postpartum course: the positive experiences will represent further resources to be installed and the negative experiences will be the targets to be reprocessed.

Summary

The goal of the EMDR Therapy Group Protocol for the Prevention of Birth Trauma and Postpartum Depression for Pregnant Women is that of conceptualizing and treating childbirth as a peak performance, promoting the women's active participation in childbirth.

This protocol integrates the use of various EMDR Therapy-related protocols for application in a group format and introduction into a delivery preparation course. In this way, it is possible to offer primary prevention intervention to a much larger number of women, in accordance with the guidelines of the World Health Organization.

References

Artigas, L., & Jarero, I. (2009). The butterfly hug. In M. Luber (Ed.), *Eye movement desensitization and reprocessing (EMDR) scripted protocols: Special populations.* New York, NY: Springer.

Artigas, L., Jarero, I., Alcalà, N., & Lopez Cano, T. (2009). The EMDR integrative group treatment protocol (IGTP). In M. Luber (Ed.), *Eye movement desensitization and reprocessing (EMDR): Basics and special situations.* New York, NY: Springer.

Artigas, L., Jarero, I., Alcalà, N., & Lopez Cano, T. (2014). The EMDR integrative group treatment protocol (IGTP). In M. Luber (Ed.), *Implementing EMDR Early Mental Health Interventions for Man-Made and Natural Disasters: Models, scripted protocols and summary sheets* (pp. 237–252). New York, NY: Springer.

Artigas, L., Jarero, I., Mauer, M., López Cano, T., & Alcalá, N. (2000, September). EMDR and traumatic stress after natural disasters: Integrative Treatment Protocol and the Butterfly Hug. Poster presented at the EMDRIA Conference, Toronto, Ontario, Canada.

Balaskas, J. (1983). *Active birth.* London, UK: Unwin Paperbacks.

Birnbaum, A. (2006). *Group EMDR: Theory and practice.* Invited presentation at EMDR Israel Humanitarian Assistance Program Conference, Netanya, Israel.

Birnbaum, A. (2009). A written workbook for individual or group EMDR. In M. Luber (Ed.), *Eye movement desensitization and reprocessing (EMDR): Basics and special situations.* New York, NY: Springer.

Birnbaum, A. (2014). A written workbook for individual or group EMDR. In M. Luber (Ed.), *Implementing EMDR Early Mental Health Interventions for Man-Made and Natural Disasters: Models, scripted protocols and summary sheets* (pp. 285–341). New York, NY: Springer.

Cox, J. L., & Holden, J. M. (Eds.), (1994). *Perinatal psychiatry: Use and misuse of the Edinburgh Postnatal Depression Scale.* London: Gaskell.

Cox, J., & Holden, J. (2003). *Perinatal mental health: A guide to Edinburgh Postnatal Depression Scale.* London, UK: The Royal College of Psychiatrists.

Cox, J. L., Holden, J. M., & Sagovsky, R. (1987). Detection of postnatal depression. Development of the 10-item Edinburgh Postnatal Depression Scale. *British Journal of Psychiatry, 150,* 782–786.

De Divitiis, A. M. (2010, June). *Application of resource development and installation (RDI) in delivery preparation in order to prevent postpartum depression.* In *Female issues.* Symposium conducted at the 11th EMDR Europe Association Conference, Hamburg, Germany.

Jarero, I., & Artigas, L. (2010). The EMDR Integrative Group Treatment Protocol: Application with adults during ongoing geopolitical crisis. *Journal of EMDR Practice and Research, 4*(4), 148–155.

Korn, D. L., & Leeds, A. M. (2002). Preliminary evidence of efficacy for EMDR resource development and installation in the stabilization phase of treatment of complex posttraumatic stress disorder. *Journal of Clinical Psychology, 58*(12), 1465–1487.

Leboyer. F. (1975). *Birth Without Violence.* New York: Alfred Knopf.

Leeds, A. M., & Shapiro, F. (2000). EMDR and resource installation: Principles and procedures for enhancing current functioning and resolving traumatic experiences. In L. Carlson & L. Sperry (Eds.), *Brief therapy strategies with individuals and couples* (pp. 469–534). Phoenix, AZ: Zeig/Tucker.

Lendl, J., & Foster, S. (2009). EMDR performance enhancement psychology protocol. In M. Luber (Ed.), *Eye movement desensitization and reprocessing (EMDR): Basics and special situations* (pp. 377–396). New York, NY: Springer.

Piscicelli, U. (1977). *Training autogeno respiratorio e psicoprofilassi ostetrica.* Padova, Italy: Piccin Editions.

Piscicelli, U. (1987). Paul Foulkes, trans. *Respiratory autogenic training and obstetric psychoprophylaxis (RAT).* Padova, Italy: Piccin.

Read, D. G. (1944). *Childbirth without fear.* New York, NY: Harper.

Shapiro, F. (1995). *Eye movement desensitization and reprocessing. Basic principles, protocols, and procedures.* New York, NY: Guilford Press.

Shapiro, F. (2001). *Eye movement desensitization and reprocessing: Basic principles, protocols, and procedures* (2nd ed.). New York, NY: Guilford Press.

Shapiro, F. (2006). *EMDR new notes on adaptive information processing with case formulation principles, forms, scripts, and worksheet.* Watsonville, CA: EMDR Institute.

Weiss, D. S. (2007). The Impact of Event Scale-Revised. In J. P. Wilson & C. S. Tang (Eds.), *Cross-cultural assessment of psychological trauma and PTSD* (pp. 219–238). New York, NY: Springer.

Weiss, D. S., & Marmar, C. R. (1996). The Impact of Event Scale—Revised. In J. Wilson & T. M. Keane (Eds.), *Assessing psychological trauma and PTSD* (pp. 399–411). New York, NY: Guilford. (NOTE: Includes measure in its entirety.)

Additional Reading

Ballard, C. G., Stanley, A. K., & Brockington, I. F. (1995). Post traumatic stress disorder (PTSD) after childbirth. *British Journal of Psychiatry, 166,* 525–528.

Foster, S. (2001b). *From trauma to triumph: EMDR and advanced performance enhancement strategies* (self-published training materials). San Francisco, CA: Success at Work.

Foster, S., & Lendl, J. (1995). Eye movement desensitization and reprocessing: Initial applications for enhancing performance in athletes. *Journal of Applied Sport Psychology, 7*(Suppl.), 63.

Foster, S., & Lendl, J. (1996). Eye movement desensitization and reprocessing: Four cases of a new tool for executive coaching and restoring employee performance after setbacks. *Consulting Psychology Journal: Practice and Research, 48,* 155–161.

Luber, M. (Ed.). (2009a). *Eye movement desensitization and reprocessing (EMDR) scripted protocols: Basics and special situations.* New York, NY: Springer.

Luber, M. (2009b). *Future template worksheet.* In M. Luber (Ed.), *Eye movement desensitization and reprocessing (EMDR): Basics and special situations* (pp. 422–429). New York, NY: Springer.

Manage, J. (1993). Posttraumatic stress disorders in women who have undergone obstetric and or gynaecological procedures: A consecutive series of 30 cases of PTSD. *Journal of Reproductive and Infant Psychology, 11,* 221–228.

Moehler, E., Brunner, R., Wiebel, A., Reck, C., & Resch, F. (2006, September). Maternal depressive symptoms in the postnatal period are associated with long-term impairment of mother-child bonding. *Archives of Women's Mental Health, 9*(5), 273–278.

Waldenstrom, U., Borg, I. M., Olsson, B., Skold, M., & Wald, S. (1996). The childbirth experience: A study of 295 new mothers. *Birth, 23,* 144–153.

World Health Organization. (1996). *Essential new-born care: Report of a technical working group, WHO/FRH/MSM/96.13.* Geneva, Switzerland: Author.

Note Sheet for Pregnant Women: EMDR Group Therapy Protocol for the Prevention of Birth Trauma and Postpartum Depression

Anna Maria De Divitiis

Name: _____ Date: _____

Develop Resources

Concentration and Body Focus

> "Now, remain concentrated on your body, listening to everything that happens. Notice what occurs in your body when you breathe. What moves? Feel the air enter and exit ... feel the weight of the body, its heat...perceive all that touches your skin... and finally ... remain concentrated on the 'full space' sensation of your body... remain concentrated on all the sensations that are occurring in your body as they happen."

_____

_____

Say, "Well, now imagine how to be better focused and concentrated on your body during the labor phase, while applying the respiratory techniques to contain the pain of contractions and while you actively look for the most favorable position to move the child forward into the birth canal.

Pay attention to how your body expands and relaxes when you breathe in.

Feel how your birth canal dilates when you breathe in.

Now, imagine how you succeed in concentrating during the expulsion phase, while you apply the respiratory techniques to strengthen your push that you learned in your course.

Remember to use the respiratory techniques you have been practicing and how to modify them, depending on what is happening. Go with that."

Say, "How did it go?"

_____

_____

Say, *"Were you able to imagine doing the techniques during delivery?"*

_____

_____

Say, *"What does your body feel when you visualize these images?"*

_____

_____

Calm/Safe Place (Shapiro, 1995, 2006)

Image

"Imagine a place, real or virtual, in which you feel a sense of refuge, well-being, freedom, and peace of mind. Perhaps being on the beach or sitting by a mountain stream. Note the details: its sights, sounds, smells, colors, temperature. Describe what you are noticing."

_____

_____

Emotions and Sensations

"Notice the emotions and physical sensations that you feel when imagining being in the place. Describe what you are noticing."

_____

_____

Safe Place Cue Word/Phrase

"Is there a word or phrase that represents your safe (or calm) place? Note it down."

_____

_____

Self-Cuing

"Now imagine yourself during those moments of respite among the contractions or while you are pushing. Do you feel disturbance? Notice what you are feeling in your body, and where you feel it. Now bring up your safe (or calm) place and notice any shifts in your body as you relive that sense of well-being. Write about it below."

_____

_____

Mastery Resource Script (Korn & Leeds, 2002)

Critical or Challenging Moment/Aspect/Situation

> *"Consider the whole process of childbirth, from the beginning of labor to the end of the delivery stage, and identify the most demanding, critical, or challenging moment that you expect. Note below."*

_____

_____

Personality Quality or Feature

> *"At that critical/challenging moment/situation, what would you like to be able to do? What would you like to believe about yourself? What would you like to feel? So, what personality quality or feature do you think would be useful to better cope with the critical moments of your childbirth? Describe below."*

_____

_____

Mastery Episode or Mastery Resource/Script

> *"Scan your memory for a positive episode or experience where you felt that particular quality you identified before. Note below."*

_____

_____

Mastery Episode Cue Word/Sentence

> *"When you go back to that experience, what are the most positive words you can say to yourself now? Write it down."*

_____

_____

Inner Advisor/Coach Resource (Lendl & Foster, 2009, pp. 390–391)

Inner Coach Resource

> *"Imagine an actual person or virtual being who can be an inner resource for you, like an Inner Coach supporting and soothing you during the critical states of childbirth. This may be some part of yourself, like your Higher or Wiser Self. Imagine this person's or being's voice, calming you when you are upset or frustrated and reminding you of your strengths, talents, and positive qualities. Go ahead and do that now and let me know what you hear. Write it down."*

_____

_____

Inner Coach Cue Word/Sentence

> *"Imagine your Coach's voice soothing or encouraging you in difficult moments/ situations of your childbirth and reminding you of your strong points and positive features. What words would you want your Inner Coach to say? Write it down."*

_____

_____

Assessment

Target

> *"Consider the whole childbirth, from the beginning of labor to the end of the delivery stage, and identify the most demanding, critical, or challenging moment that you expect. Or, which aspect worries or frightens you the most? Write it down."*

_____

_____

Image

> *"What picture represents the entire issue?"*

_____

_____

Negative Cognition

> *"What words go best with the picture that express your negative belief about yourself now? For instance: 'I'm weak'; 'I can't do it'; 'I'm powerless'; 'I'm vulnerable'; 'I'm not capable.'"*

_____

_____

Positive Cognition

> *"When you bring up that picture, or issue, what would you like to believe about yourself now? For instance, 'I'm smart'; 'I'm strong enough'; 'I can do it'; 'I'm in control'; 'I'm capable.'"*

_____

_____

Validity of Cognition

"When you think of your picture, or your issue, how true do those positive words feel to you now, on a scale of 1 to 7, where 1 feels completely false and 7 feels completely true?"

   1   2   3   4   5   6   7

(completely false)   (completely true)

Emotions

"When you bring up the picture or your issue and negative words that go with it, what emotion do you feel now? For instance: afraid, discouraged, ashamed, and so on?"

_____

_____

SUD

"On a scale of 0 to 10, where 0 is no disturbance or neutral and 10 is the highest disturbance you can imagine, how disturbing does it feel now?"

  0   1   2   3   4   5   6   7   8   9   10

(no disturbance)   (highest disturbance)

Localization

"Where do you feel it in your body?"

_____

_____

Desensitization

"Well, now go ahead and bring up the picture of the critical moment or issue that you are concerned about during your childbirth, those negative words you were saying about yourself. Notice where you are feeling it in your body."

1° set Notes

_____

_____

2° set Notes

_____

_____

3° set Notes

_____

_____

4°set Notes

_____

_____

SUD

"When you bring up the original target (critical moment or worst part of your childbirth), on a scale of 0 to 10, where 0 is no disturbance or neutral and 10 is the highest disturbance you can imagine, how disturbing does it feel to you now?

0	1	2	3	4	5	6	7	8	9	10

(no disturbance)   (highest disturbance)

1° set Notes

_____

_____

2° set Notes

_____

_____

3° set Notes

_____

_____

4° set Notes

_____

_____

SUD

"When you bring up the original target (critical moment or worst part of your childbirth), on a scale of 0 to 10, where 0 is no disturbance or neutral and 10 is the highest disturbance you can imagine, how disturbing does it feel to you now?"

0	1	2	3	4	5	6	7	8	9	10

(no disturbance)   (highest disturbance)

1° set Notes

_____

_____

2° set Notes

_____

_____

3° set Notes

_____

_____

4° set Notes

_____

_____

SUD

"When you bring up the original target (critical moment or worst part of your childbirth), on a scale of 0 to 10, where 0 is no disturbance or neutral and 10 is the highest disturbance you can imagine, how disturbing does it feel to you now?"

| 0 | 1 | 2 | 3 | 4 | 5 | 6 | 7 | 8 | 9 | 10 |

(no disturbance)   (highest disturbance)

Installation

Positive Cognition Verification

"Before we started processing, you chose a positive statement you wanted to believe about yourself. Do these positive words still fit, or is there another positive statement you feel would be more suitable?"

_____

_____

Positive Cognition Revaluation

"As you think of the original target, how true do those words feel, from 1 (completely false) to 7 (completely true)?"

| 1 | 2 | 3 | 4 | 5 | 6 | 7 |

(completely false)   (completely true)

Body Scan

"Now close your eyes and keep in mind the original target and your positive thought. (Pause) Now bring your attention to the different parts of your body, starting with your head and working downward. Any place you find tension, tightness, or unusual sensation, just notice it and then start with Butterfly Hugs."

_____

_____

Closure

"Write a few words about how you are feeling."

_____

_____

Expanded Future Template (Lendl & Foster, 2009)

Visualization

"Imagine an internal space such as a comfortable room, or a beautiful space outdoors, in which you can comfortably sit and see a large projection screen in front of you. On this screen, you can project scenes of yourself effectively dealing with all the difficulties and critical/challenging moments/situations that you think you will come across during childbirth, from the beginning of the labor to the end of the delivery phase. Visualize how you would actually use the resources to cope with these difficulties and how that feels in your body. Pay attention to your body as you competently go through the birthing process. Let me know whenever any discomfort arises and we will stop the visualization and reprocess any discomforts until you can imagine the task with a positive full-body experience."

_____

_____

Body Sensations

"What do you feel in your body?"

_____

_____

Thoughts, Beliefs

_____

_____

Final Scene Visualization of One's Own Delivery

_____

_____

SUMMARY SHEET:
EMDR Therapy Group Protocol for the Prevention of Birth Trauma and Postpartum Depression for Pregnant Women

Anna Maria De Divitiis and Marilyn Luber
SUMMARY SHEET BY MARILYN LUBER

Name: _____ Diagnosis: _____

☑ Check when task is completed, response has changed, or to indicate symptoms or diagnosis.

Note: This material is meant as a checklist for your response. Please keep in mind that it is only a reminder of different tasks that may or may not apply to your client.

Psychoprophylaxis: A method of preparing women for natural childbirth by means of special breathing and relaxation.

Logistics: 8 to 10 pregnant women; 90 to 120 minutes; protocol usually the last class; administer measurements; De Devitiis Anamnestic Questionnaire for Pregnancy; preferable for person who conducts whole class to conduct EMDR Therapy Group Protocol; staff (Lead Clinician, LC; Assistant Clinician, AC).

EMDR Therapy Group Protocol for the Prevention of Birth Trauma and Postpartum Depression for Pregnant Women Script

Phase 1: Client History

Pregnancy

History of pregnancy: _____

_____

☐ Trying to get pregnant   ☐ Unplanned pregnancy

☐ Difficult to get pregnant   ☐ Easy to get pregnant

☐ Problems in pregnancy   ☐ No problems in pregnancy

Describe: _____

Negative consequences of pregnancy: _____

_____

Experience of other pregnancies: _____

_____

_____

Delivery

Family/friends with pregnancy, delivery/postpartum issues: □ Yes   □ No

Describe: _____

Thoughts about giving birth: _____

_____

_____

Worries based on what others said about giving birth: _____

_____

Obstetric/gynecological surgery: □ Yes   □ No

Describe: _____

Experience with past deliveries: _____

Assisted at live delivery/audiovisual: □ Yes   □ No

Describe: _____

Health problems for you/baby that could complicate delivery: □ Yes   □ No

Describe: _____

Thoughts about giving birth: _____

Negative thoughts about giving birth: □ Yes   □ No

Describe: _____

Maternity: □ Yes   □ No

Thoughts about role change from daughter to mother: _____

_____

_____

Thoughts about partner being father of child: _____

_____

Worries about partner being parent: □ Yes   □ No

Describe: _____

Worries about both of you being parents: □ Yes   □ No

Describe: _____

Worries about caring for your child: □ Yes   □ No

Describe: _____

Worries about being alone with child: □ Yes   □ No

Describe: _____

Negative thoughts about self when you think about after the birth: □ Yes   □ No

Describe: _____

Know the gender of baby?   □ Yes   □ No

Happy about gender of baby?   □ Yes   □ No

What looking forward to when child arrives: _____

_____

Sexuality

Subject to sexual abuse or aggression: □ Yes   □ No

Describe: _____

Physical Safety

Accident where life at risk: □ Yes   □ No

Describe: _____

Hospitalized during life: □ Yes   □ No

Describe: _____

Subject to physical violence/assault: □ Yes   □ No

Describe: _____

Hopes, dreams, and expectations for child: _____

_____

□ Completed above interview/history
□ Assessment measures
    Beck Depression Inventory (BDI):
    State-G Trait Anxiety Inventory (STAI—Y1 and Y2):
    Separation Anxiety Test (SAT):
□ Divitiis Anamnestic Questionnaire for Pregnancy

Phase 2: Preparation

□ Explanations of the modality, objectives, and fundamentals of the work

> *"Today, we are going to work on reinforcing the resources that you have, or add to them, to increase your strength, support your dealing with the stress that you will encounter during those difficult times that might occur during the delivery process. Since you are each unique, with your own strengths and weaknesses, I will encourage you to find the resources that will be most suitable to you and assist you in preparing for this process."*

□ Teach self-administered bilateral stimulation (BLS): Butterfly Hug (BH)

Develop Resources

☐ Emphasize the importance of learning these new resources to assist in the delivery:

"During this course, you are all moving toward the birthing of your baby. It is important for you to know that no one can make you deliver your baby; it is a process that occurs and works best when your body and mind work together. With this in mind, I will be teaching you ways to support your learning how to stay concentrated on yourself by listening to the signals that your body will be sending so that you can respond during each moment of the birthing process."

Instructions to the Group

"Later we'll be reprocessing disturbing information, which will help us to overcome every possible physical or mental block, every doubt or fear, which could interfere with the carrying-out of what we learned during the delivery preparation course. We'll use the Butterfly Hug as BLS and the Notes Sheet you were given to note down briefly all your thoughts, feelings, sensations, pictures, and scenes that emerge during the process."

"Please take out your, 'Note Sheet For Expectant Mothers,' so that I can step you through how we will be using it. I suggest you reply very concisely, using only one word or one sentence because our time is limited. You can see the step-by step instruction on your Notes Sheet and can proceed at your own pace. You can keep it with you to help you remember what you have done here. I will also keep a copy to use for the follow- up that will take place after your babies are born."

Teach the following resources: (see EMDR Group Protocol for the Prevention of Birth Trauma and Postpartum Depression for Pregnant Women Notes Sheet)

CONCENTRATION AND BODY FOCUS

"Now, remain concentrated on your body, listening to everything that happens. Notice what occurs in your body when you breathe. What moves? Feel the air enter and exit … feel the weight of the body, its heat…perceive all that touches your skin… and finally… remain concentrated on the 'full space' sensation of your body… remain concentrated on all the sensations that are occurring in your body as they happen."

"Well, now imagine how to be better focused and concentrated on your body during the labor phase, while applying the respiratory techniques to contain the pain of contractions and while you actively look for the most favorable position to move the child forward into the birth canal."

"Pay attention to how your body expands and relaxes when you breathe in."

"Feel how your birth canal dilates when you breathe in."

"Now, imagine how you succeed in concentrating during the expulsion phase, while you apply the respiratory techniques to strengthen your push that you learned in your course."

"Remember to use the respiratory techniques you have been practicing and how to modify them, depending on what is happening. Go with that."

"How did it go?" _____

_____

"Were you able to imagine doing the techniques during delivery?"   ☐ Yes   ☐ No

Describe: _____

*"What does your body feel when you visualize these images?"*_____

ESTABLISH A SAFE PLACE SCRIPT

Image: _____

Emotions and sensations: _____

Safe Place cue word/phrase: _____

Self-cuing: _____

MASTERY RESOURCE SCRIPT

Critical/Challenging moment/aspect/situation: _____

Personality quality or feature: _____

Mastery episode or mastery resource/script: _____

_____

Mastery episode cue word/sentence: _____

INNER ADVISOR/COACH SCRIPT

Inner Coach resource: _____

_____

Inner Coach cue word/sentence: _____

Phase 3: Assessment

"After this work, we focus in on our target and answer a few questions about thoughts and feelings surrounding it. We will begin processing using the Butterfly Hug. After each set of Butterfly Hugs, we will briefly write something about our response, and then continue with Butterfly Hugs and processing. Some things will come up or change, and sometimes they won't. There are no 'supposed to's' in this process. Just go with the flow and let whatever happens happen, without judging it. If you have a problem or feel you have to stop, raise your hand."

"Write down each answer for the assessment on the Notes Sheet."

Target Selection

"Consider the whole childbirth, from the beginning of labor to the end of the delivery stage, and identify the most demanding, critical, or challenging moment that you expect. Or, which aspect worries or frightens you the most?" Pause.

Incident: _____

Picture: _____

Negative Cognition (NC) exs: , "I'm weak"; "I can't do it"; "I'm powerless"; "I'm vulnerable"; "I'm not capable"

Positive Cognition (PC) exs.: "I'm smart"; "I'm strong enough"; "I can do it"; "I'm in control"; "I'm capable"

VoC: _____ /7

Emotions: _____

SUD: _____ /10

Location of body sensation: _____

Phase 4: Desensitization

"Let's move on to processing. For each set, we'll do the Butterfly Hug for about 30 seconds. Then we'll pause, take a deep breath together, and briefly jot down a few words about what we noticed in the space provided on the Notes Sheet. Then we'll repeat: Butterfly Hugs. . . , deep breath. . . , writing and so on. We'll do this for about 5 to 6 minutes. I'll let you know a couple of minutes before it's time to move on together to the next stage. So we'll begin with the target, and let ourselves go with whatever comes up. Any questions?"

"Well, now go ahead and bring up the picture of the critical moment or issue that you are concerned about during your childbirth, those negative words you were saying about yourself; notice where you are feeling it in your body, and begin with your Butterfly Hugs."

After 30 seconds of processing with BH, say the following: *"Well, now let's take a deep breath. . . , and then just notice what you get now. . . , please take 30 seconds to write down a few words."*

"OK, let's continue with Butterfly Hugs and processing. Again, go with the flow, let whatever happens happen. After about 30 seconds, or when you feel a change, take a deep breath, and write something about what you noticed."

Note*:* The LC continues to do BHs and to provide positive comments during the entire session. The LC will decide on the number of sets to be used and intervenes with cognitive interweave(s) if any woman gets stuck with a dysfunctional cognition. The AC walks around among the women, offering help and clarification about how to fill in the Notes Sheet. The AC can also intervene if any woman needs emotional support.

"In two minutes we'll move on to the next stage together. So, now we can do two more sets of Butterfly Hugs. Come on, let's go!"

"Okay, deep breath, notice what you get now, and take a few moments to write your thoughts in the space provided on the Notes Sheet."

After repeating another set of BH and writing on the Notes Sheet, do SUDs.

It is possible to go to the next phase when the SUDs = 0 for all the women, or when it has at least dropped to an ecological level for all concerned.

Phase 5: Installation

"Before we started processing, you chose a positive statement you wanted to believe about yourself. Do these positive words still fit, or is there another positive statement you feel would be more suitable? When you think of the original target (critical moment or worst part of your childbirth), what would you like to believe about yourself now?"

PC: ☐ Completed

New PC (if new one is better):

VoC: _____/7

Incident + PC + BLS

Continue installation with BLS until material becomes increasingly adaptive.

If VoC = 6 or less, check and see if there is a limiting belief:

"Which thoughts or concerns prevent you from feeling those words as completely true?"

Note: If the limiting belief is not resolved quickly, explore to see whether there are any limiting beliefs or unidentified/unprocessed memory(ies)/networks that are causing this difficulty. The session is then considered incomplete; therefore, return to the incomplete target and continue the installation process in the next session.

Phase completed   ☐ Yes   ☐ No

Phase 6: Body Scan   ☐ Completed

"Now close your eyes and keep in mind the original target and your positive thought. (Pause) Now bring your attention to the different parts of your body, starting with your head and working downward. Any place you find tension, tightness, or unusual sensation, just notice it and then start to do Butterfly Hugs. Keep doing Butterfly Hugs until you sense a change, and continue tapping as long as it seems to be helping you feel better. Good. We'll do this for the next couple of minutes."

Pause. After about 90 seconds, say the following:

"Let's do another half minute of Butterfly Hugs and let go of any residual disturbance in our bodies that we don't need to hold onto right now."

"Very good. Now take a deep breath, and jot down what you noticed and how you feel now."

The Final Installation: The Expanded Future Template

"Imagine an internal space such as a comfortable room, or a beautiful space outdoors, in which you can comfortably sit and see a large projection screen in front of you. On this screen, you can project scenes of yourself effectively dealing with all the difficulties and critical/challenging moments/situations that you think you will come across during childbirth, from the beginning of the labor to the end of the delivery phase. Visualize how you would actually use the resources to cope with these difficulties and how that feels in your body. Pay attention to your body as you competently go through the birthing process. Let me know whenever any discomfort arises and we will stop the visualization and reprocess any discomforts until you can imagine the task with a positive full-body experience."

"After you do that, please describe briefly what you create on the Notes Sheet."

"Go with that and do 2 slow sets of 6 to 12 Butterfly Hugs as more positive sensations emerge in order to install all of your desired skills."

If negative sensations emerge, the LC makes sure that the participant has the time to reprocess any doubts, physical or mental blocks, or discomfort that may arise, until the expectant mother(s) can imagine the entire process of childbirth with a positive full-body experience. If any of them cannot complete this during the allotted time, the clinician either makes an individual or group appointment (depending on the number of women) in which to conclude the reprocessing.

"OK, play the movie one more time from beginning to end. Go with that and use a slow set of Butterfly Hugs."

Phase 7: Group Closure

"We will be stopping soon. You have done very good work, as individuals and as a group. Please write a few words about how you are feeling."

"Once again, I would like to urge you to practice the resources we have installed previously. The processing we have done today may continue after the session. You may or may not notice new insights, thoughts, memories, or dreams. If so, just notice what you are experiencing—take a snapshot of it—what you are seeing, feeling, thinking, and the trigger, and keep a log. Go to your Calm/Safe Place if you need to process through any disturbances. In case this isn't sufficient, you can contact me to make an appointment, and we can use the new material as targets to be reprocessed."

Phase 8: Reevaluation

Follow-up: (2–6 months after childbirth)

Past Memory Worksheet Script (Shapiro, 2001, 2006)

Incident

Say, *"The memory that we will start with today is* _____ (select the next incident to be targeted)*."*

_____

_____

_____

Say, *"What happens when you think of the* _____ (state the issue)*?"*

_____

_____

_____

Or say, *"When you think of* _____ (state the issue), *what do you get?"*

_____

_____

Picture

Say, *"What picture represents the entire* _____ (state the issue)*?"*

_____

_____

_____

If there are many choices or if the client becomes confused, the clinician assists by asking the following:

Say, "*What picture represents the most traumatic part of* _____ (state the issue)?"

_____

_____

_____

Negative Cognition

Say, "*What words best go with the picture that express your negative belief about yourself now?*"

_____

_____

Positive Cognition

Say, "*When you bring up that picture or* _____ (state the issue), *what would you like to believe about yourself now?*"

_____

_____

Validity of Cognition

Say, "*When you think of the incident* (or picture), *how true do those words* _____ (repeat the PC) *feel to you now on a scale of 1 to 7, where 1 feels completely false and 7 feels completely true?*"

1   2   3   4   5   6   7

(completely false)   (completely true)

Emotions

Say, "*When you bring up the picture or* _____ (state the issue) *and those words* _____ (state the negative cognition), *what emotion do you feel now?*"

_____

Subjective Units of Disturbance

Say, "*On a scale of 0 to 10, where 0 is no disturbance or neutral and 10 is the highest disturbance you can imagine, how disturbing does it feel now?*"

0   1   2   3   4   5   6   7   8   9   10

(no disturbance)   (highest disturbance)

Location of Body Sensation

Say, *"Where do you feel it* (the disturbance) *in your body?"*

Phase 4: Desensitization

To begin, say the following:

Say, *"Now, remember, it is your own brain that is doing the healing and you are the one in control. I will ask you to mentally focus on the target and to follow my fingers* (or any other BLS you are using). *Just let whatever happens, happen, and we will talk at the end of the set. Just tell me what comes up, and don't discard anything as unimportant. Any new information that comes to mind is connected in some way. If you want to stop, just raise your hand."*

Then say, *"Bring up the picture and the words* _____ (repeat the NC) *and notice where you feel it in your body. Now follow my fingers with your eyes* (or other BLS)."

Phase 5: Installation

Say, *"How does* _____ (repeat the PC) *sound?"*

_____

_____

_____

Say, *"Do the words* _____ (repeat the PC) *still fit, or is there another positive statement that feels better?"*

_____

_____

_____

If the client accepts the original PC, the clinician should ask for a VoC rating to see if it has improved:

Say, *"As you think of the incident, how do the words feel, from 1 (completely false) to 7 (completely true)?"*

1   2   3   4   5   6   7

(completely false)   (completely true)

Say, *"Think of the event and hold it together with the words* _____ (repeat the PC)."

Do a long set of BLS to see if there is more processing to be done.

Phase 6: Body Scan

Say, *"Close your eyes and keep in mind the original memory and the positive cognition. Then bring your attention to the different parts of your body, starting with your head and working downward. Any place you find any tension, tightness, or unusual sensation, tell me."*

_____

_____

Phase 7: Closure

Say, *"Things may come up or they may not. If they do, great. Write it down and it can be a target for next time. You can use a log to write down what triggers images, thoughts or cognitions, emotions, and sensations; you can rate them on our 0 to 10 scale where 0 is no disturbance or neutral and 10 is the worst disturbance. Please write down the positive experiences, too.*

"If you get any new memories, dreams, or situations that disturb you, just take a good snapshot. It isn't necessary to give a lot of detail. Just put down enough to remind you so we can target it next time. The same thing goes for any positive dreams or situations. If negative feelings do come up, try not to make them significant. Remember, it's still just the old stuff. Just write it down for next time. Then use the tape or the Safe Place exercise to let go of as much of the disturbance as possible. Even if nothing comes up, make sure to use the tape every day and give me a call if you need to."

Phase 8: Reevaluation

There are four ways to reevaluate our work with clients.

1. Reevaluate what has come up in the client's life since the last session.

   Say, *"OK. Let's look at your log. I am interested in what has happened since the last session. What have you noticed since our last session?"*

   _____

   _____

   _____

   Say, *"What has changed?"*

   _____

   _____

   _____

If the client has nothing to say or does not say much, say the following:

   Say, *"Have you had any dreams or nightmares?"*

   _____

   _____

   _____

   Say, *"What about _____ (state symptoms you and client have been working on) we have been working on; have you noticed any changes in them? Have they increased or decreased?"*

   _____

_____

_____

Say, _"Have you noticed any other changes, new responses, or insights in your images, thoughts, emotions, sensations, and behaviors?"_

_____

_____

_____

Say, _"Have you found new resources?"_

_____

_____

_____

Say, _"Have any situations, events, or other stimuli triggered you?"_

_____

_____

_____

Use the material from your reevaluation to feed back into your case conceptualization and help decide what to do next concerning the larger treatment plan.

2. Reevaluate the target worked on in the previous session. Has the individual target been resolved? Whether the previous processing session was complete or incomplete, use the following instructions to access the memory and determine the need for further processing.

Say, _"Bring up the memory or trigger of_ _____ (state the memory or trigger) _that we worked on last session. What image comes up?"_

_____

_____

_____

Say, _"What thoughts about it come up?"_

_____

_____

Say, _"What thoughts about yourself?"_

_____

_____

Say, _"What emotions do you notice?"_

_____

_____

Say, *"What sensations do you notice?"*

_____

_____

Say, *"On a scale of 0 to 10, where 0 is no disturbance or neutral and 10 is the highest disturbance you can imagine, how disturbing does it feel now?"*

0   1   2   3   4   5   6   7   8   9   10

(no disturbance)   (highest disturbance)

Evaluate the material to see if there are any indications of dysfunction. Has the primary issue been resolved? Is there ecological validity to the client's resolution of the issue? Is there associated material that has been activated that must be addressed?

If you are observing any resistance to resolving the issue, say the following:

Say, *"What would happen if you are successful?"*

_____

_____

If there are no indications of dysfunction, and SUD is 0, do a set of BLS to be sure that the processing is complete.

Say, *"Go with that."*

Say, *"What do you get now?"*

_____

_____

Check the PC.

Say, *"When you think of the incident* (or picture), *how true do those words* _____ (repeat the PC) *feel to you now on a scale of 1 to 7, where 1 feels completely false and 7 feels completely true?"*

1   2   3   4   5   6   7

(completely false)   (completely true)

If the VoC is 7, do a set of BLS to be sure that the processing is complete.

Say, *"Go with that."*

Say, *"What do you get now?"*

_____

_____

If there are any signs of dysfunction, such as a new negative perspective(s) or new facets of the event, or the SUD is higher than 0, say the following:

Say, *"OK, now please pay attention to the image, thoughts, and sensations associated with* _____ (state the memory or trigger) *and just go with that."*

_____

_____

Continue with the Standard EMDR Protocol until processing is complete. If the VoC is less than 7, say the following:

Say, *"What is keeping it from being a 7?"*

_____

_____

Note the associated feelings and sensations, and resume processing.

Say, *"Go with that."*

Continue with the Standard EMDR Protocol through the body scan until processing is complete.

If a completely new incident or target emerges, say the following:

Say, *"Are there any feeder memories contributing to this problem?"*

_____

_____

Do the assessment phase on the appropriate target and fully process it. It is not unusual for another aspect of the memory to emerge that has to be processed.

If the client claims that nothing or no disturbance is coming up (or he can't remember what was worked on in the previous session), and the therapist thinks that the work is probably still incomplete and that the client is simply not able to access the memory, say the following:

Say, *"When you think of _____ (state the incident that was worked on) and the image _____ (state the image) and _____ (state the NC), what body sensations do you feel now?"*

_____

_____

Say, *"Go with that."*

_____

_____

Continue processing with the Standard EMDR Protocol.

If the client wants to work on a charged trigger that came up since the last session instead of the target from the previous session, say the following:

Say, *"Yes, this IS important information. Tell me about what came up for you."*

_____

_____

Then assess the magnitude of the trigger. If it is indeed a severe critical incident, then proceed accordingly, using the assessment phase to target the new material and return to the original target when possible.

If it is not, then say the following:

Say, *"Yes, this is important; however, it is important that we finish our work on _____ (state what you are working on) before moving to another target. It is like what happens when you have too many files open on your computer and it slows down, or finishing the course of antibiotics even if you feel OK (or any other appropriate metaphor for your client)."*

Fully reprocess each target through the body scan and reevaluation before moving on to the next in order to ensure optimal results.

    3. At various critical points in treatment (before moving on to the next symptom, theme, goal, etc.), reevaluate what has been effectively targeted and resolved and what still has to be addressed.

Say, *"Now that we have finished this work, let's reevaluate our work so far."*

"Remember _____ (state the work you have done). *On a scale of 0 to 10, where 0 is no disturbance or neutral and 10 is the highest disturbance you can imagine, how disturbing does it feel now?"*

    0   1   2   3   4   5   6   7   8   9   10

(no disturbance)   (highest disturbance)

If the SUD is higher than 0, evaluate what else should be done by continuing to work with the disturbance in the framework of the Standard EMDR Protocol.

Also evaluate whether the client has been able to achieve cognitive, behavioral, and emotional goals in her life.

Say, *"Have you accomplished all of the goals that we had contracted to work on, such as* _____ (read the list of agreed-upon goals)?"

_____

_____

_____

If not, evaluate what still remains to be targeted, such as feeder memories.

Say, *"Please scan for an earlier memory that incorporates* _____ (state the NC). *What do you get?"*

_____

_____

_____

Use the Standard EMDR Protocol to process any feeder memories. Check if previously identified clusters of memories remain charged.

Say, *"Are there any memories left concerning* _____ (state the cluster of memories previously worked on)?"

_____

_____

_____

If so, work on the memory(ies), using the Standard EMDR Protocol. Make sure to incorporate the positive templates for all previously disturbing situations and projected future goals. See the Future Template Worksheet Script.

    4. Before termination, reevaluate targets worked on over the course of therapy and goals addressed during treatment.

Say, *"Before we end our treatment, let's reevaluate our work to make sure that all of the targets are resolved and goals are addressed. Are there any PAST targets that remain unresolved for you?"*

_____

_____

_____

Or say, *"These are the past targets with which we worked; do any of them remain unresolved? What about the memories that we listed during our history taking and over the course of treatment?"*

_____

_____

_____

Check with the SUDs for any disturbance.

Say, *"On a scale of 0 to 10, where 0 is no disturbance or neutral and 10 is the highest disturbance you can imagine, how disturbing does it feel now?"*

0   1   2   3   4   5   6   7   8   9   10

(no disturbance)   (highest disturbance)

Check the major NCs to see if there are any unresolved memories still active.

Say, *"These are the main negative cognitions with which we worked. Hold _____ (state one of the cognitions worked with) and scan for any unresolved memories. Does anything surface for you?"*

_____

_____

If there is more unresolved material, check with BLS to see if the charge decreases. If not, use the Standard EMDR Protocol.

Say, *"Now scan chronologically from birth until today to see if there are any other unresolved memories. What do you notice?"*

_____

_____

If there is more unresolved material, check with BLS to see if the charge decreases. If not, use the Standard EMDR Protocol.

Progressions can occur during other events or during the processing of a primary target; use your clinical judgment as to whether it is important to return and reevaluate these memories.

Clusters are related memories that were grouped together during treatment planning and can be scanned to identify any memories that were not involved through generalization of treatment effects.

Say, *"Let's check the* _____ (state the cluster) *we worked on earlier. When you think about it, are there any other memories that were not involved that you are aware of now?"*

_____

_____

If there is more unresolved material, check with BLS to see if the charge decreases. If not, use the Standard EMDR Protocol.

Participants are significant individuals in the client's life who should be targeted if memories or issues regarding them remain disturbing.

Say, *"Let's check if there are any remaining concerns or memories concerning* _____ (state whoever the client might be concerned about). *Is there anything that still is bothering you about* _____ (state the person's name)?"

_____

_____

If there is more unresolved material, check with BLS to see if the charge decreases. If not, use the Standard EMDR Protocol.

Say, *"Are there any PRESENT or RECENT triggers that remain potent?"*

_____

_____

_____

Say, *"Are there any current conditions, situations, or people that make you want to avoid them, act in ways that are not helpful, or cause you emotional distress?"*

_____

_____

If there is more unresolved material, check with BLS to see if the charge decreases. If not, use the Standard EMDR Protocol.

Say, *"Are there any future goals that have not been addressed and realized?"*

_____

_____

_____

Make sure to use the future template for each trigger, new goal(s), new skill(s), issues of memory, or incorporating the client's new sense of himself. See the Future Template Worksheet Script in this appendix.

Present Trigger Worksheet Script

Target and reprocess present triggers identified during history taking, reprocessing, and reevaluation. Steps for working with present triggers are the following.

1. Identify the presenting trigger that is still causing disturbance.
2. Target and activate the presenting trigger using the full assessment procedures (image, NC, PC, VoC, emotions, SUDs, sensations).
3. Follow phases 3 through 8 with each trigger until it is fully reprocessed (SUD = 0, VoC = 7, clear body scan) before moving to the next trigger.

Note: In some situations, a blocking belief may be associated with the present trigger, requiring a new targeting sequence plan.

4. Once all present triggers have been reprocessed, proceed to installing future templates for each present trigger (e.g., imagining encountering the same situation in the future; see future template protocols).

Present Stimuli That Trigger the Disturbing Memory or Reaction

List the situations that elicit the symptom(s). Examples of situations, events, or stimuli that trigger clients could be the following: another trauma, the sound of a car backfiring, or being touched in a certain way.

Say, *"What are the situations, events, or stimuli that trigger your trauma* _____ (state the trauma)? *Let's process these situations, events, or stimuli triggers one by one."*

Situations, Events, or Stimuli Trigger List

_____

_____

_____

_____

Target or Memory

Say, *"What situation, event, or stimulus that triggers you would you like to use as a target today?"*

_____

_____

Picture

Say, *"What picture represents the* _____ (state the situation, event, or stimulus) *that triggers you?"*

_____

_____

If there are many choices or if the client becomes confused, the clinician assists by asking the following:

Say, *"What picture represents the most traumatic part of the* _____ (state the situation, event, or stimulus) *that triggers you?"*

_____

_____

When a picture is unavailable, the clinician merely invites the client to do the following:

Say, *"Think of the* _____ (state the situation, event, or stimulus) *that triggers you."*

_____

_____

Negative Cognition

Say, *"What words best go with the picture that express your negative belief about yourself now?"*

_____

Positive Cognition

Say, *"When you bring up that picture or the* _____ (state the situation, event, or stimulus) *that triggers you, what would you like to believe about yourself now?"*

Validity of Cognition

Say, *"When you think of the* _____ (state the situation, event, stimulus, or picture that triggers), *how true do those words* _____ (repeat the PC) *feel to you now on a scale of 1 to 7, where 1 feels completely false and 7 feels completely true?"*

1   2   3   4   5   6   7

(completely false)   (completely true)

Sometimes it is necessary to explain further.

Say, *"Remember, sometimes we know something with our head, but it feels different in our gut. In this case, what is the gut-level feeling of the truth of* _____ (state the PC), *from 1 (completely false) to 7 (completely true)?"*

1   2   3   4   5   6   7

(completely false)   (completely true)

Emotions

Say, *"When you bring up the picture* (or state the situation, event, or stimulus) *that triggers you and those words* _____ (state the NC), *what emotion do you feel now?"*

_____

Subjective Units of Disturbance

Say, *"On a scale of 0 to 10, where 0 is no disturbance or neutral and 10 is the highest disturbance you can imagine, how disturbing does it feel now?"*

0   1   2   3   4   5   6   7   8   9   10

(no disturbance)   (highest disturbance)

Location of Body Sensation

Say, *"Where do you feel it* (the disturbance) *in your body?"*

_____

Continue to process the triggers according to the Standard EMDR Protocol.

Future Template Worksheet (Shapiro, 2006)

The future template is the third prong in the Standard EMDR Protocol. Work with the future template occurs after the earlier memories and present triggers are adequately resolved and the client is ready to make new choices in the future concerning the issue(s). The purpose is to address any residual avoidance, any need for further issues of adaptation, to help with incorporating any new information, and to allow for the actualization of client goals. It is another place, in this comprehensive protocol, to catch any fears, negative beliefs, inappropriate responses, and so forth; to reprocess them; and also to make sure that the new feelings and behavior can generalize into the clients' day-to-day lives.
There are two basic future templates:

1. Anticipatory Anxiety
   Anticipatory anxiety should be addressed with a full assessment (phase 3) of the future situation.

2. Skills Building and Imaginal Rehearsal
   These do not require a full assessment of target and can begin directly with "running a movie."

Future Template Script (Shapiro, 2001, pp. 210–214; 2006, pp. 51–53)

Check the Significant People and Situations of the Presenting Issues for Any Type of Distress

It is helpful to check to see if all the material concerning the issue upon which the client has worked is resolved or if there is more material that has escaped detection so far. The future template is another place to find if there is more material that requires reprocessing.

Significant People

When the client's work has focused on a significant person, ask the following:

Say, "*Imagine yourself encountering that person in the future* _____ (suggest a place that the client might see this person). *What do you notice?*"

_____

_____

_____

Watch the client's reaction to see if more work is necessary. If a client describes a negative feeling in connection with this person, check to see if it is reality based.

Say, "*Is* _____ (state the person's name) *likely to act* _____ (state the client's concern)?"

_____

_____

If the negative feeling is not matching the current reality, say the following:

Say, "*What do you think makes you have negative feelings toward* _____ (state the person in question)?"

_____

_____

If the client is unsure, use the Float-Back or affect scan to see what other earlier material may still be active.

If the negative feelings are appropriate, it is important to reevaluate the clusters of events concerning this person and access and reprocess any remaining maladaptive memories. (See Past Memory Worksheet.)

Significant Situations

It is important to have the client imagine being in significant situations in the future; this is another way of accessing material that may not have been processed.

> Say, *"Imagine a videotape or film of* _____ (state current situation client is working on) *and how it would evolve* _____ (state appropriate time frame) *in the future. When you have done that, let me know what you have noticed."*

_____

_____

If there is no disturbance, reinforce the positive experience.

> Say, *"Go with that."*

Do BLS.

Reinforce the PC with the future situation with BLS as it continues the positive associations. For further work in the future, see below.

If there is a disturbance, assess what the client needs: more education, modeling of appropriate behavior, or more past-memory reprocessing.

> Say, *"On a scale of 0 to 10, where 0 is no disturbance or neutral and 10 is the highest disturbance you can imagine, how disturbing does it feel now?"*

> 0   1   2   3   4   5   6   7   8   9   10

> (no disturbance)   (highest disturbance)

Anticipatory Anxiety

When the SUD is above 4, or when the desensitization phase is not brief, the clinician should look for a present trigger and its associated symptom and develop another targeting sequence plan using the 3-Pronged Protocol. (See worksheets on Past Memories and Present Triggers.)

When there is anticipatory anxiety at a SUD level of no more than 3 to 4 maximum, it is possible to proceed with reprocessing using the future template. The desensitization phase should be quite brief.

> Say, *"What happens when you think of* _____ (state the client's anticipatory anxiety or issue)?"*

_____

_____

_____

> Or say, *"When you think of* _____ (state the client's anticipatory anxiety or issue), *what do you get?"*

_____

_____

_____

Picture

Say, *"What picture represents the entire* _____ (state the client's anticipatory anxiety or issue)?"

_____

_____

_____

If there are many choices or if the client becomes confused, the clinician assists by asking the following:

Say, *"What picture represents the most traumatic part of* _____ (state the client's anticipatory anxiety or issue)?"

_____

_____

_____

Negative Cognition

Say, *"What words best go with the picture that express your negative belief about yourself now?"*

_____

_____

Positive Cognition

Say, *"When you bring up that picture or* _____ (state the client's anticipatory anxiety or issue), *what would you like to believe about yourself now?"*

_____

_____

Validity of Cognition

Say, *"When you think of* _____ (state the client's anticipatory anxiety or issue) *or picture, how true do those words* _____ (repeat the PC) *feel to you now on a scale of 1 to 7, where 1 feels completely false and 7 feels completely true?"*

1   2   3   4   5   6   7

(completely false)   (completely true)

Emotions

Say, *"When you bring up the picture or* _____ (state the client's anticipatory anxiety or issue) *and those words* _____ (state the NC), *what emotion do you feel now?"*

_____

Subjective Units of Disturbance

Say, *"On a scale of 0 to 10, where 0 is no disturbance or neutral and 10 is the highest disturbance you can imagine, how disturbing does it feel now?"*

0   1   2   3   4   5   6   7   8   9   10

(no disturbance)   (highest disturbance)

Location of Body Sensation

Say, *"Where do you feel it* (the disturbance) *in your body?"*

_____

_____

Phase 4: Desensitization

To begin, say the following:

Say, *"Now remember, it is your own brain that is doing the healing and you are the one in control. I will ask you to mentally focus on the target and to follow my fingers* (or any other BLS you are using). *Just let whatever happens, happen, and we will talk at the end of the set. Just tell me what comes up, and don't discard anything as unimportant. Any new information that comes to mind is connected in some way. If you want to stop, just raise your hand."*

Then say, *"Bring up the picture and the words* _____ (repeat the NC) *and notice where you feel it in your body. Now, follow my fingers with your eyes* (or other BLS)."

Continue with the desensitization phase until the SUD = 0 and the VoC = 7.

Phase 5: Installation

Say, *"How does* _____ (repeat the PC) *sound?"*

_____

Say, *"Do the words* _____ (repeat the PC) *still fit, or is there another positive statement that feels better?"*

_____

If the client accepts the original PC, the clinician should ask for a VoC rating to see if it has improved.

Say, *"As you think of the incident, how do the words feel, from 1 (completely false) to 7 (completely true)?"*

1   2   3   4   5   6   7

(completely false)   (completely true)

Say, *"Think of the event and hold it together with the words* _____ (repeat the PC)."

Do a long set of BLS to see if there is more processing to be done.

Phase 6: Body Scan

> Say, *"Close your eyes and keep in mind the original memory and the positive cognition. Then bring your attention to the different parts of your body, starting with your head and working downward. Any place you find any tension, tightness, or unusual sensation, tell me."*

_____

_____

Make sure that this anticipatory anxiety is fully processed before returning to the future template.

The future template for appropriate future interaction is an expansion of the installation phase; however, instead of linking the positive cognition with the past memory or trigger, the PC is linked to the future issues. Once the client's work has been checked and the other known issues in the past and present have been resolved, the client has the choice to do a more formal future template installation. The first option is to work with the situation or issue as an image.

Image as Future Template: Imagining Positive Outcomes

Imagining positive outcomes seems to assist the learning process. In this way, clients learn to enhance optimal behaviors, to connect them with a PC, and to support generalization. The assimilation of this new behavior and thought into a positive way to act in the future is supported by the use of BLS.

> Say, *"I would like you to imagine yourself coping effectively with or in _____ (state the goal) in the future. With the positive belief _____ (state the positive belief) and your new sense of _____ (state the quality: i.e., strength, clarity, confidence, calm), imagine stepping into this scene. Notice what you see and how you are handling the situation. Notice what you are thinking, feeling, and experiencing in your body."*

_____

_____

_____

Again, here is an opportunity to catch any disturbance that may have been missed.

> Say, *"Are there any blocks, anxieties, or fears that arise as you think about this future scene?"*

_____

_____

_____

If yes, say the following:

> Say, *"Then focus on these blocks and follow my fingers (or any other BLS)."*

> Say, *"What do you get now?"*

_____

_____

_____

If the blocks do not resolve quickly, evaluate if the client needs any new information, resources, or skills to be able to comfortably visualize the future coping scene. Introduce needed information or skills.

Say, *"What would you need to feel confident in handling the situation?"*

Or say, *"What is missing from your handling of this situation?"*

_____

_____

If the block still does not resolve and the client is unable to visualize the future scene with confidence and clarity, use direct questions, the affect scan, or the Float-Back Technique to identify old targets related to blocks, anxieties, or fears. Remember, the point of the 3-Pronged Protocol is not only to reinforce positive feelings and behavior in the future, but also, again, to catch any unresolved material that may be getting in the way of an adaptive resolution of the issue(s). Use the Standard EMDR Protocol to address these targets before proceeding with the template (see Worksheets in this appendix). If there are no apparent blocks and the client is able to visualize the future scene with confidence and clarity, say the following:

Say, *"Please focus on the image, the positive belief, and the sensations associated with this future scene and follow my fingers* (or any other BLS).*"*

_____

_____

Process and reinforce the positive associations with BLS. Do several sets until the future template is sufficiently strengthened.

Say, *"Go with that."*

_____

Then say, *"Close your eyes and keep in mind the image of the future and the positive cognition. Then bring your attention to the different parts of your body, starting with your head and working downward. Any place you find any tension, tightness, or unusual sensation, tell me."*

_____

If any sensation is reported, do BLS.

Say, *"Go with that."*
If it is a positive or comfortable sensation, do BLS to strengthen the positive feelings.

Say, *"Go with that."*
If a sensation of discomfort is reported, reprocess until the discomfort subsides.

Say, *"Go with that."*
When the discomfort subsides, check the VoC.

Say, *"When you think of the incident* (or picture), *how true do those words* _____ (repeat the PC) *feel to you now on a scale of 1 to 7, where 1 feels completely false and 7 feels completely true?"*

1   2   3   4   5   6   7

(completely false)   (completely true)

Continue to use BLS until reaching a VoC = 7 or there is an ecological resolution. When the image as future template is clear and the PC true, move on to the movie as future template.

Movie as Future Template or Imaginal Rehearsing

During this next level of future template, clients are asked to move from imagining this one scene or snapshot to imagining a movie about coping in the future, with a beginning, middle, and end. Encourage clients to imagine themselves coping effectively in the face of specific challenges, triggers, or snafus. Therapists can make some suggestions to help inoculate clients with future problems. It is helpful to use this type of future template after clients have received needed education concerning social skills and customs, assertive- ness, and any other newly learned skills.

> Say, *"This time, I'd like you to close your eyes and play a movie, imagining yourself coping effectively with or in* _____ *(state where client will be) in the future. With the new positive belief* _____ *(state positive belief) and your new sense of* _____ *(strength, clarity, confidence, calm), imagine stepping into the future. Imagine yourself coping with ANY challenges that come your way. Make sure that this movie has a beginning, middle, and end. Notice what you are seeing, thinking, feeling, and experiencing in your body. Let me know if you hit any blocks. If you do, just open your eyes and let me know. If you don't hit any blocks, let me know when you have viewed the whole movie."*

_____

_____

If the client hits blocks, address as above with BLS until the disturbance dissipates.

> Say, *"Go with that."*

If the material does not shift, use interweaves, new skills, information, resources, direct questions, and any other ways to help clients access information that will allow them to move on. If these options are not successful, it usually means that there is earlier material still unprocessed; the Float-Back and affect scan are helpful in these cases to access the material that keeps the client stuck.

If clients are able to play the movie from start to finish with a sense of confidence and satisfaction, ask them to play the movie one more time from beginning to end and introduce BLS.

> Say, *"OK, play the movie one more time from beginning to end. Go with that."*
> Use BLS.

In a sense, you are installing this movie as a future template.

After clients have fully processed their issue(s), they might want to work on other positive templates for the future in other areas of their lives using these future templates.

References

Shapiro, F. (2001). *Eye movement desensitization and reprocessing: Basic principles, protocols, and procedures* (2nd ed.). New York, NY: Guilford Press.

Shapiro, F. (2006). *EMDR: New notes on adaptive information processing with case formulation principles, forms, scripts and worksheets*. Watsonville, CA: EMDR Institute.

Appendix B: EMDR Therapy Summary Sheet and EMDR Therapy Session Form

The Eye Movement Desensitization and Reprocessing (EMDR) Therapy Summary Sheet and EMDR Therapy Session Form are helpful tools in keeping the important data, issues, and information pertinent to your client easily accessible.

The EMDR Therapy Summary Sheet creates a place to record the presenting problem(s), demographics, relevant health issues, and attachment concerns in an easily visible format.

Write down the presenting problem in an abbreviated form along with all of the relevant information pertaining to that problem, such as the worst part; the negative image; irrational belief, feelings, sensations; and urges.

The 3-Pronged Protocol is addressed by including *past memories* such as the touchstone event and places to record pertinent adverse life experiences from birth through adulthood as needed, as well as proof memories for irrational negative beliefs. Places for *present triggers* and flashforwards are included, as is an area to write in concerns about the future to assist in developing the *future template*.

There is a section to record present resources such as the Safe Place, positive attachment figures, mastery experiences, and a category for "other." Recording relevant major themes that arise to use for negative cognitions and cognitive interweaves concerning issues of safety/survival; self-judgment/guilt/blame (responsibility); self-defectiveness (responsibility); choices/control; and other concerns is helpful when formulating the case conceptualization and treatment plan with your client.

The Clinical Impressions section is a place to summarize your impression of the client, record a diagnosis, write down the results of assessment measures, assess the client's ability to regulate affect, and record your subjective response to the client. There is also a quick and easy scale (Elan Shapiro, personal communication, ca. 2007) to rate the severity of the problem, your client's motivation, your client's strengths, and level of functioning on a 1 to 5 scale, where 1 = low and 5 = high, according to the client's intake responses and your clinical impression.

The EMDR Therapy Session Form is set up to record each individual EMDR Therapy session so that you have a running record of all of the EMDR Therapy targets worked on, including the date, presenting problem/image, negative and positive cognitions, Validity of Cognition (VoC) scale, emotions, Subjective Units of Disturbance (SUDs) scale, location of body sensations, and the ending rating of the SUDs (2SUDS) and the VoC (2VoC). In this way, you will have easy access to each of the EMDR Therapy targets you have worked on, and the ability to see if it has been completed or not.

EMDR Therapy Summary Sheet

Name: _____   **Diagnosis:** _____

PRESENTING PROBLEM(S)

_____

_____

Goals: _____

DEMOGRAPHICS

Age: _____ **Gender:** ☐ Male ☐ Female   **Highest Education** _____

Family Status: ☐ Single ☐ Married ☐ Partnered ☐ Widower ☐ Separated ☐ Divorced

Work Status: ☐ Employed ☐ Unemployed ☐ Student ☐ Retired

Living Situation: ☐ Lives Alone ☐ Lives with Others_____

HEALTH

Health in General: ☐ Excellent ☐ Good ☐ Poor

Specify: _____

_____

Mood: _____

Medications:_____

Addictions: _____

Accident(s):_____

Hospitalizations: ☐ YES ☐ NO

Specify: _____

Chronic Pain: ☐ YES ☐ NO _____

Previous Psychological Treatment: ☐ YES ☐ NO   **Hospitalization(s):** ☐ YES ☐ NO

Specify: _____

Past Trauma: ☐ YES   ☐ NO

Specify: _____

ATTACHMENT

Nuclear Family Issues: _____

Mother: _____

Father: _____

Sibs: _____

_____

Major Loss(es): _____

_____

Positive Attachment Figures: _____

_____

Attachment Style/Predominant States: _____

Social Stigma Issues: _____

Violent Behavior in Family: _____

PRESENTING PROBLEM(S)

Problem

1. _____ 2. _____ 3. _____ 4. _____

Worst Part of the Problem

A. _____ B. _____ C. _____ D. _____

Negative Image Associated With Problem

A. _____ B. _____ C. _____ D. _____

Irrational Negative Beliefs Associated With Problem

A. _____ B. _____ C. _____ D. _____

Feelings Associated With Problem

A. _____ B. _____ C. _____ D. _____

Sensation/Uncomfortable Internal Negative Experience/Location

A. _____ B. _____ C. _____ D. _____

Urge Associated With Problem

A. _____ B. _____ C. _____ D. _____

PAST MEMORIES
                            TOUCHSTONE EVENT

A. _____ B. _____ C. _____ D. _____

Birth—12 years of age (Childhood)

1. _____ 1. _____ 1. _____ 1. _____
2. _____ 2. _____ 2. _____ 2. _____
3. _____ 3. _____ 3. _____ 3. _____

13 years through 19 years (Adolescence)

4. _____ 4. _____ 4. _____ 4. _____
5. _____ 5. _____ 5. _____ 5. _____
6. _____ 6. _____ 6. _____ 6. _____

20 years and higher (Adulthood)

7. _____ 7. _____ 7. _____ 7. _____
8. _____ 8. _____ 8. _____ 8. _____
9. _____ 9. _____ 9. _____ 9. _____
10. _____ 10. _____ 10. _____ 10. _____

PROOF MEMORIES
(For irrational negative beliefs—How do you know the negative belief is true?)

1. _____ 1. _____ 1. _____ 1. _____
2. _____ 2. _____ 2. _____ 2. _____
3. _____ 3. _____ 3. _____ 3. _____

PRESENT TRIGGER(S)

1. _____ 1. _____ 1. _____ 1. _____
2. _____ 2. _____ 2. _____ 2. _____
3. _____ 3. _____ 3. _____ 3. _____

FLASHFORWARD (Worst case or doom scenario*)*

1. _____ 1. _____ 1. _____ 1. _____

FUTURE TEMPLATE/ANTICIPATORY ANXIETY

1. _____ 1. _____ 1. _____ 1. _____
2. _____ 2. _____ 2. _____ 2. _____

PRESENT RESOURCES

Safe Place

1. _____ 1. _____ 1. _____ 1. _____
2. _____ 2. _____ 2. _____ 2. _____

Positive Attachment Figures

1. _____ 1. _____ 1. _____ 1. _____
2. _____ 2. _____ 2. _____ 2. _____

Mastery Experiences

1. _____ 1. _____ 1. _____ 1. _____
2. _____ 2. _____ 2. _____ 2. _____

Other

1. _____ 1. _____ 1. _____ 1. _____

MAJOR THEMES/NEGATIVE COGNITIONS/COGNITIVE INTERWEAVES

Safety/Survival

1. _____ 1. _____ 1. _____ 1. _____
2. _____ 2. _____ 2. _____ 2. _____

Self-Judgment/Guilt/Blame (Responsibility)

1. _____ 1. _____ 1. _____ 1. _____
2. _____ 2. _____ 2. _____ 2. _____

Self-Defectiveness (Responsibility)

1. _____ 1. _____ 1. _____ 1. _____
2. _____ 2. _____ 2. _____ 2. _____

Choice/Control

1. _____ 1. _____ 1. _____ 1. _____

Other Concerns

1. _____ 1. _____ 1. _____ 1. _____

CLINICAL IMPRESSIONS

Clinical Impressions: _____

_____

Diagnosis: _____

Affect Regulation (Identify, Differentiate, Manage): ☐ Good   ☐ Adequate   ☐ Poor
(Explain):_____

Do you like this client? : ☐ YES   ☐ NO

Specify: _____

Do you dislike this client? ☐ YES   ☐ NO

Specify: _____

S = Severity: (Low)   1 2 3 4 5 (High) Ratings based on all information
M = Motivation: (Low)   1 2 3 4 5 (High) and clinical impression
S = Strengths: (Low)   1 2 3 4 5 (High)
LoF = Level of Functioning: (Low) 1 2 3 4 5 (High)

EMDR Therapy Session Form:

Name: _____ Resources: _____ Safe Place: _____ EM _____ Tones _____ Tapping _____ TAC _____

Date	Presenting Problem/Image	Negative Cognition/PC	VOC	Emotions	SUDS	Location	2SUDS	2VOC

Made in the USA
Lexington, KY
11 March 2017